JOURNAL FOR THE STUDY OF THE OLD TESTAMENT SUPPLEMENT SERIES
131

Editors
David J.A. Clines
Philip R. Davies

JSOT Press
Sheffield

FORMS
OF
DEFORMITY

Lynn Holden

Journal for the Study of the Old Testament
Supplement Series 131

Copyright © 1991 Sheffield Academic Press

Published by JSOT Press
JSOT Press is an imprint of
Sheffield Academic Press Ltd
The University of Sheffield
343 Fulwood Road
Sheffield S10 3BP
England

Typeset by Sheffield Academic Press
and
Printed on acid-free paper in Great Britain
by Billing & Sons Ltd
Worcester

British Library Cataloguing in Publication Data

A catalogue record for this book is available
from the British Library

ISSN 0309-0787
ISBN 1-85075-327-X

CONTENTS

Contents

PART TWO

ACKNOWLEDGMENTS

This book is a slightly revised version of a doctoral thesis submitted to the University of Edinburgh in 1988. I would like here to thank my supervisors from the School of Scottish Studies, Professor John MacQueen, for his advice, and, in particular, Margaret Bennett, for her enthusiasm and friendship. However, my greatest debt is to my friend, the artist, Koert Linde, for stimulating discussions, perceptive criticism and a facility with ancient computers which allowed the typing of the final manuscript. The mistakes, of course, are mine.

ABBREVIATIONS

Old Testament and Apocrypha

Gen.	Genesis
Exod.	Exodus
Lev.	Leviticus
Num.	Numbers
Deut.	Deuteronomy
Josh.	Joshua
Judg.	Judges
Ruth	Ruth
1 Sam.	1 Samuel
2 Sam.	2 Samuel
1 Kgs	1 Kings
2 Kgs	2 Kings
1 Chron.	1 Chronicles
2 Chron.	2 Chronicles
Ezra	Ezra
Neh.	Nehemiah
Tob.	Tobit *
Jdt.	Judith *
Est.	Esther *
1 Macc.	1 Maccabees *
2 Macc.	2 Maccabees *
Job	Job
Ps.	Psalms
Prov.	Proverbs
Eccl.	Ecclesiastes
Song	Song of songs
Wis.	Wisdom *
Sir.	Ecclesiasticus *
Isa.	Isaiah
Jer.	Jeremiah
Lam.	Lamentations
Bar.	Baruch *
Ezek.	Ezekiel

Dan.	Daniel *
Hos.	Hosea
Joel	Joel
Amos	Amos
Obad.	Obadiah
Jon.	Jonah
Mic.	Micah
Nah.	Nahum
Hab.	Habakkuk
Zeph.	Zephaniah
Hag.	Haggai
Zech.	Zechariah
Mal.	Malachi

* These books (or part of books: in the case of Esther the passages 1.1a-1f; 2a, 2b; 3.13a-13g; 4.17a-17z; 5.1a-1f; 8.12a-12v; 10.3a-3l, and in Daniel the passages 3.24-90; 13; 14) are not included in the canon and constitute the Apocrypha.

Pseudepigrapha

Apoc. Abr.	*Apocalypse of Abraham*
T. Abr.	*Testament of Abraham*
Apoc. Adam	*Apocalypse of Adam*
T. Adam	*Testament of Adam*
LAE	*Life of Adam and Eve*
Ahiquar	*Ahiqar*
Anon. Sam.	*An Anonymous Samaritan Text*
Ep. Arist.	*Letter of Aristeas*
Arist. Exeg.	Aristeas the Exegete
Aristob.	*Aristobulus*
Art.	*Artapanus*
2 Bar.	*2 (Syriac Apocalypse of) Baruch*
3 Bar.	*3(Greek Apocalypse of) Baruch*
4 Bar.	*4 Baruch*
Cav. Tr.	*Cave of Treasures*
Cl. Mal.	Cleodemus Malchus
Apoc. Dan.	*Apocalypse of Daniel*
Dem.	*Demetrius*
El. Mod.	*Eldad and Modad*
Apoc. Elij.	*Apocalypse of Elijah*
Heb. Apoc. Elij.	*Hebrew Apocalypse of Elijah*
1 En.	*1 (Ethiopic Apocalypse of) Enoch*
2 En.	*2 (Slavonic Apocalypse of) Enoch*

3 En.	*3 (Hebrew Apocalypse of) Enoch*
Eupol.	*Eupolemus*
Ps-Eupol.	Pseudo-Eupolemus
Apocr. Ezek.	*Apocryphon of Ezekiel*
Apoc. Ezek.	*Apocalypse of Ezekiel*
Ezek. Trag.	Ezekiel the Tragedian
4 Ezra	*4 Ezra*
Gk. Apoc. Ezra	*Greek Apocalypse of Ezra*
Ques. Ezra	*Questions of Ezra*
Rev. Ezra	*Revelation of Ezra*
Vis. Ezra	Vision of Ezra
Hec. Ab.	Hecataeus of Abdera
Ps.-Hec.	Pseudo-Hecataeus
Hell. Syn. Pr.	*Hellenistic Synagogal Prayers*
T. Hez.	*Testament of Hezekiah*
Fr. Hist. Wk.	*Fragments of Historical Works*
T. Isaac	*Testament of Isaac*
Asc. Isa.	*Ascension of Isaiah*
Mart. Isa.	*Martyrdom of Isaiah*
Vis. Isa.	*Vision of Isaiah*
Lad. Jac.	*Ladder of Jacob*
Pr. Jac.	*Prayer of Jacob*
T. Jac.	*Testament of Jacob*
Jan. Jam.	*Jannes and Jambres*
T. Job	*Testament of Job*
Jos. Asen.	*Joseph and Aseneth*
Hist. Jos.	*History of Joseph*
Pr. Jos.	*Prayer of Joseph*
Jub.	*Jubilees*
LAB	*Liber Antiquitatum Biblicarum*
Lost Tr.	*The Lost Tribes*
3 Macc.	*3 Maccabees*
4 Macc.	*4 Maccabees*
5 Macc.	*5 Maccabees*
Pr. Man.	*Prayer of Manasseh*
Syr. Men.	Syriac Menander
Apoc. Mos.	*Apocalypse of Moses*
Ass. Mos.	*Assumption of Moses*
Pr. Mos.	*Prayer of Moses*
T. Mos.	*Testament of Moses*
Bk Noah	*Book of Noah*
Ps.-Orph.	*Pseudo-Orpheus*
Par. Jer.	Paraleipomena Jeremiou
Ph. E. Poet	Philo the Epic Poet
Ps.-Philo	Pseudo-Philo

Ps.-Phoc.	Pseudo-Phocylides
Fr. Poet. Wk.	*Fragments of Poetical Works*
Liv. Proph.	*Lives of the Prophets*
Hist. Rech.	*History of the Rechabites*
Apoc. Sedr.	*Apocalypse of Sedrach*
Tr. Shem	*Treatise of Shem*
Sib. Or.	*Sibylline Oracles*
Odes	*Odes of Solomon*
Pss. Sol.	*Psalms of Solomon*
T.Sol.	*Testament of Solomon*
5 Apoc. Syr. Pss.	*Five Apocryphal Syriac Psalms*
Thal.	Thallus
Theod.	Theodotus
Test. XII Patr.	*Testaments of the Twelve Patriarchs*
T. Reub.	*Testament of Reuben*
T. Sim.	*Testament of Simeon*
T. Levi	*Testament of Levi*
T. Jud.	*Testament of Judah*
T. Iss.	*Testament of Issachar*
T. Zeb.	*Testament of Zebulun*
T. Dan	*Testament of Dan*
T. Naph.	*Testament of Naphtali*
T. Gad	*Testament of Gad*
T. Ash.	*Testament of Asher*
T. Jos.	*Testament of Joseph*
T. Benj.	*Testament of Benjamin*
Apoc. Zeph.	*Apocalypse of Zephaniah*
Apoc. Zos.	*Apocalypse of Zosimus*

Midrashim

Gen. R.	*Bereshit Rabba—Midrash Rabba to Genesis*
Exod. R.	*Shemot Rabba—Midrash Rabba to Exodus*
Lev. R.	*Wayikra Rabba—Midrash Rabba to Leviticus*
Num. R.	*Bamidbar Rabba—Midrash Rabba to Numbers*
Deut. R.	*Debarim Rabba—Midrash Rabba to Deuteronomy*
Cant. R.	*Shir Hashirim Rabba—Midrash Rabba to Song of Songs*
Ruth R.	*Ruth Rabba —Midrash Rabba to Ruth*
Lam. R.	*Eka Rabba—Midrash Rabba to Lamentations*
Qoh. R.	*Kohelot Rabba—Midrash Rabba to Ecclesiastes*
Est. R.	*Esther Rabba—Midrash Rabba to Esther*
Mek.	*Mekilta de Rabbi Ishmael—Tannaitic Midrash to Exodus*
PRE	*Pirke (Chapters of) Rabbi Eliezer*
BHM	*Bet HaMidrash*

Modern Works

GL	L. Ginzberg, *Legends of the Jews*
Vermes	G. Vermes, *The Dead Sea Scrolls in English*
Mel.	R. Mellinkoff, *The Mark of Cain*
	R. Mellinkoff, *The Horns of Moses*

INTRODUCTION

'In the kingdom of the blind, the one-eyed man is king' runs a familiar saw. Other curious expressions: 'Walls have ears', 'He has eyes at the back of his head', 'He has two left feet' manifest the same preoccupation with deviations from the human form. It is the nature of proverbs to employ a symbolic language which imaginatively, and therefore powerfully, presents an abstract idea. Expressions frequently use a similar figurative language, while riddles cloak the familiar in a fantastic or poetic image. Witness the following description of a one-eyed seller of onions:

> He had two ears and only one eye, he had two feet and twelve hundred heads, a back, two hands, a belly, two shoulders and sides, a neck and two arms.[1]

In contrast to these symbolic literary modes, traditional narratives, whether myths, legends or folktales, are to be taken literally, at least for the duration of their presentation. Whatever their moral or symbolic implications, in them the fantastic is a fact, and the extraordinary is the norm: in the kingdom of the two-eyed, the one-eyed man may well be king.

Whether the intention of a genre is to generalize a multitude of particular cases, elucidate, confuse, or transform the world, it is remarkable how frequently a fantastic anatomy fulfills the aim of the storyteller. 'The body', observes the surrealist artist Hans Bellmer, 'is comparable to a sentence that invites us to disarticulate it, so that, through a series of endless anagrams, its true contents may be recombined'.[2]

It is evident that a vigorous imagination—and an unceasing delight

1. *The Exeter Book of Riddles* (trans. and ed. K. Crossley-Holland; Harmondsworth: Penguin, 1979), p. 99.
2. Quoted in J.H. Matthews, *The Imagery of Surrealism* (New York: Syracuse University Press, 1977), p. 210.

in its application—is the principal source for many of the abnormalities of fictional characters. The imagination, however, is not without its sources, many of a prosaic kind. Deformities and disabilities are frequent in the natural world, a result of accident, disease or birth defect. F. Gonzalez-Crussi, a pathologist with a lively interest in teratology, observes: 'There are human beings with one eye in the forehead, without nose, or with 'flippers' in place of limbs... children covered by a scaly integument that ... resembles that of a fish; ... double-headed, four limbed creatures... mouthless individuals'.[1] In a fascinating chapter, he argues that the Egyptian gods Ptah and Bes were afflicted with achondroplasia, the most common form of human dwarfism and that, rather than abhorring such deformities, the Egyptian society of the time believed that '... a congenitally malformed being maintain[ed] a special relationship with the Great Unknown—call it demon, deity, chance or genetic aberration ...'[2]

Many of the motifs in this index clearly derive from such medical aberrations. Even such an archetypal motif as the twinship of Jacob and Esau, and Esau's blood-red colour at birth, has a parallel in the medical condition called 'twin to twin transfusion syndrome'.[3]

Less spectacular, though more common, are the disfigurements caused by diseases such as smallpox, polio and leprosy, or by accidents resulting in the loss of an organ, in burn marks or scars. The Jewish material collected here generally views the deformities caused by diseases in a negative light, judging them to be a punishment or a retribution for some evil act, committed however unwittingly, and not a misfortune. Conversely, the disappearance of a normally permanent disfigurement or disease can be safely attributed to divine favour. Some of the deformities in traditional narratives may well be related to the impairment, not of the body itself, but of the body image as a result of mental disturbance caused by cerebral damage or diseases

---

1.   F. Gonzalez-Crussi, 'Teratology', in *Notes of an Anatomist* (London: Picador, 1986), p. 94.
2.   Gonzalez-Crussi, 'Teratology', p. 104.
3.   Gonzalez-Crussi, 'Twins', in *Notes of an Anatomist*, p. 19. On the subject of twins in myth, see D. Ward, *The Divine Twins: An Indo-European Myth in Germanic Tradition* (Berkeley: University of California Press, 1968).

such as brain lesions and cancer.[1] It has been suggested that the familiar and widespread motif of the unilateral figure has such origins.[2]

Psychologists consider certain images of deformity to be projections of inborn or acquired mental pressures or tendencies. The fear of castration, for example, is thought to be responsible for that aggressive motif of the toothed vagina, while 'the desire and pursuit of the whole' provides the inspiration for the image of the androgyne.[3]

Mutilation as the result of an accident, or inflicted upon self or others, requires no further discussion here, except that which is an intrinsic part of ritual. In fact, many of the motifs in traditional narratives bear some relation to the rituals practised by the people among whom they are current, or the memory of rituals practised at one time. Rituals in which mutilations play a crucial role are well documented by anthropologists, historians, travellers and other observers. The reason for the practise of mutilation may be given in an etiological myth, it may be given by members of the society involved, or it may remain an unspeakable subject to them; the observer will add a theory of his own, whether from a psychological, social-anthropological or historical perspective, which may be superimposed upon, explain or flatly contradict the society's own understanding. Thus it has been suggested a ritual mutilation can be a substitute for, or a relic of, human sacrifice, a symbolic death, a magical act, a payment for superior powers, an appeal for divine sympathy, a mark of distinction, a test of endurance, or a seal upon a social or religious allegiance.[4] The mutilation, which may take the form of a brand, a tattoo,

1. O. Sacks, *The Man who Mistook His Wife for a Hat* (London: Picador, 1986), pp. 7-80
2. R. Needham, 'Unilateral Figures', in *Reconnaissances* (Toronto: University of Toronto Press, 1980), pp. 36-37.
3. For a Freudian interpretation of the motif of the toothed vagina, see J. Campbell, *The Masks of God* (4 vols; New York: Viking, 1959–68), I, pp. 73-78. On the subject of the androgyne see C.G. Jung, *Mysterium Coniunctionis* (trans. R.F.C. Hull; Princeton: Princeton University Press 1977 [1955–56]).
4. See, for example, M. Eliade, *The Sacred and the Profane* (trans. W. R. Trask; Chicago: Chicago University Press, 1959 [1957]), pp. 188-190 (mutilation as symbolic death); H. Maccoby, *The Sacred Executioner* (London: Thames & Hudson 1982) (circumcision as a substitute for child sacrifice); R. Graves, *The White Goddess* (London: Faber & Faber, 1971 [1961]), pp. 327-34

the removal of a tooth or a finger, but most often of the foreskin, may be practised upon all the members of a society, upon the males only, upon a select group, or upon certain chosen individuals. Most commonly it is an intrinsic part of a rite of passage.[1] Ritual mutilations such as circumcision (ubiquitous in the material presented here) are invariably judged positively.[2] As a special sign of distinction, certain patriarchs are even born mutilated. An important source for the deformities of characters in traditional narratives can be found in the reports of the existence of 'monstrous races', those creatures who, living distantly in time, place, or state of being, embody the very notion of 'the Other'. While in specific cases the myopic observer may have confused a man on horseback with a centaur, or viewed a man with an ornamented shield or chest armour as a member of the Blemmyae (men with faces on their chest), these stories are too seductive and widespread to be attributed to confusion alone.[3] In fact, they would seem to represent the very essence of the folktale. Just as in a game of 'Chinese whispers', each story, as it travels, produces another story which, in turn, produces a third, and so on, and whether the ultimate source of a particular story is another story, taken at face

(mutilation as a relic of sacrifice); M. Delcourt, *Héphaistos, ou la légende du magicien* (Paris: Société d' L'Edition 'Les Belles Lettres', 1957), pp. 114-36 (on mutilation as a payment for magical powers); R. Mellinkoff, *The Mark of Cain* (Berkeley: University of California Press, 1970), pp. 23-29; A. van Gennep, *The Rites of Passage* (trans. M. B. Vizedom and G. L. Caffee; London: Routledge & Kegan Paul, 1977 [1908]), pp. 70-74 (mutilation as a mark of differentiation and a seal of allegiance). See also below, note 2.

    1.   The classic study on the subject is van Gennep, *The Rites of Passage*.

    2.   There does not seem to be a recent comparative study of the subject. In general, see 'Circumcision', in *The Encyclopaedia of Religion and Ethics* (ed. J. Hastings, Edinburgh: T. & T. Clark, 1908–21), pp. 659-80; more recently, T.O. Beidelman, 'Circumcision', in *The Encyclopedia of Religion* (ed. M. Eliade, New York: Macmillan, 1987), III, pp. 511-14. On Semitic circumcision, see 'Circumcision', (*Enc Jud* V, 1971), 567-76; H. Maccoby, *The Sacred Executioner* pp. 87-96; E. R. Wolfson, 'Circumcision, Vision of God and Textual Interpretation', in *History of Religions* 27/2 (1987), pp. 189-215; also van Gennep, *The Rites of Passage*, pp. 70-74.

    3.   This subject is studied mainly from the view point of iconography. See, for example, J. B. Friedman, *The Monstrous Races in Medieval Art and Thought* (Cambridge, MA: Harvard University Press 1981); also H. Mode, *Fabeltiere und Dämonen* (Leipzig: Edition Leipzig, 1977).

value, a garbled piece of information, a description of statuary, or a mistranslation of a written text, is perhaps of less importance than the fact that it is the natural proclivity of the human mind to invest all its imaginative powers in the unknown, which is responsible for its transmission.[1]

These deformities can take several forms. The first of these is that of reversal, or inversion.[2] In Jewish legend, for example, the dwellers of Paradise walk on their heads. The second is that of an addition of, or replacement by, animal features. Anah, when he goes to pasture his father's asses in the wilderness, meets beasts from the middle down in the shape of a man, and from the middle up resembling an ape, and with a tail reaching from the shoulders to the ground. Finally, human features may be enlarged or reduced in size, removed or multiplied in number, or exchange places on the body. The Cainites, for instance, whose locality varies from legend to legend but is always beyond the horizon, are depicted as giants and dwarfs with two heads.

A fourth source for the abnormalities of characters in traditional narratives can be found in symbolism. Symbolism, of course, plays an important role in all aspects of the generation of narratives, particularly those that can be explained as resulting from psychic pressures or ritual, but here I mean the utilization of what may be termed 'natural symbolism': the attribution to certain individuals or groups of those elements from the natural world which excite wonder, fear or awe in order to express their special status, power, quality or origin.[3] Thus, luminosity is associated with perfection and righteousness.[4] When Moses is born, he fills the house with light. Hairiness is associated with bestiality: thus the evil Cain and Esau, as well as the demons,

1. On the transmission of images, see R. Wittkower, 'Marvels of the East: A Study in the History of Monsters', in *Allegory and the Migration of Symbols* (London: Thames & Hudson, 1977).

2. Inversions and reversals play a major role in all ritual processes. See B. Babcock (ed.), *The Reversible World* (Ithaca: Cornell University Press, 1978).

3. All aspects of symbolism are discussed in R. Firth, *Symbols: Public and Private* (London: George Allen & Unwin, 1973).

4. For the symbolism of sun-like qualities in Near Eastern thought, see G. E. Mendenhall, *The Tenth Generation* (Baltimore: John Hopkins University Press, 1973), pp. 32-66. See also M. Eliade, 'Spirit, Light and Seed', in *Occultism, Witchcraft and Cultural Fashions* (Chicago: University of Chicago Press, 1976), pp. 93-142.

are said to be hairy all over. The natural symbolism of stature is ambivalent. To indicate their greatness, kings stand head and shoulders above their subjects; but adversaries are giants to indicate the courage of the hero who fights them. Jacob's loins are huge because he is a powerful patriarch; but that the penes of the Egyptians are huge merely reveals their carnal nature. According to certain theories, natural symbolism also operates on a more abstruse level. For example, the deformity of a character may point to his role as a mediator between opposing forces of nature or modes of being (Lévi-Strauss), to his social status (Dumézil), or to a state of disorder, both threatening and powerful (Douglas).[1] Since I am concerned with the function of deformity within narratives, not with the function of the narrative within society, this is not the place to elaborate or criticize these theories.

Finally, certain deformities may be a part of an etiological myth or legend, or may be invented to illustrate certain philosophical or theological concepts.

Considering the extraordinary variety of sources from which particular abnormalities, deformities and disabilities of characters in traditional narrative may derive, and the equally extraordinary number of functions these deformities may perform within particular narratives, it is difficult to envisage a comprehensive theory. There are two principal reasons for the construction of a motif-index of the subject.

1. Although characters with some kind of abnormality, deformity or disability are so familiar a feature in traditional narratives as to be almost characteristic, there has been no synoptic survey of the subject. There have been studies of inividual motifs, usually of their historical development or geographical distribution within a limited region or specific culture, but sometimes in a wider context.[2]

---

1. C. Lévi-Strauss, 'The Structural Study of Myth', in *Structural Anthropology* (trans. C. Jacobson and B. Grundfest; New York: Basic Books, 1963), p. 215; *idem, The Raw and the Cooked* (trans. J. and D. Weightman; New York: Harper & Row, 1975), p. 53; G. Dumézil, *Gods of the Ancient Norsemen,* (Berkeley: University of California Press, 1973 [1959]), pp. 45-47, 118-25; M. Douglas, *Purity and Danger* (London: Routledge & Kegan Paul 1984 [1966]), esp. ch. 2.

2. For instance, Mellinkoff, *The Mark of Cain; idem The Horned Moses in Medieval Art and Thought* (Berkeley: University of California Press, 1970);

There have been studies of individual characters as well as studies of certain types of beings, such as monsters, hybrids and angels.[1] There have been studies of pictorial iconography.[2] The present survey, though necessarily limited in scope, should go some way towards the recognition of a more general area of study.

2. I have chosen the format of a motif-index, first of all, to allow an easy access to the whole range of motifs that occur within traditional narrative, the reasons for their occurrence, and the interplay between motifs and reasons, and secondly, to prepare a framework for the insertion of material from different cultures and regions and make possible comparative study. Stith Thompson's *Motif-index of Folk Literature* is of little use in this particular context, for though it does include characters with deformities of various kinds, these are dispersed throughout the work in an arbitrary fashion, and, more importantly, omit the reasons or functions they perform within the tale. Hence the relationship between that work and the present one is an oblique one.

Scope and Format

This work is a motif-index in that it identifies, isolates and arranges pertinent tale elements within a system that permits a network of cross-references between a motif and the reason for its presence in a tale, between different motifs relating to the same character, and

W. Deonne, *Le symbolisme de l'oeil* (Paris: Editions E. de Boccard, 1965); M. Delcourt, *Hermaphrodite* (Paris: Presses Universitaires de France, 1956); P. Lambrechts and L. Vanden Berghe, 'La divinité-oreille dans les religions antiques', *Bulletin de l'Institut Historique* 29 (1955); Needham, 'Unilateral Figures' pp. 16-40; L. Holden, *Lame Gods* (unpub BA diss., Stirling University, 1982).

1. For example, P. Radin, *The Trickster* (New York: Schocken Books, 1976); J. B. Russell, *The Devil* (Ithaca: Cornell University Press, 1977); R. Patai, *The Hebrew Goddess* (New York: Avon Books, 1977), pp. 59-98 (on the Cherubim); G. Benwell and A. Waugh, *Sea Enchantress* (London: Hutchinson, 1961) (on the mermaid); G. Davidson, *A Dictionary of Angels* (London: Collier MacMillan, 1968); R. Merz, *Die Numinose Mischgestalt* (Berlin: de Gruyter, 1978); C.J. Thompson, *The Mystery and Lore of Monsters* (London: Williams and Norgate, 1930).

2. For example, E. R. Goodenough, *Jewish Symbols in the Greco-Roman Period* (New York: Pantheon Books 1958), VIII, pp. 59-70, on the demon with cock's feet; H. Mode *Fabeltiere und Dämonen*; J. B. Friedman, *The Monstrous Races*.

between different reasons for the same motif. As a rule, only those abnormalities and deformities that are visible or apparent to the other senses are included. However, in the case of disabilities, this limitation would have led to ambiguity—blindness, for example, is often, but not necessarily, visible—and inconsistency—since one would have to include most cases of blindness but exclude deafness altogether. This motif-index consists, therefore, almost, but not entirely, of sensible abnormalities, deformities and disabilities.

Several observations may be made at this point.[1]

1.   The abnormality, deformity or disability may be natural or fantastic, common or extraordinary.

2.   What constitutes an abnormality, deformity or disability may be affected by cultural determinants. For instance, a white person may be considered an anomaly in a black society, or vice versa. It may also be affected by stereotyping. Where, for example, an old woman becomes the 'loathly lady', she is regarded as exceptionally hideous instead of merely aged. In these cases, the narrator's viewpoint is the deciding factor.

3.   To be included here, a character (or part thereof) must be in some way animate. Thus this motif-index contains a vital thigh-bone, an animated statue and a disembodied hand.

4.   The abnormality, deformity or disability may be present at birth, acquired during life or after death, may be temporary or permanent, and may occur in a dream or vision within the narrative.

5.   Abnormalities, deformities and disabilities in the subjunctive mode or the future tense are not generally included, except in a few cases such as the Messiah and the Antichrist, who are of such importance and described in such detail that they can hardly be omitted. A pretence of deformity may also be included.

6.   Metaphors are not included, but similes sometimes imply a motif and must at times be taken literally. Consider the difference between the descriptions 'he is white as snow' and 'his eyes are like flaming torches'. Both contain a motif, but whereas in the first case the comparative conjunction stands, and the simile simply means 'he is extraordinarily white', in the second, the distinction between simile and

1.   For the sake of completeness, I have included a number of motifs under the heading 'Absence of body'; in any case, it is possible to argue that the absence of a character's body is clearly apparent to the senses.

description becomes quite meaningless: surely it means 'his eyes emit flames'. It should be added that the distinction between a metaphor, a simile and a literal description is often difficult to draw, and that, moreover, what frequently happens in this material, a metaphor from one text may be incorporated in a subsequent text as a description. Only those subjects that feature some aspect of the human physiognomy appear in this index. Whereas a beast-man and even a wheel with human eyes are included, animals or fantastic creatures are not, except where they appear as the result of a transformation from a being with a human form. By the term 'traditional narrative' I mean myths, folk tales, legends, fables, epics, sagas and ballads which have an identifiable scenario with a plot and development of action. Not included are works featuring no chain of events, but a static image or single event, such as proverbs, jokes and riddles.[1] This motif-index is applicable to all traditional narratives—and is indeed intended as an instrument for comparative studies—although confined here to Jewish narratives in, or relating to, the Bible. The kinds of traditional narrative found in biblical material will be discussed later.

The motif-index is divided into two main sections; the first part lists the abnormality, deformity or disability, while the second part gives the reason for its appearance in the narrative. Part One is divided into the various parts of the body, with certain limbs or organs being subdivided into their component parts. The principal parts are identified by a capital letter and the components are marked by a capital letter followed by a lower case letter, as follows:

A	THE BODY AS A WHOLE
B	THE SKIN AND FLESH
Ba	PERSPIRATION
C	THE BODY DIVIDED
Ca	VERTICAL DIVISION INTO RIGHT AND LEFT
Cb	VERTICAL DIVISION INTO FRONT AND BACK
Cc	HORIZONTAL DIVISION INTO UPPER AND LOWER
Cd	OTHER DIVISIONS
D	THE HEAD AND SKULL
E	THE HAIR AND BEARD
F	THE FACE

1.   On all aspects of terminology, see H. Jason, *Ethnopoetry*, (Bonn: Linguistica Biblica, 1977).

Fa	THE CHEEKS
Fb	THE FOREHEAD
Fc	THE CHIN AND JAW
G	THE EYES
Ga	THE PUPILS
Gb	THE EYEBROWS
Gc	THE EYELASHES
Gd	THE EYELIDS
Ge	THE CORNEA
Gf	TEARS
H	THE NOSE
Ha	THE NOSTRILS
Hb	MUCUS
I	THE MOUTH
Ia	THE LIPS
Ib	THE TONGUE
Ic	THE TEETH
Id	THE TONSILS
Ie	SPITTLE
If	THE VOICE
J	THE EARS
Ja	THE EARLOBES
K	THE NECK AND THROAT
L	THE TORSO
M	THE BACK AND SHOULDERS
N	THE BREAST
Na	THE MALE CHEST
Nb	THE FEMALE BREASTS
Nc	THE NIPPLES
Nd	MILK
O	THE ARMS
Oa	THE ELBOWS
Ob	THE WRISTS
P	THE HANDS
Pa	THE PALMS
Pb	THE KNUCKLES
Pc	THE FINGERS AND THUMBS
Pd	THE FINGERNAILS
Q	THE STOMACH AND WAIST
Qa	THE NAVEL
R	THE BUTTOCKS
Ra	THE ANUS
Rb	EXCREMENT
S	THE GENITALS

Sa	THE MALE GENITALS
Sb	THE FEMALE GENITALS
Sc	URINE
Sd	SEMEN
T	THE LEGS
Ta	THE THIGHS
Tb	THE KNEES
Tc	THE CALVES
Td	THE SHINS
Te	THE ANKLES
U	THE FEET
Ua	THE HEELS
Ub	THE TOES
Uc	THE TOENAILS
V	THE INTERNAL PARTS
Va	THE BONES
Vb	THE BRAIN
Vc	THE HEART
Vd	THE LIVER
Ve	THE LUNGS
Vf	THE INTESTINES
Vg	THE WOMB
Vh	THE MUSCLES
Vi	THE SPLEEN
W	THE BLOOD

Each one of these parts is subdivided into the following twenty-seven categories, marked by a numeral, indicating the type of abnormality, deformity or disability:

1	ABSENCE OF PART
2	PARTIAL ABSENCE OF PART
3	VITAL PART
4	PART IN UNUSUAL POSITION ON BODY
5	UNUSUAL NUMBER OF PARTS
6	ABNORMAL SIZE OF PART
7	PART FACING UNUSUAL DIRECTION
8	INVERTED PART
9	PART OF OPPOSITE SEX
10	UNUSUAL EMISSION OR EMANATION FROM PART
11	UNUSUAL COLOUR OF PART
12	UNUSUAL SHAPE OF PART
13	PECULIARITY OF SKIN OF PART
14	UNUSUAL PROTUBERANCE OR PROTRUSION ON PART
15	ABNORMAL PUNCTURE OR OPENING IN PART

16	PART OF UNUSUAL SUBSTANCE
17	SUBSTITUTION FOR PART
18	ANIMAL PART IN PLACE OF HUMAN, OR PART WITH ANIMAL ATTRIBUTES
19	FISH PART IN PLACE OF HUMAN, OR PART WITH FISH ATTRIBUTES
20	BIRD PART IN PLACE OF HUMAN, OR PART WITH BIRD ATTRIBUTES
21	HUMAN PART ON UNUSUAL CREATURE
22	UNUSUALLY HIDEOUS OR FRIGHTFUL PART
23	DISEASE, PARALYSIS OR MALFUNCTION OF PART
24	WOUNDED OR MUTILATED PART
25	UNUSUAL ABILITY OF PART
26	PART OF DIFFERENT AGE GROUP
27	TRANSFORMATION OF PART

Further specifications are indicated by a succeeding numeral, proceeding from the most common to the more abstruse kinds of abnormalities, deformities or disabilities. In this particular material gaps are sometimes left, firstly to create a certain uniformity between related motifs in different categories, and, secondly to allow insertion of new material.

There are several observations to be made. The divisions of the body are pragmatic rather than systematic: the stress lies on those parts of the anatomy that can be expected to play a more dominant role in folklore. Though there is an inevitable amount of overlap between categories, the aim has been to be as precise as possible and to avoid crossing categorical borders (for example, the absence of an eye is not classified as an absence of a part of the head). The overlap that does occur is occasioned first of all by the anatomical ambiguities in many narratives and, secondly, by the coincidence of certain headings both in general and with regard to specific motifs. For instance, the whole of section B (The Skin) is identical with subsection A.13 (Peculiarity of Skin of Body), except that section B, having twenty-six subsections itself, can accommodate a more accurate description of certain motifs. As for specific motifs that fit in more than one place, wings, for example, are subsumed under both M.14 (Unusual Protrusions on Back) and M.20 (Back with Bird Attributes).

A motif, as it appears in the first part of the index, is categorized as follows:

F.11.3.2

where F designates 'The Face'; 11, 'Unusual Colour of Face'; 3, 'Red Face', and 2 is the number of the individual motif. This is followed by a description of the motif itself, and, often, by cross-references to the same motif in a different place, or to different motifs concerning the same character. Next comes the source of the motif and finally, an arrow pointing to the right, followed by the cross-reference to Part Two.

The second part of the motif-index presents the reasons for the abnormality, deformity or disability. In contrast to Part One, which is organized around a limited whole—that is, the human form—the heterogeneous nature of the reasons for abnormalities, deformities and disabilities allows no hierarchic structure to be imposed on the material. Within the five principal divisions, therefore, the categories are not placed in any significant order and further categories could be added should the need arise. (The only exception is section 1, where the order partly follows the life-cycle of the individual.) Of the five parts into which Part Two is divided, the sections 1 and 2 contain textual reasons, that is, reasons given in the narrative; and 3, 4 and 5 contain extra-textual reasons. In section 1, the abnormality, deformity or disability is the result of a certain event or condition; in 2, it is the means to achieving a certain end. Section 3 embraces those abnormalities, deformities or disabilities that are either symbolic or manifestations of certain qualities of the characters, while 4 contains those motifs that have no reasons but are necessitated by the plot. A particular abnormality, deformity or disability may be necessary insofar as there would be no story without it; it may be part of an allegory without being itself symbolic; or it may be introduced in the narrative to elicit a certain response in the audience. Section 4 also contains those motifs that appear to be purely contingent. Finally, section 5 contains those motifs that are inspired by etymology. Since the main concern of this index is to identify and classify the reasons for abnormalities, deformities and disabilities as they appear in the text, motifs are assigned to sections 1 or 2 except in those cases where this is impossible.

The following points should be noted:

1. A reason may be a reason for a particular abnormality, deformity or disability, or it may be a reason for the appearance of a character thus afflicted.

2. There is a marked difference in the specificity of categories.

Certain rather general categories such as 'Abnormality, Deformity or Disability as the Result of a Certain Taste, Touch, Smell, Sight or Sound' are necessary to embrace a wide range of motifs which could not be otherwise classified, although as a result there is a certain amount of overlap with other categories.

3. The reason for an abnormality, deformity or disability may be explicit in the text, implicit in the text, or may have to be deduced from the wider context. An example of an explicit reason is that for the wings of the angel Ben Nez, which, it is stated, serve to keep back the south wind, which would otherwise destroy the world. In other words, they prevent destruction (2.15.b). Wings are a common attribute of the angels; often angels are described as winged for no other reason than to indicate that they are angels. Here, the reason is implicit: they are members of an unusual race (1.1.a). Although deduction has been kept to a minimum, in such cases where it is necessary, comparative factors may have some influence. The motif of Adam and Eve as a single androgynous being, for example, is assigned to the category 'Abnormality, Deformity or Disability as a Result of Incomplete Development' because, firstly, God immediately separates them, and the divided form is, clearly, the final one; secondly, because the motif of the ancestor who is androgynous until the accident or punishment of division is familiar and widespread.

4. With regard to section 1, there is a notable variation in the degree of directness. To be blinded by a bright light or mutilated by a sword involves a direct physical cause and effect. A more oblique cause and effect is evident in such categories as 'Abnormality, Deformity or Disability as a Result of Violation of Taboo'. Here there is an intermediate stage:

Violation of Taboo → variable → Abnormality.

Similarly with 'Abnormality, Deformity or Disability as a Result of Trickery or Deception', where the trickery does not directly cause the deformity. A third type of cause and effect is found in the category 'Abnormality, Deformity or Disability as a Result of Old Age'. No immediate action is evident here, only a slow natural process. And even that is absent with the Old Hag familiar from many folk tales: she is eternally old, an archetype of the decrepitude of age. Another level of cause and effect is found in 'Abnormality, Deformity or Disability as a Result of Unusual Environment'. Here, the reason is inherent in the circumstances.

As a result there is often more than one reason. For instance, the dust thrown in the air by Moses and Aaron descends on the Egyptians and gives them boils and leprosy. But the reason that the dust gives them boils and leprosy is to punish them for the maltreatment of the Israelites. And, finally, the disease is also intended as a means to persuade the Egyptians to release the Israelites from slavery.

5. Two further points arise from the theological nature of some of the material used. Firstly, in most of the narratives, God is the ultimate instigator of all the action. However, for obvious reasons, motifs are only subsumed under 'Abnormality, Deformity or Disability as a Result of Supernatural Intervention or Agent' when God or one of his messengers is mentioned by name. Demons and angels, whose abnormalities, deformities or disabilities are an aspect of the species, are placed in 1.1, unless the character is individually named and his abnormality, deformity or disability is peculiar to himself, when he is categorized as 3.1, 'Symbol of Identity'.

A motif in Part Two is defined as follows:

1.26.a.5

where 1 signifies 'Abnormality, Deformity or Disability as a Result, 26.a indicates 'Punishment for Evil Act', and 5 is the number of the individual motif. This is followed by a summary of the motif, and sometimes by one or more cross-references to other motifs in Part Two giving different reasons for the same motif. After this the source is given, and finally there is an arrow which points to the left, followed by the reference to Part One.

The motif-index draws upon the following Jewish material dating from before 1,000 BCE to approximately the twelfth century CE and centres on legends about Old Testament characters.

The Old Testament
Although the Hebrew canon achieved its final form in the years between 100 BCE and 100 CE, the texts were written down between 1,000 BCE and CE 100 and the oral material upon which much of it is based is even older.[1]

I have used the English translation in The Jerusalem Bible as its intention is to keep as close as possible to the literal meaning of the ancient texts. Where there is any ambiguity, I have referred directly to the Hebrew Massoretic text of the Old Testament.

The Jewish Apocryphal and Apocalyptic, or Pseudepigraphical, Books
These books were composed between 200 BCE and 100 CE. The word Apocrypha means hidden or secret. Composed after the canon of the Old Testament had been established, they were excluded from it, though the material is similarly composed of legendary, historical, prophetic, moral and didactic elements. I have used the translations in the The Jerusalem Bible. The Apocalyptic books are also known as the Pseudepigrapha because many of the books were attributed to, or claimed to be revealed by, biblical characters. The material is largely eschatological and describes visions and ascensions to heaven. My source is the two volume translation, *The Old Testament*

---

1. An excellent introduction to the subject is G. Fohrer, *Introduction to the Old Testament* (trans. D. E. Green; London: SPCK, 1968). See also N.K. Gottwald, *The Hebrew Bible* (Philadelphia Fortress Press, 1985); and, most recently, W. H. Schmidt, *Introduction to the Old Testament* (trans. M. J. O'Connell; London: SCM Press, 1984 [1979]).

Pseudepigrapha, edited by James Charlesworth, which also contains detailed introductions to each text.[1]

The Dead Sea Scrolls and The Nag Hammadi Library

The Dead Sea scrolls were written between 150 BCE and 70 CE, probably by the Essenes, a sect living at Qumran on the shores of the Dead Sea. The texts translated so far contain little legendary material, and only a single motif has been extracted from them, a description of the Messiah. The translation used is that of Vermes, *The Dead Sea Scrolls in English*.

The Nag Hammadi Library, predominantly gnostic in character, was composed within the first five centuries CE. A single motif has been taken from the Jewish text, *The Apocalypse of Adam*, translated by George W. MacRae in Robinson, *The Nag Hammadi Library in English*.

The Mishna

This is the first collection of the rabbinic law, developed by the Tannaim (scholars living in the period from the first century BCE to the second century CE) and compiled by Rabbi Jehuda Hanasi around 200 CE in Palestine.[2]

The Talmud

This is the designation for the Mishna and the Gemara—the discussion of the Mishna by the Amoraim (the name applied to those rabbis active from the second to the fifth centuries CE). There are two Talmudim, the Babylonian Talmud and the smaller Palestinian Talmud, known after the places of their composition. Since relatively little of the Talmud is pertinent to this motif-index—containing far less narrative than the Midrashim—it has not been used as a primary source; instead, Dov Neuman's *Motif-index of Talmudic-Midrashic Literature*[3] and Louis Ginzberg's *Legends of the Jews*[4] have been

1. Meyer Waxman's *A History of Jewish Literature*, I (New York: Bloch Publishing, 1930) gives a valuable insight into the social, historical and religious motivations for these texts.
2. See Hermann L. Strack, *Introduction to the Talmud and Midrash*; (Philadelphia: Jewish Publication Society of America, 1931 [1887]).
3. Unpublished thesis, University of Indiana, 1954.
4. Trans. H. Szold; 7 vols.; Philadelphia: The Jewish Publication Society of

employed, which deal adequately with this material.

The Midrashim
Midrash is the generic term for those compilations of biblical commentaries that are largely aggadic (narrative) in character and which were written down and compiled from about the second to the twelfth centuries CE. The Midrashim may be expositional/exegetical, homiletic, 'historical', ethical or mystical. The most important cycle of these is known as the Midrash Rabba and contains ten books, five of which are concerned with the Pentateuch and five with what are called the Megillot (scrolls): Canticles, Ruth, Lamentations, Ecclesiastes and Esther. The earliest of these books is *Genesis Rabba* (also known as *Bereshit Rabba*), written down before the beginning of the sixth century CE, and the last is *Bamidbar Rabba* (on Numbers) of the twelfth century. An important collection of smaller Midrashim and Midrash fragments is *Bet HaMidrash*, compiled by Adolph Jellinek[1]. Material from other Midrashim is derived from *Mekilta de Rabbi Ishmael*, a tannaitic Midrash to Exodus, Louis Ginzberg's *Legends of the Jews* and Dov Neuman's *Motif-index of Talmudic-Midrashic Literature*.

Legends of the Jews, Louis Ginzberg
This exhaustive compilation of legends was first published between 1909 and 1938 and remains the definitive work in the field. It includes material from an immense variety of sources including the Talmud, the Midrashim, the Apocryphal and Apocalyptic writings, cabbalistic texts such as the Zohar, and also contains a wealth of relevant comparative information.

Motif-index of Talmudic-Midrashic Literature, Dov Neuman
The material in this motif-index has been included in the most recent edition of Stith Thompson's *Motif-index of Folk Literature*. These indexes have no special facilities for incorporating and classifying deformities, diseases and disabilities and hence omit many of the motifs included here.

America, 1909–38.

1   *Bet HaMidrash* (6 vols.; Jerusalem: Wahrmann Books, 1967 [Vienna, 1887]).

PART ONE

A. The Entire Body

A.1. *Absence of Body*

A.1.1. *Invisible body*

(1) God speaks to Moses from a burning bush in the voice of Amram, Moses' father.
see F.5.10.1; G.10.5.1; A.11.2.1; A.11.2.2; A.11.3.1; D.16.3.1; E.11.1.1; E.11.2.1; E.12.3.1; F.16.12.1; P.10.1.1; P.10.7.1; Pc.10.7.1; Gf.4.1.1; Gf.27.2.1; A.10.1.1; I.10.5.1; If.6.1.1; Pc.10.3.1
Ia.16.12.1
GL 2, 303-305; GL 5, 416 n.115-117   [→ *2.15.b.1*

(2) Michael, disguised as a commander-in-chief, becomes invisible when he consults God concerning the death of Abraham.
see A.16.10.1; A.16.12.1; A.10.1.3; Gf.27.2.2
***T. Abr.* 8.1**   [→ *2.6.a.4*

(3) The angel who visits Sarah is invisible to Pharaoh.
GL 1, 223; GL 5, 221 n.73   [→ *2.22.b.4; 2.6.a.5*

(4) Demons have a soul but no body.
***Gen. R.* 7.5**   [→ *1.8.a.1*

(5) Jochebed becomes invisible (as does her daughter, Miriam) when the king sends his hangmen for Jochebed and Miriam.
see A.26.3.1; F.10.1.18
GL 2, 261; GL 5, 396 n.35   [→ *2.18.a.10*

(6) Phinehas makes himself invisible in Rahab's house.
see I.23.3.7; J.23.1.6; A.22.1.4
***Num. R.* 16.1**   [→ *2.18.a.7*

A.2. *Absence of Part of Body*

A.2.1. *Absence of shadow*

(1) No creature casts a shadow on the first day of the summer season.
Gen. R. 6.6 [→ *1.16.a.1*

A.2.4. *Absence of half of body*

(1) Nebuchadnezzar is half consumed by the fire of the furnace into which he orders Hananiah, Mishael and Azariah to be cast.
see A.6.2.5; A.27.2.3; Cc.27.1.1; Cc.27.4.1; T.24.3.1; U.23.1.4; Pd.6.5.1; Pd.12.1.1; E.6.5.6; Ib.1.1.2
Cant. R. 7.9 §1 [→ *1.26.b.53*

A.2.5. *Absence of head*

(1) The demon called Envy has all the limbs of a man but no head.
see D.1.1
GL 4, 152; GL 6, 292 n.55 [→ *3.9.3*

(2) The demon called Murder has all the limbs of a man but no head, and sees through his breast.
see D.1.2; G.4.5.2
T. Sol. 9.1-7 [→ *3.9.4*

A.4 *Body(ies) in Unusual Position on Body*

A.4.1. *Body(ies) on head, hair, face and parts of face*

(1) The bodies of the righteous who will descend from Adam hang on his head, hair, forehead, ears, earlobes, eyes, nose and mouth while he is still a lifeless mass.
see D.14.10.1; E.14.10.1; Fb.14.10.1; G.14.10.1; H.14.10.1; I.14.10.1; J.14.10.1; Ja.14.10.1; J.23.1.1; G.23.5.1; Ca.9.1.1; Cb.9.1.1; A.10.1.9; A.10.1.10; A.6.1.19; A.6.1.20; A.6.3.4; A.13.10.1; A.16.9.1; A.9.1.2; B.13.10.1; Sa.2.3.3; Sa.24.3.3; A.6.5.20; A.6.5.21; A.12.1.1; R.14.1.1; R.18.1.1
Exod. R. 40.3 [→ *2.4.3*

A.6. *Abnormal Size of Body*

A.6.1. *Abnormally large body*

(1) The size of the angel with whom Jacob struggles is one third of the world.
Gen. R. 97.4; Gen. R. 68.12 [→ *3.3.a.16; 3.4.a.5*

(2) The guardians of the gates of hell are as large as serpents; they have faces like very large snakes, with eyes aflame or eyes like extinguished lamps, and fangs exposed down to their breasts.

see F.18.6.1; G.16.12.6; Ic.18.2.1

2 En. **42.1 (J and A);** *2 En.* **42.1 (Appendix);** *Apoc. Zeph.* **6.8**

[→ *2.24.7; 2.22.a.10*

(3) The 200 myriads of Grigori, who lust after the daughters of men and descend to earth, have the forms of human beings but are larger than giants.

see F.13.11.1

2 En. **18.1-5 (J and A)** [→ *1.1.a.4*

(4) The Cainites are giant genii with two heads.

see A.6.1.8; A.6.2.1; D.5.1.2

GL 1, 114; GL 5, 143 n.34; GL 4, 132

[→ *1.1.a.17; 1.16.b.2; 3.2.2*

(5) The ancestors of Abraham were giants. They built the Tower of Babel (or alternatively, one of them, Belos, built it) and the city of Babylon and taught astrology. They were scattered when the Tower was destroyed, or perished for lack of wisdom.

Ps.-Eupol. Preparatio Evangelica 9.17.2-3; 9.18.2; Bar. 3.26

[→ *1.1.a.16*

(6) The generation of Noah are giants in stature and strength.

GL 1, 151, 158-160; GL 5, 172-173 n.13-15; GL 5, 181 n.35

[→ *1.1.a.11*

(7) The seventh generation are giants.

Sib. Or. **1.9** [→ *1.1.a.9*

(8) The Cainites are giants with two heads.

see A.6.1.4; A.6.2.1; D.5.1.2

GL 1, 114; GL 5, 143 n.34; GL 4, 132

[→ *1.1.a.17; 1.16.b.2; 3.2.2*

(9) The Philistines are giants.

Gen. R. **37.5** [→ *1.6.b.1*

(10) Giants, 300 cubits tall (or, in a variant, 3,000 ells tall) are born as a result of the union between mortal women and 200 angels who have descended to earth to seduce them.

1 En. **6-7;** *1 En.* **9.7-9;** *1 En.* **15.3;** *1 En.* **15.8f.;** *2 En.* **18.5 (J);**
Gen. R. **26.7;** *Jub.* **5.1-2;** *Jub.* **7.21-22** [→ *1.1.b.1*

(11) Four hundred and nine thousand giants, or, in a variant, one hundred and four thousand giants, are destroyed in the Flood.
3 Bar. **4.10 (Slavonic and Greek)** [→ *1.1.a.10*

(12) Giants put their feet over the Great Deep at the time of the Flood and keep the water shut up.
Gen. R. **31.12** [→ *4.1.b.3*

(13) Giants are born to women who lust in their minds after the angels.
T. Reub. **5.6** *(Test. XII Patr.);* *Gen. R.* **26.7; GL 5, 155 n.57**
[→ *1.5.1; 1.14a.14*

(14) The three giants Ahiman, Sheshai and Talmai, sons of Anak, are consulted by Sarah who asks them to look into the distance to try and see Abraham and Isaac.
GL 5, 256 n.259 [→ *4.1.b.4*

(15) Giants (Nephilim), sons and daughters of Anak, are seen by Caleb and his party in the land of Canaan.
see A.6.5.18
Num. **13.33;** *Num. R.* **16.11; GL 3, 268** [→ *1.1.b.5*

(16) Og, king of Bashan, is the last survivor of the Rephaim and of immense size: his bed of iron is nine cubits long and four wide.
see A.6.5.19; A.6.3.3; Va.6.5.1; Ic.6.5.2; Ic.7.2.1; Ic.7.3.1; Sa.2.3.2; Sa.24.3.2; Ic.2.8.1; Ic.5.11.1; U.6.5.3
Deut. 3.1-18 [→ *1.1.a.15*

(17) Abner, the son of the witch of Endor, is a giant of extraordinary size.
GL 4, 73; GL 6, 239 n.84,85 [→ *1.1.b.6*

(18) Ishbi, the brother of Goliath, and his three brothers, are giants.
Ruth R. **2.20; GL 4, 107; GL 6, 268 n.110** [→ *1.6.c.1; 1.6.c.2*

(19) Adam's body is of gigantic dimensions reaching from heaven to earth and the same distance from east to west and north to south.
see A.6.3.4; A.6.5.20; A.6.5.21; A.10.1.9; F.5.1.1; A.13.10.1; B.13.10.1; A.10.1.10; A.9.1.2; Sa.2.3.3; Sa.24.3.3; J.23.1.1; A.16.9.1; A.6.1.20; G.23.5.1; Ca.9.1.1; Cb.9.1.1; Cb.5.1.1; A.4.1.1; D.14.10.1; E.14.10.1; Fb.14.10.1; G.14.10.1; H.14.10.1; I.14.10.1; J.14.10.1; Ja.14.10.1; A.12.1.1; R.14.1.1; R.18.1.1
Gen. R. **19.9;** *Gen. R.* **21.3;** *Gen. R.* **8.1;** *Gen. R.* **24.2; Job 20.6;** *Apoc. Abr.* **23.5;** *Lev. R.* **14.1;** *Lev. R.* **18.2** [→ *1.16.a.2; 3.5.a.2*

(20) The size of Adam's body is reduced to one hundred ells after the Fall.

> see A.6.3.4; A.6.5.20; A.6.5.21; A.10.1.9; F.5.1.1; A.13.10.1; B.13.10.1;
> A.10.1.10; A.9.1.2; Sa.2.3.3; Sa.24.3.3; J.23.1.1; A.16.9.1; A.6.1.19;
> G.23.5.1; Ca.9.1.1; Cb.9.1.1; Cb.5.1.1; A.4.1.1; D.14.10.1; E.14.10.1;
> Fb.14.10.1; G.14.10.1; H.14.10.1; I.14.10.1; J.14.10.1; Ja.14.10.1; A.12.1.1;
> R.14.1.1; R.18.1.1
> ***Gen. R.* 19.8; *Gen. R.* 12.6; *Num. R.* 13.2; *Num. R.* 13.12**
> [→ *1.26.a.1; 1.14.d.1; 3.6.b.5*

(21) Eve's body in Paradise is incomparable in aspect and size.

> see A.6.3.5; A.6.5.22; A.10.1.11; A.13.10.2; B.13.10.2; A.16.8.1; A.16.9.2
> ***Apoc. Abr.* 23.5** [→ *3.5.a.3; 1.16.a.3*

(22) Eliezer, Abraham's servant, is a giant of a man, able to carry two camels across a stream.

> see Fb.24.1.1
> **GL 1, 295; GL 5, 261 n.292** [→ *4.1.b.8*

(23) Jacob is transformed into a giant when he is blessed by Isaac and is bathed in celestial dew which fills his bones with marrow.

> see G.23.4.7; K.13.10.1; Ta.23.1.1; Ta.24.1.1; Sa.2.3.12; Sa.24.3.12; O.6.1.1;
> Q.6.1.1; T.23.1.3; G.23.5.3
> **GL 1, 332, 336; GL 5, 283, 285 n.88, 98** [→ *1.14.c.8; 1.17.5*

(24) Achor, king of Tappual, a giant of a man, is killed by Judah.

> ***T. Jud.* 3.3-4 (*Test. XII Patr.*)** [→ *4.1.b.11*

(25) Men of enormous size are seen by Caleb and his party on their reconnaissance mission into Canaan.

> **Num. 13.32** [→ *2.5.9*

(26) Goliath, son of Orpah, is of a gigantic size.

> see A.23.1.15; A.23.6.4; A.6.5.30; N.13.2.1
> ***Ruth R.* 2.20; GL 4, 31; GL 6, 190 n.44** [→ *1.6.c.3*

(27) Absalom is of such gigantic proportions that a man, Abba Saul, himself of extraordinary size, standing in the eye-sockets of Absalom's skull, sinks in down to his nose.

> see E.5.1.1; E.6.5.5
> ***Num. R.* 9.24** [→ *3.4.a.9*

(28) One of the Philistines, a descendant of Rapha, who fights at Gath, is of a huge stature, with six fingers on each hand and six toes on each foot.

see Pc.5.5.1; Ub.5.5.1

2 Sam. 21.20; 1 Chron. 20.6   [→ *1.1.b.8*

(29) Samson's body is gigantic—he measures sixty ells between the shoulders—and his strength is superhuman.
 see M.6.3.1; U.23.1.2; E.25.5.1; I.10.20.1; Ie.17.3.1; G.24.1.2; T.25.1.2; G.1.3; E.8.1.2; E.6.5.4; G.13.4.15
 GL 4, 47; GL 6, 206-207 n.114, 115   [→ *3.4.a.8*

(30) The general Sisera has a body of vast dimensions; if he takes a bath in the river and dives beneath the surface, enough fish are caught in his beard to feed a multitude, and at the sound of his voice the strongest of walls fall in a heap.
 GL 4, 35; GL 6, 195 n.72   [→ *4.1.b.25*

(31) Daniel is a giant in appearance.
 see Sa.2.1.27; Sa.24.2.27
 Liv. Proph. (Daniel) **4.2**   [→ *3.3.a.34*

A.6.2. *Abnormally small body*

(1) Cainites are dwarfs with two heads.
 see A.6.1.4; A.6.1.4; D.5.1.2
 GL 1, 114; GL 5, 143 n.34; GL 4, 132
                            [→ *1.1.a.17; 1.16.b.2; 3.2.2*

(2) The Caphtorim are dwarfs.
 Gen. R. **37.5**   [→ *1.6.b.1.*

(3) The Neshiah, the fifth earth, is inhabited by dwarfs without noses.
 see H.1.1.1
 GL 1, 114; GL 5, 143 n.36   [→ *1.1.a.19; 3.2.4; 1.16.b.3*

(4) Aaron's body shrinks when he becomes aware of his approaching death.
 see A.23.1.8; E.6.1.2; A.6.5.26; E.12.10.2; F.10.1.12; Ga.10.2.2; I.10.1.4.
 GL 6, 111 n.636   [→ *1.12.a.25*

(5) Nebuchadnezzar is as small as a midget dwarf, smaller than a handbreadth.
 see A.27.2.3; Cc.27.1.1; Cc.27.4.1; U.23.1.4; T.24.3.1; A.2.4.1; Pd.6.5.1; Pd.12.1.1; E.6.5.6; Ib.1.1.2.
 Gen. R. **16.4**   [→ *3.6.b.11; 4.2.d.3*

A.6.3. *Abnormally broad or fat body*

(1) Kerubi'el, prince of the cherubim, is as broad and as tall as the seven heavens. His body is full of burning coals and emits lightning flashes. Flames blaze on his hands, his mouth, tongue, face and eyes; his eyelashes are like lightning, and lightning flickers from the rays of his head and his wheels. His whole body is covered with wings and eyes.

> see A.6.5.2; A.14.5.1; A.14.10.2; A.16.17.1; F.16.12.2; G.4.1.3; G.5.15.1; G.16.12.2; Gc.16.12.1; I.16.12.1; Ib.16.12.1; P.10.3.1
> **3 *En.* 22.3-9**   [→ *3.3.a.7*

(2) The breadth and height of Enoch become equal to that of the world when he is transformed into Metatron.

> see A.6.5.12; G.5.13.2; G.10.2.3; M.14.2.13; M.20.1.13; A.16.12.6; B.16.12.1; E.16.4.1; G.16.12.5; V.16.12.1; Va.16.12.1; A.10.1.7
> **3 *En.* 9.2; 3 *En.* 48c.5 (Appendix); *T. Abr.* 10.8 (Recension B)**
> [→ *1.35.2*

(3) The giant Og, who is of enormous stature, has a breadth which is one half of his height.

> see A.6.5.19; Va.6.5.1; Ic.6.5.2; Ic.7.2.1; Sa.2.3.2; Sa.24.3.2; Ic.2.8.1; Ic.5.11.1; U.6.5.3; A.6.1.16
> **GL 3, 344; GL 6, 119 n.687**   [→ *1.1.a.15.*

(4) Before the Fall, Adam's body is extraordinarily wide and reaches from east to west and north to south.

> see A.6.1.19; A.6.5.20; A.6.5.21; A.10.1.9; F.5.1.1; A.13.10.1; B.13.10.1; A.10.1.10; A.9.1.2; Sa.2.3.2; Sa.24.3.2; J.23.1.1; A.16.9.1; A.6.1.20; G.23.5.1; Ca.9.1.1; Cb.9.1.1; Cb.5.1.1; A.4.1.1; D.14.10.1; E.14.10.1; Fb.14.10.1; G.14.10.1; H.14.10.1; I.14.10.1; J.14.10.1; Ja.14.10.1; A.12.1.1; R.14.1.1; R.18.1.1
> ***Gen. R.* 21.3; *Gen. R.* 8.1; *Gen. R.* 24.2; Job 20.6; *Apoc. Abr.* 23.5; *Lev. R.* 14.1; *Lev. R.* 18.2**   [→ *3.5.a.2; 1.16.a.2*

(5) Before the Fall, Eve's body is of a terrible breadth and a very great height, incomparable in aspect and size.

> see A.6.1.21; A.6.5.22; A.10.1.11; A.13.10.2; B.13.10.2; A.16.8.1; A.16.9.2
> ***Apoc. Abr.* 23.5**   [→ *3.5.a.3; 1.16.a.3*

(6) Simon is so fat and rotund after his sojourn in Joseph's house in Egypt that he resembles a leather bottle.

> see P.23.7.1
> **GL 2, 95; GL 5, 350 n.240**   [→ *1.12.c.1*

(7) Adikam, the second son of Pharaoh, is very fleshy.
see A.6.6.1; E.6.5.2
GL 2, 298-299; GL 5, 413 n.104 [→ *3.6.b.13*

A.6.4. *Abnormally thin body*

(1) After seven days of fasting Aseneth is emaciated, with fallen face, straggly hair, cracked lips and eyes inflamed and burning from the tears of shame she has shed.
see E.22.2; G.11.3.2; Ia.15.1.1; Ba.11.3.1; F.10.1.10; Fa.11.3.1; G.10.2.8; Ia.11.3.1
Jos. Asen. **11.1.1;** *Jos. Asen.* **13.9.8;** *Jos. Asen.* **18.3**
[→ *1.13.3; 2.31.b.2*

(2) Moses is slender like a palm tree.
see Sa.2.3.19; Sa.24.3.19; A.6.5.25; P.25.4.1; P.23.1.1; F.10.1.5; Fb.10.1.11; F.11.3.2; G.10.2.9; I.10.1.5; G.25.4.1; A.25.9.1; If.6.1.3; E.6.1.1; Ga.10.2.1; E.12.10.1; I.23.3.3; Ia.13.2.1; Ia.24.4.1; Ib.13.2.1; Ib.24.4.1; P.13.2.1; P.24.4.1; K.13.10.2; B.16.12.2; Ib.16.12.3; G.17.20.1; P.11.2.2; I.23.3.3; Fb.14.2.3
GL 2, 285 [→ *3.3.a.29*

(3) The boy who is helping Solomon to build the Temple grows thin and emaciated because a demon, Ornias, sucks the thumb of his right hand (and takes half of his provisions and wages).
T. Sol. **1.2-4** [→ *1.19.b.16*

A.6.5. *Abnormally tall or long body*

(1) Serapi'el, prince of the seraphim, is as tall as the seven heavens and his body is full of eyes that resemble stars of lightning in their brightness. He has the face of an angel and the body of an eagle.
see F.21.7.1; G.4.1.1; G.5.15.1; G.10.2.1
3 En. **27.3-7** [→ *3.3.a.5*

(2) Kerubi'el, prince of the cherubim, is as tall, broad and wide as the seven heavens. His body is full of burning coals and emits lightnings; his mouth, tongue, face and eyes are also of fire; his eyelashes are like lightning, and lightning flickers from the rays of his head and his wheels. His whole body is covered with eyes and wings and flames blaze on both his hands.
see A.6.3.1; A.14.5.1; A.14.10.2; A.16.17.1; A.20.1.1; F.16.12.2; G.4.1.3; G.5.15.2; G.16.12.2; Gc.16.12.1; I.16.12.1; Ib.16.12.1; P.10.3.1
3 En. **22.3-9** [→ *3.3.a.7*

(3) The height of Opanni'el, prince of the ophanim, is a journey of 2,500 years. He has one hundred wings on each side, sixteen faces, 8,766 eyes, corresponding to the number of hours in a year, and in each pair of eyes lightnings flash and torches blaze, consuming all who look at him.

see F.5.10.2; G.10.1.1; G.10.5.2; G.5.13.1; M.14.2.14; M.20.1.14

3 En. 25.2-4   [→ *3.3.a.4*

(4) Soperi'el and Soperi-el, two princes of angels, are as tall as the seven heavens. They have appearances like lightning, eyes like the sun, bodies full of eyes, wings as numerous as the days of the year and as broad as heaven, lips like the gates of the east, tongues as high as the sea's waves; flames and lightnings issue from their mouths, fire is kindled from their sweat, and their tongues are blazing torches.

see Ba.16.4.1; G.4.1.2; G.5.15.3; G.16.12.1; I.10.1.3; I.10.5.2; Ib.6.5.1; Ib.16.12.2; M.14.2.15; M.20.1.15

3 En. 18.25   [→ *3.3.a.6*

(5) Samuil and Raguil, the two angels who transport Enoch to heaven, are very tall.

see Ia.10.1.1; F.10.1.4; P.11.2.1; G.10.1.2; M.14.2.4; M.20.1.4

2 En. 1.4-6 (J and A); 2 En. 3.1-3 (J and A); 2 En. 33.6 (J and A)
                                                             [→ *3.3.a.14*

(6) The angel Hadarniel is sixty myriads of parasangs taller than his fellows.

see I.10.5.3

GL 3, 110; GL 6, 46 n.247   [→ *3.3.a.3*

(7) The angel Nuriel is 300 parasangs tall.

see A.16.12.8; A.16.15.1

GL 2, 306-307; GL 5, 416-418 n.117   [→ *3.3.a.13*

(8) The chief of the angels called Irin and Kadishim ('Watchers' and 'Holy Ones') is so tall that it would take 500 years to walk a distance equal to his height.

see A.16.11.1

GL 2, 308; GL 5, 416-418 n.117   [→ *3.3.a.12*

(9) The angel Sammael is so tall that it would take 500 years to cover a distance equal to his height. He is covered with eyes, at the sight of which the spectator falls prostrate in awe.

see G.5.15.4; G.4.1.5; M.14.2.17; M.20.1.17
GL 2, 308; GL 5, 416-418 n.117   [→ *2.24.1*

(10) The angels Af and Hemah ('Anger' and 'Wrath') are 500
parasangs tall and forged out of chains of black fire and red fire.
GL 2, 308; GL 5, 416-418 n.117   [→ *2.24.2*

(11) The angel Sandalfon, one of the ophanim, towers above his fellows by so great a height that it would take 500 years to cross a distance equal to it. Standing on earth, his head reaches the holy Hayyot.
see D.5.13.1; I.5.14.1; Ib.5.14.1
3 En. 1.7-8; *1 En.* 71.1-7; GL 2, 307; GL 5, 416-418, n.117; GL
3, 111; GL 6, 46 n.247   [→ *3.3.a.2; 2.22.a.3*

(12) The height and breadth of Enoch become equal to that of the
world when he is transformed into Metatron. His stature is increased
by 70,000 parasangs.
see A.6.3.2; A.16.12.6; G.5.13.2; G.10.2.3; M.14.2.13; M.20.1.13; B.16.12.1;
E.16.4.1; G.16.12.5; V.16.12.1; Va.16.12.1; A.10.1.7
3 En. 9.2; *3 En.* 48c.5 (Appendix); *T. Abr.* 10.8 (Recension B)
                                        [→ *1.35.2*

(13) The Antichrist is ten cubits tall. The track of his feet is three
cubits long, as is his right arm. His hair reaches to his feet and he is
three-crested. His eyes are like the star which rises in the morning and
his right eye like a lion's. His lower teeth are made of iron, his lower
jaw of diamond; his right arm is made of iron, his left of copper. He
is long-faced, long-nosed and disorderly, and has three letters on his
forehead: A, K and T, signifying denial, rejection and the befouled
dragon. His mother conceives him by touching the head of a fish.
see E.6.5.1; Fb.13.2.3; Fc.16.5.1; G.10.2.6; G.18.1.1; Ic.16.1.1; O.16.1.1;
O.16.2.3; U.6.5.2
Apoc. Dan. 9.11, 16-26   [→ *3.1.25; 1.3.c.1*

(14) The Raphaim were giants seven, eight, nine or ten cubits tall.
They dwelt in the region between the land of the Ammonites and
Mount Hermon but were destroyed on account of their evil deeds.
Jub. 29.9-11   [→ *1.1.a.13*

(15) The Amorites are eighteen cubits tall.
see G.23.4.13; G.23.4.14; W.25.2.2
GL 3, 346; GL 6, 120 n.699   [→ *1.1.a.14*

(16) Sihon, the king of the Amorites, is a giant taller than any tower, his thighbone alone measures eighteen cubits; he is so tall that the waters of the Flood do not reach him.

see A.23.2.1
Deut. R. 11.7; GL 3, 339-342; GL 6, 117, 118 n.668, 669, 677
[→ *1.1.b.3.*

(17) Anak the giant is so tall that the sun only reaches to his ankles. After living a long time, half his body withers away because, descending as he does from the union of the fallen angels and women, he is half mortal, half immortal.

see Cd.23.1.1
Num. R. 16.11; GL 3, 268-270; GL 6, 94 n.512-516   [→ *1.1.b.4*

(18) Ahiman, Sheshai and Talmai, the three sons of Anak, are immensely tall and strong as marble; their steps make ridges in the earth.

see A.6.1.15
Num. R. 16.11; GL 3, 268-270; GL 6, 94 n.512-516   [→ *1.1.b.5*

(19) The giant Og is of immense stature: he sits on a city wall with his feet touching the ground. Moses, who is himself ten cubits tall, can, by jumping ten cubits, just reach Og's ankles. By another account, Og measures eighteen cubits, or his feet measure eighteen cubits, and he is so tall that the waters of the Flood do not reach him.

see A.6.3.3; Va.6.5.1; Ic.6.5.2; Ic.7.2.1; Sa.2.3.2; Sa.24.3.2; Ic.2.8.1; Ic.5.11.1; U.6.5.3; A.6.1.16
Deut. R. 1.24; *Deut. R.* 11.7; GL 3, 343-348; GL 6, 119-121 n.685-68, 691, 694, 695, 704   [→ *1.1.a.15*

(20) Before the Fall, Adam's body is extraordinarily tall and reaches from earth to heaven.

see A.6.1.19; A.6.1.20; A.6.3.4; F.5.1.1; A.13.10.1; A.10.1.9; A.10.1.10; B.13.10.1; A.9.1.2; Sa.2.3.3; Sa.24.3.3; J.23.1.1; A.16.9.1; A.6.5.21; G.23.5.1; Ca.9.1.1; Cb.9.1.1; A.4.1.1; D.14.10.1; E.14.10.1; Fb.14.10.1; G.14.10.1; H.14.10.1; I.14.10.1; J.14.10.1; Ja.14.10.1; A.12.1.1; R.14.1.1; R.18.1.1
Gen. R. 21.3; *Gen. R.* 8.1; *Gen. R.* 24.2; Job 20.6; *Apoc. Abr.* 23.5; *Lev. R.* 14.1; *Lev. R.* 18.2   [→ *3.5.a.2; 1.16.a.2*

(21) After the Fall, the size of Adam's body is reduced to one hundred cubits.

see A.6.1.19; A.6.1.20; A.6.3.4; F.5.1.1; A.13.10.1; A.10.1.1; A.10.1.2; B.13.10.1; A.9.1.9; Sa.2.3.3; Sa.24.3.3; J.23.1.1; A.16.9.1; A.6.5.20; G.23.5.1; Ca.9.1.1; Cb.9.1.1; A.4.1.1; D.14.10.1; E.14.10.1; Fb.14.10.1; G.14.10.1; H.14.10.1; I.14.10.1; J.14.10.1; Ja.14.10.1; A.12.1.1; R.14.1.1; R.18.1.1

Num. R. **13.2;** *Num. R.* **13.12;** *Gen. R.* **12.6;** *Gen. R.* **19.8;** *Gen. R.* **7.6;** *Cant. R.* **3.7** §5   [→ *1.14.d.1; 1.26.a.1; 3.6.b.5*

(22) Before the Fall, Eve's body is of very great height and terrible breadth, incomparable in aspect and size.

see A.6.1.21; A.6.3.5; A.10.1.11; A.13.10.2; B.13.10.2; A.16.8.1; A.16.9.2

Apoc. Abr. **23.5**   [→ *3.5.a.3; 1.16.a.3*

(23) Abraham is as tall as seventy men set on end.

see T.25.1.1; A.10.1.12; Sa.2.3.9; Sa.24.3.9; Pc.10.5.1; Pc.10.6.1; F.10.1.8

GL 1, 232; GL 5, 225 n.97; GL 5, 267 n.317   [→ *3.3.a.27*

(24) Belisath, a giant of a man in strength, twelve cubits tall, is killed by Jacob.

T. Jud. **3.7** *(Test. XII Patr.)*   [→ *4.1.b.12*

(25) Moses is like a cedar of Lebanon in stature: he is ten cubits tall.

see E.6.1.1; E.12.10.1; F.10.1.11; Ga.10.2.1; Sa.2.3.19; Sa.24.3.19; Ia.13.2.1; Ia.24.4.1; Ib.13.2.1; Ib.24.4.1; P.13.2.1; P.24.4.1; K.13.10.2; B.16.12.2; Ib.16.12.3; G.17.20.1; P.23.1.1; P.11.2.2; I.23.3.3; G.10.2.9; A.6.4.2; P.25.4.1; Fb.10.1.1; G.25.4.1; A.25.9.1; If.6.1.3; I.10.1.5; Fb.14.2.3; F.11.3.2

GL 2, 332; GL 5 425 n.157; GL 6, 120 n.695   [→ *3.3.a.29*

(26) Aaron is like a cedar of Lebanon in stature.

see E.6.1.2; E.12.10.2; F.10.1.12; Ga.10.2.2; I.10.1.4; A.23.1.8; A.6.2.3

GL 2, 332; GL 5, 425 n.157   [→ *3.3.a.30*

(27) Joshua is five ells tall.

see F.10.1.15; I.23.2.1

GL 4, 14; GL 6, 179 n.45   [→ *3.3.a.31*

(28) The Israelites who go on a reconnaissance mission into Canaan are sixty cubits in height.

GL 3, 268; GL 6, 94 n.513   [→ *2.22.b.5*

(29) An Egyptian who is five cubits tall is killed by Benaiah, son of Jehoiada, a hero from Kabzeel.

1 Chron. **11.22-23**   [→ *4.1.b.14*

(30) Goliath is six cubits and one span tall.
  see A.6.1.26; A.23.1.15; A.23.6.4; Na.13.2.1
  1 Sam. 17.4   [→ *4.1.b.17*

(31) Saul stands head and shoulders taller than the rest of the people.
  1 Sam. 9.2; 1 Sam. 10.23   [→ *3.3.a.32*

(32) David becomes as tall as Saul when he wears the latter's royal garments. Seeing this, Saul puts the evil eye on David, and David removes the clothes.
  Lev. R. **26.9**   [→ *1.14.c.16; 3.3.a.33*

(33) The Messiah is one hundred cubits tall. Alternatively, he is two, three or nine hundred cubits tall.
  Gen. R. **12.6**   [→ *3.3.a.42*

A.6.6. *Abnormally short body*

(1) Adikam, the second son of Pharaoh, is very short: his height is one cubit and a space.
  see A.6.3.7; E.6.5.2.
  GL 2, 298-299; GL 5, 413 n.104   [→ *3.6.b.13*

A.8 *Inverted Body*

(1) The dead walk with their heads downward and their feet in the air; spirits appear likewise in necromancy except when they are summoned by a king.
  Lev. R. **26.7; GL 4, 70; GL 6, 236 n.75**   [→ *1.34.2*

(2) The dwellers of Paradise walk on their heads.
  GL 5, 263 n.301   [→ *1.16.b.4; 1.34.5; 3.2.5*

(3) Isaac continues to walk on his head after he leaves Paradise.
  see A.25.3.2; G.23.4.6; Sa.2.3.11; Sa.24.3.11
  GL 5, 263 n.301   [→ *1.16.b.5*

A.9. *Body of, or including, Opposite Sex*

A.9.1. *Androgynous body*

(1) A muse who desires herself becomes androgynous and gives birth.
  Apoc. Adam **V, 5.81**   [→ *2.14.a.3; 2.23.a.1*

(2) Adam is an androgyne before he is separated into man and woman.

    see A.6.1.19; A.6.1.20; A.6.3.4; F.5.1.1; A.13.10.1; A.10.1.9; A.10.1.10; B.13.10.1; A.6.5.21; Sa.2.3.3; Sa.24.3.3; J.23.1.1; A.16.9.1; A.6.5.20; G.23.5.1; Ca.9.1.1; Cb.9.1.1; A.4.1.1; D.14.10.1; E.14.10.1; Fb.14.10.1; G.14.10.1; H.14.10.1; I.14.10.1; J.14.10.1; Ja.14.10.1; A.12.1.1; R.14.1.1; R.18.1.1

    Lev. R. **14.1;** *Gen. R.* **8.1;** *Apoc. Adam* **1.2-5**   [→ *1.8.b.3*

A.9.2. *Man in the form of woman*

(1) Elijah appears in the guise of a harlot to accompany Rabbi Meir who is being pursued by Roman bailiffs. The latter desist from their pursuit as they cannot believe Rabbi Meir would choose such a companion.

    see M.20.1.5; M.14.2.5; A.22.1.1; Pc.10.7.2; A.10.1.17

    GL 4, 204; GL 6, 326 n.51   [→ *2.18.a.2; 2.9.3; 2.6.a.6*

A.10. *Unusual Emission or Emanation from Body*

A.10.1. *Body that emits light*

(1) The lustre of God's presence nourishes Moses for forty days and nights when he is on Mount Sinai.

    see A.1.1.1; F.5.10.1; G.10.5.1; Ia.16.12.1; A.11.2.1; A.11.2.2; A.11.3.1; D.16.3.1; E.11.1.1; E.11.2.1; E.12.3.1; F.16.12.1; P.10.1.1; Pc.10.7.1; Gf.4.1.1; Gf.27.2.1; A.17.6.1; A.17.7.1

    Exod. R. **47.5**   [→ *2.32.1*

(2) Abel in heaven is a wondrous man, bright as the sun, who sits on a throne between two gates leading to destruction, and judges and sentences souls.

    see W.25.1.1

    T. Abr. **12.5**   [→ *1.35.1*

(3) The angel Michael, though disguised as a commander-in-chief when he meets Abraham, is as bright as the sun.

    see A.16.10.1; A.16.12.1; A.1.1.2; Gf.27.2.2

    T. Abr. **2.4;** *T. Abr.* **7.3-5 (Recension A and B)**   [→ *3.1.7*

(4) When the adversaries of the Jews send elephants to trample them, two angels appear, clothed in glory and of awe-inspiring appearance, and fill them with confusion and timidity.

    3 Macc. **6.18**   [→ *2.24.4; 2.15.b.3*

(5) Angels of a shining white appearance greet Sobacha, Elijah's father, when Elijah is about to be born. They wrap Sobacha in fire and give him flames of fire to eat.

see A.11.2.4

Liv. Proph. (Elijah) 21.2 [→ *3.1.9*

(6) The three hundred angels who look after Paradise are very bright.

2 En. 8.8 (J) [→ *3.6.a.4*

(7) Enoch's body becomes radiant when he is anointed with the oil which is greater than the greatest light and like the rays of the glittering sun, and he is clothed in garments of glory.

see A.6.3.2; A.6.5.12; G.5.13.2; G.10.2.3; M.14.2.13; M.20.1.13; A.16.12.6; B.16.12.1; E.16.4.1; G.16.12.5; V.16.12.1; Va.16.12.1

2 En. 22.8-10 (J and A) [→ *1.14.c.1; 1.35.2*

(8) Satan assumes the brightness of angels and, pretending to be an angel, tells Eve that her penance—standing for thirty-nine days in the river Tigris—has been accepted after eighteen days, and thus lures her out of the water.

LAE (Vita) 6.1-2; 7, 9.1-5; 10.1; *LAE (Apoc. Mos.)* 16

[→ *2.9.2; 2.6.a.3*

(9) Adam is luminous, as a 'garment of light' is made for him which is like a lamp, broad at the bottom, narrow at the top, smooth as a fingernail, lovely as pearl and like fine linen.

see A.6.1.19; A.6.1.20; A.6.3.4; F.5.1.1; A.13.10.1; A.9.1.2; A.10.1.10; B.1.10.1; A.6.5.21; Sa.2.3.3; Sa.24.3.3; J.23.1.1; A.16.9.1; A.6.5.20; G.23.5.1; Ca.9.1.1; Cb.9.1.1; A.4.1.1; D.14.10.1; E.14.10.1; Fb.14.10.1; G.14.10.1; H.14.10.1; I.14.10.1; J.14.10.1; Ja.14.10.1; A.12.1.1; R.14.1.1; R.18.1.1

Gen. R. 20.12 [→ *1.19.b.1; 5.1.2*

(10) Adam's beauty—which reflects the wisdom with which God had endowed him—makes his face shine. Even the balls of his feet outshine the sun.

see A.6.1.19; A.6.1.20; A.6.3.4; F.5.1.1; A.13.10.1; A.9.1.2; A.10.1.9; B.13.10.1; A.6.5.21; Sa.2.3.3; Sa.24.3.3; J.23.1.1; A.16.9.1; A.6.5.20; G.23.5.1; Ca.9.1.1; Cb.9.1.1; A.4.1.1; D.14.10.1; E.14.10.1; Fb.14.10.1; G.14.10.1; H.14.10.1; I.14.10.1. J.14.10.1; Ja.14.10.1; A.12.1.1; R.14.1.1; R.18.1.1.

Qoh. R. 8.1 §2; *Lev. R.* 20.2 [→ *3.6.a.6*

(11) Eve's body is luminous, as a 'garment of light' is made for her by God.
see A.6.1.21; A.6.3.5; A.6.5.22; A.13.10.2; B.13.10.2; A.16.8.1; A.16.9.2
Gen. R. **20.12**   [→ *1.19.b.1; 5.1.2*

(12) Abraham is born with a luminous body.
see Sa.2.3.9; Sa.24.3.9; Pc.10.5.1; Pc.10.6.1; A.6.5.23; T.25.1.1; F.10.1.8
Exod. R. **15.26**   [→ *3.3.a.35*

(13) Sarai's lustre makes the whole land of Egypt sparkle when the box in which Abram has hidden her is opened.
see F.10.1.9; Vg.1.1.; Vg.23.1.3; Nd.5.1.1
Gen. R. **40.5**   [→ *3.3.a.36*

(14) Rays emanating from Joseph illuminate the house of Aseneth like 'the splendour of the sun'.
see Sa.2.3.14; Sa.24.3.14; Va.3.1.2; Va.27.2.1; Va.3.1.3; Va.10.10.1
GL 2, 171; GL 5, 374 n.432   [→ *3.3.a.37*

(15) Judah becomes luminous like the moon, with twelve rays under his feet.
see I.23.3.2; J.23.1.2; F.11.6.2; E.8.1.1; E.13.1.2; G.10.4.1; Gf.16.3.1; Ic.18.5.1; F.18.5.3; If.6.1.2; Va.3.1.1
T. Naph. **5.5** (*Test. XII Patr.*)   [→ *3.10.20*

(16) The Rechabites, sons of Jonadab, possess a shining appearance after they are transported to the Isles of the Blessed.
Hist. Rech. **11.5b;** *Hist. Rech.* **12.(2)3**   [→ *1.35.9*

(17) Elijah shines after fighting the Antichrist.
see M.20.1.5; M.14.2.5; A.22.1.1; Pc.10.7.2; A.9.2.1
Apoc. Elij. **4.19**   [→ *1.35.12*

(18) Enoch shines after fighting the Antichrist.
see A.10.1.17
Apoc. Elij. **4.19**   [→ *1.35.12*

(19) Isaiah witnesses Adam, Abel, Enoch and all the righteous from the time of Adam without robes of flesh, but in the robes of above, like angels in glory.
Asc. Isa. (*Vis. Isa.*) **9.7-9**   [→ *1.35.3*

(20) A pious man has a radiance of glory at the time of his death.
GL 6, 61 n.309   [→ *1.14.c.24*

(21) At the time of the resurrection the learned and the virtuous shine as brightly as the vault of heaven and the stars.

1 En. **104.2;** *2 En.* **65.10** (J); *2 En.* **65.11** (A); *2 En.* **66.7** (J); *2 Bar.* **51.5,** 9f; **Dan. 12.3,10; Dan. 11.35;** *Lev. R.* **30.2** [→*1.35.15*

(22) The bodies of the righteous in Paradise emit a shining light.

GL 1, 20 [→*1.35.14; 3.6.a.12*

(23) The rays that emanate from the countenance of the Messiah spread a stronger lustre than those from the countenances of Moses and Joshua.

GL 6, 141-142 n.836 [→*3.3.a.43*

(24) Death assumes the form of a beautiful archangel, with an appearance like sunlight and cheeks flashing with fire, when he appears before Abraham.

see Fa.10.2.1; A.23.8.1; D.5.1.6; D.5.6.1; D.17.1.1; D.18.6.2; F.17.1.1; F.17.2.1; F.17.3.1; F.17.4.1; F.17.5.1; F.17.6.1; F.17.10.1; F.18.5.4; F.18.6.2; D.5.21

T. Abr. **16.6-8** [→*2.21.6*

A.10.2. Emission of fire or flames from body

(1) A man with fire emanating from his body, which is made of bronze (literally 'electrum'), is seen by Ezekiel in a vision.

see A.16.2.1; Cc.16.2.1; Cc.16.12.2

Ezek. 1.27 [→*3.1.15*

A.10.5. Emission of lightning from body

(1) The Hayyot emit lightnings and sparks.

see Pc.6.5.1

3 En. **29.2** [→*3.3.a.8*

A.10.10. Unusual fragrance emanating from body

(1) Job's body emits a stench.

see A.23.1.20; A.23.20.2; B.24.1.4; Cc.23.3.1; Cc.23.3.2; Pc.2.1.1; Pd.1.1.1; B.11.1.3; B.23.20.1; B.15.1.2

T. Job **31.2;** *T. Job* **34.4** [→ *1.10.5*

(2) The stench of the decay of Antiochus Epiphanes sickens the whole army.

see B.23.6.1; G.23.20.1; Va.24.1.2

2 Macc. 9.5-10 [→ *1.26.b.50; 2.4.15*

(3) Elisha's body exudes a fragrance.
see G.25.2.2
GL 4 242; GL 6, 346 n.12 [→ *3.6.a.10*

A.10.15. *Other bodily issue*

(1) Rehoboam, the son of Solomon, is afflicted with an issue (gonorrhoea) after Solomon has transferred David's curse against Joab's descendants to his own descendants.
GL 4, 127; GL 6, 278 n.10 [→ *1.7.a.7*

A.11 *Unusual Colour of Body*

A.11.1. *Black body*

(1) The fallen angels have the appearance of darkness itself.
2 En. **7.2,5 (J)** [→ *3.6.b.1*

(2) Ham comes out of the ark 'dusky' because he has had sexual relations with a dog whilst in the ark.
see B.11.1.1.
Gen. R. **36.7** [→ *1.26.a.2*

(3) Ham's descendants are black.
see B.11.1.2; E.12.3.1; G.11.3.1; Ia.12.1.1
Gen. R. **36.7** [→ *1.6.a.2; 1.2.b.1*

A.11.2. *White body*

(1) A snow-white being coming from heaven is seen by Enoch during his ascension.
see E.11.2.1; A.11.2.2; A.11.3.1; D.16.3.1; E.11.1.1; E.12.3.1; F.5.10.1; F.16.12.1; G.10.5.1; Ia.16.12.1; P.10.1.1; P.10.7.1; Pc.10.7.1; Gf.4.1.1; A.1.1.1; Gf.27.2.1; A.10.1.1; Pc.10.3.1; I.10.5.1; If.6.1.1
1 En. **87.2** [→ *3.6.a.1*

(2) God is white and ruddy. (He exercises mercy, symbolized by white, and justice, symbolized by ruddy.)
see E.11.2.1; A.11.2.1; A.11.3.1; D.16.3.1; E.11.1.1; E.12.3.1. F.5.10.1; F.16.12.1; G.10.5.1; Ia.16.12.1; P.10.1.1; P.10.7.1; Pc.10.7.1; Gf.4.1.1; A.1.1.1; Gf.27.2.1; A.10.1.1; Pc.10.3.1; I.10.5.1; If.6.1.1
Cant. R. **5.9 §1** [→ *3.9.1*

(3) The first angels are also known as the seven snow-white ones.
 1 En. **90.21-22**   [→ *3.6.a.2*

(4) Angels of a shining white appearance greet Sobacha, the father of
Elijah, when Elijah is about to be born. They wrap Sobacha in fire
and give him flames of fire to eat.
 see A.10.1.12
 Liv. Proph. (Elijah) **21.2**   [→ *3.1.9*

(5) At birth Noah's body is as white as snow and as red as a blooming
rose.
 see A.11.3.2; E.11.2.1; G.10.2.7; Sa.2.3.6; Sa.24.3.6; Sa.2.1.1; Sa.24.10.1;
 Sa.24.2.1; T.23.1.1; I.10.4.1; Va.24.1.1; If.26.1.1; B.11.3.2; B.11.2.1
 1 En. 106.2-3, 5, 10-11   [→ *3.10.17*

(6) A white son is born to the king of the Arabs and his wife, who
are both black, after she fixes her eyes upon some white-painted
figures in their house during intercourse.
 see B.11.2.5
 Num. R. **9.34**   [→ *1.5.2; 1.14.a.12*

A.11.3. *Red body*

(1) God is ruddy and white. (He exercises justice, symbolized by red,
and mercy, symbolized by white.)
 see E.11.2.1; A.11.2.2; A.11..1; D.16.3.1; E.11.1.1; E.12.3.1; F.5.10.1;
 F.16.12.1; G.10.5.1; Ia.16.12.1; P.10.1.1; P.10.7.1; Pc.10.7.1; Gf.4.1.1;
 A.1.1.1; Gf.27.2.1; A.10.1.1; Pc.10.3.1; I.10.5.1; If.6.1.1
 Cant. R. **5.9 §1**   [→ *3.9.1*

(2) At birth Noah's body is as red as a blooming rose and as white as
snow.
 see A.11.2.5; E.11.2.1; G.10.2.7; Sa.2.3.6; Sa.24.3.6; Sa.2.1.1; T.23.1.1;
 I.10.4.1; Sa.24.10.1; Va.24.1.1; If.26.1.1; B.11.3.2; B.11.2.1; Sa.24.2.1
 1 En. **106.2-3, 5, 10-11**   [→ *3.10.17*

(3) Esau is reddish from birth (and as though wrapped in a hairy
cloak).
 see A.13.6.3; B.18.3.1; E.4.1.3; O.13.6.1; P.13.6.1; B.11.3.1; B.13.6.3;
 E.26.1.1; Ic.26.1.1; Sa.2.3.4; Sa.24.3.4; A.13.1.1; B.13.1.1
 Gen. 25.25; *Gen. R.* **75.4;** *Gen. R.* **63.6;** *Gen. R.* **64.8;** *Gen. R.*
 63.12   [→ *3.7.2; 3.10.16*

A.12. *Unusual Shape of Body*

A.12.1. *Amorphous body*

(1) Adam is created as an unformed mass, spread out from one end of the world to the other.

see Cb.9.1.1; F.5.1.1; A.9.1.2; R.14.1.1; R.18.1.1; A.6.1.19; A.6.1.20; A.6.3.4; A.6.5.20; A.6.5.21; A.13.10.1; B.13.10.1; A.10.1.9; A.10.1.2; Sa.2.3.10; Sa.24.3.3; A.16.9.1; Ca.9.1.1; Cb.5.1.1; G.23.5.1; J.23.1.1; A.4.1.1; D.14.10.1; E.14.10.1; Fb.14.10.1; G.14.10.1; H.14.10.1; I.14.10.1; J.14.10.1; Ja.14.10.1

Gen. R. 8.1; Gen. R. 14.8; Gen. R. 21.3; Gen. R. 24.2; Job 20.6
[→ *1.8.b.1*

A.13. *Body with Peculiarity of Skin*

A.13.1. *Tattooed skin*

(1) Esau is born with a figure of a serpent tattooed upon his body, 'symbol of all that is wicked and hated of God'.

see A.13.6.3; B.18.3.1; E.4.1.3; O.13.6.1; P.13.6.1; B.11.3.1; B.13.6.3; E.26.1.1; Ic.26.1.1; Sa.2.3.4; Sa.24.3.4; A.11.3.3; B.13.1.1

GL 1, 315; GL 5, 274 n.27   [→ *3.6.b.7; 3.10.23*

(2) Johoiakim's body is tattooed with the names of idols (and his penis with the name of God).

see Sa.13.1.1; B.13.1.2

Lev. R. 19.6; GL 4, 284; GL 6, 379 n.125   [→ *2.13.a.21*

A.13.2. *Brand or burn (or other indelible mark) on skin*

(1) Yahweh puts a mark on Cain.

see A.23.1.1; F.11.1.2; F.10.1.7; Fb.13.2.4; Fb.14.2.2; Fb.18.11.2; O.13.2.1; F.11.3.1; B.13.2.1

Gen. 4.13-16   [→ *2.2.c.3; 2.6.b.2; 2.11.e.1; 2.15.b.4*

(2) The Israelites are engraved with the ineffable name when they leave Egypt.

Num. R. 14.24   [→ *2.11.e.3*

(3) The names of the plagues of Egypt are engraved upon the bodies of the Egyptians, including the words 'dam' (blood), 'zefardea' (frog) and 'kinnin' (vermin).

Deut. R. 7.9   [→ *1.26.b.30*

(4) The bodies of the Israelites are branded with an ivy leaf at the time of the census during the reign of Ptolemy.

3 Macc. 2.29   [→ *2.13.a.22; 2.6.b.11*

A.13.4. *Leprous skin*

(1) The skin of King Uzziah is leprous.

see A.23.1.14; B.13.4.1; B.23.1.2; Fb.13.4.1; Fb.23.1.1
2 Kgs 15.5; 2 Chron. 26.19-23; *Lev. R.* **17.3**
                                    [→ *1.19.b.17; 1.26.a.12; 1.7.a.5*

A.13.6. *Hairy skin*

(1) The demon Keteb, or Keteb Meriri ('Bitter Destruction' or 'Pestilence') is covered with hair. He is also covered in scales, full of eyes, with the head of a calf and a single horn on his forehead. He has a single eye set on his heart that kills whoever looks at it.

see D.18.4.1; E.4.1.2; Fb.14.2.1; G.5.15.6; G.4.1.6; G.4.5.1; B.13.7.1; B.13.6.1; Fb.18.11.1
Num. R. **12.3;** *Lam. R.* **1.3** §29; **GL 3, 186; GL 6, 74 n.381**
                                    [→ *3.1.22*

(2) Both male and female demons have bodies and faces covered with hair, but bald heads.

see F.13.12.1; E.1.1.2; E.4.1.1; E.4.2.1; B.13.6.2
GL 6, 192 n.58   [→ *1.1.a.6*

(3) Esau is born hairy (as though wrapped in a hairy cloak) and reddish.

see A.11.3.3; B.18.3.1; E.4.1.3; O.13.6.1; P.13.6.1; B.11.3.1; B.13.6.3; E.26.1.1; Ic.26.1.1; Sa.2.3.4; Sa.24.3.4; A.13.1.1; B.13.1.1
Gen. 25.25; Gen. 27.11,23; *Gen. R.* **63.6,8;** *Gen. R.* **73.8;**
Gen. R. **65.15**   [→ *3.7.2; 3.6.b.8; 3.10.16*

(4) The Persians are hairy like bears.

see B.18.1.1; E.18.1.1
b. Qid. 72a; *Est. R.* **1.17**   [→ *3.7.4*

A.13.10. *Horny or hard skin*

(1) Adam has a horny skin before the Fall (and is wrapped in a cloud of glory).

see Cb.9.1.1; F.5.1.1; A.9.1.2; R.14.1.1; R.18.1.1; A.6.1.19; A.6.1.20; A.6.3.4; A.6.5.20; A.6.5.21; A.12.1.1; B.13.10.1; A.10.1.9; A.10.1.10;

Sa.2.3.3; Sa.24.3.3; A.16.9.1; Ca.9.1.1; Cb.5.1.1; G.23.5.1; J.23.1.1; A.4.1.1;
D.14.10.1; E.14.10.1; Fb.14.10.1; G.14.10.1; H.14.10.1; I.14.10.1; J.14.10.1;
Ja.14.10.1
GL 1, 74; GL 5, 97 n.69 [→ *3.5.a.1; 1.16.a.4*

(2) Eve has a horny skin before the Fall
see A.6.1.3; A.6.3.2; A.6.5.3; A.10.1.3; B.13.10.2; A.16.8.1; A.16.9.2
GL 1, 74; GL 5, 97 n.69 [→ *3.5.a.1; 1.16.a.5*

A.13.11. *Abnormally dry, withered or shrunken skin*

(1) The skin of the sons of Zion is shrunken against their bones and
dry as a stick, and their faces are darker than blackness itself, after the
fall of Jerusalem in 587 BCE.
see B.13.11.1; F.11.1.4
Lam. 4.8; Lam. R. 4.8-11 [→ *1.13.4*

A.13.20. *Transparent body*

(1) The bodies of pregnant women become transparent as glass when
God agrees to accept the children as bondsmen and asks the babies in
the womb if they will be surety for the observance of the Torah.
GL 3, 90; GL 6, 35 n.196 [→ *2.2.a.2*

A.14. *Unusual Protuberances or Protusions on Body*

A.14.1. *Tumours on body*

(1) The Philistines who have brought the ark to Ashdod (as well as
the citizens of Ashdod, Gath and Ekron) are afflicted with tumours.
1 Sam. 5.6-12; 1 Sam. 6.4-11 [→ *2.24.15; 1.26.b.37*

A.14.5. *Body covered in wings*

(1) Kerubi'el, prince of the cherubim, is covered from head to toe
with wings and eyes. His entire body is full of burning coals, and rays
emanate from his wheels.
see A.20.1.1; A.6.3.1; A.6.5.2; A.14.10.2; A.16.17.1; F.16.12.2; G.4.1.3;
G.5.15.2; G.16.12.2; Gc.16.12.1; I.16.12.1; Ib.16.12.1; P.10.3.1
3 En. 22.3-9 [→ *3.3.a.7*

A.14.10. *Wheels attached to body*

(1) The four creatures seen by Ezekiel have wheels on the ground
beside them and the rims of the wheels have eyes all the way round.

see F.5.3.1; F.18.5.2; F.20.1.1; F.18.4.1; M.20.1.8; M.14.2.8; U.18.3.1;
P.21.1.1; G.4.1.4; G.5.15.5
Ezek. 1.15-21; Ezek. 3.13; Ezek. 10.9,12,16,17,19; Ezek. 11.22
[→ *3.1.16*

(2) Kerubi'el, prince of the cherubim, has wheels. His whole body is
full of burning coals and he is covered with wings and eyes.
see A.6.3.1; A.6.5.2; A.14.5.1; A.16.17.1; A.20.1.1; F.16.12.2; G.4.1.3;
G.5.15.2; G.16.12.2; Gc.16.12.1; I.16.12.1; Ib.16.12.1; P.10.3.1
3 En. **22.3-9** [→ *3.3.a.7*

A.16. *Body of Unusual Substance*

A.16.2. *Body of bronze, copper or brass*

(1) A man who appears to be made of bronze (literally 'electrum') is
seen by Ezekiel in a vision.
see A.10.2.1; Cc.16.2.1; Cc.16.12.2.
Ezek. 40.3; Ezek. 1.27 [→ *3.1.15*

(2) Idols of brass, stone and wood speak for three days to give wise
men news of future events at the time of the coming of the Messiah
(and then they fall flat on their faces).
see A.16.5.1; A.16.7.1
Lad. Jac. **7.17** [→ *1.3.d.5; 2.2.c.1*

A.16.5. *Body of stone*

(1) Idols of stone, brass and wood speak for three days to give wise
men news of future events at the time of the coming of the Messiah
(and then they fall flat on their faces).
see A.16.2.2; A.16.7.1
Lad. Jac. **7.17** [→ *1.3.d.5; 2.2.c.1*

A.16.6. *Body of clay*

(1) An image of dust and clay, made by Enosh, is animated by Satan
entering it.
see A.16.13.1
GL 1, 122-123; GL 5, 150-151 n.54 [→ *1.3.d.4; 1.32.1*

A.16.7. *Body of wood*

(1) Idols of wood, brass and stone speak for three days to give wise
men news of future events at the time of the coming of the Messiah

(and then they fall flat on their faces).
see A.16.2.2; A.16.5.1
Lad. Jac. 7.17 [→ *1.3.d.5; 2.2.c.1*

A.16.8. *Body of grass*

(1) Eve's body becomes like grass or algae after she stands for a long time in water as a penance for her sins.
see A.16.9.2; A.13.10.2; B.13.10.2; A.6.1.21; A.6.3.5; A.6.5.22; A.10.1.11
LAE (Vita) **6.1-2. 7;** *LAE (Vita)* **9.1-5;** *LAE (Vita)* **10.1;** see also
GL 5, 115 n.106 [→ *1.14.c.5*

A.16.9. *Body of sponge*

(1) Adam's body becomes like sponge as a result of his penance of standing in water.
see Cb.9.1.1; F.5.1.1; A.9.1.2; R.14.1.1; R.18.1.1; A.6.1.19; A.6.1.20;
A.6.3.4; A.6.5.20; A.6.5.21; A.13.10.1; B.13.10.1; A.10.1.9; A.10.1.10;
Sa.2.3.3; Sa.24.3.3; A.12.1.1; Ca.9.1.1; Cb.5.1.1; G.23.5.1; J.23.1.1; A.4.1.1;
D.14.10.1; E.14.10.1; Fb.14.10.1; G.14.10.1; H.14.10.1; I.14.10.1; J.14.10.1;
Ja.14.10.1
PRE 20 [→ *1.14.c.3*

(2) Eve's body becomes like sponge after she stands for a long time in water as a penance for her sins.
see A.16.8.1; A.13.10.2; B.13.10.2; A.10.1.11; A.6.1.21; A.6.5.22; A.6.3.5
GL 5, 115 n.106 [→ *1.14.c.4*

A.16.10. *Body of snow*

(1) Michael's body is made of snow, Gabriel's of fire, yet when they stand near each other they do not injure one another.
see A.16.12.1; A.1.1.2; A.10.1.3; Gf.27.2.2
Num. R. 12.8; *Deut. R* **5.12** [→ *3.1.5; 4.2.d.1*

(2) Gabriel's body is made of snow, Michael's of fire, yet when they stand beside each other they do one another no injury.
see A.16.12.2
Cant. R. 3.2 §1 [→ *3.1.5; 4.2.d.1*

(3) An angel with an appearance like snow (and hands like ice) chills Enoch's face after he has ascended to heaven, so that men are able to endure the sight of him.
see P.16.11.1
2 En. 37.1 (J); 2 En. 37. (A); GL 1, 136-137 [→ *2.22.b.3*

A.16.11. *Body of ice or hail*

(1) The chief of the angels called Irin and Kadishim, 'Watchers' and 'Holy Ones', is made of hail.
   see A.6.5.8
   GL 2, 308; GL 5, 416-418 n.117   [→ *3.3.a.12*

(2) Some of the Angels of Destruction are made of hail, others of flames.
   see A.16.12.9; G.25.2.1
   GL 2, 366; GL 5, 433-434 n.213   [→ *2.15.a.8; 2.22.a.11*

A.16.12. *Body of fire*

(1) The body of Michael is made of fire, Gabriel's of snow, yet when they stand near each other, they do each other no injury.
   see A.16.10.1; A.1.1.2; A.10.1.3; Gf.27.2.2
   Cant. R. 3.2 §1   [→ *3.1.5; 4 2.d.1*

(2) The body of Gabriel is made of fire, Michael's of snow, yet when they stand near each other, they do each other no injury.
   see A.16.10.2
   Num. R. 12.8; Deut. R. 5.12   [→ *3.1.5; 4.2.d.1*

(3) Purouel, an archangel of fire, holds a trumpet with which he tests sinners.
   T. Abr. 12.9-13   [→ *2.1.a.1*

(4) Angels of flaming fire are seen by Enoch during his ascension.
   1 En. 17.1   [→ *3.1.4*

(5) Angels of flame guard the paradise of Eden.
   2 En. 42.4   [→ *2.19.b.1*

(6) Enoch's body turns into celestial fire after his transformation into Metatron.
   see A.6.3.2; A.6.5.12; G.5.13.2; G.10.2.3; M.14.2.13; M.20.1.13; B.16.12.1;
   E.16.4.1; G.16.12.5; V.16.12.1; Va.16.12.1; A.10.1.7
   3 En. 15.1; 3 En. 48c.6 (Appendix.)   [→ *1.35.2*

(7) The angels Af and Hemah, 'Anger' and 'Wrath', are forged out of chains of black fire and red fire, and are 500 parasangs in height.
   see A.6.5.10
   GL 2, 308; GL 5, 416-418 n.117   [→ *2.24.2*

(8) The angel Nuriel and his retinue of fifty myriads of angels are made out of water and fire.
see A.6.5.7; A.16.15.1
GL 2, 306-307; GL 5, 416-418 n.117 [→ *3.3.a.13*

(9) Some of the Angels of Destruction are made of flames and some of hail.
see A.16.11.2; G.25.2.1
GL 2, 366; GL 5, 433-434 n.213 [→ *2.15.a.8; 2.22.a.11*

A.16.13. *Body of dust*

(1) An image of dust and clay, made by Enosh, is animated by Satan entering it.
see A.16.6.1
GL 1, 122-123; GL 5, 150-151 n.54 [→ *1.3.d.4; 1.32.1*

A.16.14. *Body of wax*

(1) Moulded wax figures of men (representing the army of Agnias and the army of the Egyptians) are animated by being plunged into magic water and allowed to swim. In this way Balaam hopes to foretell the outcome of the war between the African and the Egyptian armies.
GL 2, 159; GL 5, 372 n.425 [→ *1.3.d.1; 2.11.b.1; 1.14.c.2*

A.16.15. *Body of water*

(1) The angel Nuriel and his retinue of fifty myriads of angels are fashioned out of fire and water.
see A.6.5.7; A.16.12.8
GL 2, 306-307; GL 5, 416-418 n.117 [→ *3.3.a.13*

A.16.16. *Body of light*

(1) The soul when it leaves the body resembles a body of glorious light, spiritually flying.
Hist. Rech. 15.10 [→ *1.34.3*

A.16.17. *Body of coal*

(1) The body of Kerubi'el, prince of the cherubim, is full of burning coals, and he is as tall and wide as the seven heavens, and is covered in burning eyes and wings. He also has wheels.
see A.6.3.1; A.6.5.2; A.14.10.2; A.20.1.1; F.16.12.1; G.4.1.3; G.5.15.2;

G.16.12.2; Gc.16.12.1; I.16.12.1; Ib.16.12.1; P.10.3.1; A.14.5.1

3 En. 22.3-9   [→ *3.3.a.7*

A.16.18. *Body of precious stone or jewel*

(1) A man with a body like beryl, chrysolite or topaz, a face like lightning, eyes like fiery torches, and arms and legs like burnished bronze (and a voice like the voice of a crowd) is seen by Daniel in a vision.

see F.16.12.3; G.16.12.3; O.16.2.1; T.16.2.1

Dan. 10.6   [→ *3.1.14*

(2) The body and legs of Iaoel, the angel who takes the right hand of Abraham, are like sapphire, his face is like chrysolite and his hair like snow.

see E.11.2.1; F.16.18.1; T.16.18.1

Apoc. Abr. 11.2   [→ *3.3.a.11*

A.16.20. *Body of unspecified matter*

(1) A life-like statue calls out in a loud voice, 'Hither, ye satans, Solomon has come to undo you' when Solomon approaches it.

GL 4, 165; GL 6, 298 n.79   [→ *1.3.d.2; 2.10.a.1; 1.32.2*

(2) An idol speaks, saying 'I am thy God' when Nebuchadnezzar places the golden diadem of the high priest, inscribed with the holy name, into its mouth.

see If.21.1.1

Cant. R. 7.9 §1   [→ *1.3.d.3; 1.11.a.1; 2.9.5*

A.17. *Substitute for Body*

A.17.1. *Shadow in place of body*

(1) A spirit with the shadowy form of a man and gleaming eyes is summoned by Solomon.

T. Sol. 17.1-4   [→ *1.34.4*

A.17.2. *Stone in place of body*

(1) A stone takes on the appearance of Jeremiah and is stoned in his place. Later, when Jeremiah is ready to die, the stone cries out, 'O stupid children of Israel, why do you stone me thinking that I am Jeremiah? Behold, Jeremiah stands in your midst.'

4 Bar. 9.27-30   [→ *2.9.4; 2.18.a.1*

A.17.6. *Fire in place of body*

(1) The angels called Erelim have white fire in place of a body.
GL 2, 307; GL 5, 416-418 n.117   [→ *3.1.13*

A.20. *Body with Bird Attributes*

A.20.1. *Body with wings*

(1) The body of Kerubi'el, prince of the cherubim, is covered from head to toe with wings and eyes. His entire body is full of burning coals and rays emanate from his wheels.
see A.14.5.1; A.6.3.1; A.6.5.2; A.14.10.2; A.16.17.1; F.16.12.2; G.4.1.3; G.5.15.2; G.16.12.2; Gc.16.12.1; I.16.12.1; Ib.16.12.1; P.10.3.1.
3 En. 22.3-9   [→ *3.3.a.7*

A.22. *Unusually Hideous Body*

(1) Elijah takes the form of a hideously ugly man to meet Eliezer and correct his overweening conceit.
see A.9.2.1; M.20.1.5; M.14.2.5; Pc.10.7.2; A.10.1.17
GL 4, 216; GL 6, 331 n.72, 73   [→ *2.7.2*

(2) A dirty, ragged beggar with hair like nails seats himself before the bridegroom at a wedding banquet: he is the angel of death.
see E.13.1.1
GL 4, 227-229; GL 6, 335-336 n.96,97   [→ *2.6.a.1*

(3) The forbidding ugliness of the demon Asmodeus terrifies those who behold him.
see U.20.1.1
GL 4, 172; GL 6, 301 n.73   [→ *2.24.10*

(4) The husbands of the she-devils Lilith and Mahlah take possession of Caleb and Phinehas and transform them so frightfully that the residents of Jericho are struck with fear.
see I.23.3.7; J.23.1.6; I.23.2.2; If.6.1.4; A.1.1.6
GL 4, 5; GL 6, 171 n.11   [→ *1.32.3; 2.24.14*

(5) Esther becomes very ugly as a result of the witchcraft of her enemies, but she regains her former beauty through a miracle.
GL 6, 460 n.78   [→ *1.11.a.5*

(6) Haman's daughter is made repulsive by a disease so that she cannot be chosen as a successor to Vashti.
GL 6, 477 n.173   [→ *1.10.4; 2.21.4*

(7) The coquettish maidens of Jerusalem are disfigured and made repulsive by diseases sent by God.
GL 4, 312-313; GL 6, 404 n.45
[→ *1.10.6; 1.19.b.23; 1.26.b.61*

A.23. *Disease, Paralysis or Malfunction of Body*

A.23.1. Leprous body

(1) Cain is afflicted with leprosy.
see F.11.1.2; Fb.13.2.4; F.10.1.7; Fb.14.2.2; Fb.18.11.2; O.13.2.1; F.11.3.1; B.13.2.1; A.13.2.1
Num. R. 7.5; *Gen. R.* 22.12   [→ *3.6.b.6; 2.2.c.4; 1.26.b.3*

(2) Abimelech, king of Gerar, is stricken with leprosy and covered in scabs for having instigated Isaac's removal from Gerar.
Gen. R. **64.9**   [→ *1.26.b.11*

(3) Miriam becomes leprous and white as snow (but is cured after a week through the intercession of Aaron and Moses).
see B.11.2.3
Num. **12.10;** *Lev. R.* **17.3;** *Num. R.* **7.5**   [→ *1.26.b.20*

(4) The Egyptians suffer from leprosy and smarting boils when Moses is abandoned in the water. When Pharaoh's daughter discovers, and touches, the ark of Moses, she is instantly cured.
see B.23.2.2
Exod. R. **1.23;** GL 2, 266; GL 5, 398 n.48   [→ *4.1.b.15*

(5) Pharaoh and his court are afflicted with leprosy when he desires to sleep with Sarah, Abraham's wife; or, more specifically, Pharaoh is smitten with a skin disease (ra'athan) which is harmful to sexual intercourse, or with lupus, another disease of the skin, which leaves deep scars.
Gen. R. **41.2;** *Gen. R.* **52.13;** *Lev. R.* **16.1;** GL 1, 224; GL 5, 221
n.75-77   [→ *1.26.a.6; 2.23.b.1*

(6) Pharaoh is afflicted with leprosy which covers his whole body from the crown of his head to the soles of his feet; after ten years the leprosy is replaced by boils.

see B.23.2.3; B.24.1.1
Exod. R. **1.34** [→ *1.26.b.29*

(7) Two lepers, marching outside the pillar of clouds, are able to witness and report the miracle of the levelling of the mountains and the annihilation of the Amorites.
GL **6, 116 n.662** [→ *4.1.b.16*

(8) Aaron is afflicted with leprosy after he has spoken out against Moses (but the affliction lasts a moment only).
see A.6.2.4; A.6.5.26; E.6.1.2; E.12.10.2; F.10.1.12; Ga.10.2.2; I.10.1.4
GL **3, 259;** GL **6, 91 n.494,495** [→ *1.26.b.21*

(9) The Israelites suffer from leprosy and gonorrhoea after the making of the golden calf.
see Sa.10.1.1
Lev. R. **17.3;** *Num. R.* **7.1-6;** *Num. R.* **8.3;** *Num. R.* **13.8**
[→ *1.26.a.11*

(10) Gehazi is leprous and white as snow.
see B.11.2.4; F.23.1.1
2 Kgs 5.25-27; *Lev. R.* **16.1;** *Lev. R.* **17.3;** *Num. R.* **7.5**
[→ *1.26.b.43; 1.11.b.1*

(11) Gehazi's chidren and descendants are cursed 'for evermore' with leprosy by Elisha.
see F.23.1.1
2 Kgs 5.25-27; *Num. R.* **7.5** [→ *1.7.a.8; 1.6.b.3*

(12) Naaman is leprous (but is healed after following Elisha's instructions to bathe seven times in the Jordan river).
2 Kgs 5 [→ *4.1.b.19; 1.26.b.42*

(13) Four lepers discover the abandonment of the Aramaean camp during the siege of Samaria.
2 Kgs 7.3-8 [→ *4.1.b.22*

(14) King Uzziah is stricken with leprosy when he goes into the temple to burn incense upon the altar.
see A.13.4.1; B.13.4.1; B.23.1.2; Fb.13.4.1; Fb.23.1.1
2 Kgs 15.5; 2 Chron. 26.19-23; *Lev. R.* **17.3;** *Num. R.* **23.13**
[→ *1.19.b.17; 1.26.a.12; 1.7.a.5*

(15) Goliath is stricken with leprosy.
see A.6.1.26; A.23.6.4; A.6.5.30; Na.13.2.1
Lev. R. **17.3;** *Num. R.* **7.5** [→ *1.26.b.38; 1.14.a.9*

(16) David suffers from leprosy for half a year after his transgression with Bath-sheba.

see Sa.2.3.25; Sa.24.3.25; E.11.3.1; B.11.3.3; G.25.1.1; T.23.2.1; O.23.2.1; A.25.15.3; F.11.1.7; A.25.9.2

GL 4, 104; GL 6, 266 n.96 [→ *1.26.b.40*

(17) Joab and his descendants are cursed with leprosy and gonorrhoea by David after Joab has killed Abner, the son of Ner.

see Sa.10.1.2

2 Sam. 3.28-29; *Lev. R.* 16.1; *Lev. R.* 17.3; *Num. R.* 8.5

[→ *1.26.b.41*

(18) Haman becomes a leper on the day that Mordecai is honoured.

GL 6, 477 n.174 [→ *1.26.b.58*

(19) A leper bathes in the Sea of Tiberias and is instantly healed when he comes into contact with the water of Miriam's well.

see B.23.2.5

GL 3, 54; GL 6, 22 n.135 [→ *4.1.b.28*

(20) Job is smitten with leprosy from the soles of his feet to the crown of his head (and his body swarms with vermin).

see A.23.20.2; B.24.1.4; Cc.23.3.1; Pc.2.1.1; Pd.1.1; Cc.23.3.2; B.11.1.3; B.23.20.1; B.15.1.2; A.10.10.1

GL 2, 235; GL 5, 386 n.24 [→ *2.1.a.2*

(21) Shebnah, a high priest, is punished with leprosy for his evil deeds.

Lev. R. 5.5; *Lev. R.* 17.3 [→ *1.26.b.56*

(22) Doeg dies a leper (or is eaten alive by worms).

see A.23.20.3

GL 4, 76; GL 6, 242 n.106 [→ *1.26.b.39*

A.23.2. *Convulsions*

(1) Sihon and his warriors are seized with convulsions so terrible that they roll up and writhe in pain, and are unable to stand in the battle lines.

see A.6.5.16

GL 3, 342; GL 6, 118 n.679 [→ *2.16.2*

(2) The high priest of Jerusalem is overwhelmed by trembling when

Heliodorus, chancellor to the king, insists on confiscating the Temple funds for the royal exchequer.
2 Macc. 3.17   [→ *1.12.a.28*

A.23.3. *Boils*

(1) The Egyptians are covered in boils that break out into sores: this is the sixth plague of Egypt.
see B.23.2.4; Sa.2.1.7; Sa.24.2.7; W.4.2.2; P.23.1.2; Ie.27.1.1; B.24.3.1; B.24.3.2; B.24.4.2; B.23.1.1; A.23.6.1
Exod. 9.8-12; Ezek. Trag. Exagoge 137 [→ *2.5.6; 2.4.6; 1.14.c.14*

A.23.6. *Paralysis*

(1) The Egyptians are paralysed and 'clamped to the spot' in the darkness during the ninth plague of Egypt.
see Sa.2.1.7; Sa.24.2.7; W.4.2.2; P.23.1.2; B.24.3.1; B.24.3.2; B.23.2.4; B.24.4.2; B.23.1.1; A.23.3.1; Ie.27.1.1
Wis. 17.14,15,18   [→ *1.12.a.26*

(2) Sinners remain rooted to the soil, without being able to move a step, when Joshua makes the people pass before the ark.
GL 6, 176 n.28   [→ *2.6.b.6*

(3) The enemies of Israel become as still as stone in the war between Joshua and the united kings of Canaan.
GL 6, 179 n.44   [→ *2.16.6*

(4) Goliath is rooted to the ground, unable to move, after David casts his evil eye on him.
see A.23.1.15; A.6.1.26; A.6.5.30; Na.13.2.1.
GL 4, 87; GL 6, 251 n.40   [→ *1.14.a.9*

(5) Alcimus suffers a stroke, his mouth becomes obstructed and his paralysis makes him incapable of giving directions.
see I.23.2.5
1 Macc. 9.54-56   [→ *2.22.c.4; 2.15.b.12*

(6) Theodotus Ptolemy IV Philopater, king of Egypt, is tossed to the ground with a stroke, and becomes paralysed and unable to speak when he tries to enter the temple in Jerusalem.
see I.23.2.6
3 Macc. 2.22   [→ *1.26.b.51; 2.15.b.13; 1.19.b.26*

(7) Zimri and Cozbi are unable to move and separate from each other

after being pierced by Phinehas's lance during copulation.
    see I.23.2.4; W.1.1.1
    Num. R. 20.25   [→ *1.19.b.11; 2.3.8; 2.18.b.2*

A.23.8. *Decaying or putrifying body*

(1) Death appears to sinners as a decaying figure with two heads, one with the face of a dragon, the other like a sword.
    see D.5.1.6; D.5.6.1; D.17.1.1; D.18.6.2; F.17.1.1; F.17.2.1; F.17.3.1;
    F.17.4.1; F.17.5.1; F.17.6.1; F.17.10.1; F.18.5.4; F.18.6.2; Fa.10.2.1;
    D.5.2.1; A.10.1.24
    T. Abr. 13.13-16; T. Abr. 14.1-4 (Recension B) [→ *2.24.20; 3.9.7*

A.23.10. *Unspecified disease of body*

(1) Marks of disease appear on the body of Vashti, Ahasuerus's wife, so that she cannot appear naked before the guests of her husband.
    see Fb.23.1.2; F.22.1.2
    GL 4, 375; GL 6, 455 n.35   [→ *2.25.b.2*

(2) Judah's whole body is diseased: from the soles of his feet to the crown of his head there are wounds, bruises and open sores.
    Isa. 1.5,6   [→ *3.9.6*

A.23.20 *Body infested with worms*

(1) Worms crawl out of the body of Delilah, Micah's mother, while she is alive.
    Ps.-Philo 44.9; Ps.-Philo 47.12   [→ *1.26.b.55*

(2) Job's body is infested with worms (and his flesh swarms with vermin).
    see A.23.1.20; B.24.1.4; Cc.23.3.1; Cc.23.3.2; Pc.2.1.1; Pd.1.1.; B.11.1.3;
    B.23.20.1; B.15.1.2; A.10.10.1
    GL 5, 386 n.26   [→ *1.10.5; 2.1.a.2*

(3) Doeg is eaten alive by worms; a fiery worm goes up into his tongue and makes him rot away. In a variant, he dies a leper.
    see A.23.1.22
    Ps.-Philo 63.4; GL 4, 76; GL 6, 242 n.106   [→ *1.26.b.39*

A.23.30. *Elephantiasis*

(1) Chenephres is attacked by elephantiasis.
    Art. Moses Fragment 3; GL 5, 412-413 n.101   [→ *1.26.b.57*

A.24. *Wounded, Mutilated or Maimed Body*

A.24.10. *Unspecified wound or mutilation*

(1) Lamech is wounded (and kills the man who wounded him).
Gen. 4.23-24 [→ *4.1.b.7*

(2) Judas, the son of Simon, high priest and ethnarch of the Jews, is wounded in the battle against Cendebaeus.
1 Macc. 16.9 [→ *1.20.10*

(3) A prophet is struck and wounded by a man at his own request so that he can pretend to be wounded in battle when he meets King Ahab.
1 Kgs 20.37 [→ *2.9.9; 2.2.c.6*

(4) Jehoram, the son of Ahab, king of Israel, is wounded in the battle with Hazael, king of Aram.
2 Chron. 22.5 [→ *1.20.9*

A.25. *Unusual Abilities of Body*

A.25.2. *Vital corpse*

(1) The corpse of Sammael's son weeps and wails even when cut up into pieces.
GL 1, 154-155; GL 5, 177 n.22 [→ *2.19.a.2*

A.25.3. *Body that revives from the dead*

(1) Abraham's dead servants (killed by fear when Death reveals his ferocious aspect) are revived by God at Abraham's request.
T. Abr. **18.11;** *T. Abr.* **14.5-6 (Recension B)** [→ *1.19.b.5*

(2) The body of Isaac comes to life again after his death by fright upon the altar.
see Sa.2.3.11; Sa.24.3.11; A.8.1.3; G.23.4.6
GL 1, 281-282; GL 5, 251 n.243 [→ *1.14.b.1*

(3) The dead body of the boy Micah, used by the Egyptians as building material, is brought to life again when Moses writes the name of God on Micah's body.
GL 4, 49; GL 6, 209 n.126 [→ *1.11.a.7*

(4) David revives from the dead when Solomon brings David's coffin

to remind God of David's good deeds (and to plead for help in getting the ark into the sanctuary).
Exod. R. **8.1**   [→ *2.8.2*

(5) The son of a woman from Shunem is brought back to life by Elisha.
2 Kgs 4, 33-35; *Cant. R.* **2.5** §3   [→ *1.14.c.20; 1.35.10*

(6) A dead man revives at the touch of Elisha's bones. Alternatively, he is brought back to life when he touches Elisha's bier.
2 Kgs 13.21; GL 4, 246; GL 6, 347 n.21   [→ *1.14.c.21*

(7) Jeremiah rises again three days after his death.
4 Bar. **9.7-14**   [→ *2.3.6*

(8) A corpse touched by an eagle comes to life as a sign that Jeremiah's mission is true.
4 Bar. **7.18; GL 4, 320**   [→ *2.3.7; 1.14.c.18*

(9) God raises the dead Jonah to life through Elijah to show that it is not possible to run away from God.
see E.1.5; Sa.2.3.28; Sa.24.3.28
Liv. Proph. (Jonah) **10.6**   [→ *2.4.10; 1.19.b.18*

(10) The son of the widow of Zarephath is revived from the dead by Elijah when Elijah stretches himself out on the child three times and prays to God.
1 Kgs 17.17-24; *Cant. R.* **2.5** §3   [→ *1.19.b.19; 1.35.11*

(11) Ezekiel revives the dead in the Valley of Dura.
Ezek. 37.7   [→ *1.19.b.22; 2.4.12*

(12) The beautiful youths who were executed in Babylon because the husbands of the Babylonian women were jealous, are revived by Ezekiel.
GL 4, 332; GL 6, 421-422 n.94,95   [→ *1.19.b.22; 2.4.12*

(13) The Ephraimites, who had perished in the attempt to escape from Egypt before Moses led the nation out of the land of bondage, are revived by Ezekiel.
GL 4, 332; GL 6, 421-422 n.94, 95   [→ *1.19.b.22*

(14) The Jews whom Nebuchadnezzar had killed because of their wicked deeds, are revived twenty years later in the Valley of Dura.

God drops the dew of heaven upon the dry bones, and then sends the four winds to the four corners of the earth to retrieve the souls from the treasure house of souls.

GL **4**, 332-333; GL **6**, 421-422 n.94, 95; see also *2 Bar.* 29.7; *2 Bar.* 73.2   [→ *1.19.b.22; 1.17.4; 1.14.c.23*

(15) The godless who had, in life, polluted the temple with heathen rites, and those who had not believed in the resurrection of the dead, are revived by Ezekiel.

GL **4**, 332; GL **6**, 421-422 n.94, 95   [→ *1.19.b.22; 2.3.5*

(16) The dead in Sheol are revived at the sound of the divine voice.

GL **3**, 95, 97; GL **6**, 39-40 n.215   [→ *1.14.b.7; 2.7.7*

A.25.9. *Corpse that remains fresh*

(1) Although Moses' body lies in the grave, it is still as fresh as when Moses was alive; his eyes do not become dim and his countenance retains the brightness it had received on Mount Sinai.

see F.10.1.11; Sa.2.3.19; Sa.24.3.19; A.6.5.25; A.6.4.2; P.23.1.1; P.25.4.1; I.10.1.5; G.10.2.9; F.11.3.2; Fb.10.1.1; F.10.1.11; G.25.4.1; If.6.1.2; Fb.14.2.3; I.23.3.3; P.11.2.2; G.17.20.1; Ib.13.2.1; Ib.24.4.1; Ia.24.4.1; E.6.1.1; Ga.10.2.1; E.12.10.1; P.13.2.1; P.24.4.1; K.13.10.2; B.16.12.2; Ib.16.12.3; Ia.13.2.1.

GL **3**, 473; GL **6**, 164 n.953   [→ *3.6.a.7*

(2) The face of David's corpse amazes Hadrian with its high colour; and when he presses the flesh with his fingers, the blood begins to circulate.

see E.11.3.1; B.11.3.3; Sa.2.3.25; Sa.24.3.25; G.25.1.1; A.23.1.16; T.23.2.1; O.23.2.1; A.25.15.3; F.11.1.7

GL **6**, 412-413 n.73   [→ *3.6.a.9*

(3) The corpse of Baruch shows no sign of decay.

GL **4**, 324; GL **6**, 412 n.73   [→ *3.6.a.11*

A.25.10. *Body with other unusual abilities*

(1) The children of the generation of the Nephilim, or ante-diluvians, run around while still connected to the mother by the navel string.

GL **1**, 151-152; GL **5**, 173 n.16   [→ *1.1.a.12*

A.25.15. *Body that can fly through the air*

(1) Balaam can fly through the air.

see If.6.1.5; U.23.1.1; G.23.4.12; I.23.3.6; Va.27.1.1; G.5.1.2; G.1.2

GL 2, 287; GL 5, 407-410 n.80; GL 3, 409-410; GL 6, 103-104
n.851,853,854   [→ *1.11.a.3; 2.18.a.5*

(2) Jannes and Jambres, the sons of Balaam, can fly through the air.
GL 2, 287; GL 5, 407-410 n.80   [→ *2.18.a.6*

(3) David is suspended in the air and thus avoids being transfixed by
Ishbi's lance.
see Sa.2.3.25; Sa.24.3.25; E.11.3.1; B.11.3.3; G.25.1.1; A.23.1.16; T.23.2.1;
O.23.2.1; F.11.1.7; A.25.9.2
GL 4, 108; GL 6, 268 n.110   [→ *1.11.a.4; 2.15.b.11*

(4) The kings of Midian practise witchcraft together with Balaam and
fly, but fall down on top of the slain Midianites when they see the
plate engraved with the holy name.
Num. R. **20.20;** *Num. R.* **22.5**   [→ *2.11.c.1*

A.25.30. *Fire-proof body*

(1) Hezekiah is fireproof after he is rubbed with the blood of a salamander.
see E.1.4; B.2.2.1; Sa.2.1.24; Sa.24.2.24; B.15.1.1
GL 4, 266; GL 6, 361 n.47   [→ *1.14.c.19*

A.26. *Body of Different Age Group*

A.26.1. *Child with characteristics of adult*

(1) In the days of the sons of Noah children can run, speak and obey
orders while still attached by the umbilical cord to their mothers.
see Qa.14.1.1
Gen. R. **36.1;** *Lev. R.* **5.1**   [→ *1.16.a.5*

(2) Melkisedek, the child born to the dead Sopanim, is fully developed physically (like a three year old), blesses God, and has the badge
of priesthood on his chest.
2 En. **71.17-19**   [→ *3.10.15*

(3) From the day of his birth Moses is able to speak, walk and con-
verse with his parents. At the age of three he prophesies.
see F.10.1.11; Sa.2.3.19; Sa.24.3.19; A.6.5.25; A.6.4.2; P.23.1.1; P.25.4.1;
I.10.1.5; G.10.2.9; F.11.3.2; Fb.10.1.1; G.25.4.1; If.6.1.3; Fb.14.2.3;
I.23.3.3; P.11.2.2; G.17.20.1; Ib.13.2.1; Ib.24.4.1; Ia.24.4.1; E.6.1.1;
Ga.10.2.1; E.12.10.1; P.13.2.1; P.24.4.1; K.13.10.2; B.16.12.2; Ib.16.12.3;
Ia.13.2.1; A.25.9.1
Deut. R **11.10**   [→ *3.10.11*

A.26.3. *Old person with youthful looks*

(1) Though she is old, Jochebed regains her youth at her re-marriage with Amram: her skin becomes soft, the wrinkles in her face disappear and the warm tints of maiden beauty return.

see A.1.1.5; F.10.1.18
GL 2, 263; GL 5, 396 n.38 [→ *1.35.8*

(2) Ruth the Moabitess is forty years old, yet she looks like a girl of fourteen.
Ruth R. 4.4 [→ *4.2.c.4*

A.27. Transformation or Partial Transformation of Body

A.27.2. *Transformation of human form into that of a land animal*

(1) Those who wanted to ascend the Tower of Babel and set up idols are transformed into apes.
GL 1, 180; GL 5, 203-204 [→ *1.26.a.3*

(2) The breakers of the Sabbath are transformed into apes by Moses.
GL 6, 85 n.452 [→ *1.26.a.8*

(3) Nebuchadnezzar is made to live like a beast for forty days (or seven years) as a punishment for deeming himself more than a man. As far down as his navel he resembles an ox and the lower part of his body resembles a lion.

see Cc.27.1.1; Cc.27.4.1; A.6.2.5; U.23.1.4; T.24.3.1; E.6.5.6; Pd.6.5.1; Pd.12.1.1; Ib.1.2
*Liv. Proph. (Daniel)*4.5 [→ *1.26.b.52; 2.7.6*

(4) The Amalekites are great sorcerers who transform themselves into animals to escape the attacks of their enemies in war.
GL 6, 233 n.61 [→ *2.18.a.11*

(5) A man is transformed into a demon in the form of a gigantic dog as a punishment for his unlawful deeds.
T. Sol. 10.1-2 [→ *1.26.b.63*

A.27.6. *Transformation of human body into a star*

(1) Istehar is transformed into a star in the constellation of the Pleiades as a reward for her chastity after she tricked the angels who wanted to seduce her into giving her their wings, and used them to fly to heaven.

see M.14.2.21; M.20.1.21
**BHM 5.21 Midrash Fragments no.4 (Hebrew text, 156; BHM 4.3
Schemchasai und Asael (Hebrew text, 127)** [→ *1.35.13*

A.27.7. *Transformation of body into salt*

(1) Lot's wife is transformed into a pillar of salt.
Gen. 19.17-26 [→ *1.26.a.4; 1.26.b.9; 1.14.a.5*

B. The Skin and the Flesh

B.2. *Partial Absence of Skin or Flesh*

B.2.1. *Gnawed skin or flesh*

(1) Men gnaw the flesh from their own bones during the famine in Samaria.
see B.15.3.1; B.24.4.3
GL 4, 191; GL 6, 314 n.55   [→ *1.13.6*

B.2.2. *Peeled skin or flesh*

(1) Hezekiah's skin peels off as a result of a disease inflicted upon him as a punishment for his having 'peeled off' the gold from the temple.
see E.1.4; A.25.30.1; Sa.2.1.24; Sa.24.2.24; B.15.1.1.
GL 4, 272; GL 6, 366 n.72   [→ *1.26.b.46; 1.10.3*

B.2.3. *Body with pieces of skin or flesh cut off*

(1) Nebuchadnezzar cuts off a piece of Hiram's flesh every day and forces Hiram to eat it, until he finally perishes.
GL 4, 336; GL 6, 424-425 n.105   [→ *1.24.2; 2.15.a.11*

B.11. *Unusual Colour of Skin*

B.11.1. *Black skin*

(1) Ham comes out of the ark 'dusky' because he has had sexual relations with a dog whilst in the ark.
see A.11.1.2
Gen. R. 36.7   [→ *1.26.a.2*

(2) Ham's descendants have a black skin.
see A.11.1.3; E.12.3.2; G.11.3.1; Ia.12.1.1
Gen. R. 36.7   [→ *1.6.a.2; 1.2.b.1*

(3) Job's skin turns black with disease.

see B.23.20.1; B.15.1.2; A.23.1.20; A.23.20.2; B.24.1.4; Cc.23.3.1; Pc.2.1.1;
Pd.1.1.; Cc.23.3.2; A.10.10.1
Job 30.30   [→ *2.1.a.2*

B.11.2. *White skin*

(1) At birth Noah is as white as snow and as red as a blooming rose.
see B.11.3.2; A.11.2.5; A.11.3.2; E.11.2.1; G.10.2.7; Sa.2.3.6; Sa.24.3.6;
Sa.2.1.1; T.23.1.1; I.10.4.1; Sa.24.10.1; Va.24.1.1; If.26.1.1; Sa.24.2.1
   1 En. **106.2-3, 5, 10-11**   [→ *3.10.17*

(2) Laban is exceptionally white (an albino).
   Gen. R. **60.7;** *Num. R.* **10.5**   [→ *3.6.b.9; 5.1.5*

(3) Miriam becomes white as snow — a leper — after she has complained about Moses taking the Cushite woman.
see A.23.1.3
Num. 12.10   [→ *1.26.b.20*

(4) Gehazi is as white as snow and leprous.
see A.23.1.10; F.23.1.1
   2 Kgs 5.25-27   [→ *1.26.b.43*

(5) A white son is born to the king of the arabs and his wife, who are both black.
see A.11.2.6
Num. R. 9.34   [→ *1.5.2; 1.14.a.12*

B.11.3. *Red skin*

(1) Esau is reddish of skin when he is born (and as though wrapped in a hairy cloak).
see A.13.6.3; A.11.3.2; B.13.6.3; B.18.3.1; E.4.1.3; A.13.1.1; P.13.6.1;
O.13.6.1; E.26.1.1; Ic.26.1.1; Sa.2.3.4; Sa.24.3.4
   Gen. 25.25; *Gen. R.* **63.6, 8, 12;** *Gen. R.* **75.4**   [→ *3.10.16; 3.7.2*

(2) At birth Noah is as red as a blooming rose and as white as snow.
see A.11.3.2; A.11.2.5; B.11.2.1; E.11.2.1; G.10.2.7; Sa.2.3.6; Sa.24.3.6;
Sa.2.1.1; T.23.1.1; I.10.4.1; Sa.24.10.1; Va.24.1.1; If.26.1.1; Sa.24.2.1
   1 En. **106.2-3, 5, 10-11**   [→ *3.10.17*

(3) David has a ruddy complexion.
see E.11.3.1; Sa.2.3.25; Sa.24.3.25; G.25.1.1; A.23.1.16; T.23.2.1; O.23.2.1;
A.25.15.3; F.11.1.7; A.25.9.2
   GL 6, 247 n.13   [→ *1.12.a.31; 3.10.18*

B.13. *Peculiarities of Skin or Flesh as a Whole*

B.13.1. *Tattooed skin*

(1) Esau is born with the figure of a serpent upon his skin, 'symbol of all that is wicked and hated of God'.
see A.13.6.3; B.18.3.1; E.4.1.3; O.13.6.1; P.13.6.1; B.11.3.1; B.13.6.3; E.26.1.1; Ic.26.1.1; Sa.2.3.4; Sa.24.3.4; A.13.1.1; A.11.3.3
GL 1, 315; GL 5, 274 n.27 [→ *3.6.b.7; 3.10.23*

(2) Jehoiakim's skin is tattooed with the names of idols (and his penis with the name of God).
see A.13.1.2; Sa.13.1.1
Lev. R. 19.6; **GL 4, 284; GL 6, 379 n.125** [→ *2.13.a.21*

B.13.2. *Brand or engraving on skin or flesh*

(1) Yahweh puts a mark on Cain.
see A.13.2.1; A.23.1.1; F.11.1.2; F.10.1.7; Fb.13.2.4; Fb.14.2.2; Fb.18.11.2; O.13.2.1; F.11.3.1
Gen. 4.13-16 [→ *2.2.c.3; 2.6.b.2; 2.11.e.1; 2.15.b.4*

(2) The plagues become engraved upon the bodies of the Egyptians including the words 'dam' (blood), 'zefardea' (frog) and 'kinnin' (vermin)
Deut. R. 7.9 [→ *1.26.b.30*

(3) The ineffable name is engraved upon the Israelites when they leave Egypt; and as long it remains no evil thing can touch them.
Num. R. 14.24 [→ *2.11.e.3*

(4) The Jews enrolled in a census by Ptolemy are branded with an ivy leaf, the emblem of Dionysus.
3 Macc. 2.29 [→ *2.13.a.22; 2.6.b.11*

B.13.4. *Leprous skin*

(1) King Uzziah's skin is leprous.
see A.23.1.14; A.13.4.1; B.23.1.2; Fb.13.4.1; Fb.23.1.1
2 Kgs 15.5; 2 Chron. 26.19-23; *Lev. R.* 17.3
[→ *1.19.b.17; 1.26.a.12; 1.7.a.5*

B.13.6. *Hairy skin*

(1) The demon Keteb or Keteb Meriri ('Bitter Destruction' or 'Pestilence') is covered with hair. He is also covered in scales and eyes, and has the head of a calf with a single horn on his forehead. He has a single eye set on his heart that kills whoever looks at it.

see A.13.6.1; D.18.4.1; E.4.1.2; Fb.14.2.1; G.5.15.6; G.4.1.6; G.4.5.1; B.13.7.1; Fb.18.11.1

Num. R. 12.3; *Lam. R.* 1.3 §29; GL 3, 186; GL 6, 74 n.381

[→ *3.1.22*

(2) Both male and female demons have bodies and faces covered with hair, but bald heads.

see A.13.6.2; F.13.12.1; E.1.2; E.4.1.1; E.4.2.1

GL 6, 192 n.58   [→ *1.1.a.6*

(3) When he is born, Esau is hairy as though wrapped in a hairy cloak and reddish in colour.

see A.13.6.3; B.18.3.1; E.4.1.3; O.13.6.1; P.13.6.1; B.11.3.1; A.11.3.3; E.26.1.1; Ic.26.1.1; Sa.2.3.4; Sa.24.3.4; A.13.1.1; B.13.1.1

Gen. 25.25; Gen. 27.11,23; *Gen. R.* 65.15; *Gen. R.* 63.6,8; *Gen. R.* 73.8   [→ *3.7.2; 3.6.b.8; 3.10.16*

B.13.7. *Scaly skin*

(1) The demon Keteb or Keteb Meriri ('Bitter Destruction' or 'Pestilence') is covered with scales and eyes, and is hairy all over. He has the head of a calf, with a single horn on his forehead. He also has an eye on his heart which kills whoever looks at it.

see D.18.4.1; E.4.1.2; Fb.14.2.1; G.5.15.6; G.4.1.6; G.4.5.1; A.13.6.1; B.13.6.1; Fb.18.11.1

Num. R. 12.3; *Lam.R.* 1.3 §29; GL 3, 186; GL 6, 74 n.381

[→ *3.1.22*

B.13.10. *Horny or hard skin*

(1) Adam has a horny skin before the Fall (and is enveloped in a cloud of glory).

see Cb.9.1.1; F.5.1.1; A.9.1.2; R.14.1.1; R.18.1.1; A.6.1.19; A.6.1.20; A.6.3.4; A.6.5.20; A.6.5.21; A.13.10.1; A.12.1.1; A.10.1.9; A.10.1.10; Sa.2.3.3; Sa.24.3.3; A.16.9.1; Ca.9.1.1; Cb.5.1.1; G.23.5.1; J.23.1.1; A.4.1.1; D.14.10.1; E.14.10.1; Fb.14.10.1; G.14.10.1; H.14.10.1; I.14.10.1; J.14.10.1; Ja.14.10.1

GL 1, 74; GL 5, 97 n.69   [→ *3.5.a.1; 1.16.a.4*

(2) Eve has a horny skin before the Fall.

see A.6.1.21; A.6.3.5; A.6.5.22; A.10.1.11; A.13.10.2; A.16.8.1; A.16.9.2

GL 1, 74; GL 5, 97 n.69   [→ *3.5.a.1; 1.16.a.4*

B.13.11. *Dry, withered or shrunken skin*

(1) After the fall of Jerusalem in 587 BCE, the skin of the sons of Zion shrinks against their bones and becomes dry as a stick; and their faces become darker than blackness itself.

see F.11.1.4; A.13.11.1

Lam. 4.8; *Lam. R.* **4.8 §11** [→ *1.13.4*

B.15. *Abnormal Puncture or Opening in Skin*

B.15.1. *Ulcers*

(1) King Hezekiah has ulcers (but recovers when Isaiah applies a fig poultice to the wound).

see A.25.30.1; B.2.2.1; E.1.4; Sa.2.1.24; Sa.24.2.24

2 Kgs 20.7; Isa. 38.1-8 [→ *1.10.2*

(2) Job is struck down with malignant ulcers from the soles of his feet to the top of his head.

see B.11.1.3; B.23.20.1; A.23.1.20; A.23.20.2; B.24.1.4; Cc.23.3.1; Pc.2.1.1; Pd.1.1; Cc.23.3.2; A.10.10.1

Job 2.7; Arist. Exeg. Preparatio Evangelica 9.25.1-4; *T. Job* **20.6-9;** *T. Job* **24.3;** *T. Job* **26.1;** *T. Job* **34.4** [→ *2.1.a.2*

B.15.3. *Gnawed or eaten skin or flesh*

(1) Men gnaw the flesh from their own bones during the famine in Samaria.

see B.2.1.1; B.24.4.3

GL 4, 191; GL 6, 314 n.55 [→ *1.13.6*

B.16. *Skin or Flesh of Unusual Substance*

B.16.12. *Skin of fire*

(1) Enoch's skin turns into flame at his transformation into Metatron.

see A.6.3.2; A.6.5.12; G.5.13.2; G.10.2.3. M.14.2.13; M.20.1.13; A.16.12.6; E.16.4.1; G.16.12.5; V.16.12.1; Va.16.12.1; A.10.1.7

3 En. 15.1; 3 En. 48c.6 (Appendix) [→ *1.35.2*

(2) Moses' flesh is changed into torches of fire (and his strength changed into an angel's).

see F.10.1.11; Sa.2.3.19; Sa.24.3.19; A.6.5.25; A.6.4.2; P.23.1.1; P.25.4.1; I.10.1.2; G.10.2.9; F.11.3.2; Fb.10.1.1; F.10.1.11; G.25.4.1; If.6.1.3;

Fb.14.2.3; I.23.3.3; P.11.2.2; G.17.20.1; Ib.13.2.1; Ib.24.4.1; Ia.24.4.1;
E.6.1.1; Ga.10.2.1; E.12.10.1; P.13.2.1; P.24.4.1; K.13.10.2; A.25.9.1;
Ib.16.12.3; Ia.13.2.1; A.26.1.3
GL 2, 306; GL 5, 416-418 n.117   [→ *2.15.b.9*

B.18. *Animal Skin or Skin with Animal Attributes*

B.18.1. *Furred skin or pelt*

(1) The Persians are hairy like bears.
see A.13.6.4; E.18.1.1
Kid 72a; *Est. R.* 1.17   [→ *3.7.4*

B.18.2. *Snake skin*

(1) Sammael (or Satanael) wears the skin of a serpent when he
deceives man.
3 *Bar.* 9.7 (Slavonic and Greek)   [→ *2.6.a.2; 2.9.1*

B.18.3. *Hairy skin*

(1) Esau is born hairy, as though wrapped in a hairy cloak.
see A.11.3.3; A.13.6.3; B.11.3.2; E.4.1.3; O.13.6.1; P.13.6.1; B.13.6.3;
E.26.1.1; Ic.26.1.1; Sa.2.3.4; Sa.24.3.4; A.13.1.1; B.13.1.1
***Gen. R.* 65.15**   [→ *3.10.16; 3.7.2; 3.6.b.8*

B.23. *Disease or Malfunction of Skin or Flesh*

B.23.1. *Leprous skin*

(1) The skin of the Egyptians turns leprous: this is the sixth plague of
Egypt.
see B.23.2.4; B.24.3.1; B.24.3.2; P.23.1.2; Ie.27.1.1; Sa.24.2.7; Sa.2.1.7;
B.24.4.2; W.4.2.2; A.23.3.1; A.23.6.1
***Exod. R.* 11.6**   [→ *1.26.b.28; 2.5.7; 1.14.c.13*

(2) King Uzziah has a leprous skin.
see A.13.4.1; A.23.1.14; B.13.4.1; Fb.23.1.1; Fb.13.4.1
2 Kgs 15.5; 2 Chron. 26.19-23; *Lev. R.* 17.3
[→ *1.19.b.17; 1.26.a.12; 1.7.a.5*

B.23.2. *Boils on skin*

(1) The Egyptian magicians are covered in boils so that they cannot
face Moses in a magical contest or perform any magic.
Gen. 9.11; Jub. 48.11   [→ *2.22.c.2*

(2) The Egyptians suffer from smarting boils and leprosy when Moses is abandoned in the water. Pharaoh's daughter is healed when she discovers Moses.

see A.23.1.4

Exod. R. **1.23** [→ *4.1.b.15*

(3) Pharaoh is afflicted with boils after having leprosy for ten years.

see A.23.1.6; B.24.1.1

Exod. R. **1.34** [→ *1.26.b.29*

(4) The Egyptians and their animals suffer from boils and blains, so that their flesh becomes inflamed and soft within and dry on top.

see B.24.3.1; B.24.3.2; B.23.1.1; P.23.1.2; Ie.27.1.1; Sa.24.2.7; Sa.2.1.7; B.24.4.2; W.4.2.2; A.23.3.1; A.23.6.1; A.23.3.1

Exod. 9.10; *Exod. R.* **11.5-6** [→ *1.26.b.28; 2.5.7; 1.14.c.13*

(5) A man with boils bathes in the Sea of Tiberias and is instantly healed when he comes into contact with the waters of Miriam's well.

see A.23.1.19

Lev. R. **22.4**; *Qoh. R.* **5.8** §5 [→ *4.1.b.28*

B.23.6. *Rotting or putrefying skin or flesh*

(1) The flesh of Antiochus Epiphanes rots away, his eyes teem with worms and he has an incurable pain in his bowels; and the stench of his decay sickens the whole army.

see A.10.10.2; G.23.20.1; Va.24.1.2

2 Macc. 9.5-10 [→ *1.26.b.50; 2.4.15*

B.23.20. *Flesh infested with worms*

(1) Worms and vermin cover Job's flesh; his skin cracks and oozes pus, his flesh rots and his bones protrude.

see B.11.1.3; B.15.1.2; A.23.1.20; A.23.20.2; B.24.1.4; Cc.23.3.1; Pc.2.1.1; Pd.1.1.; Cc.23.3.2; A.10.10.1

Job 7.5; Job 17.7; Job.18.13; Job 19.20; Job 30.17,30; *T. Job* **20.6-9;** *T. Job* **24.3;** *T. Job* **26.1;** *T. Job* **34.4** [→ *2.1.a.2*

(2) Worms breed in the flesh of the sinners in hell (while half their bodies are immersed in fire, the other half in snow).

see G.13.10.1; Ic.24.1.1; Ic.25.1.1; Ic.6.5.3

GL 2, 313; GL 5, 418-419 n.118 [→ *1.26.b.66*

B.24. *Wounded, Mutilated or Maimed Skin or Flesh*

B.24.1. *Lacerated skin or flesh*

(1) Pharaoh's flesh is torn from him when he is thrown from his horse and his chariot falls on top of him when he rides to the land of Goshen to chastise the children of Israel.
see A.23.1.6; B.23.2.3
Exod. R. 1.34   [→ *1.26.b.29*

(2) The Israelites pretend to repent by gashing themselves for the sake of corn and wine.
Hos. 7.14   [→ *2.32.9*

(3) The Israelites gash themselves with swords and spears until their blood flows during their hobbling dance to Baal.
1 Kgs 18.28   [→ *2.13.a.17*

(4) At first, Job's wounds are the size of a grain of wheat, but on the third day they have grown to the size of an ass's hoof.
see A.23.1.20; A.23.20.2; Cc.23.3.1; Cc.23.3.2; Pc.2.1.1; Pd.1.1.; B.11.1.3; B.23.20.1; B.15.1.2; A.10.10.1
GL 5, 386 n.26   [→ *1.10.5; 2.1.a.2*

B.24.3. *Burnt skin or flesh*

(1) The flesh of the Egyptians is seared by hailstones or by the fire contained within them: this is the seventh plague of Egypt.
see B.23.2.4; B.23.1.1; B.24.3.2; P.23.1.2; Ie.27.1.1; Sa.24.2.7; Sa.2.1.7; B.24.4.2; W.4.2.2; A.23.3.1; A.23.6.1
Exod. 8.24-25; *Exod. R.* 12.4
                           [→ *1.26.a.7; 1.26.b.26; 1.17.2; 2.5.4*

(2) The Egyptians have blains as a result of the hot naphtha God pours on them.
see B.23.2.4; B.23.1.1; B.24.3.1; P.23.1.2; Ie.27.1.1; Sa.2.1.7; Sa.24.2.7; B.24.4.2; W.4.2.2; A.23.3.1; A.23.6.1
Exod. R. 11.5-6   [→ *1.26.b.28; 2.5.7; 1.14.c.13*

(3) A foolhardy wight scalds himself by jumping into a scalding hot tub.
GL 3, 62; GL 6, 25 n.147   [→ *1.14.c.25; 4.1.a.5*

B.24.4. *Bitten skin*

(1) Seth is wounded by the teeth of the serpent (Satan) or of a wild beast.
  LAE (Vita) **37.1; 39.3;** *LAE (Apoc. Mos.)* **10.1; 12.2**   [→ *1.24.1*

(2) The flesh of the Egyptians is pierced by lice: this is the third plague of Egypt.
  see B.24.3.1; B.23.2.4; B.24.3.2; B.23.1.1; P.23.1.2; Sa.24.2.7; Ie.27.1.1; W.4.2.2; Sa.2.1.7; A.23.3.1; A.23.6.1
  GL 2, 342-352; GL 5, 426-429 n.171-173, 183-185
                                      [→ *1.26.b.27; 2.5.5*

(3) Men gnaw the flesh from their own bones during the famine in Samaria.
  see B.2.1.1; B.15.3.1
  GL 4, 191; GL 6, 314 n.55   [→ *1.13.6*

B.27. Transformation or Partial Transformation of Skin or Flesh

B.27.15. *Transformation of flesh or skin into vegetation or trees.*

(1) The flesh and hair torn from a martyr change into trees.
  see E.27.15.1
  GL 6, 405 n.47   [→ *1.35.16*

Ba. Perspiration

Ba.11. Unusual Colour of Perspiration

Ba.11.3. *Red perspiration*

(1) Red sweat of anger pours from the face of Aseneth when her father, Pentephres, tells her he will give her in marriage to Joseph.
  see A.6.4.1; E.22.2; Ia.15.1.1; G.11.3.2; F.10.1.10; Fa.11.3.1; G.10.2.2; Ia.11.3.1
  Jos. Asen. **4.9 (11)**   [→ *1.12.a.18*

Ba.16. Perspiration of Unusual Substance

Ba.16.4. *Perspiration of fire*

(1) Fire is kindled from the perspiration of Soperi'el and Soperi-el, two princes of angels, and lightnings and flame issue from their mouths. They have long tongues like blazing torches, lips like the gates of the east, and they are as tall as the seven heavens. Their bodies are full of eyes and they have wings as numerous as the days of the year.

see A.6.5.4; G.4.1.2; G.5.15.3; G.16.12.1; I.10.1.3; I.10.5.2; Ib.6.5.1; Ib.16.12.2; M.14.2.15; M.20.1.15

3 En. **18.25**   [→ *3.3.a.6*

(2) The holy Hayyot perspire fire from fear of God.
see I.10.1.1
Gen. R. **78.1;** *Lam. R.* **3.23**   [→ *1.12.a.3*

C. THE BODY DIVIDED

Ca. *The Body Divided into Right and Left*

Ca.9. *Right or Left Side of Opposite Sex*

(1) Man is created half male, half female. The female side is later made into a woman.

> see Cb.9.1.1; F.5.1.1; A.9.1.2; R.14.1.1; R.18.1.1; A.6.1.19; A.6.1.20; A.6.3.4; A.6.5.20; A.6.5.21; A.13.10.1; B.13.10.1; A.10.1.9; A.10.1.10; Sa.2.3.3; Sa.24.3.3; A.16.9.1; A.12.1.1; Cb.5.1.1; G.23.5.1; J.23.1.1; A.4.1.1; D.14.10.1; E.14.10.1; Fb.14.10.1; G.14.10.1; H.14.10.1; I.14.10.1; J.14.10.1; Ja.14.10.1
> *Lev. R.* **14.1;** *Gen. R.* **8.1;** *Apoc. Adam* **1.** **2-5**   [→ *1.8.b.3*

Cb. *The Body Divided into Front and Back*

Cb.5. *Unusual number of fronts or backs*

Cb.5.1. *Two fronts*

(1) Man is created a hermaphrodite, with two fronts, one male, one female. God saws him in two so that two bodies result, one male, one female.

> see Cb.9.1.1; F.5.1.1; A.9.1.2; R.14.1.1; R.18.1.1; A.6.1.19; A.6.1.20; A.6.3.4; A.6.5.20; A.6.5.21; A.13.10.1; B.13.10.1; A.10.1.9; A.10.1.10; Sa.2.3.3; Sa.24.3.3; A.16.9.1; Ca.9.1.1; A.12.1.1; G.23.5.1; J.23.1.1; A.4.1.1; D.14.10.1; E.14.10.1; Fb.14.10.1; G.14.10.1; H.14.10.1; I.14.10.1; J.14.10.1; Ja.14.10.1
> *Gen. R.* **8.1;** *Lev. R.* **14.1;** *Apoc. Adam* **1.** **2-5**   [→ *1.8.b.3*

Cb.9. *Front or Back of Opposite Sex or with Attributes of Opposite Sex*

Cb.9.1. *Androgyne*

(1) The first man is an androgyne with two faces; later God saws him in two and makes a back for each side.

see A.12.1.1; F.5.1.1; A.9.1.2; R.14.1.1; R.18.1.1; A.6.1.19; A.6.1.20; A.6.3.4; A.6.5.20; A.6.5.21; A.13.10.1; B.13.10.1; A.10.1.9; A.10.1.10; Sa.2.3.3; Sa.24.3.3; A.16.9.1; Ca.9.1.1; Cb.5.1.1; G.23.5.1; J.23.1.1; A.4.1.1; D.14.10.1; E.14.10.1; Fb.14.10.1; G.14.10.1; H.14.10.1; I.14.10.1; J.14.10.1; Ja.14.10.1

Lev. R. 14.1; *Gen. R.* **8.1; Apoc. Adam 1. 2-5**   [→ *1.8.b.3*

Cc. *Body Divided Into Upper and Lower Half*

Cc.16. *Upper or Lower Body of Unusual Substance*

Cc.16.2. *Upper or lower body of bronze*

(1) A man with an upper body of bronze and a lower part of fire is seen by Ezekiel in a vision.

see A.10.2.1; A.16.2.1; Cc.16.12.2

Ezek. 8.2   [→ *3.1.15*

Cc.16.10. *Upper or lower body of snow*

(1) The angels called Ishim have a lower body of snow and an upper body of fire.

see Cc.16.12.1

GL 2, 308; GL 5, 416-418 n.117   [→ *3.1.11*

Cc.16.12. *Upper or lower body of fire*

(1) The angels called Ishim have an upper body of fire and a lower body of snow.

see Cc.16.10.1

GL 2, 308; GL 5, 416-418 n. 117   [→ *3.1.11*

(2) A man with a lower body of fire and an upper body of bronze is seen by Ezekiel in a vision.

see A.10.2.1; A.16.2.1; Cc.16.2.1

Ezek. 8.2   [→ *3.1.15*

Cc.18.1. *Centaur*

(1) The men of the generation succeeding Enosh resemble centaurs (and apes).

see F.18.3.1

Gen. R. **23.6;** *Gen. R.* **24.6**   [→ *1.6.a.1*

Cc.18.2. *Upper or lower body of bear*

(1) Demons, from the middle down in the shape of a man and from the middle up resembling a bear (with a tail reaching from the shoulders to the ground) are met by Anah, a descendant of Esau, when he goes to pasture his father's asses in the wilderness.
    see Cc.18.3.1
    GL 1, 423; GL 5, 322 n.321, 322   [→ *3.2.1; 1.16.b.1*

Cc.18.3. *Upper or lower body of ape*

(1) Demons, from the middle down in the shape of a man and from the middle up in the shape of an ape (with a tail reaching from the shoulders to the ground) are met by Anah, a descendant of Esau, when he goes to pasture his father's asses in the wilderness.
    see Cc.18.2.1
    GL 1, 423; GL 5, 322 n.321,322   [→ *1.16.b.1; 3.2.1*

Cc.18.4. *Upper or lower body of goat*

(1) A strange creature, man above, he-goat below, is discovered and killed by Zepho, the son of Eliphaz.
    GL 2, 160; GL 5, 373 n.425   [→ *4.1.b.5*

Cc.19. *Upper or Lower Body of Fish*

Cc.19.1. *Upper or lower body of dolphin*

(1) The 'sons of the sea' (or dolphins) are half-man, half-fish.
    GL 1, 35; GL 5, 53-54 n.168   [→ *1.1.a.20; 1.9.1*

Cc.23. *Disease, Paralysis or Malfunction of Upper or Lower Body*

Cc.23.3. *Boils on upper or lower body*

(1) The upper part of Job's body is encrusted with dry boils.
    see Cc.23.3.2; A.23.1.20; A.23.20.2; B.24.1.4; Pc.2.1.1; Pd.1.1.1; B.11.1.3; B.23.20.1; B.15.1.2; A.10.10.1
    GL 2, 235; GL 5, 386 n.25   [→ *1.10.5; 2.1.a.2*

(2) The lower body of Job is covered with oozing boils.
    see Cc.23.3.1; A.23.1.20; A.23.20.2; B.24.1.4; Pc.2.1.1; Pd.1.1.1; B.11.1.3; B.23.20.1; B.15.1.2; A.10.10.1
    GL 2, 235; GL 5, 386 n.25   [→ *1.10.5; 2.1.a.2*

Cc.27. *Transformation of Upper or Lower Body*

Cc.27.1. *Transformation of upper or lower body into an ox*

(1) Nebuchadnezzar's upper body as far down as his navel is transformed into that of an ox, while the rest of his body is transformed into that of a lion.

> see Cc.27.4.1; A.27.2.3; A.6.2.2; A.2.4.1; U.23.1.4; T.24.3.1; E.6.5.6; Pd.6.5.1; Pd.12.1.1; Ib.1.1.2
> *Liv. Proph. (Daniel)* **4.5**   [→ *1.26.b.52; 2.7.6*

Cc.27.4. *Transformation of upper or lower body into lion*

(1) Nebuchadnezzar's lower body is transformed into that of a lion, while his upper body is transformed into that of an ox.

> see Cc.27.1.1; A.27.2.3; A.6.2.5; A.2.4.1; U.23.1.4; T.24.3.1; E.6.5.6; Pd.6.5.1; Pd.12.1.1; Ib.1.1.2
> *Liv. Proph. (Daniel)* **4.5**   [→ *1.26.b.52; 2.7.6*

Cd. *Other Divisions of the Body*

Cd.23. *Disease, Paralysis or Malfunction of Unspecified Half of Body*

Cd.23.1. *Withering of unspecified half of body*

(1) Half of the body of the giant Anak withers away after he has lived a very long time.

> see A.6.5.17
> **GL 3, 269; GL 6, 94 n.515**   [→ *1.1.b.4*

D. THE HEAD AND THE SKULL

D.1. *Absence of Head or Skull*

(1) The demon called Envy has the limbs of a man, but no head.
see A.2.5.1
GL 4, 152; GL 6, 292 n.55   [→ *3.9.3*

(2) The demon called Murder has the limbs of a man, but no head; he sees through his breast.
see G.4.5.2; A.2.5.2
T. Sol. **9.1-7**   [→ *3.9.4*

D.2. *Partial Absence of Head*

D.2.2 *Scalped Head*

(1) Eleazar's head is scalped, his tongue is cut out, the pupils of his eyes are pierced and his extremities are cut off as King Antiochus Epiphanes tries to force him to taste pig's flesh. He is later fried alive. His six brothers and his mother receive the same treatment.
see Ib.1.1.3; P.1.1.2; U.1.1.1; Ga.24.1.1
2 Macc. 7; *4 Macc.* **6.6,25;** *4 Macc.* **7.13-14;** *4 Macc.* **9.28;** *4 Macc.* **10.5-8,17-21;** *4 Macc.* **11.18-19;** *4 Macc.* **18.21**
[→ *2.5.12; 2.25.a.2; 1.24.4*

D.3. *Vital Head or Skull*

D.3.1. *Head that can wander off and return at will*

(1) The skull (or, alternatively, the bones) of a slain Jew made into a drinking vessel comes to life and strikes a blow into Nebuchadnezzar's face, while a voice announces 'A friend of this man is at this moment reviving the dead'.
see Va.3.1.4
GL 4, 330; GL 6, 418 n.90   [→ *1.15.3; 2.2.c.11*

D.3.2. *Head of a dead person that continues to function*

(1) The teraphim are the heads of slain men, shaved, salted and anointed with oil. When the 'name', written on a small tablet of copper or gold, is placed under their tongues, they speak and have oracular powers.

GL 1, 371-372; GL 5, 301 n.218 [→ *1.11.a.8; 2.2.c.9*

D.5. *Unusual Number of Heads or Skulls*

D.5.1. *Two heads or skulls*

(1) Enepsigos is a female demon with two heads on her shoulders and two pairs of arms. She hovers near the moon and can assume three forms.

see O.5.3.1
***T. Sol.* 15.1-5** [→ *3.1.18*

(2) The Cainites have two heads.
see A.6.1.4; A.6.2.1; A.6.1.8
GL 1, 114; GL 5, 143 n.34; GL 4, 132
[→ *1.1.a.17; 1.16.b.2; 3.2.2*

(3) A double-headed Cainite comes up when Asmodeus sticks his finger into the ground. This Cainite in turn has a son with two heads.
see D.5.1.4
GL 4, 132; GL 6, 286 n.28, 29 [→ *4.1.b.1*

(4) The double-headed son of a double-headed Cainite claims two portions of his father's property.
see D.5.1.3
GL 4, 132; GL 6, 286 n.29 [→ *4.1.b.2*

(5) The inhabitants of Tebel, the second earth, have two heads.
see D.18.4.2; D.18.5.1; D.18.6.1; D.21.4.1; D.21.5.1; D.21.6.1; O.5.3.2; P.5.3.1; T.5.3.1; U.5.3.1
GL 1, 10 [→ *1.16.b.8; 3.2.7*

(6) Death, in order to reveal his corruption, shows two heads, one with the face of a dragon, one like a sword.
see F.18.6.2; D.17.1.1; A.23.8.1; D.5.6.1; F.17.4.1; D.18.6.2; F.17.1.1; F.17.2.1; F.17.3.1; F.17.5.1; F.17.10.1; F.18.5.4; F.17.6.1; A.10.1.23; Fa.10.2.1; D.5.2.1
***T. Abr.* 13.13-16; *T. Abr.* 14.1 (Recension B)** [→ *2.24.20; 3.9.7*

D.5.2. *Three heads*

(1) Death shows Abraham his three-headed dragon face, as well as his serpent face, lion face and his faces of flaming fire, of darkness, a precipice, a sword, of thunder and lightning, a turbulent river, a mixed cup of poisons, and every fatal disease when Abraham requests him to reveal his face of ferocity, decay and bitterness.

see F.18.6.2; D.17.1.1; A.23.8.1; D.5.6.1; F.17.4.1; D.18.6.2; F.17.1.1; F.17.2.1; F.17.3.1; F.17.5.1; F.17.10.1; F.18.5.4; F.17.6.1; A.10.1.23; Fa.10.2.1; D.5.1.6

T. Abr. 17.12-17; T. Abr. 19.5f. [→ *2.24.19; 3.9.8*

D.5.6. *Seven heads*

(1) Death shows Abraham his seven fiery heads of dragons and also his serpent face, lion face and faces of flaming fire, darkness, a precipice, a sword, of thunder and lightning, a turbulent river, a mixed cup of poisons, and of every fatal disease when Abraham requests him to reveal his face of ferocity, decay and bitterness.

see F.18.6.2; D.17.1.1; A.23.8.1; D.5.2.1; F.17.4.1; D.18.6.2; F.17.1.1; F.17.2.1; F.17.3.1; F.17.5.1; F.17.10.1; F.18.5.4; F.17.6.1; A.10.1.23; Fa.10.2.1; D.5.1.6

T. Abr. 17.12-17; T. Abr. 19.5f. [→ *2.24..19; 3.9.8*

D.5.13. *Between one thousand and one million heads*

(1) The angel Sandalfon has 70,000 heads.

see A.6.5.11; I.5.14.1; Ib.5.14.1

3 En. 1.7-8; 1 En. 71.1-7 [→ *2.22.a.4*

D.7. *Head or Skull facing Unusual Direction*

D.7.1. *Head facing backwards*

(1) At the sound of Judah's outcry, the heads of Joseph's heroes remain fixed facing backwards (having turned to discover the cause of the tumult) and they lose their teeth.

see D.23.6.1; Ic.1.1.1

Gen. R. 93.7 [→ *1.14.b.3.*

D.14. *Unusual Protuberances or Protusions on Head or Skull*

D.14.2. *Horns on head*

(1) The angel Zagzagel has horns of glory.
    GL 2, 309; GL 5, 416-418 n.117   [→ *3.1.12*

(2) The cherubim have horns of glory on their heads.
    see M.14.2.8; M.20.1.8; F.18.5.2; F.20.1.1; F.18.4.1; U.18.3.1; P.21.1.1;
    A.14.10.1; G.4.1.4; G.5.15.5; G.10.2.2; F.10.1.1; F.5.3.1
    3 En. 22.13-15   [→ *31.16*

(3) Men with horns of deer, faces like cattle, feet of goats and the
loins of sheep live in the first heaven; these are the men who built the
Tower of Babel.
    see D.18.11.1; F.18.4.2; U.18.2.1; Sa.18.2.1
    3 Bar. 2.3 (Slavonic and Greek)   [→ *1.26.b.7*

(4) Men with horns of deer, faces of dogs and the feet of goats and
deer, live in the second heaven; these are the men who planned to
build the Tower of Babel and forced men and women to make bricks.
    see U.18.2.2; D.18.11.2; U.18.4.1; F.18.2.2
    3 Bar. 3.3 (Slavonic and Greek)   [→ *1.26.b.6*

(5) Zedekiah, the son of Chenaanah, makes himself iron horns.
    see D.18.11.3
    1 Kgs 22.11; 2 Chron. 18.10   [→ *2.16.10*

D.14.10. *Body(ies) on head*

(1) While Adam is still a lifeless mass, God shows him all the righteous people who will descend from him: some hang on his head, some
on his hair, his forehead, his eyes, his nose, mouth, ear and earlobes.
    see Cb.9.1.1; F.5.1.1; A.9.1.2; R.14.1.1; R.18.1.1; A.6.1.19; A.6.1.20;
    A.6.3.4; A.6.5.20; A.6.5.21; A.13.10.1; B.13.10.1; A.10.1.9; A.10.1.10;
    Sa.2.3.3; Sa.24.3.3; A.16.9.1; Ca.9.1.1; Cb.5.1.1; G.23.5.1; J.23.1.1; A.4.1.1;
    A.12.1.1; E.14.10.1; Fb.14.10.1; G.14.10.1; H.14.10.1; I.14.10.1; J.14.10.1;
    Ja.14.10.1
    Exod. R. 40.3   [→ *2.4.3*

D.16. *Head or Skull of Unusual Substance*

D.16.3. *Head or skull of gold*

(1) God's head is made of gold, his locks are curled and black as a
raven.
    see E.11.2.1; A.11.2.2; A.11.3.1; A.11.2.1; E.11.1.1; E.12.3.1; F.5.10.1;

F.16.12.1; G.10.5.1; Ia.16.12.1; P.10.1.1; P.10.7.1; Pc.10.7.1; Gf.4.1.1;
A.1.1.1; Gf.7.2.1; A.10.1.1; Pc.10.3.1; I.10.5.1; If.6.1.1
Cant. **R. 5.11 §1** [→ *3.9.1*

D.17. *Substitution for Head or Skull*

D.17.1. *Weapon in place of head or skull*

(1) Death appears with two heads, one like a sword, one with the face
of a dragon, when he approaches sinners.
see F.18.6.2; D.5.1.6; A.23.8.1; D.5.6.1; F.17.4.1; D.18.6.2; F.17.1.1;
F.17.2.1; F.17.3.1; F.17.5.1; F.17.10.1; F.18.5.4; F.17.6.1; A.10.1.24;
Fa.10.2.1; D.5.2.1
T. Abr. **13.13-16;** *T. Abr.* **14. (Recension B)** [→ *2.24.20; 3.9.7*

D.18. *Animal Head or Skull, or Head or Skull with Animal Attributes*

D.18.1. *Head of dog*

(1) There are heavenly bodies with a human form, but with heads
like dogs.
T. Sol. **18.1** [→ *3.2.3*

D.18.4. *Head of ox*

(1) The demon Keteb or Keteb Meriri ('Bitter Destruction' or
'Pestilence') has the head of a calf with a single horn on his forehead.
He is hairy all over, covered in scales, and full of eyes. He has an eye
set on his heart which kills whoever looks at it.
see E.4.1.2; Fb.14.2.1; G.5.15.6; G.4.1.6; G.4.5.1; B.13.7.1; A.13.6.1;
B.13.6.1; Fb.18.11.1
Num. **R. 12.3;** *Lam.* **R. 1.3 §29** [→ *3.1.22*

(2) Tebel, the second earth, is inhabited by creatures with a human
body but the head of an ox.
see D.5.1.5; D.18.5.1; D.18.6.1; D.21.4.1; D.21.5.1; D.21.6.1; O.5.3.2;
P.5.3.1; T.5.3.1; U.5.3.1
GL 1, 10 [→ *1.16.b.8; 3.2.7*

D.18.5. *Head of lion*

(1) Tebel, the second earth, is inhabited by creatures with a human body but the head of a lion.

> see D.5.1.5; D.18.4.2; D.18.6.1; D.21.4.1; D.21.5.1; D.21.6.1; O.5.3.2; P.5.3.1; T.5.3.1; U.5.3.1
> **GL 1, 10** [→ *1.16.b.8; 3.2.7*

D.18.6. *Head of snake or dragon*

(1) Tebel, the second earth, is inhabited by creatures with a human body but the head of a snake.

> see D.5.1.5; D.18.4.2; D.18.5.1; D.21.4.1; D.21.5.1; D.21.6.1; O.5.3.2; P.5.3.1; T.5.3.1; U.5.3.1
> **GL 1, 10** [→ *1.16.b.8; 3.2.7*

(2) Death shows Abraham his three-headed and seven-headed dragon face, as well as his faces of a viper, an asp, a cobra-headed serpent, of a precipice, of a sword, of thunder and lightning, of darkness, of a turbulent river, a mixed cup of poisons and of every fatal disease, when Abraham requests death to reveal his face of ferocity, decay and bitterness.

> see F.18.6.2; D.5.1.6; A.23.8.1; D.5.6.1; F.17.4.1; D.17.1.1; F.17.1.1; F.17.2.1; F.17.3.1; F.17.5.1; F.17.10.1; F.18.5.4; F.17.6.1; A.10.1.24; Fa.10.2.1; D.5.2.1
> *T. Abr.* **17.12-17;** *T. Abr.* **19.5f.** [→ *2.24.19; 3.9.8*

D.18.11. *Head with horns*

(1) Men with the horns of deer, faces like cattle, feet of goats and the loins of sheep inhabit the first heaven: these are the men who built the Tower of Babel.

> see D.14.2.3; F.18.4.2; U.18.2.1; Sa.18.2.1
> *3 Bar.* **2.3 (Slavonic and Greek)** [→ *1.26.b.7*

(2) Men with the horns of deer, faces of dogs and feet of deer and goats inhabit the second heaven: these are the men who planned to build the Tower of Babel and forced men and women to build bricks.

> see D.14.2.2; F.18.2.1; U.18.4.1; U.18.2.2
> *3 Bar.* **3.3 (Slavonic and Greek)** [→ *1.26.b.6*

(3) Zedekiah, the son of Chenaanah, makes himself iron horns.

> see D.14.2.5
> **1 Kgs 22.11; 2 Chron. 18.10** [→ *2.16.10*

D.21. *Human Head on Unusual Creature*

D.21.4. *Human head on body of ox*

(1) Tebel, the second earth, is inhabited by creatures with a human head, but the body of an ox.
　　see D.5.1.5; D.18.4.2; D.18.5.1; D.18.6.1; D.21.5.1; D.21.6.1; O.5.3.2; P.5.3.1; T.5.3.1; U.5.3.1
　　GL 1, 10　　　　　　　　　　　　　　　[→ *1.16.b.8; 3.2.7*

D.21.5. *Human head on body of lion*

(1) Tebel, the second earth, is inhabited by creatures with a human head but the body of a lion.
　　see D.5.1.5; D.18.4.2; D.18.5.2; D.18.6.1; D.21.4.1; D.21.6.1; O.5.3.2; P.5.3.1; T.5.3.1; U.5.3.1
　　GL 1, 10　　　　　　　　　　　　　　　[→ *1.16.b.8; 3.2.7*

D.21.6. *Human head on body of snake or dragon*

(1) Tebel, the second earth, is inhabited by creatures with a human head but the body of a serpent.
　　see D.5.1.5; D.18.4.2; D.18.5.2; D.18.6.1; D.21.4.1; D.21.5.1; O.5.3.2; P.5.3.1; T.5.3.1; U.5.3.1
　　GL 1, 10　　　　　　　　　　　　　　　[→ *1.16.b.8; 3.2.7*

D.23. *Disease, Paralysis or Malfunction of Head*

D.23.1. *Leprous head*

(1) The daughters of Zion become leprous and leprous scabs appear on their heads.
　　see E.23.1.1; W.5.1.1; Sb.10.3.1
　　Lev. R. **16.1**; *Lev. R.* **17.3**; *Num. R.* **7.5**; *Lam. R.* **4.15 §18**
　　　　　　　　　　　　　　　　　　　[→ *1.26.b.60*

D.23.6. *Paralysis of head*

(1) At the sound of Judah's outcry, the heads of Joseph's three hundred heroes remain fixed facing backwards (having turned to discover the cause of the tumult) and lose their teeth.
　　see D.7.1.1; Ic.1.1.1
　　Gen. R. **93.7**　　　　　　　　　　　[→ *1.14.b.3*

E. THE HAIR AND THE BEARD

E.1. *Absence of Hair or Beard*

(1) Spirits have no hair.
  Ruth R. **6.1**   [→ *1.1.a.2*

(2) Both male and female demons have bald heads while their bodies
and faces are covered in hair.
  see B.13.6.2; A.13.6.2; F.13.12.1; E.4.1.1; E.4.2.1
  GL 6, 192 n.58   [→ *1.1.a.6*

(3) Elisha has a bald head and is mocked by some small boys.
  2 Kgs 2.23   [→ *4.1.b.20*

(4) Hezekiah has a bald head
  see A.25.30.1; B.2.2.1; Sa.2.1.24; Sa.24.2.24; B.15.1.1
  GL 4, 277; GL 6, 370 n.94   [→ *4.1.b.18*

(5) Jonah's hair falls out as a result of the intense heat in the belly of
the fish.
  see Sa.2.3.28; Sa.24.3.28; A.25.3.9
  GL 4, 252; GL 6, 351 n.36   [→ *1.9.2; 1.14.c.17*

(6) Siti's hair is shaved off by Satan (disguised as a bread seller) in
return for three loaves of bread.
  T. Job **23.7-11**   [→ *2.32.8*

(7) A man's hair falls out when, passing through the wilderness of
Cub, he is terrified to see a sleeping serpent as thick as the beam of an
olive press.
  Exod. R. **24.4**   [→ *1.12.a.30*

(8) The head and body hair of Korah (and others) is shaved off.
  GL 3, 288; GL 6, 100 n.564   [→ *2.13.a.11*

E.2. *Partial Absence of Hair or Beard*

E.2.1. *Unusually shaped bald patch*

(1) The Antichrist has a bald head with a tuft of grey hair at the front, eyebrows reaching to his ears, a leprous bare spot on the palms of his hands, and fiery wings. He also has skinny legs and can appear as a child or an old man, but is unable to change the signs on his head.
   see E.11.4.1; Gb.6.5.1; M.14.2.19; M.20.1.19; Pa.23.1.1; T.6.4.1
   Apoc. Elij. **3.15-17**; *Apoc. Elij.* **5.20**   [→ *3.1.26*

E.2.2. *Hair torn out*

(1) Certain Israelites tear out their hair in desperation when they are told by Moses to turn back to Pi-hahiroth.
   GL 3, 10; GL 6, 3 n.12   [→ *1.12.a.11*

(2) Ezra tears out the hair from his head and beard when he hears that the Israelites have married foreigners.
   see E.2.3.1
   Ezra 9.3   [→ *1.12.a.14*

(3) Nehemiah tears out the hair of several Israelites in his anger over their marriage to foreigners.
   Neh. 13.25   [→ *1.12.a.24*

E.2.3. *Hair of beard pulled out.*

(1) Ezra tears out the hair from his beard and head when he hears that Israelites have married foreigners.
   see E.2.2.2
   Ezra 9.3   [→ *1.12.a.14*

E.4. *Hair or Beard in Unusual Place on Body*

E.4.1. *Hair on body*

(1) Both male and female demons have bodies and faces covered with hair.
   see E.4.2.1; A.13.6.2; F.13.12.1; B.13.6.2; E.1.1.2
   GL 6, 192 n.58   [→ *1.1.a.6*

(2) The demon Keteb, or Keteb Meriri ('Bitter Destruction' or 'Pestilence') is covered with hair and scales. He is also full of eyes, and has the head of a calf with a single horn on his forehead. He has a single eye set on his heart that kills whoever looks at it.

> see D.18.4.1; Fb.14.2.1; G.5.15.6; G.4.1.6; G.4.5.1; B.13.7.1; A.13.6.1; B.13.6.1; Fb.18.11.1
> *Num. R.* **12.3;** *Lam. R.* **1.3 §29; GL 3, 186; GL 6, 74 n.381**
> [→ *3.1.22*

(3) Esau is hairy all over.

> see A.13.6.3; B.18.3.1; A.11.3.3; O.13.6.1; P.13.6.1; B.11.3.1; B.13.6.3; E.26.1.1; Ic.26.1.1; Sa.2.3.4; Sa.24.3.4; A.13.1.1; B.13.1.1
> **Gen. 25.25; Gen. 27.11, 23;** *Gen. R.* **63.6-8, 8:** *Gen. R.* **73.8**
> [→ *3.7.2; 3.6.b.8; 3.10.16*

E.4.2. *Hair on face*

(1) Both male and female demons have hair on their faces and bodies.

> see E.4.1.1; A.13.6.2; F.13.12.1; B.13.6.2; E.1.1.2
> **GL 6, 192 n.58**   [→ *1.1.a.6*

E.5. *Unusual Quantity of Hair*

E.5.1. *Abundance of hair*

(1) Absalom has an abundance of hair: the small quantity he clips off each week (or year) weighs 200 shekels.

> see A.6.1.27; E.6.5.5
> **2 Sam. 14.26;** *Gen. R.* **9.24**   [→ *3.4.a.9; 2.13.a.15*

E.6. *Unusual Size of Beard or Hair*

E.6.1. *Abnormally large beard or head of hair*

(1) Moses' beard is like a palm branch.

> see F.10.1.11; Sa.2.3.19; Sa.24.3.19; A.6.5.25; A.6.4.2; P.23.1.1; P.25.4.1; I.10.1.5; G.10.2.9; F.11.3.2; Fb.10.1.1; G.25.4.1; If.6.1.2; Fb.14.2.3; I.23.3.3; P.11.2.2; G.17.20.1; Ib.13.2..1; Ib.24.4.1; Ia.24.4.1; A.25.9.1; Ga.10.2.1; E.12.10.1; P.13.2.1; P.24.4.1; K.13.10.2; B.16.12.2; Ib.16.12.3; Ia.13.2.1; A.26.1.3
> **GL 2, 332; GL 5, 425 n.157**   [→ *3.3.a.30*

(2) Aaron's beard is like a palm branch.

> see A.6.5.26; E.12.10.2; F.10.1.12; Ga.10.2.2; I.10.1.1; A.6.2.4; A.23.1.8
> **GL 2, 332; GL 5, 425 n.157**   [→ *3.3.a.30*

E.6.5. *Abnormally long hair or beard*

(1) The Antichrist's hair reaches to his feet and he is three-crested. He is ten cubits tall and the track of his feet is three cubits. His left eye is like the star which rises in the morning and his right eye is like a lion's. His lower teeth are made of iron and his lower jaw of diamond; his right arm is of iron, his left of copper. His right hand is three cubits long. He is long-faced, long-nosed and disorderly, and has three letters written on his forehead: A, K and T, signifying denial, rejection and the befouled dragon. His mother conceives him by touching the head of a fish.

    see A.6.5.13; Fb.13.2.3; Fc.16.5.1; G.10.2.6; G.18.1.1; Ic.16.1.1; O.16.1.1; O.16.2.3; U.6.5.2

    Apoc. Dan. **9.11,16-26**   [→ *3.1.25; 1.3.c.1*

(2) Adikam, the second son of Pharaoh, has a beard which flows down to his ankles.

    see A.6.6.1; A.6.3.7

    GL 2, 298-299; GL 5, 413 n.104   [→ *3.6.b.13*

(3) The babies born to Hebrew women in Egypt and abandoned in the fields (to prevent their murder by the Egyptians) have hair down to their knees to serve as a protecting garment.

    GL 2, 258; GL 5, 394 n.25   [→ *2.27.a.1*

(4) Samson's hair grows extremely long since he is a Nazirite and is forbidden to let a razor touch his head.

    see E.8.1.2; E.25.5.1; A.6.1.29; Ie.17.3.1; I.10.20.1; G.24.1.2; G.1.3; U.23.1.2; M.6.3.1; T.25.1.2; G.23.4.16

    Judg. 13.5   [→ *2.13.a.14*

(5) Absalom lets his hair grow long, and he has such an abundance of it that the small quantity he clips off each year (or week) weighs two hundred shekels.

    see E.5.1.1; A.6.1.27

    2 Sam. 14.26; Gen. R. 9.24   [→ *3.4.a.9; 2.13.a.15*

(6) Nebuchadnezzar's hair grows as long as an eagle's feathers, and his nails become like birds' claws when he is driven from human society and lives for seven years as a beast.

    see Pd.6.5.1; Pd.12.1.1; A.27.2.3; Cc.27.1.1; Cc.27.4.1; Ib.1.1.2; A.6.2.5; A.2.4.1; T.24.3.1; U.23.1.4

    Dan. 4.30   [→ *1.9.3*

E.8. *Inverted Hair (Horripilation)*

E.8.1. *Horripilation*

(1) The hair above Judah's heart grows so stiff and hot that it stands on end and pierces the five garments in which he is clothed. Judah's chest hair kills anyone who touches it.

see E.13.1.2; G.10.4.1; Gf.16.3.1; Ic.18.5.1; F.18.5.3; J.23.1.2; I.23.3.2; Va.3.1.1; F.11.6.2; If.6.1.2; A.10.1.15
Gen. R. 93.6,7; GL 2, 107-108; GL 5, 354 n.277, 278
[→ *1.12.a.19*

(2) Samson's hairs become stiff and knock against one another like bells (and their clang travels as far as from Zorah to Eshtaol) when the Holy Spirit is with him.

see E.6.5.4; E.25.5.1; A.6.1.29; Ie.17.3.1; I.10.20.1; G.24.1.2; G.1.3; U.23.1.2; M.6.3.1; T.25.1.2; G.23.4.16
Lev. R. 8.2   [→ *1.1.1; 1.19.b.9*

E.9. *Hair or Beard of Opposite Sex*

E.9.3. *Female with hairy legs or feet*

(1) The queen of Sheba has hairy legs and feet (like a man).

see T.13.6.1; U.13.6.1
GL 4, 145; GL 6, 289 n.41   [→ *1.1.a.8*

E.9.5. *Male with female hair*

(1) The hair of the ugly angels who carry off the souls of ungodly men, is loose like the hair of women; their faces are like those of a leopard, their eyes are mixed with blood and their tusks are outside their mouths like a wild boar's.

see F.18.9.1; Ic.18.1.1; W.4.1.1
Apoc. Zeph. 4.2-4; Apoc. Zeph. 6.8   [→ *2.24.9*

E.10. *Unusual Emission or Emanation from Hair or Beard*

E.10.2. *Hair that emits flames*

(1) The hair of an angel seen by Aseneth (probably Michael) is like a flaming torch, his face like lightning, his eyes like sunshine and his hands and feet like glowing iron which emits sparks.

see F.10.1.3; G.10.2.4; P.10.3.2; P.16.1.1; U.10.3.1; U.16.1.1
Jos. Asen. **14.9.8,9;** *Jos. Asen.* **16.12,13(7)** [→ *3.1.8*

E.11. *Unusual Colour of Hair or Beard*

E.11.1. *Black hair*

(1) God's hair is black as a raven, his locks are curled and his head is made of gold.
see E.11.2.1; A.11.2.2; A.11.3.1; D.16.3.1; A.11.2.1; E.12.3.1; F.5.10.1;
F.16.12.1; G.10.5.1; Ia.16.12.1; P.10.1.1; P.10.7.1; Pc.10.7.1; Gf.4.1.1;
A.1.1.1; Gf.27.2.1; A.10.1.1; Pc.10.3.1; I.10.5.1; If.6.1.1
Cant. R. **5.11 §1** [→ *3.9.1*

E.11.2. *White hair*

(1) God's hair is white like pure wool.
see A.11.2.1; A.11.2.2; A.11.3.1; D.16.3.1; E.11.1.1; E.12.3.1; F.5.10.1;
F.16.12.1; G.10.5.1; Ia.16.12.1; P.10.1.1; P.10.7.1; Pc.10.7.1; Gf.4.1.1;
A.1.1.1; Gf.27.2.1; A.10.1.1; Pc.10.3.1; I.10.5.1; If.6.1.1
Dan. 7.9; *1 En.* **46.1;** *1 En.* **71.10; 2** *En.* **28.7** [→ *3.6.a.1*

(2) The hair of the angel Iaoel is as white as snow, his face is like chrysolite, his body and legs like sapphire and he wears a headdress which looks like a rainbow.
see A.16.18.2; F.16.18.1; T.16.18.1
Apoc. Abr. **11.2** [→ *3.3.a.11*

(3) At birth Noah's hair is long and curly and as white as wool.
see A.11.2.5; A.11.3.2; G.10.2.7; Sa.2.3.6; Sa.24.3.6; Sa.2.1.1; T.23.1.1;
I.10.4.1; Sa.24.10.1; Va.24.1.1; If.26.1.1; B.11.2.1; B.11.3.2; Sa.24.2.1
1 En. **106.2, 10; GL 1, 145; GL 5, 167-169 n.1-4** [→ *3.10.17*

E.11.3. *Red hair*

(1) David has red hair.
see B.11.3.3; Sa.2.3.25; Sa.24.3.25; G.25.1.1; A.23.1.16; T.23.2.1; O.23.2.1;
A.25.15.3; F.11.1.7; A.25.9.2
GL 6, 247 n.13 [→ *1.12.a.31; 3.10.18*

(2) The Messiah has red hair and small birthmarks on his thigh.
see Ta.13.2.1
'Horoscope of the Messiah', Vermes, 270 [→ *3.1.29*

E.11.4. *Grey hair*

(1) The Antichrist has a tuft of grey hair at the front of his bald head, eyebrows reaching to his ears, a leprous bare spot on the palms of his hands and fiery wings. He can appear as an old man or a child, but cannot change the signs on his forehead.

see E.2.1.1; Gb.6.5.1; M.14.2.19; M.20.1.19; Pa.23.1.1; T.6.4.1
Apoc. Elij. **3.15-17;** *Apoc. Elij.* **5.20**   [→ *3.1.26*

E.12. *Unusual Shape of Hair or Beard,*
or Hair or Beard Worn in Unusual Style

E.12.3. *Curly, twisted hair*

(1) God's locks are curly and black as a raven, and his head is made of gold.

see E.11.2.1; A.11.2.2; A.11.3.1; D.16.3.1; E.11.1.1; A.11.2.1; F.5.10.1;
F.16.12.1; G.10.5.1; Ia.16.12.1; P.10.1.1; P.10.7.1; Pc.10.7.1; Gf.4.1.1;
A.1.1.1; Gf.27.2.1; A.10.1.1; Pc.10.3.1; I.10.5.1; If.6.1.1
Cant. R. **5.11 §1**   [→ *3.9.1*

(2) Ham's descendants have twisted, curly hair.

see G.11.3.1; Ia.12.1.1; A.11.1.3; B.11.1.2
GL 1, 169; GL 5, 191-192 n.60,61   [→ *1.7.a.3*

E.12.10. *Beard like palm branch*

(1) Moses' beard is like a palm branch.

see F.10.1.11; Sa.2.3.19; Sa.24.3.19; A.6.5.25; A.6.4.2; P.23.1.1; P.25.4.1;
I.10.1.5; G.10.2.9; F.11.3.2; Fb.10.1.1; F.10.1.11; G.25.4.1; If.6.1.3;
Fb.14.2.3; I.23.3.3; P.11.2.2; G.17.20.1; Ib.13.2.1; Ib.24.4.1; Ia.24.4.1;
E.6.1.1; Ga.10.2.1; A.25.9.1; P.13.2.1; P.24.4.1; K.13.10.2; B.16.12.2;
Ib.16.12.3; Ia.13.2.1; A.26.1.3
GL 2, 332; GL 5, 425 n.157   [→ *3.3.a.30*

(2) Aaron's beard is like a palm branch.

see E.6.1.2; A.6.5.26; F.10.1.12; Ga.10.2.2; I.10.1.4; A.23.1.8; A.6.2.4
GL 2, 332; GL 5, 425 n.157   [→ *3.3.a.30*

E.13. *Unusual Texture of Hair or Beard*

E.13.1. *Unusually rigid hair*

(1) A beggar with 'hair like nails', who is really the angel of death, seats himself before the bridegroom at a wedding banquet.

see A.22.1.2
GL 4, 227-229; GL 6, 335-336 n.96,97   [→ *2.6.a.1*

(2) The hair above Judah's heart grows so stiff and hot that it pierces the five garments in which he is clothed. Judah's chest hair kills anyone who touches it.

see E.8.1.1; G.10.4.1; Gf.16.3.1; Ic.18.5.1; F.18.5.3; J.23.1.2; I.23.3.2; Va.3.1.1; F.11.6.2; If.6.1.2; A.10.1.15
Gen. R. 93.6, 7; GL 2, 107-108; GL 5, 354 n.277, 278

[→ *1.12.a.19*

E.14. *Unusual Protuberances or Protusions on Hair or Beard*

E.14.10. *Body(ies) on hair*

(1) While Adam is still a lifeless mass, God shows him all the righteous people who will descend from him: some hang on Adam's hair, others on his head, his forehead, his eyes nose, mouth, ears and earlobes.

see Cb.9.1.1; F.5.1.1; A.9.1.2; R.14.1.1; R.18.1.1; A.6.1.19; A.6.1.20; A.6.3.4; A.6.5.20; A.6.5.21; A.13.10.1; B.13.10.1; A.10.1.9; A.10.1.10; Sa.2.3.3; Sa.24.3.3; A.16.9.1; Ca.9.1.1; Cb.5.1.1; G.23.5.1; J.23.1.1; A.4.1.1; D.14.10.1; A.12.1.1; Fb.14.10.1; G.14.10.1; H.14.10.1; I.14.10.1; J.14.10.1; Ja.14.10.1
Exod. R. 40.3

[→ *2.4.3*

E.16. *Hair or Beard of Unusual Substance*

E.16.4. *Hair of flame*

(1) Enoch's hair becomes a flaring blaze when he is transformed into Metatron.

see A.6.3.2; A.6.5.12; G.5.13.2; G.10.2.3; M.14.2.13; M.20.1.13; A.16.12.6; B.16.12.1; G.16.12.5; V.16.12.1; Va.16.12.1; A.10.1.7
3 En. 15.1; 3 En. 48c. (Appendix)

[→ *1.3.2*

E.18. *Animal Hair in Place of Human*

E.18.1. *Bear hair*

(1) The Persians are hairy like bears.

see A.13.6.4; B.18.1.1
b. Qid 72a; Est. R. 1.17

[→ *3.7.4*

E.22. *Unusually Hideous Hair or Beard*

(1) Obyzouth is a demon in the shape of a woman but with savage, dishevelled hair. She strangles newborn infants, injures eyes, condemns mouths, destroys minds and causes pain. Her body is darkness itself.

T. Sol. **13.1**; *T. Sol.* **13.5** [→ *3.1.17*

(2) After seven days of fasting as a penance for her sins, Aseneth's hair is straggly from the load of ashes she has put on it, her eyes are inflamed, her lips cracked, and her body is emaciated.

see A.6.4.1; G.11.3.2; Ia.15.1.1; Ba.11.3.1; F.10.1.10; Fa.11.3.1; G.10.2.8; Ia.11.3.1

Jos. Asen. **11.1.1**; *Jos. Asen.* **13.9.8**; *Jos. Asen.* **18.3**
[→ *1.14.c.9*; *2.31.b.2*

E.23. *Disease of Hair or Beard*

E.23.1. Hair infested with lice

(1) The daughters of Zion have hair infested with lice as a punishment for their unchastity and pride.

see D.23.1.1; W.5.1.1; Sb.10.3.1

Lev. R. **16.1**; *Lev. R.* **17.3**; *Num. R.* **7.5**; *Lam. R.* **4.15** §18
[→ *1.26.b.60*

E.25. *Unusual Abilities of Hair or Beard*

E.25.5. Hair that moves and emits sound

(1) When the spirit of God is upon him, Samson's hair becomes stiff and emits a bell-like sound which can be heard as far as from Zorah to Eshtaol.

see E.8.1.2; E.6.5.4; A.6.1.29; Ie.17.3.1; I.10.20.1; G.24.1.2; G.1.3; U.23.1.2; M.6.3.1; T.25.1.2; G.23.4.16

Lev. R. **8.2** [→ *1.18.1*; *1.19.b.9*

E.26. *Hair or Beard of Different Age Group*

E.26.1. Child with hair or beard of adult

(1) Esau is born with hair, beard and both front and back teeth.

see A.13.6.3; B.18.3.1; E.4.1.3; O.13.6.1; P.13.6.1; B.11.3.1; B.13.6.3;

A.11.3.3; Ic.26.1.1; Sa.2.3.4; Sa.24.3.4; A.13.1.1; B.13.1.1
GL 1, 315; GL 5, 273 n.23 [→ *3.10.16*

(2) Children are born with grey temples as a sign of the End.
Sib. Or. **2, 221-226;** *Jub.* **23.25** [→ *3.10.22*

E.27. *Transformation of Hair or Beard*

E.27.15. *Transformation of hair into trees*

(1) The hair and flesh torn from a martyr change into trees.
see B.27.15.1
GL 6, 405 n.47 [→ *1.35.16*

F. THE FACE

F.3. *Vital Face*

(1) Lix Tetrax, the demon of the wind, bears his face on high, while
the remaining part of his body crawls along like a snail.
  T. Sol. **7.1**   [→ *3.9.2*

F.5. *Unusual Number of Faces*

F.5.1. *Two faces*

(1) Adam has two faces until God separates them by sawing Adam in
two and making a back for each side.
  see Cb.9.1.1; A.12.1.1; A.9.1.2; R.14.1.1; R.18.1.1; A.6.1.19; A.6.1.20;
  A.6.3.4; A.6.5.20; A.6.5.21; A.13.10.1; B.13.10.1; A.10.1.9; A.10.1.10;
  Sa.2.3.3; Sa.24.3.3; A.16.9.1; Ca.9.1.1; Cb.5.1.1; G.23.5.1; J.23.1.1; A.4.1.1;
  D.14.10.1; E.14.10.1; Fb.14.10.1; G.14.10.1; H.14.10.1; I.14.10.1; J.14.10.1;
  Ja.14.10.1
  ***Gen. R.* 8.1**   [→ *1.8.b.3*

(2) The sun, represented as a bridegroom, has two faces.
  see F.16.12.4; F.16.11.1
  GL 1, 24-25; GL 5, 37 n.103   [→ *2.22.a.18*

F.5.3. *Four faces*

(1) The cherubim seen by Ezekiel and Abraham have four faces, one
human, one of a bull, one of a lion and one of an eagle. In a different
version, the bull's face is replaced by that of a cherub.
  see F.18.5.2; F.20.1.1; F.18.4.1; M.20.1.8; M.14.2.8; U.18.3.1; P.21.1.1;
  A.14.10.1; G.4.1.4; G.5.15.5
  Ezek. 1.6,10; Ezek. 10.14,21; *Apoc. Abr.* 18.3-7   [→ *3.1.16*

F.5.10. *Between ten and twenty faces*

(1) God is the twelve-faced, lightning-eyed one.
  see E.11.2.1; A.11.2.2; A.11.3.1; D.16.3.1; E.11.1.1; E.12.3.1; A.11.2.1;

F.16.12.1; G.10.5.1; Ia.16.12.1; P.10.1.1; P.10.7.1; Pc.10.7.1; Gf.4.1.1; A.1.1.1; Gf.27.2.1; A.10.1.1; Pc.10.3.1; I.10.5.1; If.6.1.1
Lad. Jac. 2.17   [→ *3.4.a.1*

(2) Opanni'el, the prince of the ophanim, has sixteen faces, four on each side; he has one hundred wings on each side, 8,766 eyes, corresponding to the number of hours in a year, and in each pair of eyes lightnings flash and torches blaze, consuming all who look at him. The height of his body is a journey of 2,500 years.
   see A.6.5.3; G.10.1.1; G.10.5.1; G.5.13.1; M.14.2.14; M.20.1.14
3 En. 25.2-4   [→ *3.3.a.4*

F.6. *Abnormal Size of Face*

F.6.1. *Abnormally large face*

(1) There are four Hayyot, and each of the Hayyot has 240 faces, and faces within these faces (as well as wings within wings).
3 En. 21.1-3   [→ *3.1.10*

(2) The face of each Seraph is as large as the rising sun, and radiates light.
   see F.10.1.1; G.10.2.2; M.20.1.12; M.14.2.12; U.18.3.2; G.4.1.4; G.5.15.5
3 En. 26.9-11   [→ *3.1.2*

F.10. *Unusual Emission or Emanation from Face*

F.10.1. *Emission of light from face*

(1) A brilliant light shines from the faces and eyes of the ophanim, cherubim and seraphim.
   see G.10.2.2; F.6.1.2; M.20.1.12; M.14.2.12; U.18.3.2; G.4.1.4; G.5.15.5.
1 En. **71.1,7;** *3 En.* **1.7-8;** *3 En.* **2.1;** *3 En.* **22.13-15;** *3 En.* **24.18**
(Appendix); *3 En.* **25.6;** *3 En.* **26.9-11**   [→ *3.1.2; 3.1.16; 3.1.3*

(2) The archangels have faces more radiant than the sun. They harmonize all existence, both heavenly and earthly.
2 En. 19.1 (J and A)   [→ *3.6.a.3*

(3) The angel seen by Aseneth (probably Michael) has a face like lightning, eyes like sunshine, hair like the flaming of a torch, and hands and feet like glowing iron, emitting sparks.
   see E.10.2.1; G.10.2.4; P.10.3.2; P.16.1.1; U.10.3.1; U.16.1.1
Jos. Asen. 14.9 (8, 9); Jos. Asen. 16.12, 13 (7)   [→ *3.1.8*

(4) The two angels Samuil and Raguil, who take Enoch to heaven, have luminous faces shining like the sun.

see P.11.2.1; Ia.10.1.1; G.10.1.2; M.14.2.4; M.20.1.4; A.6.5.5.

2 En. **1.4-6 (J and A);** *2 En.* **3.1-3 (J and A);** *2 En.* **33.6 (J and A)**
[→ *3.3.a.14*

(5) The angel Eremiel is a great angel, with a face shining like the rays of the sun in its glory. His feet are like molten bronze.

see U.16.2.1.

Apoc. Zeph. **6.11-12**   [→ *3.3.a.10*

(6) Methusalam's face is radiant like the sun at midday, or like the morning star, when he approaches the altar to offer sacrifice.

2 En. **69.10 (J and F)**   [→ *3.6.a.5*

(7) Cain is born with a luminous face.

see F.11.1.2; Fb.13.2.4; A.23.1.1; Fb.14.2.2; Fb.18.11.2; O.13.2.1; F.11.3.1; B.13.2.1; A.13.2.1.

LAE (Apoc. Mos.) **1.1-3;** *LAE (Vita)* **21.3**   [→ *1.1.b.7; 5.1.3*

(8) Abraham, after his death, appears with a face as luminous as lightning and dressed in magnificent garments studded with gems that are radiant like the sun.

see A.10.1.12; Sa.2.3.9; Sa.24.3.9; Pc.10.5.1; Pc.10.6.1; A.6.5.23; T.25.1.1

GL 1, 307; GL 5, 269 n.319   [→ *1.35.4; 2.6.b.3*

(9) Sarah's face shines like an olive when the angels tell her that she shall conceive.

see A.10.1.13; Vg.1.1.1; Vg.23.1.3; Nd.5.1.1

Gen. R. **53.3**   [→ *1.14.f.1*

(10) After eating from a honeycomb, Aseneth's face, emaciated through fasting, becomes like the sun, with eyes like the rising morning star, cheeks red like the blood of the son of man, lips like the rose of life, teeth like fighting men lined up for battle, hair like the vine in paradise, a neck like a cypress, with an appearance of light, and bones strong like cedars.

see Fa.11.3.1; G.10.2.8; Ia.11.3.1; G.11.3.2; E.22.1.2; Ia.15.1.1; A.6.4.1; Ba.11.3.1

Jos. Asen. **16.16;** *Jos. Asen.* **18.7;** *Jos. Asen.* **20.6**
[→ *1.14.d.2; 1.35.5*

(11) Moses has a luminous face.
  see A.25.9.1; Sa.2.3.19; Sa.24.3.19; A.6.5.25; A.6.4.2; P.23.1.1; P.25.4.1;
  I.10.1.5; G.10.2.9; F.11.3.2; Fb.10.1.1; G.25.4.1; If.6.1.2; Fb.14.2.3;
  I.23.3.3; P.11.2.2; G.17.20.1; Ib.13.2.1; Ib.24.4.1; Ia.24.4.1; E.6.1.1;
  Ga.10.2.1; E.12.10.1; P.13.2.1; P.24.4.1; K.13.10.2; B.16.12.2; Ib.16.12.3;
  Ia.13.2.1; A.26.1.3
  Exod. 34.29-30, 35; *Exod. R.* 1.20-22; *Exod. R.* 47.6; *Deut. R.*
  3.12; *Deut. R.* 11.10; Ps-Philo 12.1; *3 En.* 15B.5 (Appendix)
                    [→ *1.14.a.6; 1.14.a.7; 1.14.f.2; 1.35.7; 2.24.12;*
                                          3.3.a.30; 3.3.a.38

(12) Aaron has a luminous face.
  see A.6.5.26; E.6.1.2; E.12.10.2; Ga.10.2.2; I.10.1.4; A.23.1.8; A.6.2.4
  Exod. R. 1.20; *Exod. R.* 1.22   [→ *3.3.a.30*

(13) The faces of those who did not want the golden calf to be made,
but were forced to consent, begin to shine when they drink the water
Moses gives them, while the tongues of those who did want the golden
calf to be made, drop off.
  Ps-Philo 12.7; GL 6, 55 n.281   [→ *1.35.6; 26.b.5*

(14) A heavenly radiance is shed over the faces of the Israelites when
they agree to accept the Torah before they know its contents, while
Moses is given a lustrous countenance as a reward for writing down
the Law.
  Deut. R. 3.12   [→ *1.35.7*

(15) Joshua's face shines like the moon; but the rays from his face do
not reach their full intensity until he has crossed the Jordan.
  see A.6.5.27; I.23.2.1
  GL 3, 400, 438, 441; GL 6, 141-142 n.835, 836; GL 6, 151 n.901
                                                 [→ *1.14.c.11; 3.3.a.39*

(16) The faces of the circumcised men are filled with radiance when
the doors of the ark are opened and they behold the Shekinah.
  see Sa.2.3.26; Sa.24.3.26
  GL 4, 146; GL 6, 290 n.43   [→ *1.14.a.10*

(17) Barak, Deborah's husband, is so called because his face shines
like lightning.
  GL 6, 195 n.73   [→ *5.2.1*

(18) The face of Jochebed, Amram's wife, radiates a celestial light.
  see A.1.1.5; A.26.3.1
  GL 2, 261; GL 5, 396 n.34   [→ *3.6.a.8*

(19) Kings, lords and princes have radiant faces.
　GL 3, 112; GL 6, 46 n.247   [→ *1.14.a.13; 2.24.18*

(20) The face of a woman (who had previously given birth to a son after thirty years of sterility, but whose son dies on her wedding day) suddenly shines and flashes like lightning; she then utters a loud cry and becomes invisible, but is replaced by an established city.
　see Vg.23.1.8
　4 Ezra 9.43f.; *4 Ezra* 10.25-27, 44, 50   [→ *4.1.a.4*

(21) The Messiah's face spreads a stronger lustre than the faces of Moses and Joshua.
　GL 6, 141-142 n.836   [→ *3.3.a.43*

F.10.2. *Face that emits flames*

(1) Phinehas's face flames like a torch when the Holy Spirit rests upon him, so that he resembles an angel.
　Lev. R. 1.1; *Lev. R.* 21.12   [→ *1.19.b.15*

F.11. *Unusual Colour of Face*

F.11.1. *Black face*

(1) The faces of the souls of the wicked on their way to Sheol are as black as the bottom of a pot, while the faces of the souls of intermediate sinners are greenish. They have the bodies of eagles.
　see F.11.6.1; F.21.7.2
　3 En. 44.5-6   [→ *3.6.b.4*

(2) Cain's face becomes as black as smoke after his unsatisfactory offering.
　see Fb.13.2.4; A.23.1.1; F.10.1.7; Fb.14.2.2; Fb.18.11.2; O.13.2.1; B.13.2.1; A.13.2.1
　GL 1, 107-108; GL 5, 136-137 n.12, 13   [→ *1.26.b.5*

(3) The faces of the Midianite women are blackened by the Israelites.
　see F.11.2.1
　Cant. R. 4.4 §3; *Cant. R.* 6.6 §1; *Cant. R.* 1.6 §3   [→ *2.26.b.1*

(4) After the fall of Jerusalem in 587 BCE, the faces of the sons of Zion become darker than blackness itself and their skin shrinks against their bones and becomes dry as a stick.
　see B.13.11.1; A.13.11.1
　Lam. 4.8; *Lam. R.* 4.8 §11   [→ *1.13.4*

(5) The faces of the women who accompany Nehemiah from the Exile are darkened by the sun.

Gen. R. 18.5 [→ *1.17.3*

(6) Ashur makes his face black by fasting.

Exod. R. 1.17 [→ *1.13.5*

(7) David's face becomes black as a cake baked on coal when he sees Uzzah touch the ark and die.

see E.11.3.1; Sa.2.3.25; Sa.24.3.25; B.11.3.3; T.23.2.1; O.23.2.1; A.25.15.3; A.23.1.16; G.25.1.1; A.25.9.2

Num. R. 4.20 [→ *1.12.a.12*

F.11.2. *White face*

(1) The faces of the Midianite women who are ripe for marriage grow white when they are led past the gold plate of the mitre on the high priest's forehead.

see F.11.1.3

GL 3, 413; GL 6, 145 n.861 [→ *1.19.b.14; 2.2.a.1*

F.11.3. *Red face*

(1) Cain's face turns red as a torch when his offering is not accepted.

see Fb.14.2.2; F.11.1.2; Fb.18.11.2; A.23.1.1; Fb.13.2.4; F.10.1.7; O.13.2.1; B.13.2.1; A.13.2.1

Gen. R. 22.6 [→ *1.12.a.17*

(2) Moses' face reddens when he hears a revelation from God.

see F.10.1.11; Sa.2.3.19; Sa.24.3.19; A.6.5.25; A.6.4.2; P.23.1.1; P.25.4.1; I.10.1.5; G.10.2.9; A.25.9.1; Fb.10.1.1; F.10.1.11; G.25.4.1; If.6.1.3; Fb.14.2.3; I.23.3.3; P.11.2.1; G.17.20.1; Ib.13.2.1; Ib.24.4.1; Ia.24.4.1; E.6.1.1; Ga.10.2.1; E.12.10.1; P.13.2.1; P.24.4.1; K.13.10.2; B.16.12.2; Ib.16.12.3; Ia.13.2.1; A.26.1.3

Num. R. 12.1 [→ *1.14.b.5*

F.11.6. *Green face*

(1) The faces of the souls of intermediate sinners on their way to Sheol are greenish, while the faces of the souls of the wicked are black. They have the bodies of eagles.

see F.11.1.1; F.21.7.2

3 En. 44.5-6 [→ *3.6.b.4*

(2) Judah's face turns green with shame when he publicly confesses his crime with Tamar.

see E.13.1.2; G.10.4.1; Gf.16.3.1; Ic.18.5.1; F.18.5.3; J.23.1.2; I.23.3.2; Va.3.1.1; E.8.1.1; If.6.1.2; A.10.1.15

GL 3, 170; GL 6, 69 n.357 [→ *1.12.a.32*

(3) A man's face turns green with fear when he meets the angel of death and hears of his impending death.

BHM **6.14 no.8 (Hebrew text S, 133)** [→ *1.12.a.29*

F.13. *Peculiarities of Skin of Face*

F.13.2. *Burnt or blistered face*

(1) The faces of the Philistines are scorched in the battle against Samuel.

see F.24.3.1; Vf.1.1.1

GL 4, 64; GL 6, 228 n.42 [→ *2.16.7*

F.13.11. *Withered skin of face*

(1) The faces of the angels called Grigori are withered.

see A.6.1.3

GL 1, 133; GL 5, 159 [→ *3.6.b.2*

F.13.12. *Hairy skin of face*

(1) Both male and female demons have faces and bodies covered with hair, but bald heads.

see A.13.6.2; B.13.6.2; E.1.1.2; E.4.1.1; E.4.2.1

GL 6, 192 n.58 [→ *1.1.a.6*

F.16. *Face of Unusual Substance*

F.16.11. *Face of ice or hail*

(1) The sun, represented as a bridegroom, has two faces, one of hail and one of fire.

see F.16.12.4; F.5.1.2

GL 1, 24-25; GL 5, 37 n.103 [→ *2.22.a.18*

F.16.12. *Face of fire or lightning*

(1) God's face is incandescent like iron made hot by a fire, and emits sparks.

see E.11.2.1; A.11.2.2; A.11.3.1; D.16.3.1; E.11.1.1; E.12.3.1; F.5.10.1; A.11.2.1; G.10.5.1; Ia.16.12.1; P.10.1.1; P.10.7.1; Pc.10.7.1; Gf.4.1.1; A.1.1.1; Gf.27.2.1; A.10.1.1; Pc.10.3.1; I.10.5.1; If.6.1.1
2 En. 22.1-2 (J); *2 En.* 39.3 (A); *2 En.* 39.5 (J); *Ques. Ezra* (Recension A) 26   [→ *3.4.a*

(2) The face of Kerubi'el, prince of the cherubim, is like a blazing fire. His mouth, tongue and eyes are also of fire, and his body of burning coals which emit flames. He is as tall and broad as the seven heavens, covered with eyes and wings, and has wheels.
see A.6.3.1; A.6.5.2; A.14.5.1; A.14.10.2; A.16.17.1; A.20.1.1; G.4.1.3; G.5.15.2; G.16.12.2; Gc.16.12.1; I.16.12.1; Ib.16.12.1; P.10.3.1
3 En. 22.3-9   [→ *3.3.a.7*

(3) An angel with a face like lightning, eyes like fiery torches, arms and legs as if of burnished bronze, and a body like beryl, chrysolite or topaz (and a voice like the voice of a crowd) is seen by Daniel in a vision.
see A.16.18.1; G.16.12.3; O.16.2.1; T.16.2.1
Dan. 10.6   [→ *3.1.14*

(4) The sun, represented as a bridegroom, has two faces, one of fire and one of hail.
see F.16.11.1; F.5.1.2
GL 1, 24-25; *GL* 5, 37 n.103   [→ *2.22.a.18*

F.16.13. *Face of lightning*

(1) The myriads of angels inhabiting Arabot, the seventh heaven, have faces like lightning, eyes like torches of fire, and arms and feet as if of burnished bronze.
see G.16.12.4; O.16.2.2; U.16.2.2
3 En. 35.1-2; *3 En.* 22B.6 (Appendix)   [→ *3.3.a.9*

F.16.18. *Face of precious stone or jewel*

(1) The face of the angel Iaoel, who takes the right hand of Abraham, is like chrysolite, his body and legs are like sapphire and his hair like snow. He wears a headdress like a rainbow.
see A.16.18.2; E.11.2.1; T.16.18.1
Apoc. Abr. 11.2   [→ *3.3.a.11*

F.17. *Substitution for Face*

F.17.1. *Weapon in place of face*

(1) Death shows Abraham his face of a sword, as well as his faces of darkness, a precipice, a ferocious burning fire, a lion, of thunder and lightning, a turbulent river, of dragons and serpents, and of a mixed cup of poisons, great ferocity, bitterness and every fatal disease, when Abraham requests Death to reveal his face of ferocity, decay and bitterness.

> see D.17.1.1; A.23.8.1; D.5.1.6; D.5.6.1; D.18.6.2; F.17.2.1; F.17.3.1;
> F.17.4.1; F.17.5.1; F.17.6.1; F.17.10.1; F.18.5.4; F.18.6.2; A.10.1.24;
> Fa.10.2.1; D.5.2.1
> *T. Abr.* **17.12-17**; *T. Abr.* **19.5f.**; *T. Abr.* **13.13-16**; *T. Abr.* **14.1**
> (Recension B)   [→ *2.24.19; 2.24.20; 3.9.7; 3.9.8*

F.17.2 *Thunder and lightning in place of face*

(1) Death shows Abraham his face of thunder and lightning, as well as his faces of burning fire, of dragons and serpents, a lion, a sword, a turbulent river, of darkness, a precipice, a mixed cup of poisons, and great ferocity, bitterness and every fatal disease, when Abraham requests Death to reveal his face of ferocity, decay and bitterness.

> see D.17.1.1; A.23.8.1; D.5.1.6; D.5.6.1; D.18.6.2; F.17.1.1; F.17.3.1;
> F.17.4.1; F.17.5.1; F.17.6.1; F.17.10.1; F.18.5.4; F.18.6.2; A.10.1.24;
> Fa.10.2.1; D.5.2.1
> *T. Abr.* **17.12-17**; *T. Abr.* **19.5f**   [→ *2.24.19; 3.9.8*

F.17.3. *Fire in place of face*

(1) Death shows Abraham his face of burning fire, as well as his faces of thunder and lightning, of darkness, a sword, a precipice, a mixed cup of poisons, serpents and dragons, a turbulent river, and great ferocity, bitterness and every fatal disease, when Abraham requests Death to reveal his face of ferocity, decay and bitterness.

> see D.17.1.1; A.23.8.1; D.5.1.6; D.5.6.1; D.18.6.2; F.17.2.1; F.17.1.1;
> F.17.4.1; F.17.5.1; F.17.6.1; F.17.10.1; F.18.5.4; F.18.6.2; A.10.1.24;
> Fa.10.2.1; D.5.2.1
> *T. Abr.* **17.12-17**; *T. Abr.* **19.5f.**   [→ *2.24.19; 3.9.8*

F.17.4. *Water in place of face*

(1) Death shows Abraham his face of a turbulent river, as well as his faces of thunder and lightning, of darkness, of burning fire, of

serpents and dragons, a lion, a sword, a precipice, a mixed cup of poisons, great ferocity, bitterness and every fatal disease, when Abraham requests Death to reveal his face of ferocity, bitterness and decay.

see D.17.1.1; A.23.8.1; D.5.1.6; D.5.6.1; D.18.6.2; F.17.2.1; F.17.3.1; F.17.1.1; F.17.5.1; F.17.6.1; F.17.10.1; F.18.5.4; F.18.6.2; A.10.1.24; Fa.10.2.1; D.5.2.1

T. Abr. **17.12-17;** *T. Abr.* **19.5f.**   [→ *2.24.19; 3.9.8*

F.17.5. *Mountain, hill or precipice in place of face*

(1) Death shows Abraham his face of a precipice, as well as his faces of dragons and serpents, of burning fire, of darkness, of thunder and lightning, a turbulent river, a lion, a sword, a mixed cup of poisons, great ferocity, bitterness and every fatal disease, when Abraham requests Death to reveal his face of ferocity, decay and bitterness.

see D.17.1.1; A.23.8.1; D.5.1.6; D.5.6.1; D.18.6.2; F.17.2.1; F.17.3.1; F.17.4.1; F.17.1.1; F.17.6.1; F.17.10.1; F.18.5.4; F.18.6.2; A.10.1.24; Fa.10.2.1; D.5.2.1

T. Abr. **17.12-17;** *T. Abr.* **19.5f.**   [→ *2.24.19; 3.9.8*

F.17.6. *Darkness in place of face*

(1) Death shows Abraham his face of darkness, as well as his faces of dragons and serpents, of thunder and lightning, a turbulent river, a precipice, a burning fire, a lion, a sword, a mixed cup of poisons, great ferocity, bitterness and every fatal disease, when Abraham requests Death to reveal his face of ferocity, bitterness and decay.

see D.17.1.1; A.23.8.1; D.5.1.6; D.5.6.1; D.18.6.2; F.17.2.1; F.17.3.1; F.17.4.1; F.17.5.1; F.17.1.1; F.17.10.1; F.18.5.4; F.18.6.2; A.10.1.24; Fa.10.2.1; D.5.2.1

T. Abr. **17.12-17;** *T. Abr.* **19.5f.**   [→ *2.24.19; 3.9.8*

F.17.10. *Other things in place of face*

(1) Death shows Abraham his face of a mixed cup of poisons, as well as his faces of darkness, of thunder and lightning, of dragons and serpents, a lion, a burning fire, a turbulent river, a precipice, a sword, great ferocity, bitterness and every fatal disease, when Abraham requests Death to reveal his face of ferocity, decay and bitterness.

see D.17.1.1; A.23.8.1; D.5.1.6; D.5.6.1; D.18.6.2; F.17.2.1; F.17.3.1; F.17.4.1; F.17.5.1; F.17.6.1; F.17.1.1; F.18.5.4; F.18.6.2; A.10.1.24; Fa.10.2.1; D.5.2.1

T. Abr. **17.12-17;** *T. Abr.* **19.5f.**   [→ *2.24.19; 3.9.8*

F.18. *Animal Face or Face with Animal Attributes*

F.18.1. *Face of tiger or face with tiger attributes*

(1) Isaac sees creatures with the faces of tigers in the heavens. Others have faces of lions, camels, hyenas or dogs, and some have only one eye.

  see F.18.2.1; F.18.5.1; F.18.7.1; F.18.8.1; G.1.1; G.5.1.1
  T. Isaac 5.7-10   [→ *2.24.8*

F.18.2. *Face of dog or face with dog attributes*

(1) Isaac sees creatures with the faces of dogs in the heavens. Others have faces of camels, lions, hyenas or tigers, and some have only one eye.

  see F.18.1.1; F.18.5.1; F.18.7.1; F.18.8.1; G.1.1; G.5.1.1
  T. Isaac 5.7-10   [→ *2.24.8*

(2) Men with the faces of dogs, the horns of deer and the feet of goats inhabit the second heaven.

  see D.14.2.3; D.18.11.2; U.18.2.2; U.18.4.1
  3 Bar. 3.3 (Slavonic and Greek)   [→ *1.26.b.6*

(3) Baladan's father, the real king of Babylon, has a dog's face.
  GL 4, 275; GL 6, 367-368 n.81, 82   [→ *3.7.3*

F.18.3. *Face of ape or face with ape attributes*

(1) The faces of the men of the generation succeeding Enosh resemble apes and centaurs.

  see Cc.18.1.1
  Gen. R. 23.6; *Gen. R.* 24.6   [→ *1.6.a.1*

F.18.4. *Face of an ox, bull or calf, or face with ox, bull or calf attributes*

(1) The cherubim seen by Ezekiel and Abraham have four faces: a bull's face, a lion's face, an eagle's face and a human face. In a different version, the bull's face is replaced by a cherub's.

  see F.18.5.2; F.20.1.1; F.5.3.1; M.20.1.8; M.14.2.8; U.18.3.1; P.21.1.1;
  A.14.10.1; G.4.1.4; G.5.15.5
  Ezek. 1.10; Ezek. 10.14; *Apoc. Abr.* 18.3-7   [→ *3.1.16*

(2) Men with the faces of cattle, the horns of deer, the feet of goats and the loins of sheep inhabit the first heaven.

see D.14.2.3; D.18.11.1; U.18.2.1; Sa.18.2.1
3 Bar. 2.3 (Slavonic and Greek)   [→ *1.26.b.7*

F.18.5. *Face of lion or face with lion attributes*

(1) Isaac sees creatures with the faces of lions in the heavens. Others have faces of camels, dogs, hyenas or tigers, and some have only one eye.

see F.18.1.1; F.18.2.1; F.18.7.1; F.18.8.1; G.1.1.1; G.5.1.1
T. Isaac 5.7-10   [→ *2.24.8*

(2) The cherubim seen by Ezekiel and Abraham have four faces: a lion's face, a bull's face, an eagle's face and a human face. (In a different version, the bull's face is replaced by a cherub's.)

see F.5.3.1; F.20.1.1; F.18.4.1; M.20.1.8; M.14.2.8; U.18.3.1; P.21.1.1;
A.14.10.1; G.4.1.4; G.5.15.5
Ezek. 1.10; Ezek. 10.14; *Apoc. Abr.* 18.3-7   [→ *3.1.16*

(3) Judah's face and teeth are like a lion's when he attacks the army from Nineveh.

see E.13.1.2; G.10.4.1; Gf.16.3.1; Ic.18.5.1; E.8.1.1; J.23.1.2; I.23.3.2;
Va.3.1.1; F.11.6.2; If.6.1.2; A.10.1.15
GL 1, 404, 406; GL 5, 314 n.291   [→ *1.12.a.20*

(4) Death shows Abraham his face of a lion, as well as his faces of serpents and dragons, of flaming fire, of darkness, a precipice, a sword, of thunder and lightning, a turbulent river, a mixed cup of poisons and every fatal disease, when Abraham requests Death to reveal his face of ferocity, decay and bitterness.

see D.17.1.1; A.23.8.1; D.5.1.6; D.5.6.1; D.18.6.2; F.17.2.1; F.17.3.1;
F.17.4.1; F.17.5.1; F.17.6.1; F.17.10.1; F.17.1.1; F.18.6.2; A.10.1.24;
Fa.10.2.1; D.5.2.1
T. Abr. 17.12-17; *T. Abr.* 19.5f.   [→ *2.24.19; 3.9.8*

F.18.6. *Face of serpent or dragon or face with serpent or dragon attributes*

(1) The guards of the gates of hell have faces like very large snakes, with eyes aflame or eyes like extinguished lamps, fangs exposed down to their breasts, and they stand as large as serpents.

see A.6.1.2; G.16.12.6; Ic.18.2.1
2 En. 42.1 (J and A); *2 En.* 42.1 (Appendix); *Apoc. Zeph.* 6.8
                                                    [→ *2.24.7; B.22.a.10*

(2) Death appears in decay, with two heads, one with the face of a dragon, and one like a sword, when he approaches sinners.

see D.17.1.1; A.23.8.1; D.5.1.6; D.5.6.1; D.18.6.2; F.17.2.1; F.17.3.1; F.17.4.1; F.17.5.1; F.17.6.1; F.17.10.1; F.18.5.4; F.17.1.1; A.10.1.24; Fa.10.2.1; D.5.2.1

T. Abr. 13.13-16; T. Abr. 14.1 (Recension B)   [→ *2.24.20; 3.9.7*

F.18.7. *Face of camel or face with camel attributes*

(1) Isaac sees creatures with the faces of camels in the heavens. Others have the faces of dogs, lions, hyenas or tigers, and some have only one eye.

see F.18.1.1; F.18.2.1; F.18.5.1; F.18.8.1; G.1.1.1; G.5.1.1

T. Isaac 5.7-10   [→ *2.24.8*

F.18.8. *Face of hyena or face with hyena attributes*

(1) Isaac sees creatures with the faces of hyenas in the heavens. Others have the faces of lions, camels, dogs or tigers, and some have only one eye.

see F.18.1.1; F.18.2.1; F.18.5.1; F.18.7.1; G.1.1.1; G.5.1.1

T. Isaac 5.7-10   [→ *2.24.9*

F.18.9. *Face of leopard or face with leopard attributes*

(1) The ugly angels who carry off the souls of ungodly men have faces like leopards, and their tusks are outside their mouths like those of wild boars. Their eyes are mixed with blood and their hair is loose like the hair of women.

see Ic.18.1.1; W.4.1.1; E.9.5.1

Apoc. Zeph. 4.2-4   [→ *2.24.9*

F.20. *Bird Face or Face with Bird Attributes*

F.20.1. *Face of eagle*

(1) The cherubim seen by Ezekiel and Abraham have four faces: an eagle's face, a lion's face, a bull's face and a human face. In a different version, the bull's face is replaced by a cherub's.

see F.18.5.2; F.5.3.1; F.18.4.1; M.20.1.8; M.14.2.8; U.18.3.1; P.21.1.1; A.14.10.1; G.4.1.4; G.5.15.5

Ezek. 1.10; Ezek. 10.14; Apoc. Abr. 18.3-7   [→ *3.1.16*

F.21. *Human Face on Unusual Creature*

F.21.6. *Human face on body of serpent or dragon*

(1) A winged demon in the form of a dragon but with the face and feet of a man is summoned up by Solomon.
   see U.21.6.2
   T. Sol. 14.1-2   [→ *3.1.19*

F.21.7. *Human face on body of bird*

(1) Serapi'el, the prince of the seraphim, has the face of an angel on the body of an eagle. He is as tall as the seven heavens and his body is full of eyes which resemble stars of lightning in their brightness.
   see A.6.5.1; G.4.1.1; G.5.15.1; G.10.2.1
   3 En. 27.3-7   [→ *3.3.a.5*

(2) The souls of the sinners on their way to Sheol have human faces but the bodies of eagles. The faces of the intermediate sinners are greenish, while the faces of the wicked are as black as the bottom of a pot.
   see F.11.1.1; F.11.6.1
   3 En. 44.5-6   [→ *1.34.1*

F.22. *Unusually Hideous Face*

(1) A woman's monstrous face is changed into a beautiful one when Elijah gives her medicine.
   GL 6, 328 n.59   [→ *4.1.b.21*

(2) Vashti's face is marred and her beauty vanishes when Daniel pronounces the name of God.
   see Fb.23.1.2; A.23.10.1
   GL 4, 378; GL 6, 457 n.45   [→ *1.11.a.6*

F.23. *Disease, Paralysis or Malfunction of Face*

F.23.1. *Leprous face*

(1) Gehazi's face becomes leprous when Elisha rebukes him with the words 'May the disease of Naaman afflict thee and thy descendants for evermore'. His children inherit his leprosy.

see A.23.1.10; A.23.1.11; B.11.2.4
2 Kgs 5.25-27; *Lev. R.* 16.1; *Lev. R.* 17.3 [→ *1.26.b.43;   1.11.b.1*

F.24. Wounded, Mutilated or Maimed Face

F.24.3. *Burnt or blistered face*

(1) The faces of the Philistines are scorched in the battle against Samuel.
see F.13.2.1; Vf.1.1.1
GL 4, 64; GL 6, 228 n.42   [→ *2.16.7*

Fa. The Cheek(s)

Fa.2. Partial Absence of Cheek(s) or Absence of Part of Cheek(s)

Fa.2.1. *Absence of hair of cheek(s)*

(1) The hair is plucked from Micah's cheek and his cheek is wounded when Zedekiah strikes him with a rod.
see Fa.24.10.1
Mic. 4.6; *Lev. R.* 10.2   [→ *2.5.11*

Fa.10. Unusual Emission or Emanation from Cheek(s)

Fa.10.2. *Cheek(s) that emits flames*

(1) Death assumes the form of a beautiful archangel with cheeks flashing with fire and an appearance like sunlight when he appears before Abraham.
see D.17.1.1; A.23.8.1; D.5.1.6; D.5.6.1; D.18.6.2; F.17.2.1; F.17.3.1;
F.17.4.1; F.17.5.1; F.17.6.1; F.17.10.1; F.18.5.4; F.18.6.2; A.10.1.24;
F.17.1.1; D.5.2.1
T. Abr. 16.6-8   [→ *2.21.6*

Fa.11. Unusual Colour of Cheek(s)

Fa.11.3. *Red cheek(s)*

(1) After she eats from the honeycomb, Aseneth's cheeks become red like the blood of the son of man, while her face becomes like the sun, her eyes like the rising morning star, her lips like the rose of life, and her teeth, hair, neck and bones become strong as cypresses or cedars.

see F.10.1.10; G.10.2.8; Ia.11.3.1; G.11.3.2; E.22.2; Ia.15.1.1; A.6.4.1; Ba.11.3.1
Jos. Asen. **16.16;** *Jos. Asen.* **18.7;** *Jos. Asen.* **20.6**   [→ *1.14.d.2*

Fa.13. *Peculiarity of Skin of Cheek(s)*

Fa.13.3. *Scarred skin*

(1) The young men seized and bound when the enemy enters the Temple have scars on their cheeks from the tears they shed.
see Gf.25.1.2
Lam. R. **1.2** §25   [→ *1.12.a.15*

Fa.24. *Wounded, Mutilated or Maimed Cheek(s)*

Fa.24.10. *Unspecified wound or mutilation of cheek(s)*

(1) Micah's cheek is wounded and the hair plucked from it, when Zedekiah strikes him on the cheek with a rod.
see Fa.2.1.1
Lev. R. **10.2;** *Mic.* **4.6**   [→ *2.5.11*

Fb. *The Forehead*

Fb.10. *Unusual Emission or Emanation from Forehead*

Fb.10.1. *Emission of light from forehead*

(1) Beams of light radiate from the forehead of Moses when he wipes his pen on the hair of his forehead upon completing the writing of the Torah.
see F.10.1.11; Sa.2.3.19; Sa.24.3.19; A.6.5.25; A.6.4.2; P.23.1.1; P.25.4.1; I.10.1.5; G.10.2.9; F.11.3.2; Fb.10.1.1; G.25.4.1; If.6.1.3; A.25.9.1; I.23.3.3; P.11.2.2; G.17.20.1; Ib.13.2.1; Ib.24.4.1; Ia.24.4.1; E.6.1.1; Ga.10.2.1; E.12.10.1; P.13.2.1; P.24.4.1; K.13.10.2; B.16.12.2; Ib.16.12.3; Ia.13.2.1; A.26.1.3
Exod. R. **47.6;** *Deut. R.* **3.12**   [→ *1.14.c.12*

Fb.13. *Peculiarity of Skin of Forehead*

Fb.13.1. *Tattoo on forehead*

(1) The man created by Ben Sira and his father after studying the Book of Yezirah for three years, has 'Emet' (truth) written on his forehead. He tells them to erase the first letter, leaving 'Met' (dead), and he immediately turns into dust.

GL 6, 402 n.42   [→ *3.9.5*

Fb.13.2. *Branded or engraved forehead or other indelible mark on forehead*

(1) A heavenly being has the name 'Israel' engraved on its forehead.

GL 5, 307 n.253   [→ *2.6.b.1*

(2) The Antichrist has the inscription 'Antichrist' on his forehead. His mouth is one cubit in size, his teeth are a span long, and the soles of his feet two spans; his fingers are like scythes and his right eye is like the rising morning star, while his other eye is fixed.

see G.10.2.5; G.23.3.1; I.6.1.1; Ic.6.5.1; Pc.12.1.1; Pc.12.2.1; U.6.5.1

Gk Apoc. Ezra **4.29f.**   [→ *3.1.24*

(3) The Antichrist has three letters written on his forehead: A, K and T, signifying denial, rejection and the befouled dragon. His eyes are like the rising morning star and his right eye like a lion's. He is ten cubits tall and his feet and right hand measure three cubits. His hair reaches to his feet and he is three-crested. His left arm is made of copper and his right arm and lower teeth are made of iron. His lower jaw is diamond. He is long-faced, long-nosed and disorderly. His mother conceives him by touching the head of a fish.

see A.6.5.13; E.6.5.1; Fc.16.5.1; G.10.2.6; G.18.1.1; Ic.16.1.1; O.16.1.1; O.16.2.3; U.6.5.2

Apoc. Dan. **9.11,16-26**   [→ *3.1.25; 1.3.c.1; 3.6.b.3*

(4) The letters of God's holy name are placed upon Cain's forehead.

see F.11.1.2; A.23.1.1; F.10.1.7; Fb.14.2.2; Fb.18.11.2; O.13.2.1; F.11.3.1; B.13.2.1; A.13.2.1

GL 1, 111-112; GL 5, 141 n.27,28   [→ *2.11.e.2; 1.19.b.2*

(5) The foreheads of those who disapprove of the filth practised in Jerusalem are marked with a cross by a man with a scribe's ink horn (the Angel Gabriel). In a different version, the name of God is written on their foreheads, while in yet another version, the letter 'tav' is written on their foreheads in ink, while the same letter is written in blood on the foreheads of the damned.

Ezek. 9.4-6; *Apoc. Elij.* 1.9; *Pss. Sol.* 15.6; *Lam. R.* 2.1 §3; **GL 1, 6; GL 6, 392 n.26**   [→ *2.6.b.10; 2.2.c.7; 2.15.b.14; 2.15.a.10*

Fb.13.4. *Leprous forehead*

(1) King Uzziah's forehead becomes leprous when he tries to offer sacrifices upon the altar.
   see A.13.4.1; A.23.1.14; B.13.4.1; B.23.1.2; Fb.23.1.1
   2 Chron. 26.19-23   [→ *1.19.b.17; 1.26.a.12; 1.7.a.5*

Fb.14. Unusual Protuberances or Protusions on Forehead

Fb.14.2. *Horns on forehead*

(1) The demon Keteb or Keteb Meriri ('Bitter Destruction' or 'Pestilence') has a single horn on his forehead and the head of a calf. He is hairy all over, covered in scales and full of eyes, with a single eye set on his heart which kills whoever looks at it.
   see D.18.4.1; E.4.1.2; G.5.15.6; G.4.5.1; B.13.7.1; A.13.6.1; B.13.6.1; Fb.18.11.1; G.4.1.6
   Num. R. **12.3;** *Lam. R.* **1.3 §29; GL 3, 186; GL 6, 74 n.381**
                                                              [→ *3.1.22*

(2) Cain has a horn on his forehead.
   see Fb.18.11.2; A.23.1.1; Fb.13.2.4; F.11.1.2; F.10.1.7; O.13.2.1; F.11.3.1; B.13.2.1; A.13.2.1
   Gen. R. **22.12**   [→ *1.19.b.3; 1.26.b.4*

(3) Moses has horns on his forehead when he descends from Sinai.
   see F.10.1.11; Sa.2.3.19; Sa.24.3.19; A.6.5.25; A.6.4.2; P.23.1.1; P.25.4.1; I.10.1.5; G.10.2.9; F.11.3.2; Fb.10.1.1; G.25.4.1; If.6.1.3; A.25.9.1; I.23.3.3; P.11.2.2; G.17.20.1; Ib.13.2.1; Ib.24.4.1; Ia.24.4.1; E.6.1.1; Ga.10.2.1; E.12.10.1; P.13.2.1; P.24.4.1; K.13.10.2; B.16.12.2; Ib.16.12.3; Ia.13.2.1; A.26.1.3
   Mell. 1, 79f.; Exod. 34.29, 35   [→ *5.1.4*

Fb.14.10. *Body(ies) on forehead*

(1) While Adam is still a lifeless mass, God shows him all the righteous people to descend from him: some hang on Adam's forehead, some on his head, some on his hair, eyes nose, mouth, ears and earlobes.
   see Cb.9.1.1; F.5.1.1; A.9.1.2; R.14.1.1; R.18.1.1; A.6.1.19; A.6.1.20; A.6.3.4; A.6.5.20; A.6.5.21; A.13.10.1; B.13.10.1; A.10.1.9; A.10.1.10; Sa.2.3.3; Sa.24.3.3; A.16.9.1; Ca.9.1.1; Cb.5.1.1; G.23.5.1; J.23.1.1; A.4.1.1;

D.14.10.1; E.14.10.1; A.12.1.1; G.14.10.1; H.14.10.1; I.14.10.1; J.14.10.1;
Ja.14.10.1
Exod. R. **40.3**   [→ *2.4.3*

Fb.18. *Forehead with Animal Attributes*

Fb.18.11. *Horn on forehead*

(1) The demon Keteb or Keteb Meriri ('Bitter Destruction' or
'Pestilence') has a single horn on his forehead and the head of a calf.
He is hairy all over, covered in scales, and full of eyes, with a single
eye set on his heart which kills whoever looks at it.
    see D.18.4.1; E.4.1.2; G.5.15.6; G.4.5.1; B.13.7.1; A.13.6.1; B.13.6.1;
    Fb.14.2.1
    Num. R. **12.3**; *Lam. R.* **1.3** §29; GL 3, 186; GL 6, 74 n.381
                                                       [→ *3.1.22*

(2) Cain has a horn on his forehead.
    see Fb.14.2.2; A.23.1.1; Fb.13.2.4; F.11.1.2; F.10.1.7; O.13.2.1; F.11.3.1;
    B.13.2.1; A.13.2.1
    Gen. R. **22.12**   [→ *1.19.b.3; 1.26.b.4*

Fb.23. *Disease or Paralysis of Forehead*

Fb.23.1. *Leprous forehead*

(1) King Uzziah's forehead becomes leprous when he tries to offer
sacrifices upon the altar.
    see A.13.4.1; A.23.1.14; B.13.4.1; B.23.1.2; Fb.13.4.1
    2 Chron. 26.19-23   [→ *1.19.b.17; 1.26.a.12; 1.7.a.5*

(2) Vashti's forehead becomes leprous, and marks of other diseases
appear on her body, so that she cannot appear naked before the guests
of her husband.
    see A.23.10.1; F.22.1.2
    GL 4, 375; GL 6, 455 n.35   [→ *2.25.b.2*

Fb.24. *Wounded or Mutilated Forehead*

Fb.24.1. *Lacerated forehead*

(1) Eliezer, a bondsman of Abraham, is wounded on the forehead by
a stone thrown at him by a Sodomite.
    see A.6.1.22
    GL 1, 247-248   [→ *1.20.1*

(2) Pharaoh's son is wounded on the forehead by a pebble thrown by Benjamin.

GL 2, 177; GL 5, 374-375 n.432 [→ *1.20.5*

Fc. *The Chin and the Jaw*

Fc.16. *Chin or Jaw of Unusual Substance*

Fc.16.5. *Chin or jaw of stone or precious stone*

(1) The lower jaw of the Antichrist is made of diamond and his lower teeth of iron. His right arm is made of iron and his left of copper. He is ten cubits tall and his feet and right hand are three cubits long. His hair reaches to his feet and he is three-crested. His eyes are like the rising morning star and his right eye like a lion's. He is long-faced, long-nosed and disorderly, and has three letters written on his forehead: A, K and T, signifying denial, rejection and the befouled dragon. His mother conceives him by touching the head of a fish.

see A.6.5.13; E.6.5.1; Fb.13.2.3; G.10.2.6; G.18.1.1; Ic.16.1.1; O.16.1.1; O.16.2.3; U.6.5.2

Apoc. Dan. 9.11,16-26 [→ *3.1.25; 1.3.c.1*

G. THE EYES

G.1. *Absence of Eye(s)*

(1) Isaac sees creatures with only one eye and the faces of lions, tigers, dogs, camels or hyenas in his vision of the heavens.
  see G.5.1.1; F.18.1.1; F.18.2.1; F.18.5.1; F.18.7.1; F.18.8.1
  T. Isaac **5.7-10**   [→ *2.24.8*

(2) One of Balaam's eyes drops out when he gazes upon the camps of the Israelites.
  see G.5.1.2; G.23.4.12; U.23.1.1; If.6.1.5; A.25.15.1; I.23.3.6; Va.27.1.1
  Num. R. **2.4;** *Num. R.* **20.6;** *Num. R.* **20.10**   [→ *1.12.a.21*

(3) Samson's eyes are put out.
  see E.8.1.2; E.25.5.1; A.6.1.29; Ie.17.3.1; I.10.20.1; G.24.1.2; E.6.5.4;
  U.23.1.2; M.6.3.1; T.25.1.2; G.23.4.16
  Judg. 16.21; Ps-Philo 43.5-6; *Num. R.* **9.24** [→ *2.18.b.1; 1.12.c.2*

(4) Zedekiah's eyes are put out at the order of the king of Babylon.
  see G.23.4.24; G.24.1.3
  2 Kgs 25.7; Jer. 39.7; Jer. 52.11   [→ *1.24.3*

(5) The eyes of the sinners are pricked out by the angels of hell.
  Vis. Ezra **40**   [→ *1.26.b.67*

G.3. *Vital Eye(s)*

(1) The physician who has recommended a milk cure for the Persian king has a dream in which his eyes, mouth, tongue, feet and hands quarrel with one another, each claiming the greatest credit in procuring the remedy for the Persian king.
  see I.3.1.1; Ib.3.1.1; P.3.1.1; U.3.1.1
  GL 4, 174; GL 6, 302 n.97   [→ *2.5.13*

G.4. *Eye(s) in Unusual Place on Body*

G.4.1. *Eyes covering entire body*

(1) Eyes which resemble stars of lightning in their brightness cover the entire body of Serapi'el, the prince of the seraphim. He has the face of an angel on an eagle's body, and is as tall as the seven heavens.
see G.5.15.1; A.6.5.1; F.21.7.1; G.10.2.1
   3 En. 27.3-7   [→ *3.3.a.5*

(2) Soperi'el and Soperi-el, two princes of angels, have bodies full of eyes, appearances like lightning, and eyes like the sun; they are as tall as the seven heavens, and their wings are the breadth of heaven; their lips are like the gates of the east, their tongues are like blazing torches as high as the sea's waves; flames and lightnings issue from their mouths, and fire is kindled from their sweat.
   see G.5.15.3; G.16.12.1; A.6.5.4; Ba.16.4.1; I.10.1.3; I.10.5.2; Ib.6.5.1;
   Ib.16.12.2; M.14.2.15; M.20.1.15
   3 En.18.25   [→ *3.3.a.6*

(3) Kerubi'el, prince of the cherubim, has a body full of eyes and is covered with wings. He is as tall and wide as the seven heavens, and has a body of burning coals and a mouth, a tongue, a face and eyes of fire; lightning flickers from the rays of his head and his wheels.
   see A.6.3.1; A.6.5.2; A.14.5.1; A.14.10.2; A.16.17.1; A.20.1.1; F.16.12.2;
   G.5.15.2; G.16.12.2; Gc.16.12.1; I.16.12.1; Ib.16.12.1; P.10.3.1
   3 En. 22.3-9   [→ *3.3.a.7*

(4) The cherubim seen by Ezekiel, Abraham and Enoch, as well as the ophanim and the seraphim seen by Enoch, have bodies, backs, hands, wings and wheels covered with eyes.
   see F.18.5.2; F.20.1.1; F.18.4.1; M.20.1.8; M.14.2.8; U.18.3.1; P.21.1.1;
   A.14.10.1; G.5.15.5; F.5.3.1
   Ezek. 10.12; Ezek. 1.18; Apoc. Abr. 18.3-7; Lad. Jac. 2.7-8; 2 En. 1a.4 (Recension A and J); 2 En. 20.1 (J); 2 En. 19.6 (A); 2 En. 21.1 (J); 3 En. 25.6; 3 En. 24.18 (Appendix)
                                    [→ *3.1.2; 3.1.16; 3.1.3*

(5) The angel Sammael is covered with eyes from the crown of his head to the soles of his feet, at the sight of which the spectator falls prostrate in awe. He is also immensely tall.
   see A.6.5.9; G.5.15.14; M.14.2.17; M.20.1.17
   GL 2, 308; GL 5, 416-418 n.117   [→ *2.24.1*

(6) The demon Keteb or Keteb Meriri ('Bitter Destruction' or 'Pestilence') is covered in eyes and scales, and is hairy all over. He has the head of a calf with a single horn on his forehead, and an eye set on his heart that kills whoever looks at it.

see G.5.15.6; G.4.5.1; D.18.4.1; E.4.1.2; Fb.14.2.1; B.13.7.1; A.13.6.1; B.13.6.1; Fb.18.11.1

Num. R. 12.3; *Lam. R.* 1.3 §29; GL 3, 186; GL 6, 74 n.381

[→ *3.1.22*

G.4.5. *Eye(s) on chest or heart*

(1) The demon Keteb or Keteb Meriri ('Bitter Destruction' or 'Pestilence') has an eye set on his heart that kills whoever looks at it. He is covered in eyes and scales, and is hairy all over. He has the head of a calf with a single horn on his forehead.

see G.5.15.6; G.4.1.6; D.18.4.1; E.4.1.2; Fb.14.2.1; B.13.7.1; A.13.6.1; B.13.6.1; Fb.18.11.1

Num. R. 12.3; *Lam. R.* 1.3 §29; GL 3, 186; GL 6, 74 n.381

[→ *3.1.22; 2.15.a.9*

(2) The demon called Murder sees through his breast and has the limbs of a man, but no head.

see D.1.1.2; A.2.5.2

T. Sol. 9.1-7   [→ *1.13.1*

G.5. *Unusual Number of Eyes*

G.5.1. *Single eye*

(1) Isaac sees creatures with only one eye and the faces of lions, tigers, dogs, hyenas or camels in his vision of the heavens.

see G.1.1; F.18.1.1; F.18.5.1; F.18.2.1; F.18.7.1; F.18.8.1

T. Isaac 5.7-10   [→ *2.24.8*

(2) Balaam has only one eye after the other one drops out when he gazes upon the camps of the Israelites and realizes he is unable to touch them.

see G.1.2; G.23.4.12; U.23.1.1; If.6.1.5; A.25.15.1; I.23.3.6; Va.27.1.1

Num. R. 2.4; *Num. R.* 20.6   [→ *1.12.a.21*

G.5.13. *Between one thousand and one million eyes*

(1) Opanniel, the prince of the ophanim, has 8,766 eyes, corresponding to the number of hours in a year, while in each pair of eyes lightnings flash and torches blaze, consuming all who look at him. The height of his body is a journey of 2,500 years; he has one hundred wings on each side and sixteen faces, four on each side.

see G.10.1.1; G.10.5.2; A.6.5.3; F.5.10.2; M.14.2.14; M.20.1.14

3 En. 25.2-4   [→ *3.12.2*

(2) Enoch has 365,000 eyes after his transformation into Metatron.

see A.6.3.2; A.6.5.12; G.10.2.3; M.14.2.13; M.20.1.13; A.16.12.6; B.16.12.1; E.16.4.1; G.16.12.5; V.16.12.1; Va.16.12.1; A.10.1.7

3 En. 9.4-5   [→ *1.35.2*

G.5.15. *Unspecified number of eyes*

(1) Serapi'el, the prince of the seraphim, has a body covered with eyes, resembling stars of lightning in their brightness. He has the face of an angel and an eagle's body, and is as tall as the seven heavens.

see G.4.1.1; A.6.5.1; F.21.7.1; G.10.2.1

3 En. 27.3-7   [→ *3.3.a.5*

(2) Kerubi'el, the prince of the cherubim, has a body full of eyes, and these eyes, as well as his mouth, tongue and face, are made of fire. He is as tall as the seven heavens, and has a body of burning coals. He is covered with wings, and lightnings flash from the rays from his head and his wheels.

see A.6.3.1; A.6.5.2; A.14.5.1; A.14.10.2; A.16.17.1; A.20.1.1; F.16.12.2; G.4.1.3; G.16.12.2; Gc.16.12.1; I.16.12.1; Ib.16.12.1; P.10.3.1

3 En. 22.3-9   [→ *3.3.a.7*

(3) Soperi'el and Soperi-el, two princes of angels, have bodies full of eyes, appearances like lightning, with eyes like the sun, lips like the gates of the east, tongues like blazing torches as high as the sea's waves; their height is that of the seven heavens, and they have wings as numerous as the days of the year and as broad as heaven. Flames issue from their mouths, and fire is kindled from their sweat.

see G.4.1.2; G.16.12.1; A.6.5.4; Ba.16.4.1; I.10.1.3; I.10.5.2; Ib.6.5.1; Ib.16.12.2; M.14.2.15; M.20.1.15

3 En. 18.25   [→ *3.3.a.6*

(4) The angel Sammael is covered with glaring eyes from the crown of his head to the soles of his feet, at the sight of which the beholder falls prostrate in awe. He is also immensely tall.

see A.6.5.9; G.4.1.5; M.14.2.17; M.20.1.17

GL 2, 308; GL 5, 416-418 n.117   [→ *2.24.1*

(5) The cherubim seen by Ezekiel, Abraham and Enoch, as well as the seraphim and ophanim seen by Enoch, have bodies, backs, hands, wings and wheels covered with eyes.

see F.18.5.2; F.20.1.1; F.18.4.1; M.20.1.8; M.14.2.8; U.18.3.1; P.21.1.1; A.14.10.1; G.4.1.4; F.5.3.1

Ezek. 10.12; Ezek. 1.18; *Apoc. Abr.* **18.3-7;** *Lad. Jac.* **2.7-8; 2** *En.* **1a.4 (Recension J and A); 2** *En.* **20.1 (J); 2** *En.* **19.6 (A); 2** *En.* **21.1 (J); 3** *En.* **25.6; 3** *En.* **24.18 (Appendix)**

[→ *3.1.2; 3.1.16; 3.1.3*

(6) The demon Keteb or Keteb Meriri ('Bitter Destruction' or 'Pestilence') is covered with eyes and scales. He has one eye set on his heart that kills whoever looks at it. He has the head of a calf, with a single horn on his forehead.

see G.4.5.1; G.4.1.6; D.18.4.1; E.4.1.2; Fb.14.2.1; B.13.7.1; A.13.6.1; B.13.6.1; Fb.18.11.1

Num. R. **12.3;** *Lam. R.* **1.3 §29; GL 3, 186; GL 6, 74 n.381**

[→ *3.1.22*

G.10.1 *Eye(s) that emits fire or flame*

(1) Torches blaze and lightnings flash from the 8,766 eyes of Opanniel, the prince of the ophanim, consuming all who look at him. The height of his body is a journey of 2,500 years; he has one hundred wings on each side, and sixteen faces, four on each side.

see G.10.5.2; G.5.13.1; A.6.5.3; F.5.10.2; M.14.2.14; M.20.1.14

3 *En.* **25.2-4**   [→ *2.15.a.4*

(2) The eyes of the two angels Samuil and Raguil, who take Enoch to heaven, are like burning lamps.

see F.10.1.4; P.11.2.1; Ia.10.1.1; M.14.2.4; M.20.1.4; A.6.5.5

2 *En.* **1.4-6 (J and A); 2** *En.* **3.1-3 (J and A); 2** *En.* **33.6 (J and A)**

[→ *3.3.a.14*

(3) Scorching fire and thick cloud pour from the eyes of the Angel of the Face.

see G.10.3.1

GL 1, 14; GL 5, 17-18 n.50   [→ *2.15.a.7; 2.22.b.1*

G.10.2 *Eye(s) that emits light or luminous eye(s)*

(1) The eyes of Serapi'el, the prince of the seraphim, resemble stars of lightning in their brightness and cover his whole body. He has the

G. *The Eyes*

face of an angel and the body of an eagle, and is as tall as the seven heavens.

see A.6.5.1; F.21.7.1; G.4.1.1; G.5.15.1
3 En. **27.3-7**   [→ *3.3.a.5*

(2) A brilliant light shines from the eyes and faces of the ophanim, seraphim and cherubim.

see F.10.1.1; F.6.1.2; M.20.1.12; M.14.2.12; U.18.3.2; G.4.1.4; G.5.15.5
3 En. **25.6;** *3 En.* **24.18** (Appendix); *3 En.* **1.7-8;** *3 En.* **2.1**
                                   [→ *3.1.2; 3.1.3; 3.1.16*

(3) The 365,000 eyes bestowed upon Enoch at his transformation into Metatron are as brilliant as the sun.

see A.6.3.2; A.6.5.12; G.5.13.2; M.14.2.13; M.20.1.13; A.16.12.6; B.16.12.1;
E.16.4.1; G.16.12.5; V.16.12.1; Va.16.12.1; A.10.1.7
3 En. **9.4-5**   [→ *1.35.2*

(4) The eyes of the angel seen by Aseneth (probably Michael) shine like the sun, while his face is like lightning, the hairs of his head like a flaming torch, and his hands and feet like glowing iron emitting sparks.

see E.10.2.1; F.10.1.3; P.10.3.2; P.16.1.1; U.10.3.1; U.16.1.1
Jos. Asen. **14.9 (8, 9);** *Jos. Asen.* **16.12,13(7)**   [→ *3.1.8*

(5) The right eye of the Antichrist shines like the star rising at dawn, while the other is unmoving. His mouth is one cubit in size, his teeth are a span long, the soles of his feet two span. His fingers are like scythes. On his forehead is the inscription 'Antichrist'.

see G.23.3.1; Fb.13.2.2; I.6.1.1; Ic.6.5.1; Pc.12.1.1; Pc.12.2.1; U.6.5.1
Gk Apoc. Ezra **4.29f.**   [→ *3.1.24*

(6) The eyes of the Antichrist shine like the rising morning star, while his right eye is like a lion's. His lower teeth are made of iron and his lower jaw of diamond. His right arm is made of iron, his left of copper. His right hand is three cubits long, as are his feet. He is ten cubits tall, with hair reaching down to his feet, and he is three-crested. He is long-faced, long-nosed and disorderly, with three letters written on his forehead: A, K and T, signifying denial, rejection and the befouled dragon. His mother conceives him by touching the head of a fish.

see G.18.1.1; A.6.5.13; E.6.5.1; Fb.13.2.3; Fc.16.5.1; Ic.16.1.1; O.16.1.1;
O.16.2.3; U.6.5.2
Apoc. Dan. **9.11, 16-26**   [→ *3.1.25; 1.3.c.1*

(7) At birth, Noah's eyes are like the rays of the sun: the whole house glows when he opens them.

> see A.11.2.5; A.11.3.2; E.11.2.1; Sa.2.3.6; Sa.24.3.6; Sa.2.1.1; T.23.1.1; I.10.4.1; Sa.24.10.1; Va.24.1.1; If.26.1.1; B.11.2.1; B.11.3.2; Sa.24.2.1
> *1 En.* **106.2, 5, 10**   [→ *3.10.17*

(8) Aseneth's eyes, dulled and inflamed through fasting, become like the rising morning star when she eats from a honeycomb, while her face becomes like the sun, her cheeks red like blood, her lips like the rose of life, and her teeth, hair, neck and bones become strong as cypresses or cedars.

> see F.10.1.10; Fa.11.3.1; Ia.11.3.1; G.11.3.2; E.22.1.2; Ia.15.1.1; A.6.4.1; Ba.11.3.1
> *Jos. Asen.* **16.16;** *Jos. Asen.* **18.7;** *Jos. Asen.* **20.6**   [→ *1.14.d.2*

(9) Moses' eyes and face shine like the sun when he writes down the Ineffable Name shortly before his death, and his mouth emits darts of fire and lightning flashes.

> see F.10.1.11; Sa.2.3.19; Sa.24.3.19; A.6.5.25; A.6.4.2; P.23.1.1; P.25.4.1; I.10.1.5; A.25.9.1; F.11.3.2; Fb.10.1.1; G.25.4.1; If.6.1.3; Fb.14.2.3; I.23.3.3; P.11.2.2; G.17.20.1; Ib.13.2.1; Ib.24.4.1; Ia.24.4.1; E.6.1.1; Ga.10.2.1; E.12.10.1; P.13.2.1; P.24.4.1; K.13.10.2; B.16.12.2; Ib.16.12.3; Ia.13.2.1; A.26.1.3
> *Deut. R.* **11.10**   [→ *2.24.12*

(10) The eyes of Jonathan brighten after he eats honey from a honeycomb.

> **1Sam. 14.27-29**   [→ *1.14.d.3*

G.10.3. *Eye(s) that emits smoke or clouds*

(1) Thick clouds and scorching fires pour from the eyes of the Angel of the Face.

> see G.10.1.3
> **GL 1, 14; GL 5, 17-18 n.50**   [→ *2.15.a.7; 2.22.b.1*

G.10.4 *Eye(s) that emits tears of blood*

(1) Judah's right eye sheds tears of blood in his rage with Joseph over the release of Benjamin. At other times, both his eyes shed blood when he is enraged.

> see E.13.1.2; E.8.1.1; Gf.16.3.1; Ic.18.5.1; F.18.5.3; J.23.1.2; I.23.3.2; Va.3.1.1; F.11.6.2; If.6.1.1; A.10.1.15
> **BR 93.7; GL 2, 107; GL 5, 354 n.277**   [→ *1.12.a.19*

G.10.5 *Eye(s) that emits lightning*

(1) Lightning flashes from God's eye for both creative and destructive ends.

see E.11.2.1; A.11.2.2; A.11.3.1; D.16.3.1; E.11.1.1; E.12.3.1; F.5.10.1;
F.16.12.1; A.11.2.1; Ia.16.12.1; P.10.1.1; P.10.7.1; Pc.10.7.1; Gf.4.1.1;
A.1.1.1; Gf.27.2.1; A.10.1.1; Pc.10.3.1; I.10.5.1; If.6.1.1
2 En. **22.1-2 (J)**; *2 En.* **29.1 (J)**; *2 En.* **39.3-4 (A)**; *2 En.* **39.5 (J)**;
Lad. Jac. **2.17**; *Sib. Or.* **7.124-128**   [→ *2.14.a.1; 2.15.a.1*

(2) Lightnings flash and torches blaze from the 8,766 eyes of Opanni'el, the prince of the ophanim, consuming all who look at him. The height of his body is a journey of 2,500 years; he has one hundred wings on each side and sixteen faces, four on each side.

see G.10.1.1; G.5.13.1; A.6.5.3; F.5.10.2; M.14.2.14; M.20.1.14
3 En. **25.2-4**   [→ *2.15.a.4*

G.11. *Unusual Colour of Eye(s)*

G.11.2. *White eye(s)*

(1) White spots form on Tobit's eyes when hot droppings from a sparrow fall on them. He is cured when the gall of a fish is placed on his eyes and the white spots are blown away.

see G.23.4.23
Tob. **2.10**; *Tob.* **11.7-8, 10-14**   [→ *1.14.c.22; 1.30.1*

G.11.3. *Red eye(s)*

(1) Ham's descendants have red eyes.
see E.12.3.2; Ia.12.1.1; A.11.1.3; B.11.1.2
GL 1, 169; GL 5, 191-192 n.60, 61   [→ *1.7.a.1*

(2) After seven days of fasting, Aseneth's eyes are inflamed from the tears she has shed, while her lips are cracked, her hair is straggly, her face has fallen, and her body is emaciated.

see A.6.4.1; E.22.2; Ia.15.1.1; Ba.11.3.1; F.10.1.10; Fa.11.3.1; G.10.2.8;
Ia.11.3.1
Jos. Asen. **11.1.1**; *Jos. Asen.* **13.9.8**; *Jos. Asen.* **18.3**
                                          [→ *1.12.a.10; 2.31.b.2*

(3) Haman has eyes inflamed like those of a serpent because of his deranged hatred of Israel.
Gen. R. **16.4**   [→ *1.12.a.22*

G.11.11. *Translucent or abnormally clear eye(s)*

(1) The Messiah's eyes are clearer than pure wine.
see Ic.11.2.1
GL 2, 143; GL 5, 367 n.388　　　　　　　　　[→ *1.13.7*

G.13. *Peculiarities of Skin or Cornea of Eye(s)*

G.13.10. *Melted eye(s)*

(1) The eyes of the sinners in hell melt in their sockets.
see B.23.20.2; Ic.24.1.1; Ic.25.1.1; Ic.6.5.3
GL 2, 312; GL 5, 418-419 n.118　　　　[→ *1.14.d.6; 1.26.b.64*

G.14. *Unusual Protuberances or Protusions on Eye(s)*

G.14.10. *Body(ies) on eye(s)*

(1) While Adam is still a lifeless mass, God shows him all the right-eous people to descend from him: some hang on Adam's eyes, some on his head, others on his hair, nose, mouth, ear and earlobes.
see Cb.9.1.1; F.5.1.1; A.9.1.2; R.14.1.1; R.18.1.1; A.6.1.19; A.6.1.20; A.6.3.4; A.6.5.20; A.6.5.21; A.13.10.1; B.13.10.1; A.10.1.9; A.10.1.10; Sa.2.3.3; Sa.24.3.3; A.16.9.1; Ca.9.1.1; Cb.5.1.1; G.23.5.1; J.23.1.1; A.4.1.1; D.14.10.1; E.14.10.1; Fb.14.10.1; A.12.1.1; H.14.10.1; I.14.10.1; J.14.10.1; Ja.14.10.1
Exod. R. **40.3**　　　　　　　　　　[→ *2.4.3*

G.16. *Eye(s) of Unusual Substance*

G.16.12. *Eye(s) of fire*

(1) Soperi'el and Soperi-el, two princes of angels, have eyes that burn like the sun. Their appearances are like lightning, and they are as tall as the seven heavens, with bodies full of wings and eyes, lips like the gates of the east, tongues like blazing torches as high as the sea's waves, with flames and lightnings issuing from their mouths and fire kindling from their sweat.
see G.4.1.2; G.5.15.3; A.6.5.4; Ba.16.4.1; I.10.1.3; I.10.5.2; Ib.6.5.1; Ib.16.12.2; M.14.2.15; M.20.1.15;
3 En. **18.25**　　　　　　　　　　[→ *3.3.a.6*

G. *The Eyes*

(2) Eyes of fire cover the body of Kerubi'el, the prince of the cherubim. He is as tall and wide as the seven heavens, with a body of burning coals emitting flames, while lightnings flicker from the rays from his head and wheels. He is also covered in wings.

see A.6.3.1; A.6.5.2; A.14.5.1; A.14.10.2; A.16.17.1; A.20.1.1; F.16.12.3; G.5.15.2; G.4.1.3; Gc.16.12.1; I.16.12.1; Ib.16.12.1; P.10.3.1
3 En. 22.3-9   [→ *3.3.a.7*

(3) An angel with eyes like fiery torches, arms and legs like burnished bronze, a face like lightning, and a body like beryl, chrysolite or topaz (and a voice like the voice of a crowd) is seen by Daniel in a vision.

see A.16.18.1; F.16.12.3; O.16.2.1; T.16.2.1
Dan. 10.6   [→ *3.1.14*

(4) The myriads of angels in the seventh heaven (called Arabot) have eyes like torches of fire, faces like lightning, and arms and feet like burnished bronze.

see F.16.13.1; O.16.2.2; U.16.2.2
3 En. 35.1-2; *3 En.* 22B.6 (Appendix)   [→ *3.3.a.9*

(5) Enoch's eyes become torches of fire when he is transformed into Metatron.

see A.6.3.2; A.6.5.12; G.5.13.2; G.10.2.3; M.14.2.13; M.20.1.13; A.16.12.6; B.16.12.1; E.16.4.1; V.16.12.1; Va.16.12.1; A.10.1.7
3 En. 15.1; *3 En.* 48c.6 (Appendix)   [→ *1.35.2*

(6) The guardians of the gates of hell have eyes aflame, or eyes like extinguished lamps, with fangs exposed down to their breasts and faces like very large snakes. They stand as large as serpents.

see A.6.1.2; F.18.6.1; Ic.18.2.1
2 En. 42.1 (J and A); *2 En.* 42.1 (Appendix)   [→ *2.24.7; 2.22.a.10*

G.17. *Substitution for Eye(s)*

G.17.20. *Wheels in place of eye(s)*

(1) Moses' eyes are changed into Merkabah wheels, and his strength is changed into an angel's by the angel Metatron.

see F.10.1.11; Sa.2.3.19; Sa.24.3.19; A.6.5.25; A.6.4.2; P.23.1.1; P.25.4.1; I.10.1.5; G.10.2.9; F.11.3.2; Fb.10.1.1; F.10.1.11; G.25.4.1; If.6.1.3; Fb.14.2.3; I.23.3.3; P.11.2.2; A.25.9.1; Ib.13.2.1; Ib.24.4.1; Ia.24.4.1; E.6.1.1; Ga.10.2.1; E.12.10.1; P.13.2.1; P.24.4.1; K.13.10.2; B.16.12.2;

Ib.16.12.3; Ia.13.2.1; A.6.1.21

GL 2, 306; GL 5, 416-418 n.117   [→ *2.15.b.9*

G.18. Animal Eye(s) or Eye(s) with Animal Attributes

G.18.1. *Eye(s) of lion*

(1) The right eye of the Antichrist is like a lion's, and both his eyes shine like the rising morning star. He is ten cubits tall and his feet and right hand are three cubits long. His hair reaches to his feet and he is three-crested. His left arm is made of copper, his right arm and lower teeth of iron, while his lower jaw is made of diamond. He is long-faced, long-nosed and disorderly, with three letters written on his forehead: A, K and T, signifying denial, rejection and the befouled dragon. His mother conceives him by touching the head of a fish.

see G.10.2.6; A.6.5.13; E.6.5.1; Fb.13.2.3; Fc.16.5.1; Ic.16.1.1; O.16.1.1;
O.16.2.3; U.6.5.2

Apoc. Dan. 9.11, 16-26   [→ *3.1.25; 1.3.c.1*

G.21. Human Eye(s) on Unusual Creature

G.21.1. *Eye(s) on wheels*

(1) Eyes cover the fiery wheels of the chariot which Abraham sees during his apocalypse.

Apoc. Abr. 18.12   [→ *3.1.27*

G.21.10. *Human eye(s) on fabulous beast*

(1) In a vision Daniel sees a beast with a single horn full of eyes and a mouth 'that is full of boasts'. The beast also has iron teeth, bronze claws and ten other horns.

see I.21.10.1

Dan. 7.7-8,19f.; Gen. R. 76.6   [→ *4.1.a.6*

G.23. Disease, Paralysis or Malfunction of Eye(s)

G.23.3. *Paralysis of eye(s)*

(1) The Antichrist's left eye is fixed, while his right eye resembles the rising morning star. His mouth is one cubit long, his teeth a span long, the soles of his feet two span, and his fingers are like scythes; on his forehead is the inscription 'Antichrist'.

see G.10.2.5; Fb.13.2.2; I.6.1.1; Ic.6.5.1; Pc.12.1.1; Pc.12.2.1; U.6.5.1
Gk Apoc. Ezra **4.29f.**   [→ *3.1.24*

(2) Eli's gaze becomes fixed when he is ninety-eight years old.
see G.23.4.15
1 Sam. 3.15   [→ *1.31.4*

G.23.4 *Blindness*

(1) The angel Sammael is blind.
Deut. R. **11.10; GL 5, 121 n.116; GL 6, 449 n.57**
                                         [→ *5.1.1; 1.14.a.1; 3.4.b.1*

(2) Lamech, Cain's great-grandson, is blind and kills his ancestor by
accidentally shooting him with his bow and arrow.
GL 1, 116-117; GL 5, 145-147 n.42, 44   [→ *4.1.b.6*

(3) The builders of the Tower of Babel are struck blind by God.
3 Bar. **3.8** (Greek)   [→ *1.26.b.8; 1.19.b.4; 2.22.c.1*

(4) The men of Sodom are struck blind.
Gen. 19.11; *Gen. R.* **50.8**   [→ *2.19.b.2*

(5) All the blind are made to see at Isaac's birth.
see I.23.3.1; T.23.1.4
GL 1, 262; GL 5, 245 n.203   [→ *2.4.5*

(6) Isaac becomes blind in old age (or, in a variant, at the time of the
Akedah).
Gen. 27.1; *T. Isaac* **4.8-9;** *Gen. R.* **65.5-10; GL 1, 328; GL 3, 479;**
GL 5, 281-282n.73, 74; GL 6, 166 n.962   [→ *1.14.a.2; 1.14.a.3;*
1.14.a.4; 1.19.b.6; 2.6.a.7; 1.31.1; 2.7.3; 2.20.1; 4.1.b.10;
1.14.c.6; 1.12.a.8; 1.7.a.4; 1.26.a.5; 1.26.b.12

(7) Jacob's eyes become dull from weeping over the fate of Joseph
(but when he goes to Egypt he sees clearly again).
see G.23.5.3; Sa.2.3.12; Sa.24.3.12; K.13.10.1; Ta.24.1.1; O.6.1.1; Q.6.1.1;
A.6.1.23; Ta.23.1.1; T.23.1.3
T. Jac. **1.12**   [→ *1.12.a.9*

(8) Jacob blinds the enemy army by grinding huge rocks into lime
powder and throwing them at his opponents.
GL 1, 406; GL 5, 314 n.291   [→ *2.16.3*

(9) All the Pharaoh's counsellors become blind, deaf or dumb, and
are therefore unable to tell Pharaoh where Moses has gone when they
are ordered to pursue him.

see I.23.3.5; J.23.1.4

Exod. R. 1.31; *Deut. R.* 2.26-27; GL 2, 282; GL 5, 406 n.76

[→ *2.2.b.2; 2.19.b.3; 2.22.c.3*

(10) Many Israelites are blinded while working in Egypt because wood or clay gets in their eyes. Others are maimed in a similar way. (But all the lame, blind, deaf, dumb and maimed are healed in the time between the Exodus and the Revelation on Mount Sinai so that they are fit to receive the Torah.)

see J.23.1.3; I.23.3.4; P.1.1.1; T.23.1.2

Num. R. 7.1; GL 3, 13, 78; GL 6, 30 n.176   [→ *1.23.1*

(11) Ahasuerus is blind, but his eyes become bright as soon as he directs them towards Esther.

GL 6, 474 n.149   [→ *4.1.b.24*

(12) Balaam becomes blind in one eye when he boasts to God about how King Balak wishes him to curse the Israelites. Alternatively, his eye drops out when he gazes upon the camp of the Israelites and realizes he is unable to touch them.

see U.23.1.1; If.6.1.5; A.25.15.1; I.23.3.6; Va.27.1.1; G.1.2; G.5.1.2

Num. R. 2.4; GL 3, 359; GL 6, 125-126 n.730, 731   [→ *1.26.b.33*

(13) The Amorites are struck blind by the angel Gabriel, the angel Ingethel, or by hornets stinging their eyes, so that they fall upon and kill one another.

see G.23.4.14; A.6.5.15; W.25.2.2

Ps-Philo 25.12; *Gen. R.* 18.22; GL 4, 26; GL 6, 184 n.18

[→ *1.19.b.12; 2.16.9*

(14) When a blind Amorite kisses one of the seven idols made of precious stones from Havilah and at the same time touches his eyes, his sight is restored; alternatively, his sight is restored when he looks at his precious stones, which include crystal and prase.

see G.23.4.13; A.6.5.15; W.25.2.2

Ps-Philo 25.12; GL 4, 23; GL 6, 182 n.10   [→ *4.1.b.27*

(15) When Eli is ninety-eight years old, his gaze becomes fixed, leaving him blind or dim-sighted.

see G.23.3.2

1 Sam. 3.2,15; *1 Sam.* 2.27-36; GL 6, 221 n.27

[→ *1.31.4; 1.26.b.34*

(16) Samson is blinded when he is captured by the Philistines.
see E.8.1.2; E.25.5.1; A.6.1.29; Ie.17.3.1; I.10.20.1; G.24.1.2; G.1.3;
U.23.1.2; M.6.3.1; T.25.1.2; E.6.5.4
Judg. 16.21; Ps-Philo 43.5-6; *Num.R.* **9.24** [→ *2.18.b.1; 1.12.c.2*

(17) A blind man, going astray, is set on the right path by Asmodeus.
GL 4, 167-168 [→ *4.1.b.23*

(18) Ahijah, the prophet, is blind.
1 Kgs 14.4 [→ *1.31.5*

(19) Jair and his servants are blinded by the angel Nathaniel when
they try to burn the seven pious men for refusing to worship Baal.
Ps-Philo 38.3 [→ *2.18.a.8; 1.19.b.13*

(20) At Shihin a blind man bathes in the water of Miriam's well and
is healed.
Num. R. **18.22** [→ *4.1.b.29*

(21) A scholar loses his eyesight when he looks at the fiery chariots
in which the pious ascend to the heavenly academy and sees the lustre
of the chariot of Rabbi Hiyyah.
GL 6, 332 n.84 [→ *1.14.a.11*

(22) The Aramaean warriors are smitten with blindness after Elisha
prays for this to happen.
2 Kgs 6.18 [→ *2.9.8; 2.18.a.9; 2.18.c.1; 1.19.b.20*

(23) Tobit is blinded when hot droppings from sparrows fall into his
eyes, forming white spots which are aggravated by ointments pre-
scribed by the doctors.
see G.11.2.1
Tob. 2.10; Tob. 3.16-17; Tob. 5.10; Tob. 6.9; Tob. 11.7-8,10-14
[→ *1.14.c.22; 1.30.1*

(24) Zedekiah is blinded.
see G.24.1.3; G.1.1.4
Jer. 39.7; Jer. 52.11; 2 Kgs 25.7 [→ *1.12.a.13; 1.26.b.48; 1.24.3*

(25) A ravager of Ezekiel's grave becomes blind and sick.
GL 4, 326; GL 6, 413 n.75 [→ *1.26.b.59*

(26) King Darius is blinded by an angel because he keeps Daniel in
prison. His sight is restored when he releases Daniel and, on the

advice given to Daniel by an angel, washes his eyes.

GL 4, 347; GL 6, 434 n.9 [→ *1.26.b.54*

(27) Children are blinded and made deaf and dumb, and their ears turned around backwards while they are still in the womb, by a demon in the form of a three-headed dragon with awful skin.

see J.7.1.1; J.23.1.9; I.23.3.12

T. Sol. **12.1-2** [→ *1.19.b.24*

(28) A parable: a blind man is helped home by a sighted man, then the sighted man asks the blind man to light a lamp for him (so that the blind man is under no obligation).

Num. R. **15.5**; *Exod. R.* **36.2** [→ *4.1.a.3*

(29) A parable: the blind walk on an evil road so that thorns add wound to wound. Those who see walk on a good road and so they and their clothes become scented.

Exod. R. **30.20** [→ *4.1.a.1*

(30) A parable: a blind man and a lame man guard the king's orchard; the lame man rides on the blind man's back and thus they manage to steal the king's early figs. The king realizes what has happened and takes both men to task.

see T.23.1.6

Lev. R. **4.5**; *Apoc. Ezek.* **1.1f.** [→ *4.1.a.2*

G.23.5. *Partial blindness*

(1) Adam is subjected to an affliction of the eyes, of the hearing and sixty-eight other plagues as a punishment for his sins.

see Cb.9.1.1; F.5.1.1; A.9.1.2; R.14.1.1; R.18.1.1; A.6.1.19; A.6.1.20; A.6.3.4; A.6.5.20; A.6.5.21; A.13.10.1; B.13.10.1; A.10.1.9; A.10.1.10; Sa.2.3.3; Sa.24.3.3; A.16.9.1; Ca.9.1.1; Cb.5.1.1; A.12.1.1; J.23.1.1; A.4.1.1; D.14.10.1; E.14.10.1; Fb.14.10.1; G.14.10.1; H.14.10.1; I.14.10.1; J.14.10.1; Ja.14.10.1

LAE (Apoc. Mos.) **8.2**; *LAE (Apoc. Mos.)* **5.2-4**; *LAE (Vita)* **30**; *LAE (Vita)* **34.1-2** [→ *1.26.b.2*

(2) Leah's eyes are weak, or have no sparkle.

see Gc.1.1.1

Gen. 29.17; *Jub.* **28.5** [→ *1.12.a.7*

(3) Jacob's eyes grow dim with age (while he is still in the land of Goshen).

see G.23.4.7; Sa.2.3.12; Sa.24.3.12; K.13.10.1; Ta.24.1.1; O.6.1.1; Q.6.1.1;
A.6.1.23; Ta.23.1.1; T.23.1.3
Gen. 48.10; *T. Jac.* **2.3;** *T. Jac.* **4.10** [→ *1.31.2*

G.23.20. *Worm-infested eyes*

(1) The eyes of Antiochus Epiphanes teem with worms, he has an
incurable pain in his belly and his flesh rots away so that the stench of
his decay sickens the whole army.
see A.10.10.2; B.23.6.1; Va.24.1.2
2 Macc. 9.5-10 [→ *1.26.b.50; 2.4.15*

G.24. *Wounded, Mutilated or Maimed Eye(s)*

G.24.1. *Lacerated eye(s)*

(1) King Nimrod dreams that his eye is lacerated by a chicken which
hatches from an egg thrown at him by a man resembling Abraham.
GL 1, 204; GL 5, 215-216 n.45 [→ *3.10.21*

(2) Samson's eyes are torn.
see E.8.1.2; E.25.5.1; A.6.1.29; Ie.17.3.1; I.10.20.1; G.1.3; U.23.1.2;
M.6.3.1; T.25.1.2; E.6.5.4
Judg. 16.21; Ps-Philo 43.5-6; *Num. R.* **9.24** [→ *1.12.c.2; 2.18.b.1*

(3) Zedekiah's eyes are pierced with iron lances when he is captured
by King Nebuchadnezzar and carried off to Babylon.
see G.1.4; G.23.4.24
GL 4, 293-294; GL 6, 283 n.6-8; 2 Kgs 25.7; Jer. 39.7; Jer. 52.11
[→ *1.24.3; 1.26.b.48*

G.25. *Unusual Abilities of Eye(s)*

G.25.1. *'The Evil Eye'*

(1) David has the Evil Eye, by means of which he afflicts Goliath
with leprosy and paralysis.
see E.11.3.1; Sa.2.3.25; Sa.24.3.25; B.11.3.3; T.23.2.1; O.23.2.1; A.25.15.3;
A.23.1.16; F.11.1.7; A.25.9.2
GL 4, 87; GL 6, 251 n.37 [→ *2.16.8*

(2) People cast the Evil Eye on Hananiah, Mishael and Azariah when
they emerge from the furnace unharmed.
Gen. R. **56.11; GL 6, 419 n.92** [→ *1.12.a.23; 2.15.a.12*

G.25.2. *Awesome eyes*

(1) The glance of the angel of destruction causes terror and trembling in the heart of the beholder.

see A.16.11.2; A.16.12.9
GL 2, 366; GL 5, 433-434 n.213   [→ *2.24.5*

(2) The eye of the prophet Elisha is so awe-inspiring that no woman can look him in the face and live.

see A.10.10.3
GL 4, 242; GL 6, 346 n.11   [→ *3.3.a.40*

G.25.4. *Eye(s) with extraordinary powers of sight*

(1) Moses' eyes are strengthened so that he can see the entire length and breadth of Israel (a square of 400 parasangs) before he dies.

see F.10.1.11; Sa.2.3.19; Sa.24.3.19; A.6.5.25; A.6.4.2; P.23.1.1; P.25.4.1; I.10.1.5; G.10.2.9; F.11.3.2; Fb.10.1.1; F.10.1.5; A.25.9.1; If.6.1.3; Fb.14.2.3; I.23.3.3; P.11.2.2; G.17.20.1; Ib.13.2.1; Ib.24.4.1; Ia.24.4.1; E.6.1.1; Ga.10.2.1; E.12.10.1; P.13.2.1; P.24.4.1; K.13.10.2; B.16.12.2; Ib.16.12.3; Ia.13.2.1; A.26.1.3
GL 3, 442; GL 6, 151 n.901   [→ *2.23.a.3*

Ga. *The Pupil(s)*

Ga.10. *Unusual Emission or Emanation from Pupil(s)*

Ga.10.2. *Emanation of light from pupil(s)*

(1) The pupils of Moses' eyes are like the sphere of the morning star.

see F.10.1.11; Sa.2.3.19; Sa.24.3.19; A.6.5.25; A.6.4.2; P.23.1.1; P.25.4.1; I.10.1.5; G.10.2.9; F.11.3.2; Fb.10.1.1; F.10.1.11; G.25.4.1; If.6.1.3; Fb.14.2.3; I.23.3.3; P.11.2.2; G.17.20.1; Ib.13.2.1; Ib.24.4.1; Ia.24.4.1; E.6.1.1; A.25.9.1; E.12.10.1; P.13.2.1; P.24.4.1; K.13.10.2; B.16.12.2; Ib.16.12.3; Ia.13.2.1; A.26.1.3
GL 2, 332; GL 5, 425 n.157   [→ *3.3.a.30*

(2) The pupils of Aaron's eyes are like the sphere of the morning star.

see A.6.5.26; E.12.10.2; E.6.1.2; F.10.1.12; I.10.1.4; A.23.1.8; A.6.2.4
GL 2, 332; GL 5, 425 n.157   [→ *3.3.a.30*

Ga.23. *Disease, Paralysis or Malfunction of Pupil(s)*

Ga.23.2. *Closed up pupil(s)*

(1) The pupils of the eyes of the Philistines and their beasts and all the other apertures of their bodies are closed up when King Abimelech takes Sarah as a wife.
see Ha.23.1.1; I.23.4.1; J.23.2.1; Ra.23.1.1; Sa.23.2.1; Sb.23.2.1
GL 1, 258; GL 5, 243 n.190; GL 5, 244 n.202 [→ *2.10.a.2*

Ga.24. *Wounded or Mutilated Pupil(s)*

Ga.24.1. *Lacerated pupil(s)*

(1) The pupils of the eyes of seven martyrs and their mother are pierced when they are tortured by King Antiochus Epiphanes; their tongues are cut out, their heads scalped and their extremities cut off.
see Ib.1.1.3; D.2.2.1; P.1.1.2; U.1.1.1
4 Macc. 18.21; *4 Macc.* 6.6,25; *4 Macc.* 7.13-14; *4 Macc.* 9.28; *4 Macc.* 10.5-8,17-21; *4 Macc.* 11.18-19 [→ *2.5.12; 2.25.a.2; 1.24.4*

Gb. *The Eyebrow(s)*

Gb.6. *Abnormal Size of Eyebrow(s)*

Gb.6.5. *Exceptionally long eyebrow(s)*

(1) The Antichrist has eyebrows reaching to his ears, a tuft of grey hair on the front of his bald head, skinny legs, fiery wings, and a leprous bare spot on the palms of his hands; he can appear like an old man or a child, but cannot change the signs on his head.
see E.2.1.1; E.11.4.1; M.14.2.19; M.20.1.19; Pa.23.1.1; T.6.4.1
Apoc. Elij. 3.15-17; *Apoc. Elij.* 5.20 [→ *3.1.26*

Gc. *The Eyelash(es)*

Gc.1. *Absence of Eyelash(es)*

(1) Leah's eyelashes drop from their lids when she weeps over her prospective marriage to the villainous Esau.
see G.23.5.2
GL 1, 359; GL 5, 294 n.163 [→ *1.12.a.6*

(2) Rabbi Gamaliel weeps until his eyelashes fall out when he hears a woman weeping in the night and is reminded of the destruction of the Temple of Jerusalem.

Lam. R. 1.2 §24   [→ *1.12.a.16*

Gc.16. *Eyelash(es) of Unusual Substance*

Gc.16.12. *Eyelash(es) of lightning*

(1) Kerubi'el, the prince of the cherubim, has eyelashes of lightning, and his entire body is full of burning coals and covered with eyes and wings, while rays flash from his wheels.

see A.6.3.1; A.6.5.2; A.14.5.1; A.14.10.2; A.16.17.1; A.20.1.1; F.16.12.2; G.5.15.2; G.16.12.2; G.4.1.3; I.16.12.1; Ib.16.12.1; P.10.3.1
3 En. 22.3-9   [→ *3.3.a.7*

Gd. *The Eyelid(s)*
[No reference in sources]

Ge. *The Cornea*
[No reference in sources]

Gf. *The Tear(s)*

Gf.4. *Tear(s) in Unusual Position on Body*

Gf.4.1. *Tear(s) on hand(s) or finger(s)*

(1) Rivers of tears flow from the fingers of God's right hand, such is his sorrow over the destruction of the temple.

see E.11.2.1; A.11.2.2; A.11.3.1; D.16.3.1; E.11.1.1; E.12.3.1; F.5.10.1; F.16.12.1; G.10.5.1; Ia.16.12.1; P.10.1.1; P.10.7.1; Pc.10.7.1; A.11.2.1; A.1.1.1; Gf.27.2.1; A.10.1.1; Pc.10.3.1; I.10.5.1; If.6.1.1
3 En. 48a.4   [→ *1.12.a.2*

Gf.16. *Tear(s) of Unusual Substance*

Gf.16.3. *Tear(s) of blood*

(1) Judah's right eye sheds tears of blood when he is enraged with Joseph over the release of Benjamin; at other times, both his eyes shed blood when he is enraged.

see E.13.1.2; G.10.4.1; E.8.1.1; Ic.18.5.1; F.18.5.3; J.23.1.2; I.23.3.2;

Va.3.1.1; F.11.6.2; If.6.1.2; A.10.1.15
Gen. R. **93.7; GL 2, 107; GL 5, 354 n.277** [→ *1.12.a.19*

Gf.25. *Unusual Abilities or Properties of Tears*

Gf.25.1. *Tear(s) with abrasive properties*

(1) The tears of the ministering angels fall on the knife which is to be used for the sacrifice of Isaac, and dissolve it.
Gen. R. **56.7** [→ *1.12.a.4*

(2) The tears of the young men seized and bound when the enemy enter the temple run down their cheeks and leave scars.
see Fa.13.3.1
Lam. R. **1.2 §25** [→ *1.12.a.15*

Gf.27. *Transformation of Tear(s)*

Gf.27.2. *Transformation of tear(s) into jewel(s) or precious stone(s)*

(1) God's tears, shed for the suffering of Israel after the destruction of the temple, turn into pearls.
see E.11.2.1; A.11.2.2; A.11.3.1; D.16.3.1; E.11.1.1; E.12.3.1; F.5.10.1; F.16.12.1; G.10.5.1; Ia.16.12.1; P.10.1.1; P.10.7.1; Pc.10.7.1; Gf.4.1.1; A.1.1.1; A.11.2.1; A.10.1.1; Pc.10.3.1; I.10.5.1; If.6.1.1
GL 6, 398 n.39 [→ *1.12.a.1*

(2) The angel Michael's tears turn into precious stones when he weeps with compassion over the forthcoming death of Abraham.
see A.16.10.1; A.16.12.1; A.1.1.2; A.10.1.3
T. Abr. **3.9-12;** *T. Abr.* **6.7 (Recension A and B)** [→ *3.1.6; 1.12.a.3*

Gf.27.5 *Transformation of tear(s) into fountain(s)*

(1) Two tears falling from the eyes of Jeremiah become two fountains.
see Sa.2.3.31; Sa.24.3.31; If.26.1.3
GL 6, 405 n.47 [→ *4.2.c.3*

H. THE NOSE

H.1 *Absence of Nose*

(1) The Neshiah, the fifth earth, is inhabited by dwarfs without noses.
see A.6.2.3
GL 1, 114; GL 5, 143 n.36   [→ *1.1.a.19; 3.2.4*

H.14. *Unusual Protuberances or Protusions on Nose*

H.14.10. *Body(ies) on nose*

(1) While Adam is still a lifeless mass, God shows him the righteous people who descend from him: some hang on Adam's nose, others on his mouth, ears, earlobes, forehead, head, hair and eyes.
see Cb.9.1.1; F.5.1.1; A.9.1.2; R.14.1.1; R.18.1.1; A.6.1.19; A.6.1.20;
A.6.3.4; A.6.5.20; A.6.5.21; A.13.10.1; B.13.1.1; A.10.1.9; A.10.1.10;
Sa.2.3.3; Sa.24.3.3; A.16.9.1; Ca.9.1.1; Cb.5.1.1; G.23.5.1; J.23.1.1; A.4.1.1;
D.14.10.1; E.14.10.1; Fb.14.10.1; G.14.10.1; A.12.1.1; I.14.10.1; J.14.10.1;
Ja.14.10.1
Exod. R. 40.3   [→ *2.4.3*

H.15. *Abnormal Puncture or Opening in Nose*

H.15.1. *Pierced nose*

(1) Rebecca's nose is pierced by a nose-ring which Abraham's servants give her.
Gen. 24.22, 47   [→ *2.26.a.1*

Ha. *The Nostril(s)*

Ha.23. *Disease or Malfunction of Nostril(s)*

Ha.23.1. *Closed-up nostril*

(1) The nostrils of the Philistines and their beasts and all the other

apertures of their bodies are closed up when King Abimelech takes
Sarah as a wife.

see Ga.23.2.1; I.23.4.1; J.23.2.1; Ra.23.1.1; Sa.23.2.1; Sb.23.2.1
GL 1, 258; GL 5, 243, n.190; GL 5, 244 n.202   [→ *2.10.a.2*

I. THE MOUTH

I.3. *Vital Mouth*

(1) A physician who has recommended a milk cure for the Persian king has a dream in which his mouth, eyes, tongue, feet and hands quarrel with one another, each claiming the greatest credit in procuring the remedy for the king.

    see G.3.1.1; Ib.3.1.1; P.3.1.1; U.3.1.1

    GL 4, 174; GL 6, 302 n.97   [→ *2.5.13*

I.5. *Unusual Number of Mouths*

I.5.14. *Over one million mouths*

(1) The angel Sandalfon has 4,900,000,000 mouths (70,000 mouths in each of his 70,000 heads).

    see A.6.5.11; D.5.13.1; Ib.5.14.1

    3 En. **1.7-8;** *1 En.* **71.1-7**   [→ *2.22.a.4*

I.6. *Abnormal Size of Mouth*

I.6.1. *Abnormally large mouth*

(1) The Antichrist's mouth is one cubit in size, his teeth are a span long, his feet two span; his fingers are like scythes, his right eye like the rising morning star and his left eye fixed, while on his forehead is the inscription 'Antichrist'.

    see Ic.6.5.1; Fb.13.2.2; G.10.2.5; G.23.3.1; Pc.12.1.1; Pc.12.2.1; U.6.5.1

    Gk Apoc. Ezra **4.29f.**   [→ *3.1.24*

I.10. *Unusual Emission or Emanation from Mouth*

I.10.1. *Emission of fire from mouth*

(1) The holy Hayyot breathe fire.

see Ba.16.4.2
Gen. R. **78.1** [→ *1.12.a.3*

(2) The angels of terror have a fiery breath.
 GL 3, 112; GL 6, 46 n.247 [→ *2.24.6; 2.19.b.1*

(3) Flames and lightnings issue from the mouths of Soperi'el and Soperi-el, two princes of angels, and fire is kindled from their sweat. They have long tongues like blazing torches, lips like the gates of the east, and they are as tall as the seven heavens, with bodies full of eyes, and wings as numerous as the days in the year.
 see I.10.5.2; Ib.6.5.1; Ib.16.12.2; A.6.5.4; Ba.16.4.1; G.4.1.2; G.5.15.3; G.16.12.1; M.14.2.15; M.20.1.15
 3 En. **18.25** [→ *3.3.a.6*

(4) Aaron's mouth emits flames when he opens it to speak.
 see A.6.5.26; E.6.1.2; E.12.10.2; F.10.1.12; Ga.10.2.2; A.23.1.8; A.6.2.4
 GL 2, 332; GL 5, 425 n.157 [→ *3.3.a.30*

(5) Moses' mouth emits flames when he opens it to speak, and darts of fire shoot from it when he writes down the Ineffable Name shortly before his death.
 see F.10.1.11; Sa.2.3.19; Sa.24.3.19; A.6.5.25; A.6.4.2; P.23.1.1; P.25.4.1; A.25.9.1; G.10.2.9; F.11.3.2; Fb.10.1.1; G.25.4.1; If.6.1.3; Fb.14.2.3; I.23.3.3; P.11.2.2; G.17.20.1; Ib.13.2.1; Ib.24.4.1; Ia.24.4.1; E.6.1.1; Ga.10.2.1; E.12.10.1; P.13.2.1; P.24.4.1; K.13.10.2; B.16.12.2; Ib.16.12.3; Ia.13.2.1; A.26.1.3
 Deut. R. **11.10; GL 2, 332; GL 5, 425 n.157; GL 3, 467; GL 6, 160 n.947** [→ *3.3.a.30; 2.24.12*

(6) Fire streams from the mouth, lips and tongue of the Messiah: this fire burns up a multitude so that only dust, ashes and smoke remain.
 see Ia.10.1.6; Ib.10.1.1
 4 Ezra **13.4, 10-11, 37-39** [→ *2.15.a.14; 2.10.a.4*

I.10.4. *Emission of blood from mouth*

(1) Noah coughs up blood while in the ark as a result of the cold.
 see A.11.2.6; A.11.3.2; G.10.2.7; Sa.2.3.6; Sa.24.3.6; Sa.2.1.1; T.23.1.1; E.11.2.1; Sa.24.10.1; Va.24.1.1; If.26.1.1; B.11.2.1; B.11.3.2; Sa.24.2.1
 Gen. R. **32.10** [→ *1.17.1*

I.10.5. *Emission of lightning or thunder from mouth*

(1) Thunder and lightning issue from God's mouth when he pronounces the first commandment.

see E.11.2.1; A.11.2.2; A.11.3.1; D.16.3.1; E.11.1.1; E.12.3.1; F.5.10.1;
F.16.12.1; G.10.5.1; Ia.16.12.1; P.10.1.1; P.10.7.1; Pc.10.7.1; Gf.4.1.1;
A.1.1.1; Gf.27.2.1; A.10.1.1; Pc.10.3.1; If.6.1.1; A.11.2.1

Exod. R. **5.14**   [→ *3.4.a.3*

(2) Lightning and fire issue from the mouths of Soperi'el and Soperi-el, two princes of angels, and fire is also kindled from their sweat. They have long tongues like blazing torches, lips like the gates of the east, and they are as tall as the seven heavens, with bodies full of eyes, and wings as numerous as the days of the year.

see I.10.1.3; Ib.6.5.1; Ib.16.12.2; A.6.5.4; Ba.16.4.1; G.4.1.2; G.5.15.3;
G.16.12.1; M.14.2.15; M.20.1.15

3 En. **18.25**   [→ *3.3.a.6*

(3) Twelve thousand fiery lightning flashes issue from the mouth of the angel Hadarniel with every word that he speaks.

see A.6.5.6

GL 3, 110; GL 6, 46 n.247   [→ *2.22.a.7; 2.15.a.6*

I.10.10. *Unusual fragrance from mouth*

(1) The breath of the Israelites is putrid as a result of the blows they have received.

Exod. R. **5.21**   [→ *1.20.6*

I.10.20. *Emission of water or spring from mouth*

(1) Water begins to flow from Samson's mouth when he is about to perish from thirst after his first victory over the Philistines.

see E.8.1.2; E.25.5.1; A.6.1.29; Ie.17.3.1; E.6.5.4; G.24.1.2; G.1.3; U.23.1.2;
M.6.3.1; T.25.1.2; G.23.4.16

Gen. R. **98.13;** *Num. R.* **9.24; GL 4, 48; GL 6, 207 n.119**

[→ *2.32.5*

I.14. Unusual Protuberances or Protusions from Mouth

I.14.10. *Body(ies) on mouth*

(1) While Adam is still a lifeless mass, God shows him all the righteous people to descend from him: some hang on Adam's mouth, others on his ear, earlobes, head, hair, eyes and forehead.

see Cb.9.1.1; F.5.1.1; A.9.1.2; R.14.1.1; R.18.1.1; A.6.1.19; A.6.1.20;
A.6.3.4; A.6.5.20; A.6.5.21; A.13.10.1; B.13.10.1; A.10.1.9; A.10.1.10;

Sa.2.3.3; Sa.24.3.3; A.16.9.1; Ca.9.1.1; Cb.5.1.1; G.23.5.1; J.23.1.1; A.4.1.1; D.14.10.1; E.14.10.1; Fb.14.10.1; G.14.10.1; H.14.10.1; A.12.1.1; J.14.10.1; Ja.14.10.1

Exod. R. **40.3**

[→ *2.4.3*

I.16. *Mouth of Unusual Substance*

I.16.12. *Mouth of fire*

(1) The mouth of Kerubi'el, prince of the cherubim, blazes like a fiery torch, and his whole body is full of burning coals from which lightnings flash. He is as tall and wide as the seven heavens, and eyes and wings cover his body, while rays emanate from his wheels.

see A.6.3.1; A.6.5.2; A.14.5.1; A.14.10.2; A.16.17.1; A.20.1.1; F.16.12.2; G.5.15.2; G.16.12.2; Gc.16.12.1; G.4.1.3; Ib.16.12.1; P.10.3.1

3 En. **22.3-9**

[→ *3.3.a.7*

I.21. *Human Mouth on Unusual Creature*

I.21.10. *Human mouth on fabulous beast*

(1) In a vision Daniel sees a mouth 'full of boasts', and eyes on a horn which grows on a beast with great iron teeth, bronze claws and ten other horns.

see G.21.10.1

Dan. 7.7, 8, 19f.; *Gen. R.* **76.6**

[→ *4.1.a.6*

I.23. *Disease, Paralysis or Malfunction of Mouth*

I.23.2. *Paralysis of mouth*

(1) Sammael stops Joshua's mouth so that he cannot pray for Moses' life.

see F.10.1.15; A.6.5.27

GL 3, 433; GL 6, 150 n.896

[→ *2.19.b.4*

(2) Sammael stops Caleb's mouth so that he cannot pray for Moses' life.

see If.6.1.4; J.23.1.6; I.23.3.7; A.22.1.4

GL 3, 433; GL 6, 150 n.896

[→ *2.19.b.4*

(3) Sammael stops Eleazar's mouth so that he cannot pray for Moses' life.

GL 3, 433; GL 6, 150 n.896

[→ *2.19.b.4*

(4) An angel stops the mouths of Zimri and Cozbi so that they cannot cry for help.
    see A.23.6.7; W.1.1.1
    Num. R. 20.25   [→ *1.19.b.11; 2.18.b.2*

(5) Alcimus suffers a stroke, his mouth becomes obstructed, and the paralysis makes him incapable of speech.
    see A.23.6.5
    1 Macc. 9.54-56   [→ *2.22.c.4; 2.15.b.12*

(6) Theodotus, Ptolemy IV Philopator, king of Egypt, is tossed to the ground with a stroke, and becomes paralysed and unable to speak when he tries to enter the temple in Jerusalem.
    see A.23.6.6
    3 Macc. 2.22   [→ *1.26.b.51; 2.15.b.13; 1.19.b.26*

I.23.3. *Inability to speak or speech impediment*

(1) All the dumb are made to speak at the birth of Isaac.
    see G.23.4.5; T.23.1.4
    GL 1, 262; GL 5, 245 n.203   [→ *2.4.5*

(2) Judah sits deaf and dumb in the heavenly academy, unable to participate in the dispute of the learned.
    see E.13.1.2; G.10.4.1; Gf.16.3.1; Ic.18.5.1; F.18.5.3; J.23.1.2; E.8.1.1;
    Va.3.1.1; F.11.6.2; If.6.1.2; A.10.1.15
    GL 3, 456; GL 6, 155 n.922   [→ *1.26.b.14*

(3) Moses has a speech impediment.
    see F.10.1.11; Sa.2.3.19; Sa.24.3.19; A.6.5.25; A.6.4.2; P.23.1.1; P.25.4.1;
    I.10.1.5; G.10.2.9; F.11.3.2; Fb.10.1.1; G.25.4.1; If.6.1.3; Fb.14.2.3;
    A.25.9.1; P.11.2.2; G.17.20.1; Ib.13.2.1; Ib.24.4.1; Ia.24.4.1; E.6.1.1;
    Ga.10.2.1; E.12.10.1; P.13.2.1; P.24.4.1; K.13.10.2; B.16.12.2; Ib.16.12.3;
    Ia.13.2.1; A.26.1.3
    Exod. 4.10; Exod. 6.12, 30; *Exod. R.* **1.26;** *Ezek. Trag. Exagoge*
    113-115   [→ *1.14.c.10; 2.3.3; 2.6.a.8; 2.9.6; 2.20.2; 3.3.b.3;*
                                    1.14.b.6; 1.26.b.22; B.4.7.

(4) Many Israelites become dumb as a result of accidents during the building work in Egypt.
    see J.23.1.3; G.23.4.10; P.1.1.1; T.23.1.2
    Num. R. 7.1; GL 3, 13, 78; GL 6, 30 n.176   [→ *1.23.1*

(5) All the counsellors of the Pharaoh become dumb, deaf or blind,

so that they cannot tell where Moses has gone when they are ordered to pursue Moses.

see G.23.4.9; J.23.1.4

Exod. R. 1.31; *Deut. R.* 2.26-27; GL 2, 282; GL 5, 406 n.76

[→ *2.2.b.2; 2.19.b.3; 2.22.c.3*

(6) Balaam is unable to speak when he wants to curse Israel.

see If.6.1.5; U.23.1.1; G.23.4.12; Va.27.1.1; G.5.1.2; G.1.2

GL 3, 372; GL 6, 130 n.762   [→ *1.32.4; 2.21.3*

(7) Caleb and Phinehas pretend to be dumb and deaf when they go as spies to Canaan so as not to arouse suspicions.

see J.23.1.6; A.22.1.4; If.6.1.4; I.23.2.2; A.1.1.6

GL 6, 171 n.11   [→ *2.6.a.9; 2.9.7*

(8) Yahweh causes Ezekiel to be struck dumb (literally, Ezekiel's tongue sticks to the roof of his mouth) so that he will stop warning the Israelites and only speak as Yahweh's mouthpiece.

see Ib.23.2.1

Ezek. 3.26-27; *Ezek.* 24.27; *Ezek.* 33.22   [→ *2.10.b.1; 1.19.b.21*

(9) Amos has a speech impediment: he stammers.

Lev. R. 10.2; *Qoh. R.* 1.1 §2   [→ *3.3.b.3; 4.2.d.4*

(10) A deaf-mute points with one hand to his eye and with the other to a staple on the bolt of a door. Since 'eye' and 'spring' are the same word in Aramaic, as are 'staple' and 'spring', Mordecai understands that he means a place called En Soker, 'Dry Well'.

see J.23.1.8

GL 4, 383; GL 6, 459 n.63   [→ *4.1.b.26; 2.2.c.8*

(11) A deaf-mute points to a roof and a cottage, and Mordecai, who understands the language of the deaf-mute, realizes that these signs indicate a locality by the name of 'Cottage-roofs' and grain is found there for the Omer offering.

see J.23.1.7

GL 4, 383; GL 6, 459 n.63   [→ *4.1.b.26; 2.2.c.8*

(12) Children are made dumb, deaf and blind, and their ears are turned around backward while they are still in the womb by a demon in the form of a three-headed dragon with an awful skin.

see J.7.1.1; J.23.1.9; G.23.4.27

T. Sol. 12.1-2   [→ *1.19.b.24*

I.23.4. *Mouth closed up*

(1) The mouths and all the other apertures of the bodies of the Philistines and their beasts are closed up when King Abimelech takes Sarah as a wife.

see Ga.23.2.1; Ha.23.1.1; J.23.2.1; Ra.23.1.1; Sa.23.2.1; Sb.23.2.1
GL 1, 258; GL 5, 243 n.190; GL 5, 244 n.202   [→ *2.10.a.2*

Ia. *The Lip(s)*

Ia.10. *Unusual Emission or Emanation from Lip(s)*

Ia.10.1. *Emission of fire from lip(s)*

(1) Fire issues from the lips of the two angels Raguil and Samuil, who take Enoch to heaven.

see F.10.1.4; P.11.2.1; A.6.5.5; G.10.1.2; M.14.2.4; M.20.1.4
2 En. **1.4-6 (J and A);** *2 En.* **3.1-3 (J and A);** *2 En.* **33.6 (J and A)**
                                                    [→ *3.3.a.14*

(2) Fire streams from the lips, mouth and tongue of the Messiah.

see I.10.1.6; Ib.10.1.1
4 Ezra **13.4, 10-11, 37-39**   [→ *2.15.a.14; 2.10.a.4*

Ia.11. *Unusual Colour of Lip(s)*

Ia.11.3. *Unusually red lip(s)*

(1) Aseneth's lips (which had paled and cracked through fasting) become like the rose of life after she eats from the honeycomb, while her cheeks become red like blood, her face like the sun, her eyes like the rising morning star, and her teeth, hair, neck and bones become as strong as cypresses or cedars.

see F.10.1.10; G.10.2.8; Fa.11.3.1; G.11.3.2; E.22.1.2; Ia.15.1.1; A.6.4.1;
Ba.11.3.1
Jos. Asen. **16.16;** *Jos. Asen.* **18.7;** *Jos. Asen.* **20.6**   [→ *1.14.d.2*

Ia.12. *Unusual Shape of Lip(s)*

Ia.12.1. *Misshapen lip(s)*

(1) Ham's descendants have misshapen lips.

see E.12.3.2; G.11.3.1; A.11.1.3; B.11.1.2
GL 1, 169; GL 5, 191-192 n.60, 61   [→ *1.7.a.2*

Ia.13. *Peculiarity of Skin of Lip(s)*

Ia.13.2. *Burnt lip(s)*

(1) Moses' lips are partly burnt by a burning coal which he grasps and puts to his mouth.

see F.10.1.11; Sa.2.3.19; Sa.24.3.19; A.6.5.25; A.6.4.2; P.23.1.1; P.25.4.1; I.10.1.5; G.10.2.9; F.11.3.2; Fb.10.1.1; G.25.4.1; If.6.1.3; Fb.14.2.3; I.23.3.3; P.11.2.2; G.17.20.1; Ib.13.2.1; Ib.24.4.1; Ia.24.4.1; E.6.1.1; Ga.10.2.1; E.12.10.1; P.13.2.1; P.24.4.1; K.13.10.2; B.16.12.2; Ib.16.12.3; A.25.9.1; A.26.1.3

Exod. R. **1.26**   [→ *1.14.c.10; 2.3.3; 2.6.a.8; 2.9.6; 2.20.2*

(2) Isaiah's lips are burnt by a live coal which a seraph has taken from the altar and touched him with.

Isa. **6.6-7**   [→ *2.31.b.4*

Ia.15. *Abnormal Opening or Puncture in Lip(s)*

Ia.15.1. *Cracked lip(s)*

(1) Aseneth's lips are cracked after seven days of fasting, while her eyes become inflamed, her hair scraggly, her face fallen, and her body emaciated.

see A.6.4.1; E.22.1.2; G.11.3.2; Ba.11.3.1; F.10.1.10; Fa.11.3.1; G.10.2.8; Ia.11.3.1

Jos. Asen. **11.1.1;** *Jos. Asen.* **13.9.8;** *Jos. Asen.* **18.3**
          [→ *1.13.3; 2.31.b.2*

Ia.16. *Lip(s) of Unusual Substance*

Ia.16.12. *Lip(s) of fire*

(1) God's lips are a furnace of fire. His angels, or, in a variant, his words, are the flames issuing from them.

see E.11.2.1; A.11.2.2; A.11.3.1; D.16.3.1; E.11.1.1; E.12.3.1; F.5.10.1; F.16.12.1; G.10.5.1; A.11.2.1; P.10.1.1; P.10.7.1; Pc.10.7.1; Gf.4.1.1; A.1.1.1; Gf.27.2.1; A.10.1.1; Pc.10.3.1; I.10.5.1; If.6.1.1

2 En. **39.3 (A);** *2 En.* **39.5 (J)**   [→ *3.4.a.2*

Ia.23. *Disease, Paralysis or Malfunction of Lip(s)*

Ia.23.3. *Sealed lip(s)*

(1) The lips of those who have devotedly worshipped the golden calf become tightly sealed, 'like gold'.

GL 6, 54-55 n.281   [→ *1.26.a.9*

(2) Idolaters are unable to open their lips after drinking the water that Samuel gives them.

GL 4, 64; GL 6, 225-226 n.40   [→ *2.6.b.8; 1.14.d.4*

Ia.24. *Wounded or Mutilated Lip(s)*

Ia.24.4. *Burnt lip(s)*

(1) Moses' lips are partly burnt by a burning coal which he grasps and puts to his mouth.

> see F.10.1.11; Sa.2.3.19; Sa.24.3.19; A.6.5.25; A.6.4.2; P.23.1.1; P.25.4.1;
> I.10.1.5; G.10.2.9; F.11.3.2; Fb.10.1.1; G.25.4.1; If.6.1.3; Fb.14.2.3;
> I.23.3.3; P.11.2.2; G.17.20.1; Ib.13.2.1; Ib.24.4.1; A.25.9.1; E.6.1.1;
> Ga.10.2.1; E.12.10.1; P.13.2.1; P.24.4.1; K.13.10.2; B.16.12.2; Ib.16.12.3;
> Ia.13.2.1; A.26.1.3
> *Exod. R.* **1.26**   [→ *1.14.c.10; 2.3.3; 2.6.a.8; 2.9.6; 2.20.2*

Ib. *The Tongue*

Ib.1. *Absence of Tongue*

(1) The tongues of those who wanted the golden calf made are cut off when they drink the water into which they are thrown. Alternatively, their tongues drop off when they drink the water into which the broken calf has been thrown.

> see Ib.24.1.1
> **Ps-Philo 12.7; GL 6, 55 n.281**   [→ *1.26.a.10; 2.6.b.5*

(2) Nebuchadnezzar's tongue is taken from him when he is reduced to living like a beast.

> see A.27.2.3; Cc.27.4.1; Cc.27.1.1; A.6.2.5; Pd.6.5.1; Pd.12.1.1; E.6.5.6;
> A.2.4.1; T.24.3.1; U.23.1.4
> *Liv. Proph. (Daniel)* **4.10**   [→ *2.23.b.3; 1.26.b.52*

(3) Eliezer, his six brothers, and his mother are tortured by having their tongues cut out, their heads scalped, their extremities cut off and their pupils pierced, by King Antiochus Epiphanes, to make them taste pig's flesh.

see D.2.2.1; P.1.1.2; U.1.1.1; Ga.24.1.1

2 Macc. 7; *4 Macc.* 6.6,25; *4 Macc.* 7.13-14; *4 Macc.* 11.18-19; *4 Macc.* 9.28; *4 Macc.* 10.5-8,17-21; *4 Macc.* 18.21

[→ *2.5.12; 2.25.a.2; 1.24.4*

Ib.3. *Vital Tongue*

(1) A physician who has recommended a milk cure for the Persian king has a dream in which his tongue, mouth, eyes, feet and hands quarrel with one another, each claiming the greatest credit in procuring the remedy for the king.

see G.3.1.1; I.3.1.1; P.3.1.1; U.3.1.1

GL 4, 174; GL 6, 302 n.97   [→ *2.5.13*

Ib.5. *Unusual Number of Tongues*

Ib.5.14. *Over one million tongues*

(1) The angel Sandalfon has three hundred and forty-three billion tongues (70,000 tongues in each of his 70,000 mouths in each of his 70,000 heads) and each tongue has as many sayings.

see A.6.5.11; D.5.13.1; I.5.14.1

3 En. 1.78; *1 En.* 71.1-7   [→ *2.22.a.4*

Ib.6. *Abnormal Size of Tongue*

Ib.6.5. *Abnormally long tongue*

(1) Soperi'el and Soperi-el, two princes of angels, have tongues like blazing torches as long as the sea's waves, lips like the gates of the east; flames and lightnings issue from their mouths, fire is kindled from their sweat, and they are as tall as the seven heavens, with bodies full of eyes, and wings as numerous as the days of the year.

see Ib.16.12.2; I.10.1.3; I.10.5.2; A.6.5.4; Ba.16.4.1; G.4.1.2; G.5.15.3; G.16.12.1; M.14.2.15; M.20.1.15

3 En. 18.25   [→ *3.3.a.6*

(2) The tongues of the spies who have tried to dissuade the Israelites from entering Canaan are stretched to such a length that they touch their navels (and worms crawl out of their tongues and pierce their navels).

see Ib.23.20.1; Qa.15.1.1
GL 3, 283; GL 6, 98 n.552 [→ *1.26.b.31*

Ib.10. *Unusual Emission or Emanation from Tongue*

Ib.10.1. *Emission of fire from tongue*

(1) Fire streams from the tongue, lips and mouth of the Messiah.
see I.10.1.6; Ia.10.1.2
4 Ezra 13.4, 10-11, 37-39 [→ *2.15.a.14; 2.10.a.4*

Ib.13 *Peculiarity of Skin of Tongue*

Ib.13.2 *Burnt tongue*

(1) Moses' tongue is partly burnt by a burning coal which he grasps and puts to his mouth.
see F.10.1.11; Sa.2.3.19; Sa.24.3.19; A.6.5.25; A.6.4.2; P.23.1.1; P.25.4.1; I.10.1.5; G.10.2.9; F.11.3.2; Fb.10.1.1; G.25.4.1; If.6.1.3; Fb.14.2.3; I.23.3.3; P.11.2.2; G.17.20.1; A.25.9.1; Ib.24.4.1; Ia.24.4.1; E.6.1.1; Ga.10.2.1; E.12.10.1; P.13.2.1; P.24.4.1; K.13.10.2; B.16.12.2; Ib.16.12.3; Ia.13.2.1; A.26.1.3
Exod. R. 1.26 [→ *1.14.c.10; 2.3.3; 2.6.a.8; 2.9.6; 2.20.2*

Ib.16. *Tongue of Unusual Substance*

Ib.16.12. *Tongue of fire*

(1) The tongue of Kerubi'el, the prince of the cherubim, is a consuming fire, as are his face, eyes and mouth. His body is made of burning coals and he is covered with eyes and wings, while rays emanate from his wheels.
see A.6.3.1; A.6.5.2; A.14.5.1; A.14.10.2; A.16.17.1; A.20.1.1; F.16.12.2; G.5.15.2; G.16.12.2; Gc.16.12.1; I.16.12.1; G.4.1.3; P.10.3.1
3 En. 22.3-9 [→ *3.3.a.7*

(2) Soperi'el and Soperi-el, two princes of angels, have tongues like blazing torches as high as the sea's waves, lips like the gates of the east, while flames and lightnings issue from their mouths and fire is

kindled from their sweat. They are as tall as the seven heavens, with
bodies full of eyes, and wings as numerous as the days of the year.
   see Ib.6.5.1; I.10.1.3; I.10.5.2; A.6.5.4; Ba.16.4.1; G.4.1.2; G.5.15.3;
   G.16.12.1; M.14.2.15; M.20.1.15
   3 En. 18.25
                                              [→ *3.3.a.6*

(3) Moses' tongue is changed into a flame by Metatron (and his
strength changed into an angel's).
   see F.10.1.11; Sa.2.3.19; Sa.24.3.19; A.6.5.25; A.6.4.2; P.23.1.1; P.25.4.1;
   I.10.1.5; G.10.2.9; F.11.3.2; Fb.10.1.1; G.25.4.1; If.6.1.3; Fb.14.2.3;
   I.23.3.3; P.11.2.2; G.17.20.1; Ib.13.2.1; Ib.24.4.1; Ia.24.4.1; E.6.1.1;
   Ga.10.2.1; E.12.10.1; P.13.2.1; P.24.4.1; K.13.10.2; B.16.12.2; A.25.9.1;
   Ia.13.2.1; A.26.1.3
   GL 2, 306; GL 5, 416-418 n.117
                                              [→ *2.15.b.9*

Ib.21. *Human Tongue on Unusual Creature*

Ib.21.6. *Serpent with human tongue*

(1) The serpent has a tongue and the power of speech (as well as
hands, feet, wings and ears) before he slanders God, his creator.
   see P.21.6.2; U.21.6.3; J.21.6.1
   Deut. R. 5.10; *LAE (Vita)* 38.1   [→ *3.3.a.44; 1.16.a.6*

Ib.23. *Disease, Paralysis or Malfunction of Tongue*

Ib.23.2. *Paralysis of tongue*

(1) Yahweh makes Ezekiel's tongue stick to the roof of his mouth so
that he will stop warning the Israelites and only speak as the mouthpiece of Yahweh.
   see I.23.3.8
   Ezek. 3.26-27; Ezek. 24.27; Ezek. 33.22   [→ *2.10.b.1; 1.19.b.21*

Ib.23.20. *Worm-infested tongue*

(1) Worms crawl from the tongues of the spies who have tried to dissuade the Israelites from entering the land of Canaan.
   see Ib.6.5.2; Qa.15.1.1
   GL 3, 283; GL 6, 98 n.552   [→ *1.26.b.31*

Ib.24. *Wounded or Mutilated Tongue*

Ib.24.1. *Severed tongue*

(1) The tongues of those who wanted the golden calf made are cut off

when they drink the water into which they are thrown (or, alternatively, into which the broken calf has been thrown).

see Ib.1.1.1; Ia.23.3.1

Ps-Philo 12.7; GL 6, 55 n.281   [→ *1.26.a.10; 2.6.b.5*

Ib.24.4. *Burnt tongue*

(1) Moses' tongue is partly burnt by a burning coal which he grasps and puts to his mouth.

see F.10.1.11; Sa.2.3.19; Sa.24.3.19; A.6.5.25; A.6.4.2; P.23.1.1; P.25.4.1; I.10.1.5; G.10.2.9; F.11.3.2; Fb.10.1.1; G.25.4.1; If.6.1.3; Fb.14.2.3; I.23.3.3; P.11.2.2; G.17.20.1; Ib.13.2.1; A.25.9.1; Ia.24.4.1; E.6.1.1; Ga.10.2.1; E.12.10.1; P.13.2.1; P.24.4.1; K.13.10.2; B.16.12.2; Ib.16.12.2; Ia.13.2.1; A.26.1.3

Exod. R. 1.26   [→ *1.14.c.10; 2.3.3; 2.6.a.8; 2.9.6; 2.20.2*

Ic. *The Tooth/Teeth*

Ic.1. *Absence of Tooth/Teeth*

(1) Joseph's three hundred heroes lose their teeth at the sound of Judah's outcry, and their heads remain fixed facing backwards, as they have turned to discover the cause of the tumult.

see D.7.1.1; D.23.6.1

Gen. R. 93.7; **GL 2, 106, 112; GL 5, 354-355 n.275, 281**
                    [→ *1.14.b.3*

(2) The teeth of Simon's assailants are knocked out when they fall to the ground upon hearing his loud cry.

GL 2, 86; GL 5, 348 n.218   [→ *1.14.b.2*

Ic.2. *Partial Absence of Tooth/Teeth*

Ic.2.8. *Absence of tooth or part of tooth*

(1) Eliezer, also known as the giant Og, loses a tooth when Abraham shouts at him.

see Ic.5.11.1; Ic.6.5.2; Ic.7.2.1; Ic.7.3.1; Sa.2.3.2; Sa.24.3.2; A.6.5.2; A.6.3.19; Va.6.5.1; U.6.5.3; A.6.1.16

GL 3, 344; GL 6, 119 n.688, 689   [→ *1.12.a.5*

Ic.5. *Unusual Number of Tooth/Teeth*

Ic.5.11. *Between eleven and thirty-one teeth*

(1) Eliezer, also known as the giant Og, loses a tooth when Abraham shouts at him, leaving only 31.

> see Ic.2.8.1; Ic.6.5.2; Ic.7.2.1; Ic.7.3.1; Sa.2.3.2; Sa.24.3.2; A.6.5.19; A.6.3.3; Va.6.5.1; U.6.5.3; A.6.1.16
> **GL 3, 344; GL 6, 119 n.688, 689** [→ *1.12.a.5*

Ic.6 *Abnormal Size of Tooth/Teeth*

Ic.6.5 *Abnormally Long Tooth/Teeth*

(1) The Antichrist's teeth are a span long, his mouth is one cubit in size, his feet two span; his fingers are like scythes, his right eye is like the rising morning star, his left eye unmoving, while on his forehead is the inscription 'Antichrist'.

> see I.6.1.1; Fb.13.2.2; G.10.2.5; G.23.3.1; Pc.12.1.1; Pc.12.2.1; U.6.5.1
> *Gk Apoc. Ezra* **4.29f.** [→ *3.1.24*

(2) The teeth of the giant Og are sixty cubits long.

> see Ic.5.11.1; Ic.7.2.1; Ic.7.3.1; Sa.2.3.2; Sa.24.3.2; A.6.5.19; A.6.3.3; Va.6.5.1; U.6.5.3; A.6.1.16; Ic.2.8.1
> **GL 6, 120 n.695** [→ *1.1.a.15*

(3) The teeth of the sinners in hell grow to the length of one parasang during the night.

> see Ic.25.1.1; Ic.24.1.1; B.23.20.2; G.13.10.1
> **GL 2, 312; GL 5, 418-419 n.118**
> [→ *1.19.b.25; 2.22.b.7; 1.26.a.14; 1.26.b.65*

Ic.7. *Tooth/Teeth Facing Unusual Direction*

Ic.7.2. *Tooth/teeth facing right*

(1) The teeth of the giant Og are pushed out and extend to the left and right, so that Og is unable to throw a mountain at the Israelites.

> see Ic.5.11.1; Ic.7.3.1; Ic.6.5.1; Sa.2.3.2; Sa.24.3.2; A.6.5.19; A.6.3.3; Va.6.5.1; U.6.5.3; A.6.1.16; Ic.2.8.1
> **GL 3, 346; GL 6, 120 n.695, 696** [→ *2.16.1*

Ic.7.3 *Tooth/teeth facing left*

(1) The teeth of the giant Og are pushed out and extend to the left and right, so that Og is unable to throw a mountain at the Israelites.

> see Ic.5.11.1; Ic.7.2.1; Ic.6.5.1; Sa.2.3.2; Sa.24.3.2; A.6.5.19; A.6.3.3;

Va.6.5.1; U.6.5.3; A.6.1.16; Ic.2.8.1
GL 3, 346; GL 6, 120 n.695, 696   [→ *2.16.1*

Ic.11. *Unusual Colour of Tooth/Teeth*

Ic.11.2. *Abnormally white teeth*

(1) The Messiah's teeth are whiter than milk.
see G.11.11.1
GL 2, 143; GL 5, 367 n.388   [→ *1.13.7*

Ic.16. *Tooth/Teeth of Unusual Substance*

Ic.16.1. *Iron teeth*

(1) The lower teeth of the Antichrist are made of iron, his lower jaw of diamond. His right arm is made of iron, his left of copper. He is ten cubits tall, and his feet and right hand measure three cubits. His hair reaches to his feet and he is three-crested. His eyes are like the rising morning star, his right eye like a lion's. He is long-faced, long-nosed and disorderly, with three letters written on his forehead: A, K and T, signifying denial, rejection and the befouled dragon. His mother conceives him by touching the head of a fish.
see A.6.5.13; E.6.5.1; Fb.13.2.3; Fc.16.5.1; G.10.2.6; G.18.1.1; O.16.1.1; O.16.2.3; U.6.5.2
Apoc. Dan. **9.11, 16-26**   [→ *3.1.25; 1.3.c.1*

Ic.18. *Animal Tooth/Teeth in Place of Human*

Ic.18.1. *Tusk(s)*

(1) The ugly angels, who carry off the souls of ungodly men, have tusks like those of a wild boar, their faces are like those of a leopard, their eyes are mixed with blood, and their hair is loose like the hair of women.
see F.18.9.1; W.4.1.1; E.9.5.1
Apoc. Zeph. **4.2-4;** *Apoc. Zeph.* **6.8**   [→ *2.24.9*

Ic.18.2 *Fang(s)*

(1) The guards of the gates of hell have fangs exposed down to their breasts, faces like very large snakes, eyes aflame or eyes like extinguished lamps, and they stand large as serpents.

see A.6.1.2; F.18.6.1; G.16.12.6
2 En. **42.1** (J and A); *2 En.* **42.1** (Appendix) [→ *2.24.7; 2.22.a.10*

Ic.18.5. *Lion's tooth/teeth or tooth/teeth with lion attributes*

(1) When Judah attacks the army of Nineveh his teeth and face are like a lion's.

see E.13.1.2; G.10.4.1; Gf.16.3.1; E.8.1.1; F.18.5.3; J.23.1.2; I.23.3.2; Va.3.1.1; F.11.6.2; If.6.1.2; A.10.1.15
GL 1, 404-406; GL 5, 314 n.291   [→ *1.12.a.20*

Ic.23. *Disease, Paralysis or Malfunction of Tooth/Teeth*

Ic.23.1. *Toothache*

(1) Judah the Patriarch has toothache for thirteen years as a punishment for not having sympathy for a heifer going to slaughter.
Gen. R. **33.3**   [→ *1.26.b.19*

Ic.24. *Mutilated Tooth/Teeth*

Ic.24.1. *Broken tooth/teeth*

(1) The teeth of the sinners in hell are broken by the Angels of Destruction with fiery stones from morning until evening.
see Ic.25.1.1; B.23.20.2; Ic.6.5.3; G.13.10.1
GL 2, 312; GL 5, 418-419 n.118   [→ *1.26.b.65; 1.26.a.14*

Ic.25. *Unusual Abilities of Tooth/Teeth*

Ic.25.1. *Tooth/teeth that regrows when broken*

(1) The teeth of the sinners in hell regrow to the length of one parasang during the night.
see Ic.24.1.1; B.23.20.2; Ic.6.5.3; G.13.10.1
GL 2, 312; GL 5, 418-419 n.118
                    [→ *1.19.b.25; 2.22.b.7; 1.26.a.14; 1.26.b.65*

Ic.26. *Tooth/Teeth of Different Age Group*

Ic.26.1. *Child born with teeth*

(1) Esau is born with teeth, hair and a beard.
see A.13.6.3; B.18.3.1; E.4.1.3; O.13.6.1; P.13.6.1; B.11.3.1; B.13.6.3;

E.26.1.1; A.11.3.3; Sa.2.3.4; Sa.24.3.4; A.13.1.1; B.13.1.1
GL 1, 315; GL 5, 273 n.23   [→ *3.10.16*

Id. *The Tonsil(s)*

[No reference in sources]

Ie. *The Spittle*

Ie.17. Substitution for Spittle

Ie.17.3. *Water in place of spittle*

(1) Water begins to flow from Samson's mouth, as from a spring, when Samson is about to perish from thirst after his first victory over the Philistines.

see E.8.1.2; E.25.5.1; A.6.1.29; E.6.5.4; I.10.20.1; G.24.1.2; G.1.3; U.23.1.2; M.6.3.1; T.25.1.2; G.23.4.16
GL 4, 48; GL 6, 207 n.119   [→ *2.32.5*

Ie.27 *Transformation of Spittle*

Ie.27.1 *Transformation of spittle to blood*

(1) The spittle from the Egyptians' mouths turns to blood as soon as it is ejected.

see W.4.2.2; B.24.3.1; B.23.2.4; B.24.3.2; B.23.1.1; P.23.1.2; Sa.24.2.7; B.24.4.2; Sa.2.1.7; A.23.3.1; A.23.6.1
Exod. R. 9.10-11   [→ *1.26.b.24; 2.5.8; 2.24.13*

If. *The Voice*

If.6.1. Abnormally Loud Voice

(1) God's voice reverberates throughout the world.

see E.11.2.1; A.11.2.2; A.11.3.1; D.16.3.1; E.11.1.1; E.12.3.1; F.5.10.1; F.16.12.1; G.10.5.1; Ia.16.12.1; P.10.1.1; P.10.7.1; Pc.10.7.1; Gf.4.1.1; A.1.1.1; Gf.27.2.1; A.10.1.1; Pc.10.3.1; I.10.5.1; A.11.2.1
Exod. R. 5.9   [→ *3.3.a.1*

(2) Judah's roar, when Joseph seizes Benjamin, travels 400 parasangs until Hushim, son of Dan, hears it and goes to help him.

see E.13.1.2; G.10.4.1; Gf.16.3.1; Ic.18.5.1; F.18.5.3; J.23.1.2; I.23.3.2; Va.3.1.1; F.11.6.2; E.8.1.1; A.10.1.15
Gen. R. 93.7   [→ *2.19.a.5*

(3) Moses' voice is of supernatural strength: it carries for twelve miles, from the house of study to the end of the camp of the Israelites.

see F.10.1.11; Sa.2.3.19; Sa.24.3.19; A.6.5.25; A.6.4.2; P.23.1.1; P.25.4.1;
I.10.1.5; G.10.2.9; F.11.3.2; Fb.10.1.1; G.25.4.1; A.25.9.1; Fb.14.2.3;
I.23.3.3; P.11.2.2; G.17.20.1; Ib.13.2.1; Ib.24.4.1; Ia.24.4.1; E.6.1.1;
Ga.10.2.1; E.12.10.1; P.13.2.1; P.24.4.1; K.13.10.2; B.16.12.2; Ib.16.12.3;
Ia.13.2.1; A.26.1.3
    GL 6, 95 n.521   [→ *3.3.a.41*

(4) Caleb's voice is so powerful it can be heard twelve miles away
and makes the three giants Ahiman, Sheshai and Talmai fall down in a
swoon.
    see I.23.2.2; J.23.1.6; I.23.3.7; A.22.1.1
    GL 3, 273-274; GL 6, 95-96 n.527   [→ *3.4.a.7*

(5) Balaam's voice is so powerful it carries as far as sixty miles.
    see A.25.15.1; U.23.1.1; G.23.4.12; I.23.3.6; Va.27.1.1; G.1.2; G.5.1.2
    GL 6, 133 n.781   [→ *3.4.a.6*

If.21. *Human Voice from Unusual Creature*

If.21.1. *Human voice from idol*

(1) An idol speaks, saying 'I am thy God' when Nebuchadnezzar
places a golden diadem in its mouth, on which is inscribed the holy
name.
    see A.16.20.2
    Cant. R. **7.9 §1**   [→ *1.11.a.1*

If.21.2. *Voice from fire or flame*

(1) God's voice is heard from a fire.
    Deut. 4.12, 15, 33, 36   [→ *2.7.1*

If.21.10. *Voice from vegetation*

(1) Ezra hears a voice from a thorn-bush which admonishes him to
guard in his heart the secrets revealed to him.
    GL 4, 357; GL 6, 445 n.50   [→ *2.2.c.12*

If.26. *Voice of Different Age Group*

If.26.1. *Child speaks coherently from birth*

(1) Noah rises from the hands of the midwife and blesses the Lord of
Heaven.
    see A.11.2.5; A.11.3.2; G.10.2.7; Sa.2.3.6; Sa.24.3.6; Sa.2.1.1; T.23.1.1;

I.10.4.1; Sa.24.10.1; Va.24.1.1; E.11.2.1; B.11.2.1; B.11.3.2; Sa.24.2.1
1 En. **106.3, 10** [→ *3.10.17*

(2) Moses' voice is like a child's though he is only a baby.

see F.10.1.11; Sa.2.3.19; Sa.24.3.19; A.6.5.25; A.6.4.2; P.23.1.1; P.25.4.1;
I.10.1.5; G.10.2.9; F.11.3.2; Fb.10.1.1; G.25.4.1; If.6.1.3; Fb.14.2.3;
I.23.3.3; P.11.2.2; G.17.20.1; Ib.13.2.1; Ib.24.4.1; Ia.24.4.1; E.6.1.1;
Ga.10.2.1; E.12.10.1; P.13.2.1; P.24.4.1; K.13.10.2; B.16.12.2; Ib.16.12.3;
Ia.13.2.1; A.26.1.3
Exod. R. **1.24** [→ *3.10.12*

(3) Jeremiah speaks with the voice of a youth when he is barely out
of the womb crying 'The walls of my heart are disquieted, my limbs
quake, destruction upon destruction I bring upon earth'.

see Sa.2.3.31; Sa.24.3.31; Gf.27.5.1
GL 4, 294; GL 6, 385 n.13 [→ *3.10.13*

(4) Ben Sira, the 'son of Jeremiah', speaks immediately after his
birth.

GL 6, 401 n.42 [→ *3.10.14*

J. THE EARS

J.7. Ear(s) Facing Unusual Direction

J.7.1. Ear(s) facing backwards

(1) The ears of children are turned around backwards and they are made deaf, dumb and blind while still in the womb by a demon in the form of a three-headed dragon with awful skin.

see J.23.1.9; I.23.3.12; G.23.4.27

T. Sol. **12.1-2**   [→ *1.19b.24*

J.14. Unusual Protuberances or Protusions on Ear(s)

J.14.10. Body(ies) on ear(s)

(1) While Adam is still a lifeless mass, God shows him all the righteous people to descend from him: some hang on Adam's ears, others on his earlobes, his head, hair, mouth, eyes and forehead.

see Cb.9.1.1; F.5.1.1; A.9.1.2; R.14.1.1; R.18.1.1; A.6.1.19; A.6.1.20; A.6.3.4; A.6.5.20; A.6.5.21; A.13.10.1; B.13.10.1; A.10.1.9; A.10.1.10; Sa.2.3.3; Sa.24.3.3; A.16.9.1; Ca.9.1.1; Cb.5.1.1; G.23.5.1; J.23.1.1; A.4.1.1; D.14.10.1; E.14.10.1; Fb.14.10.1; G.14.10.1; H.14.10.1; I.14.10.1; A.12.1.1; Ja.14.10.1

Exod. R. **40.3**   [→ *2.4.3*

J.21. Human Ear(s) on Unusual Creature

J.21.6. Human ear(s) on serpent

(1) The serpent has human ears, hands, feet, and tongue, as well as wings, before the Fall.

see P.21.6.2; U.21.6.3; Ib.21.6.1

LAE (Apoc. Mos.) **26.2-3**   [→ *3.3.a.44; 3.5.a.4; 1.16.a.6*

J.23. *Disease, Paralysis or Malfunction of Ear(s)*

J.23.1. *Deafness*

(1) Adam is subjected to an affliction of the hearing, of the sight, and sixty-eight other plagues as a punishment for his sin.

see Cb.9.1.1; F.5.1.1; A.9.1.2; R.14.1.1; R.18.1.1; A.6.1.19; A.6.1.20; A.6.3.4; A.6.5.20; A.6.5.21; A.13.10.1; B.13.10.1; A.10.1.9; A.10.1.10; Sa.2.3.3; Sa.24.3.3; A.16.9.1; Ca.9.1.1; Cb.5.1.1; G.23.5.1; A.12.1.1; A.4.1.1; D.14.10.1; E.14.10.1; Fb.14.10.1; G.14.10.1; H.14.10.1; I.14.10.1; J.14.10.1; Ja.14.10.1

LAE (Apoc. Mos.) **8.2;** *LAE (Apoc. Mos.)* **5.2-4;** *LAE (Vita)* **30;**
LAE (Vita) **34.1-2**   [→ *1.26.b.2*

(2) Judah sits deaf and dumb in the heavenly academy, unable to participate in the disputes of the learned.

see E.13.1.2; G.10.4.1; Gf.16.3.1; Ic.18.5.1; F.18.5.3; E.8.1.1; I.23.3.2; Va.3.1.1; F.11.6.2; If.6.1.2; A.10.1.15
GL 3, 456; GL 6, 155 n.922   [→ *1.26.b.14*

(3) Many Israelites become deaf or otherwise incapacitated during the building work in Egypt. (But all the deaf, dumb, blind and maimed are healed in the time between the Exodus and the Revelation on Mount Sinai so that they are fit to receive the Torah.)

see I.23.3.4; G.23.4.9; P.1.1.1; T.23.1.2
Num. R. **7.1; GL 3, 78; GL 6, 30 n.176; GL 3, 13**   [→ *1.23.1*

(4) All the counsellors of the Pharaoh become deaf, dumb and blind so that they cannot tell Pharaoh where Moses has gone when they are ordered to pursue him.

see G.23.4.9; I.23.3.5
Exod. R. **1.31;** *Deut. R.* **2.26-27; GL 2, 282; GL 5, 406 n.76**
                                              [→ *2.2.b.2; 2.19.b.3; 2.22.c.3*

(5) Hushim, the son of Dan, is deaf.
GL 2, 154; GL 5, 371 n.422   [→ *4.1.b.13*

(6) Caleb and Phinehas pretend to be deaf and dumb so as not to arouse suspicion when they go as spies to Jericho.

see I.23.3.7; A.22.1.4; If.6.1.4; I.23.2.2; A.1.1.6
GL 6, 171 n.11   [→ *2.6.a.9; 2.9.7*

(7) A deaf-mute points to a roof and to a cottage, and Mordecai, who understands the language of deaf-mutes, realizes that these signs indicate a locality by the name of 'Cottage-roofs' and grain is found there for the Omer offering.

> see I.23.3.11
> **GL 4, 383; GL 6, 459 n.63**   [→ *4.1.b.26; 2.2.c.8*

(8) A deaf-mute points with one hand to his eye and with the other to a staple of a bolt on a door. Since 'eye' and 'spring' are the same word in Aramaic, as are 'staple' and 'exhaustion', Mordecai, who understands the language of deaf-mutes, realizes the man means a place called En Soker, 'Dry Well'.

> see I.23.3.10
> **GL 4, 383; GL 6, 459 n.63**   [→ *4.1.b.26; 2.2.c.8*

(9) Certain children are made deaf, dumb and blind, and their ears are turned around backwards while still in the womb by a demon in the form of a three-headed dragon with awful skin.

> see J.7.1.1; I.23.3.12; G.23.4.27
> *T. Sol.* **12.1-2**   [→ *1.19.b.24*

J.23.2 *Ear(s) closed up*

(1) The ears of the Philistines and their beasts, as well as all the other apertures of their bodies, are closed up when King Abimelech takes Sarah as a wife.

> see Ga.23.2.1; Ha.23.1.1; I.23.4.1; Ra.23.1.1; Sa.23.2.1; Sb.23.2.1
> **GL 1, 258; GL 5, 243 n.190; GL 5, 244 n.202**   [→ *2.10.a.2*

Ja *The Earlobes*

Ja.14 *Unusual Protuberances or Protusions on Earlobe(s)*

Ja.14.10 *Body(ies) on earlobe(s)*

(1) While Adam is still a lifeless mass, God shows him all the righteous people to descend from him: some hang on his earlobes and ears, others on his mouth, head, forehead, hair and eyes.

> see Cb.9.1.1; F.5.1.1; A.9.1.2; R.14.1.1; R.18.1.1; A.6.1.19; A.6.1.20; A.6.3.4; A.6.5.20; A.6.5.21; A.13.10.1; B.13.10.1; A.10.1.9; A.10.1.10; Sa.2.3.3; Sa.24.3.3; A.16.9.1; Ca.9.1.1; Cb.5.1.1; G.23.5.1; J.23.1.1; A.4.1.1; D.14.10.1; E.14.10.1; Fb.14.10.1; G.14.10.1; H.14.10.1; I.14.10.1; J.14.10.1; A.12.1.1
> *Exod. R.* **40.3**   [→ *2.4.3*

K THE NECK AND THROAT

K.13 *Peculiarity of Skin of Neck or Throat*

K.13.10 *Abnormally hard or horny neck or throat*

(1) The flesh of Jacob's neck becomes as hard as ivory (or becomes stone or marble) when Esau tries to sink his long teeth into it, so that Esau's teeth are set on edge and melt like wax.

see A.6.1.23; G.23.4.7; Ta.23.1.1; Ta.24.1.1; Sa.2.3.12; Sa.24.3.12; O.6.1.1; Q.6.1.1; K.16.5.1; T.23.1.3; G.23.5.3

Gen. R. **78.9**; *Cant. R.* **7.5** §1 [→ *2.15.b.7*

(2) Moses' neck becomes as hard as ivory or turns into marble when the executioner strikes it ten times with a sharp sword.

see F.10.1.11; Sa.2.3.19; Sa.24.3.19; A.6.5.25; A.6.4.2; P.23.1.1; P.25.4.1; I.10.1.5; G.10.2.9; F.11.3.2; Fb.10.1.1; G.25.4.1; If.6.1.3; Fb.14.2.3; I.23.3.3; P.11.2.2; G.17.20.1; Ib.13.2.1; Ib.24.4.1; Ia.24.4.1; E.6.1.1; Ga.10.2.1; E.12.10.1; P.13.2.1; P.24.4.1; A.25.9.1; B.16.12.2; Ib.16.12.3; Ia.13.2.1; A.26.1.3; K.16.5.2

Exod. R. **1.31**; *Cant. R.* **7.5** §1; *Deut. R.* **2.26-27** [→ *2.15.b.8*

K.16 *Neck or Throat of Unusual Substance*

K.16.5 *Neck or throat of stone*

(1) Jacob's neck turns to stone or marble (or becomes like ivory) so that when Esau tries to bite him, his teeth are set on edge and melt like wax.

see A.6.1.23; G.23.4.7; Ta.23.1.1; Ta.24.1.1; Sa.2.3.12; Sa.24.3.12; O.6.1.1; Q.6.1.1; K.13.10.1; T.23.1.3; G.23.5.3

Gen. R. **78.9**; *Cant. R.* **7.5** §1 [→ *2.15.b.7*

(2) Moses' neck turns to marble when the executioner strikes it, so that the sword slides off his neck and hits the executioner.

see F.10.1.11; Sa.2.3.19; Sa.24.3.19; A.6.5.25; A.6.4.2; P.23.1.1; P.25.4.1;

I.10.1.5; G.10.2.9; F.11.3.2; Fb.10.1.1; G.25.4.1; If.6.1.3; Fb.14.2.3;
I.23.3.3; P.11.2.2; G.17.20.1; Ib.13.2.1; Ib.24.4.1; Ia.24.4.1; E.6.1.1;
Ga.10.2.1; E.12.10.1; P.13.2.1; P.24.4.1; K.13.10.2; B.16.12.2; Ib.16.12.3;
Ia.13.2.1; A.26.1.3; A.25.9.1
Exod. R. **1.31;** *Deut. R.* **2.26-27;** *Cant. R.* **7.5** §1   [→ *2.15.b.8*

L THE TORSO
[No references in sources]

M. THE BACK AND THE SHOULDERS

M.1. *Absence of Back or Shoulders*

(1) Angels have no backs.
Gen. R. 49.7   [→ *1.1.a.1*

M.6. *Abnormal Size of Back or Shoulders*

M.6.3. *Abnormally wide back or shoulder(s)*

(1) Samson measures sixty ells between the shoulders.
see E.8.1.2; E.25.5.1; A.6.1.29; Ie.17.3.1; I.10.20.1; G.24.1.2; G.1.3;
U.23.1.2; E.6.5.4; T.25.1.2; G.23.4.17
GL 4, 47; GL 6, 206-207 n.114, 115   [→ *3.4.a.8*

M.14. *Unusual Protuberances or Protrusions on Back or Shoulders*

M.14.2 *Wings on shoulder(s)*

(1) Angels have wings.
see M.20.1.1
1 En. **93.12;** *Gen. R.* **65.21**   [→ *1.1.a.5*

(2) The angel Ben Nez has wings.
see M.20.1.2
GL 1, 12; GL 5, 14 n.36   [→ *2.22.a.2; 2.15.b.2*

(3) Two hundred winged angels govern the stars.
see M.20.1.3
2 En. **4.2 (J and A)**   [→ *2.22.a.6*

(4) The two angels Samuil and Raguil, who take Enoch to heaven,
have wings more glistening than gold.
see M.20.1.4; F.10.1.4; P.11.2.1; Ia.10.1.1; G.10.1.2; A.6.5.5
2 En. **1.4-6 (J and A);** *2 En.* **3.1-3 (J and A);** *2 En.* **33.6 (J and A)**
                                                      [→ *2.22.b.2; 3.3.a.14*

(5) Elijah, after his removal from earth, has wings with four beats of which he can traverse the world.

see M.20.1.5; A.22.1.1; A.9.2.1; Pc.10.7.1; A.10.1.17

GL 4, 203; GL 6, 326 n.46   [→ *2.19.a.3; 2.22.a.9*

(6) The angel Gallizur, also called Raziel, stands before the throne with outspread wings.

see M.20.1.6

GL 3, 112; GL 6, 46 n.247   [→ *2.22.a.8; 2.21.1*

(7) The angel Gabriel claps together his wings and the noise this produces is so terrific that the Assyrians give up the ghost.

see M.20.1.7

GL 6, 363 n.58; GL 4, 269   [→ *2.15.a.5*

(8) The four cherubim seen by Ezekiel (and by Enoch, who names them Hayyot) each have four wings, two of which touch each other above their heads while the other two cover their bodies.

see F.18.5.2; F.20.1.1; F.18.4.1; M.20.1.8; F.5.3.1; U.18.3.1; P.21.1.1; A.14.10.1; G.4.1.4; G.5.15.5

Ezek. 1.6, 8, 9, 11, 23, 24; Ezek. 3.13; Ezek. 11.22; Ezek. 10.5, 8, 11, 16-21; 3 *En.* 21.1-3   [→ *3.1.16*

(9) The Lord of Spirits has four wings, on which a multitude of angels stand and beneath which the righteous will dwell.

see M.20.1.9

1 En. **39.7;** *1 En.* **40.1-2**   [→ *3.3.a.15*

(10) Angels have six wings, including the angels who accompany the sun and the moon.

see M.20.1.10

2 En. **11.4-5 (J);** *2 En.* **16.7 (J and A);** *Gen. R.* **65.21**   [→ *1.1.a.3*

(11) The cherubim seen by Enoch and Abraham have six wings. (Those seen by Ezekiel have four.)

see M.20.1.11

2 En. **19.6 (A);** *2 En.* **21.1 (J);** *Apoc. Abr.* **18.3-7;** *Ques. Ezra* **(Recension A) 29**   [→ *3.1.16*

(12) The seraphim seen by Isaiah, Moses and Enoch have six wings. Those seen by Enoch and Moses also have calves' feet.

see M.20.1.12; U.18.3.2; F.10.1.1; F.6.1.2; G.10.2.2; G.4.1.4; G.5.15.5

Isa. 6.2; 2 *En.* 21.1 (J); 3 *En.* 26.9-11; 2 *En.* 20.1 (J); *Lad. Jac.*

2.15; *Ques. Ezra* (Recension A) 29; *LAE (Apoc. Mos.)* 37.3; *B H M*
5.21 (Midrash Fragments 21; HelSynPro 82); GL 6, 359 n.36; GL
2, 309; GL 5, 416-418 n.117

[→ *2.22.a.5; 2.21.2; 2.13.a.1; 2.8.1; 2.2.b.1*

(**13**) Seventy-two wings are attached to Enoch's body, thirty-six to
the left and thirty-six to the right, at his transformation into Metatron.
　　see A.6.3.2; A.6.5.12; G.5.13.2; G.10.2.3; M.20.1.13; A.16.12.6; B.16.12.1;
　　E.16.4.1; G.16.12.5; V.16.12.1; Va.16.12.1; A.10.1.7
　　3 En. 9.3; *3 En.* 42.2   [→ *1.35.2*

(**14**) Opanni'el, the prince of the ophanim, has one hundred wings on
each side of his body. He also has sixteen faces with 8,766 eyes, corresponding to the number of hours in a year, while in each pair of eyes
lightning flashes and torches blaze, consuming all who look at him.
The height of his body is a journey of 2,500 years.
　　see M.20.1.14; A.6.5.3; F.5.10.2; G.10.1.1; G.10.5.2; G.5.13.1
　　3 En. 25.2-4   [→ *3.3.a.4*

(**15**) Soperi'el and Soperi-el, two princes of angels, have wings as
numerous as the days of the year and as wide as the breadth of heaven.
They are as tall as the seven heavens, with appearances like lightning,
bodies full of eyes, eyes like the sun, lips like the gates of the east,
tongues like blazing torches as high as the sea's waves, while flames
and lightnings issue from their mouths and fire is kindled from their
sweat.
　　see M.20.1.15; A.6.5.4; Ba.16.4.1; G.4.1.2; G.5.15.3; G.16.12.1; I.10.1.3;
　　I.10.5.2; Ib.6.5.1; Ib.16.12.2
　　3 En. 18.25   [→ *3.12.1; 3.3.a.6*

(**16**) Demons have wings.
　　see M.20.1.16
　　GL 5, 108 n.98   [→ *1.1.a.5*

(**17**) The angel Sammael (Satan) has twelve wings before his fall
(instead of the usual six).
　　see M.20.1.17; A.6.5.9; G.5.15.4; G.4.1.5
　　GL 1, 63; GL 5, 52 n.155; GL 5, 84 n.34   [→ *3.3.a.18*

(**18**) Abezethibou is a one-winged demon, an adversary of Moses in
Egypt, who is trapped in the Red Sea when the parted waters return.
　　see M.20.1.18
　　T. Sol. 6.3; *T. Sol.* 25.2-3   [→ *3.1.21*

(19) The Antichrist has fiery wings, skinny legs, a tuft of grey hair on the front of his bald head, eyebrows reaching to his ears, and a leprous bare spot on the palms of his hands. He can appear as a child or an old man, but cannot change the signs on his head.

see M.20.1.19; E.2.1.1; E.11.4.1; Gb.6.5.1; Pa.23.1.1; T.6.4.1

Apoc. Elij. **3.15-17;** *Apoc. Elij.* **5.20**   [→ *3.1.26*

(20) The angel Azazel has twelve wings and human hands and feet attached to the body of a dragon.

see M.20.1.20; P.21.6.1; U.21.6.1

Apoc. Abr. **23.7; GL 5, 123-124 n.131**   [→ *3.1.28*

(21) A woman called Istehar is given wings by the angels who want to seduce her, and with the help of these wings she escapes her seducers and ascends to heaven, where she is changed into the constellation Virgo.

see M.20.1.1; A.27.6.1

BHM **4.3 Shemchasai and Asael (Hebrew text, p.156);** *BHM* **5.21 (Midrash Fragments); 4 (Hebrew text S, p.156)**   [→ *2.18.a.12*

(22) The two Egyptian magicians Jannes and Jambres make wings for themselves with which to fly to heaven and escape drowning in the Red Sea.

see M.20.1.22

GL 3, 28-29; GL 6, 10 n.53   [→ *2.18.a.3*

(23) Two women with wings like a stork raise a bushel containing another woman (the personification of wickedness) midway between earth and heaven before taking it to the land of Shinar where they are to build a temple for it.

see M.20.1.3

Zech. 5.5f.   [→ *2.22.b.8*

M.20. *Shoulder(s) or Back with Bird Attributes*

M.20.1. Shoulder(s) or back with wings

(1) Angels have wings.

see M.14.2.1

1 En. **93.12;** *Gen. R.* **65.21**   [→ *1.1.a.5*

(2) The angel Ben Nez has wings.

see M.14.2.2

GL 1, 12; GL 5, 14 n.36   [→ *2.22.a.2; 2.15.b.2*

(3) Two hundred winged angels govern the stars.

   see M.14.2.3

   2 En. **4.2 (J and A)**   [→ *2.22.a.6*

(4) The two angels Samuil and Raguil, who take Enoch to heaven, have wings more glistening than gold.

   see M.14.2.4; F.10.1.4; P.11.2.1; Ia.10.1.1; G.10.1.2; A.6.5.5

   2 En. **1.4-6 (J and A)**; *2 En.* **3.1-3 (J and A)**; *2 En.* **33.6 (J and A)**

                                 [→ *2.22.b.2; 3.3.a.14*

(5) Elijah, after his removal from earth, has wings with four beats of which he can traverse the world.

   see M.14.2.5; A.22.1.1; A.9.2.1; Pc.10.7.1; A.10.1.17

   GL 4, 203; GL 6, 326 n.46   [→ *2.19.a.3; 2.22.a.9*

(6) The angel Gallizur, also called Raziel, stands before the throne with outspread wings.

   see M.14.2.6

   GL 3, 112; GL 6, 46 n.247   [→ *2.22.a.8; 2.21.1*

(7) The angel Gabriel claps his wings together and the noise this produces is so terrific that the Assyrians give up the ghost.

   see M.14.2.7

   GL 6, 363 n.58; GL 4, 269   [→ *2.15.a.5*

(8) The four cherubim seen by Ezekiel (and by Enoch, who names them Hayyot) each have four wings, two of which touch each other above their heads while the other two cover their bodies.

   see F.18.5.2; F.20.1.1; F.18.4.1; M.14.2.8; F.5.3.1; U.18.3.1; P.21.1.1;

   A.14.10.1; G.4.1.4; G.5.15.5

   Ezek. 1.6, 8, 9, 11, 23, 24; Ezek. 3.13; Ezek. 10.5, 8, 11, 16-21;

   Ezek. 11.22; *3 En.* **21.1-3**   [→ *3.1.16*

(9) The Lord of Spirits has four wings, on which a multitude of angels stand and beneath which the righteous will dwell.

   see M.14.2.9

   1 En. **39.7;** *1 En.* **40.1-2**   [→ *3.3.a.15*

(10) Angels have six wings, including the angels who accompany the sun and the moon.

   see M.14.2.10

   2 En. **11.4-5 (J);** *2 En.* **16.7 (J and A);** *Gen. R.* **65.21**   [→ *1.1.a.3*

(11) The cherubim seen by Enoch and Abraham have six wings. (Those seen by Ezekiel have four.)

see M.14.2.11

2 En. **19.6 (A);** *2 En.* **21.1 (J);** *3 En.* **22.13-15** *Apoc. Abr.* **18.3-7;**
Ques. Ezra (Recension A) 29 [→ *3.1.16*

(12) The seraphim seen by Isaiah, Moses and Enoch have six wings. Those seen by Enoch and Moses also have calves' feet.

see M.14.2.12; U.18.3.2; F.10.1.1; F.6.1.2; G.10.2.2; G.4.1.4; G.5.15.5
Isa. 6.2; *2 En.* **21.1 (J);** *3 En.* **26.9-11;** *2 En.* **20.1 (J);** *Lad. Jac.*
2.15; *Ques. Ezra* (Recension A) 29; *LAE (Apoc. Mos.)* **37.3;** *B H M*
5.21 (Midrash Fragments 21; HelSynPro 82); GL 6, 359 n.36;
GL. 2, 309; GL 5, 416-418 n.117
[→ *2.22.a.5; 2.21.2; 2.13.a.1; 2.8.1; 2.2.b.1*

(13) Seventy-two wings are attached to Enoch's body, thirty-six to the left and thirty-six to the right, at his transformation into Metatron.

see A.6.3.2; A.6.5.12; G.5.13.2; G.10.2.3; M.14.2.13; A.16.12.6; B.16.12.1;
E.16.4.1; G.16.12.5; V.16.12.1; Va.16.12.1; A.10.1.6
3 En. **9.3;** *3 En.* **42.2** [→ *1.35.2*

(14) Opanni'el, the prince of the ophanim, has one hundred wings on each side of his body. He also has sixteen faces, 8,766 eyes, corresponding to the number of hours in a year, while in each pair of eyes lightning flashes and torches blaze, consuming all who look at him. The height of his body is a journey of 2,500 years.

see M.14.2.14; A.6.5.3; F.5.10.1; G.10.1.1; G.10.5.2; G.5.13.1
3 En. **25.2-4** [→ *3.3.a.4*

(15) Soperi'el and Soperi-el, two princes of angels, have wings as numerous as the days of the year and as wide as the breadth of heaven. They are as tall as the seven heavens, with appearances like lightning, bodies full of eyes, eyes like the sun, lips like the gates of the east, tongues like blazing torches as high as the sea's waves, while flames and lightnings issue from their mouths and fire is kindled from their sweat.

see M.14.2.15; A.6.5.4; Ba.16.4.1; G.4.1.2; G.5.15.3; G.16.12.1; I.10.1.3;
I.10.5.2; Ib.6.5.1; Ib.16.12.2
3 En. **18.25** [→ *3.12.1; 3.3.a.6*

(16) Demons have wings.

see M.14.2.16
GL 5, 108 n.98 [→ *1.1.a.5*

(17) The angel Sammael (Satan) has twelve wings before his fall (instead of the usual six).

see M.14.2.17; A.6.5.9; G.5.15.4; G.4.1.5
GL 1, 63; GL 5, 52 n.155; GL 5, 84 n.34 [→ *3.3.a.18*

(18) Abezethibou is a one-winged demon, an adversary of Moses in Egypt, who is trapped in the Red Sea when the parted waters return.

see M.14.2.18
T. Sol. **6.3;** *T. Sol.* **25.2-3** [→ *3.1.21*

(19) The Antichrist has fiery wings, skinny legs, a tuft of grey hair on the front of his bald head, eyebrows reaching to his ears, and a leprous bare spot on the palms of his hands. He can appear as a child or an old man, but cannot change the signs on his head.

see M.14.2.19; E.2.1.1; E.11.4.1; Gb.6.5.1; Pa.23.1.1; T.6.4.1
Apoc. Elij. **3.15-17;** *Apoc. Elij.* **5.20** [→ *3.1.26*

(20) The angel Azazel has twelve wings and human hands and feet attached to the body of a dragon.

see M.14.2.20; P.21.6.1; U.21.6.1
Apoc. Abr. **23.7; GL 5, 123-124 n.131** [→ *3.1.28*

(21) A woman called Istehar is given wings by the angels who want to seduce her, and with the help of these wings she escapes her seducers and ascends to heaven, where she is changed into the constellation Virgo.

see M.14.2.21; A.27.6.1
BHM **4.3 Shemchasai and Asael (Hebrew text, p.156);** *BHM* **5.21 Midrash Fragments 4 (Hebrew text S, p.156)** [→ *2.18.a.12*

(22) The two Egyptian magicians Jannes and Jambres make wings for themselves with which to fly to heaven and escape drowning in the Red Sea.

see M.14.2.22
GL 3, 28-29; GL 6, 10 n.53 [→ *2.18.a.3*

(23) Two women with wings like a stork raise a bushel containing another woman (the personification of wickedness) midway between earth and heaven before taking it to the land of Shinar where they are to build a temple for it.

see M.14.2.23
Zech. 5.5f. [→ *2.22.b.8*

M.24. *Wounded or Mutilated Shoulders or Back*

M.24.1. *Slashed shoulder(s)*

(1) The shoulder of Dositheus, a Tubian, is slashed by one of the Thracian cavalry when he grasps Gorgias.

2 Macc. 12.35 [→ *1.20.11*

N. THE BREAST

Na. *The Male Breast*

Na.13. *Peculiarity of Skin of Breast*

Na.13.2 *Engraving on breast*

(1) The name of Dagon, Goliath's god, is engraved upon Goliath's breast.

see A.23.1.15; A.23.6.4; A.6.1.26; A.6.5.30

Cant. R. **4.4** §5   [→ *2.13.a.16*

Nb *The Female Breast(s)*
[No references in sources]

Nc *The Nipples*

Nc.10 *Unusual Emission from Nipples*

Nc.10.1 *Emission of milk from nipple(s) of male*

(1) Milk flows from the nipples of Mordecai to feed the baby Esther.

see Nd.9.1.1

Gen. R. **30.8**   [→ *2.32.7*

Nd *Milk*

Nd.5 *Unusual Quantity of Milk*

(1) Sarah has enough milk in her breasts to suckle all the babies present at Isaac's circumcision.

see A.10.1.13; F.10.1.9; Vg.1.1.1; Vg.23.1.3

GL 1, 263; GL 5, 246 n.208   [→ *2.32.3; 2.3.1*

Nd.9 *Milk from Person of Opposite Sex*

Nd.9.1 *Milk from male*

(1) Milk flows from the breasts of Mordecai to feed the baby Esther.
see Nc.10.1.1
Gen. R. **30.8** [→ *2.32.7*

Nd.26 *Milk of Unusual Age Group*

Nd.26.4 *Milk from mother although son is adult*

(1) Milk flows from the breasts of Joshua's mother when, unwittingly, he is about to marry her, having killed his father.
GL 4, 3; GL 6, 169 n.2 [→ *2.10.a.3; 2.6.b.7*

O. THE ARMS

O.5. *Unusual Number of Arm(s)*

O.5.3. *Four arms*

(1) Enepsigos, a female demon, has two pairs of arms and two heads on her shoulders. She hovers near the moon and can assume three forms.

see D.5.1.1
T. Sol. **15.1-5** [→ *3.1.18*

(2) Tebel, the second earth, is inhabited by humans with four arms.
see D.5.1.5; P.5.3.1; T.5.3.1; U.5.3.1; D.18.4.2; D.18.5.1; D.18.6.1; D.21.4.1; D.21.5.1; D.21.6.1
GL 1, 10 [→ *1.16.b.8; 3.2.7*

O.6. *Unusual Size of Arm(s)*

O.6.1. *Unusually large arm(s)*

(1) Jacob's arms are as large as 'the pillars supporting the bath-house in Tiberias'.
see A.6.1.23; G.23.4.7; Ta.23.1.1; Ta.24.1.1; Sa.2.3.12; Sa.24.3.12; K.13.10.1; Q.6.1.1; K.16.5.1; T.23.1.3; G.23.5.3
Gen. R. **65.17** [→ *3.3.a.28*

O.6.5 *Abnormally long arm(s)*

(1) Pharaoh's daughter's arm lengthens miraculously to reach over a distance of sixty ells and grasp the ark containing Moses.
see A.23.1.4
Cant. R. **1.23** [→ *2.19.a.6*

O.13 *Peculiarity of Skin of Arm(s)*

O.13.2 *Brand or engraving on arm(s)*

(1) The letter 'teth' (the ninth letter of the Hebrew alphabet) is engraved upon Cain's arm.

see A.23.1.1; F.10.1.7; F.11.1.2; Fb.13.2.4; Fb.14.2.2; Fb.18.11.2; B.13.2.1; F.11.3.1; A.13.2.1
GL 5, 141 n.27 [→ *2.4.4*

O.13.6 *Hairy arm(s)*

(1) Esau has hairy arms.

see A.13.6.3; B.18.3.1; E.4.1.3; A.11.3.3; P.13.6.1; B.11.3.1; B.13.6.3; E.26.1.1; Ic.26.1.1; Sa.2.3.4; Sa.24.3.4; A.13.1.1; B.13.1.1
Gen. 27.23; *Gen. R.* 65.15; *Gen. R.* 65.22 [→ *3.7.2; 3.6.b.8*

O.16 *Arm(s) of Unusual Substance*

O.16.1 *Arm(s) of iron*

(1) The Antichrist's right arm is made of iron and his left arm of copper. His lower teeth are made of iron and his lower jaw of diamond. He is ten cubits tall, while his feet and right hand are three cubits long. His hair reaches to his feet and he is three-crested. His eyes are like the rising morning star and his right eye like a lion's. He is long-faced, long-nosed and disorderly, with three letters written on his forehead: A, K and T, signifying denial, rejection and the befouled dragon. His mother conceives him by touching the head of a fish.

see O.16.2.3; A.6.5.13; E.6.5.1; Fb.13.2.3; Fc.16.5.1; G.10.2.6; G.18.1.1; Ic.16.1.1; U.6.5.2
Apoc. Dan. 9.11, 16-26 [→ *3.1.25; 1.3.c.1*

O.16.2 *Arm(s) of copper or bronze*

(1) An angel with arms and legs as if of burnished bronze, a body like beryl, chrysolite or topaz, a face like lightning and eyes like fiery torches (and a voice like the voice of a crowd) is seen by Daniel in a vision.

see A.16.18.1; F.16.12.3; G.16.12.3; T.16.2.1
Dan. 10.6 [→ *3.1.14*

(2) The myriads of angels in the seventh heaven (called Arabot) have arms and feet like burnished bronze, eyes like torches of fire and faces like lightning.

see F.16.13.1; G.16.12.4; U.16.2.2

3 En. 35.1-2; *3 En.* 22B.6 (Appendix)   [→ *3.3.a.9*

(3) The Antichrist's left arm is made of copper and his right arm of iron. His lower teeth are made of iron and his lower jaw of diamond. He is ten cubits tall, while his feet and right hand are three cubits long. His hair reaches to his feet and he is three-crested. His eyes are like the rising morning star and his right eye like a lion's. He is long-faced, long-nosed and disorderly, with three letters written on his forehead: A, K and T, signifying denial, rejection and the befouled dragon. His mother conceives him by touching the head of a fish.

see O.16.1.1; A.6.5.13; E.6.5.1; Fb.13.2.3; Fc.16.5.1; G.10.2.6; G.18.1.1; Ic.16.1.1; U.6.5.2

Apoc. Dan. 9.11, 16-26   [→ *3.1.25; 1.3.c.1*

O.23 *Disease, Paralysis or Malfunction of Arm(s)*

O.23.2 *Trembling or agitation of arm(s)*

(1) David's limbs never cease from trembling after the day he sees an angel slay his four sons, the prophet Gad and the elders who accompany him, and then wipe his dripping sword on the king's garments.

see E.11.3.1; Sa.2.3.25; Sa.24.3.25; B.11.3.3; T.23.2.1; F.11.1.7; A.25.15.3; A.23.1.16; G.25.1.1; A.25.9.2

GL 4, 113; GL 6, 271 n.124   [→ *1.12.a.27; 1.14.a.8*

Oa. The Elbow(s)
[No References in sources]

Ob. The Wrist(s)
[No References in sources]

P. THE HANDS

P.1. *Absence of Hands*

(1) Many Israelites are maimed by falling masonry and lose their hands during the building work in Egypt.

> see T.23.1.2; G.23.4.10; I.23.3.4; J.23.1.3
>
> *Num. R.* **7.1; GL 3, 78; GL 6, 30 n.176; GL 3, 13**   [→ *1.23.1*

(2) The hands of Eleazar, his six brothers and his mother are cut off, as well as their feet and tongues; their eyes are pierced, their heads scalped, and then they are fried alive by King Antiochus Epiphanes who wants them to taste pig's flesh.

> see U.1.1.1; D.2.2.1; Ib.1.1.3; Ga.24.1.1
>
> **2 Macc. 7;** *4 Macc.* **6.6, 25;** *4 Macc.* **7.13-14;** *4 Macc.* **9.28;** *4 Macc.* **10.5-8,17-21;** *4 Macc.* **11.18-19;** *4 Macc.* **18.21**
>
> [→ *2.5.12; 2.25.a.2; 1.24.4*

P.2. *Absence of Part of Hands*

P.2.1. *Absence of finger(s) or thumb(s)*

(1) The Levites bite off their own fingers when they are asked to play their harps for the Babylonians.

> see Pc.1.1.1
>
> **GL 4, 316-317; GL 6, 407 n.55**   [→ *2.25.b.1*

(2) Two hundred thousand men amputate a finger when their commander, Bar Koziba, orders them to.

> see Pc.1.1.2
>
> *Lam. R.* **2.2 §4**   [→ *2.1.a.3; 2.4.13*

P.3. *Vital Hands*

(1) A fiery hand appears and takes the keys from Jeconiah when he stands on the temple roof, offering the keys back declaring that his people are no fit custodians of the temple.

see P.16.12.1

Lev. R. **19.6** [→ *2.19.a.1*

(2) A physician who has recommended a milk cure for the Persian king has a dream in which his hands, feet, eyes, mouth and tongue quarrel with one another, each claiming the greatest share of credit in procuring the remedy for the king.

see G.3.1.1; I.3.1.1; Ib.3.1.1; U.3.1.1

GL 4, 174; GL 6, 302 n.97 [→ *2.5.13*

P.5. *Unusual Number of Hands*

P.5.3. *Four hands*

(1) The inhabitants of Tebel, the second earth, have four hands.

see D.5.1.5; O.5.3.2; T.5.3.1; U.5.3.1; D.18.4.2; D.18.5.1; D.18.6.1; D.21.4.1; D.21.5.1; D.21.6.1

GL 1, 10 [→ *1.16.b.8; 3.2.7*

P.6. *Unusual Size of Hand(s)*

P.6.5. *Abnormally long hand(s)*

(1) An angel, whose size is one-third of the world, can stretch his hand from heaven to earth at the behest of God.

Exod. R. **3.6** [→ *3.4.a.4*

P.10 *Unusual Emission or Emanation from Hand(s)*

P.10.1 *Hand(s) that emits light*

(1) A brilliant light shines from the right hand of the Omnipotent One, from which the 955 heavens were created (but the right hand is banished behind him because of the destruction of the temple and cannot function again until its restoration).

see E.11.2.1; A.11.2.2; A.11.3.1; D.16.3.1; E.11.1.1; E.12.3.1; F.5.10.1; F.16.12.1; G.10.5.1; Ia.16.12.1; A.11.2.1; P.10.7.1; Pc.10.7.1; Gf.4.1.1; A.1.1.1; Gf.27.2.1; A.10.1.1; Pc.10.3.1; I.10.5.1; If.6.1.1

3 En. **48a.1**; *3 En.* **5.3**; Hab. 3.3-4 [→ *2.15.a.2; 2.14.a.3*

P.10.3 *Hand(s) that emits flames*

(1) The hands of Kerubi'el, the prince of the cherubim, emit flames, while his body is full of burning coals and covered with eyes and wings. Rays flash from his wheels.

see A.6.3.1; A.6.5.2; A.14.5.1; A.14.10.2; A.16.17.1; A.20.1.1; F.16.12.2; G.5.15.2; G.16.12.2; Gc.16.12.1; I.16.12.1; Ib.16.12.1; G.4.1.3

3 En. 22.3-9 [→ *3.3.a.7*

(2) Sparks fly from the hands and feet of the angel (probably Michael) seen by Aseneth, and his appearance is like molten iron, while the hairs of his head are like a flaming torch, his face is like lightning and his eyes like sunshine.

see E.10.2.1; F.10.1.3; G.10.2.4; P.16.1.1; U.10.3.1; U.16.1.1

***Jos. Asen.* 14.9 (8, 9); *Jos. Asen.* 16.12, 13 (7)** [→ *3.1.8*

P.10.7 Hand(s) that emits tears

(1) God's right hand weeps because of the destruction of the temple, and rivers of tears flow from the five fingers, falling into the Great Sea.

see E.11.2.1; A.11.2.2; A.11.3.1; D.16.3.1; E.11.1.1; E.12.3.1; F.5.10.1; F.16.12.1; G.10.5.1; Ia.16.12.1; P.10.1.1; A.11.2.1; Pc.10.7.1; Gf.4.1.1; A.1.1.1; Gf.27.2.1; A.10.1.1; Pc.10.3.1; I.10.5.1; If.6.1.1

3 En. 48a.4 [→ *1.12.a.2*

P.11 Unusual Colour of Hand(s)

P.11.2 *White hand(s)*

(1) The hands of the two angels Samuil and Raguil, who take Enoch to heaven, are whiter than snow.

see F.10.1.4; Ia.10.1.1; G.10.1.2; M.14.2.4; M.20.1.4; A.6.5.5

2 En. 1.4-6 (J and A); 2 En. 3.1-3 (J and A); 2 En. 33.6 (J and A) [→ *3.3.a.14*

(2) Moses' hand turns leprous and white as snow when he puts it in his bosom and then takes it out again. When he repeats the operation, it returns to normal.

see F.10.1.11; Sa.2.3.19; Sa.24.3.19; A.6.5.25; A.6.4.2; P.23.1.1; P.25.4.1; I.10.1.5; G.10.2.9; F.11.3.2; Fb.10.1.1; G.25.4.1; If.6.1.3; Fb.14.2.3; I.23.3.3; A.25.9.1; G.17.20.1; Ib.13.2.1; Ib.24.4.1; Ia.24.4.1; E.6.1.1; Ga.10.2.1; E.12.10.1; P.13.2.1; P.24.4.1; K.13.10.2; B.16.12.2; Ib.16.12.3; Ia.13.2.1; A.26.1.3

Exod. 4.6; *Num. R.* 7.5; *Ezek. Trag. Exagoge* 129-131
[→ *1.26.b.23; 2.7.4; 2.3.2; 2.5.2*

P.12. *Unusual Shape of Hand(s)*

P.12.1. *Hand(s) of one piece, with fingers unseparated*

(1) Until the time of Noah, human hands consisted of one piece, without separate fingers.

GL 5, 168   [→ *1.8.a.2*

P.13. *Peculiarity of Skin of Hand(s)*

P.13.2. *Burnt hand(s)*

(1) Moses' hand is burnt by a burning coal which he grasps and puts to his mouth.

see F.10.1.11; Sa.2.3.19; Sa.24.3.19; A.6.5.25; A.6.4.2; P.23.1.1; P.25.4.1; I.10.1.5; G.10.2.9; F.11.3.2; Fb.10.1.1; G.25.4.1; If.6.1.3; Fb.14.2.3; I.23.3.3; P.11.2.1; G.17.20.1; Ib.13.2.1; Ib.24.4.1; Ia.24.4.1; E.6.1.1; Ga.10.2.1; E.12.10.1; A.25.9.1; P.24.4.1; K.13.10.2; B.16.12.2; Ib.16.12.3; Ia.13.2.1; A.26.1.3

Cant. R. **1.26**   [→ *1.14.c.10; 2.3.3; 2.6.a.8; 2.9.6; 2.20.2*

P.13.6. *Hairy hand(s)*

(1) Esau has hairy hands.

see A.13.6.3; B.18.3.1; E.4.1.3; O.13.6.1; A.11.3.3; B.11.3.1; B.13.6.3; E.26.1.1; Ic.26.1.1; Sa.2.3.4; Sa.24.3.4; A.13.1.1; B.13.1.1

Gen. 27.23; Gen. R. 65.15; Gen. R. 65.22   [→ *3.7.2; 3.6.b.8*

P.16. *Hand(s) of Unusual Substance*

P.16.1. *Hand(s) of iron*

(1) The hands and feet of the angel (probably Michael) seen by Aseneth are like glowing iron and emit sparks, while his face is like lightning, the hairs of his head like a flaming torch, and his eyes like sunshine.

see E.10.2.1; F.10.1.3; G.10.2.4; P.10.3.2; U.10.3.1; U.16.1.1

Jos. Asen. **14.9 (8, 9);** *Jos. Asen.* **16.12, 13 (7)**   [→ *3.1.8*

P.16.11. *Hand(s) of ice or hail*

(1) An angel with hands of ice is sent to Enoch to chill him before he returns to earth.

see A.16.10.3

2 En. **37.1-2 (J);** *2 En.* **37.1 (A)**   [→ *2.22.b.3*

P.16.12. *Hand(s) of fire*

(1) A fiery hand appears and takes the keys from Jeconiah when he stands on the temple roof offering them back, declaring that his people are no fit custodians of the temple.
see P.3.1.1
Lev. R. **19.6** [→ *3.1.1*

P.18. *Animal Parts in Place of Hand(s) or Hand(s) with Animal Attributes*

P.18.5. *Horse hoof(s) in place of hand(s)*

(1) The stars (who are fallen angels) have hoofs in place of hands and feet, and the sexual organs of horses.
see U.18.5.1; Sa.18.5.1
1 En. **88.1**; *1 En.* **88.3** [→ *3.7.1*

P.21. *Human Hand(s) on Unusual Creature*

P.21.1. *Cherub or angel with human hand(s)*

(1) The cherubim have human hands under their wings.
see F.18.5.2; F.20.1.1; F.18.4.1; M.20.1.8; M.14.2.8; U.18.3.1; F.5.3.1; A.14.10.1; G.4.1.4; G.5.15.5
Ezek. **10.8**; *Ezek.* **1.8** [→ *3.1.16*

P.21.6. *Body of dragon or serpent with human hand(s)*

(1) The angel Azazel has human hands and feet and the body of a dragon with twelve wings.
see U.21.6.1; M.14.2.20; M.20.1.20
Apoc. Abr. **23.7** [→ *3.1.28*

(2) Before the Fall, the serpent has human hands, feet, ears and tongue, as well as wings.
see U.21.6.3; Ib.21.6.1; J.21.6.1
Gen. R. **19.1**; *Gen. R.* **20.5**; *LAE (Apoc. Mos.)* **26.2-3**; *Qoh. R.* **10.11** §1 [→ *3.3.a.44; 3.5.a.4; 1.16.a.6*

P.23. *Disease, Paralysis or Malfunction of Hand(s)*

P.23.1. *Leprous hand(s)*

(1) Moses' hand turns leprous and white as snow when he puts it in his bosom and takes it out again. When he repeats the operation it returns to normal.

see F.10.1.11; Sa.2.3.19; Sa.24.3.19; A.6.5.25; A.6.4.2; A.25.9.1; P.25.4.1; I.10.1.5; G.10.2.9; F.11.3.2; Fb.10.1.1; G.25.4.1; If.6.1.3; Fb.14.2.3; I.23.3.3; P.11.2.1; G.17.20.1; Ib.13.2.1; Ib.24.4.1; Ia.24.4.1; E.6.1.1; Ga.10.2.1; E.12.10.1; P.13.2.1; P.24.4.1; K.13.10.2; B.16.12.2; Ib.16.12.3; Ia.13.2.1; A.26.1.3

Exod. 4.6; *Num. R.* **7.5;** *Ezek. Trag. Exagoge* **129-131**

[→ 1.26.b.23; 2.7.4; 2.3.2; 2.5.2

(2) The Egyptians have leprous hands after placing them in their bosoms and taking them out again in imitation of Moses.

see B.23.1.1; B.24.3.2; B.23.2.4; B.24.3.1; Ie.27.1.1; Sa.24.2.7; B.24.4.2; W.4.2.2; Sa.2.1.7; A.23.3.1; A.23.6.1

GL 2, 355; GL 5, 431 n.193   *[→ 1.15.2*

P.23.6. Paralysis of hand(s)

(1) The hands of the Ishmaelites are paralysed when they raise them to inflict a blow upon Joseph.

GL 2, 20; GL 5, 330 n.59   *[→ 2.15.b.6*

(2) Joab's right hand is paralysed and stuck to his sword (until he kills a pregnant woman and the blood of the unborn baby separates his hand from his sword).

see W.25.2.1; U.13.1.1

GL 4, 100; GL 6, 258-259 n.77   *[→ 1.12.b.1; 1.14.c.15*

(3) King Jeroboam is unable to withdraw his withered hand when he stretches it out to seize a man of God.

see P.23.7.2

1 Kgs 13.4   *[→ 2.3.10; 1.26.b.44*

P.23.7. Withered hand(s)

(1) Simon's right hand withers for seven days after Joseph is sold to the Ishmaelites.

see A.6.3.6

T. Sim. **2.12 (T12P)**   *[→ 1.26.b.17; 2.15.b.5*

(2) King Jeroboam's hand withers when he stretches it out to seize a man of God, and he is unable to withdraw it.

see P.23.6.3

1 Kgs 13.4   *[→ 2.3.10; 1.26.b.44*

P.24. *Wounded or Mutilated Hand(s)*

P.24.4. *Burnt hand(s)*

(1) Moses' hand is burnt by a burning coal which he grasps and puts to his mouth.

see F.10.1.11; Sa.2.3.19; Sa.24.3.19; A.6.5.25; A.6.4.2; P.23.1.1; P.25.4.1;
I.10.1.5; G.10.2.9; F.11.3.2; Fb.10.1.1; G.25.4.1; If.6.1.3; Fb.14.2.3;
I.23.3.3; P.11.2.1; G.17.20.1; Ib.13.2.1; Ib.24.4.1; Ia.24.4.1; E.6.1.1;
Ga.10.2.1; E.12.10.1; P.13.2.1; A.25.9.1; K.13.10.2; B.16.12.2; Ib.16.12.3;
Ia.13.2.1; A.26.1.3

Cant. R. **1.26**   [→ *1.14.c.10; 2.3.3; 2.6.a.8; 2.9.6; 2.20.2*

P.25. *Unusual Abilities of Hand(s)*

P.25.4. *Hand(s) that speaks*

(1) Moses' hand proclaims what has happened to it after it has turned leprous in his bosom.

see F.10.1.11; Sa.2.3.19; Sa.24.3.19; A.6.5.25; A.6.4.2; P.23.1.1; A.25.9.1;
I.10.1.5; G.10.2.9; F.11.3.2; Fb.10.1.1; G.25.4.1; If.6.1.3; Fb.14.2.3;
I.23.3.3; P.11.2.2; G.17.20.1; Ib.13.2.1; Ib.24.4.1; Ia.24.4.1; E.6.1.1;
Ga.10.2.1; E.12.10.1; P.13.2.1; P.24.4.1; K.13.10.2; B.16.12.2; Ib.16.12.3;
Ia.13.2.1; A.26.1.3

GL 5, 421 n.132   [→ *2.2.c.5*

Pa. *The Palm(s)*

Pa.23. *Disease, Paralysis or Malfunction of Palm(s)*

Pa.23.1. *Leprous palm(s)*

(1) The Antichrist has a leprous bare spot on the palms of his hands, eyebrows reaching to his ears, fiery wings, skinny legs and a tuft of grey hair on the front of his bald head. He can appear as a child or an old man, but is unable to change the signs on his head.

see E.2.1.1; E.11.4.1; Gb.6.5.1; M.14.2.19; M.20.1.19; T.6.4.1

Apoc. Elij. **3.15-17;** *Apoc. Elij.* **5.20**   [→ *3.1.26*

Pb. *The Knuckles*
[No references in sources]

Pc. *The Finger(s) or Thumb(s)*

Pc.1. *Absence of Finger(s) or Thumb(s)*

Pc.1.1 *Absence of finger(s)*

(1) The Levites bite off their own fingers when they are asked to play their harps for the Babylonians.
    see P.2.1.1
    GL 4, 316-317; GL 6, 407 n.55   *[→ 2.25.b.1*

(2) Two hundred thousand men amputate a finger when their commander, Bar Koziba, orders them to.
    see P.2.1.2
    Lam. R. 2.2 §4   *[→ 2.1.a.3; 2.4.13*

Pc.1.2 *Absence of thumb(s)*

(1) Adoni-zedek's thumbs and big toes are cut off by the tribe of Judah.
    see Ub.1.1.1
    Judg. 1.6-7   *[→ 1.26.b.36*

Pc.2. *Absence of Part of Finger(s) or Thumb(s)*

Pc.2.1. *Absence of fingertip(s) or nail(s)*

(1) Job's fingertips and nails drop off (and his body swarms with vermin).
    see Pd.1.1.1; A.23.1.20; A.23.20.2; B.24.1.4; Cc.23.3.1; Cc.23.3.2; B.11.1.3; B.23.20.1; B.15.1.2; A.10.10.1
    GL 2, 235; GL 5, 386 n.25   *[→ 1.10.5; 2.1.a.2*

Pc.3. *Vital Finger(s) or Thumb(s)*

(1) Balshazzar sees the awesome fingers of an angel writing 'Mene, Mene, Tekel, Upharsin', while the rest of the angel remains invisible.
    Dan. 5.5; GL 4, 343; GL 6, 430 n.1, 2   *[→ 2.24.3*

Pc.5. *Unusual Number of Fingers or Thumbs*

-
Pc.5.5. *Six fingers on hand(s)*

(1) One of the Philistines who fights at Gath has six fingers on each hand and six toes on each foot.

see Ub.5.5.1; A.6.1.14
2 Sam. 21.20; 1 Chron. 20.6 [→ *1.1.b.8*

Pc.6. *Abnormal Size of Finger(s) or Thumb(s)*

Pc.6.5. *Abnormally long finger(s) or thumb(s)*

(1) The fingers of the Hayyot (who bear the throne of God) have a length of 8,766 parasangs.

see A.10.5.1
3 En. 33.3; 3 En. 34.1 [→ *3.3.a.8*

Pc.10 *Unusual Emission or Emanation from Finger(s) or Thumb(s)*

Pc.10.3 *Finger(s) or thumb(s) that emits fire*

(1) God's little finger emits a devouring fire, which falls on the ranks of the angels and splits them into 496,000 myriads of parts and then devours them, when the angels fail to recite the 'Holy'.

see E.11.2.1; A.11.2.2; A.11.3.1; D.16.3.1; E.11.1.1; E.12.13.1; F.5.10.1; F.16.12.1; G.10.5.1; Ia.16.12.1; P.10.1.1; P.10.7.1; Pc.10.7.1; Gf.4.1.1; A.1.1.1; Gf.27.2.1; A.10.1.1; A.11.2.1; I.10.5.1; If.6.1.1
3 En. 40.3; 3 En. 47.1-3; 3 En. 35.6 [→ *1.26.b.1; 2.15.a.3*

(2) When the angel meets Jacob at the ford he sticks his finger into the ground and the ground begins to emit fire.

Gen. R. 77.2 [→ *2.4.1; 3.8.1*

Pc.10.5. *Finger(s) or thumb(s) that emits milk*

(1) Milk flows from the little finger of Abraham's right hand when he is a baby.

see Pc.10.6.1; A.10.1.12; Sa.2.3.9; Sa.24.3.9; A.6.5.23; T.25.1.1; F.10.1.8
GL 1, 189; GL 5, 210 n.14 [→ *2.32.2*

Pc.10.6. *Finger(s) or thumb(s) that emits honey*

(1) Honey flows from the little finger of Abraham's right hand when he is a baby.

see Pc.10.5.1; A.10.1.12; Sa.2.3.9; Sa.24.3.9; A.6.5.23; T.25.1.1; F.10.1.8
GL 1, 189; GL 5, 210 n.14 [→ *2.32.2*

190   *Forms of Deformity*

Pc.10.7 *Finger(s) or thumb(s) that emits water*

(1) The Omnipresent One's right hand weeps at the destruction of the temple, and five rivers of tears flow from his five fingers, falling into the Great Sea.

> see E.11.2.1; A.11.2.2; A.11.3.1; D.16.3.1; E.11.1.1; E.12.3.1; F.5.10.1;
> F.16.12.1; G.10.5.1; Ia.16.12.1; P.10.1.1; P.10.7.1; A.11.2.1; Gf.4.1.1;
> A.1.1.1; Gf.27.2.1; A.10.1.1; Pc.10.3.1; I.10.5.1; If.6.1.1
> **3 *En.* 48A.4**   [→ *1.12.a.2*

(2) Ten springs of water gush forth from Elijah's fingers when Elisha pours a little water over them.

> see M.14.2.5; M.20.1.5; A.9.2.1; A.22.1.1; A.10.1.17
> **GL 4, 199; GL 6, 320 n.18**   [→ *2.4.9; 2.5.10; 2.7.5*

Pc.12. *Unusual Shape of Finger(s) or Thumb(s)*

Pc.12.1. *Curved finger(s) or thumb(s)*

(1) The Antichrist's fingers are like scythes, his feet measure two span, his mouth is one cubit long and his teeth one span. His right eye is like the rising morning star, his left eye unmoving, while on his forehead is the inscription 'Antichrist'.

> see Pc.12.2.1; Fb.13.2.2; G.10.2.5; G.23.3.1; I.6.1.1; Ic.6.5.1; U.6.5.1
> ***Gk Apoc. Ezra* 4.29f.**   [→ *3.1.24*

Pc.12.2. *Pointed finger(s) or thumb(s)*

(1) The Antichrist's fingers are like scythes, his feet measure two span, his mouth one cubit and his teeth a span. His right eye is like the rising morning star, his left eye is unmoving, while on his forehead is the inscription 'Antichrist'.

> see Pc.12.1.1; Fb.13.2.2; G.10.2.5; G.23.3.1; I.6.1.1; Ic.6.5.1; U.6.5.1
> ***Gk Apoc. Ezra* 4.29f.**   [→ *3.1.24*

Pd. *The Fingernails*

Pd.1. *Absence of Fingernails*

(1) Job's nails and fingertips drop off (and his body swarms with vermin).

> see Pc.2.1.1; A.23.1.20; A.23.20.2; B.24.1.4; Cc.23.3.1; Cc.23.3.2; B.11.1.3;
> B.23.20.1; B.15.1.2; A.10.10.1
> **GL 2, 235; GL 5, 386 n.25**   [→ *1.10.5; 2.1.a.2*

Pd.6. *Abnormal Size of Fingernails*

Pd.6.1. *Abnormally large fingernail(s)*

(1) The fingernails of giants are large enough to stop up a spring of water according to a report by the Israelites who have been on a reconnaissance mission into Canaan.
  GL 3, 275-276; GL 6, 96 n.532   [→ *1.1.a.18*

Pd.6.5. *Abnormally long fingernail(s)*

(1) Nebuchadnezzar's nails become like a bird's claws when he is driven from human society and lives like a beast for seven years.
  see Pd.12.1.1; E.6.5.6; A.27.2.3; Cc.27.1.1; Cc.27.4.1; Ib.1.1.2; A.6.2.5; U.23.1.4; T.24.3.1; A.2.4.1
  Dan. 4.30   [→ *1.9.3*

Pd.10. *Unusual Emission or Emanation from Fingernails*

Pd.10.16. *Emission of semen from fingernails*

(1) Joseph's semen is diffused and emerges from his fingernails when Potiphar's wife tries to seduce him.
  see Sd.4.1.1
  Gen. R. 87.7; Gen. R. 98.20   [→ *2.14.b.3*

Pd.12. *Unusual Shape of Fingernails*

Pd.12.1. *Curved fingernail(s)*

(1) Nebuchadnezzar's nails become like a bird's claws when he is driven from human society and lives like a beast for seven years.
  see Pd.6.5.1; E.6.5.6; A.27.2.3; Cc.27.1.1; Cc.27.4.1; Ib.1.1.2; A.6.2.5; U.23.1.4; T.24.3.1; A.2.4.1
  Dan. 4.30   [→ *1.9.3*

Q. THE STOMACH AND THE WAIST

Q.6. *Abnormal Size of Stomach or Waist*

Q.6.1. *Abnormally large stomach or waist*

(1) Jacob's loins are like a giant's.
see A.6.1.23; G.23.4.7; Ta.23.1.1; Ta.24.1.1; Sa.2.3.12; Sa.24.3.12; O.6.1.1;
K.13.10.1; K.16.5.1; T.23.1.3; G.23.5.3
GL 2, 175; GL 5, 374-375 n.432   [→ *3.3.a.28*

Qa. *The Navel*

Qa.14. *Unusual Protuberances or Protusions on Navel*

Qa.14.1. *Umbilical cord attached to navel*

(1) In the days of the sons of Noah children can run, speak and obey
orders while still attached by the umbilical cord to their mothers.
see A.26.1.1
Gen. R. 36.1; Lev. R. 5.1   [→ *1.16.a.5*

(2) Adne Sadeh, the 'man of the mountain', has a human form but is
fastened to the ground by means of a string protruding from his
navel.
GL 1, 31-32; GL 5, 50 n.147-149   [→ *3.2.6; 1.16.b.7*

Qa.15. *Abnormal Puncture or Opening in Navel*

(1) The navels of the spies who have tried to dissuade the Israelites
from entering Canaan are pierced by worms that crawl out of their
tongues.
see Ib.6.5.2; Ib.23.20.1
GL 3, 283; GL 6, 98 n.552   [→ *1.26.b.31*

R. The Buttocks

R.14. *Unusual Protuberances or Protusions on Buttock(s)*

R.14.1. *Tail on buttock(s)*

(1) Adam is created with a tail, but the tail is later removed by God because of the dignity owing to man.

see Cb.9.1.1; F.5.1.1; A.9.1.2; A.12.1.1; R.18.1.1; A.6.1.19; A.6.1.20; A.6.3.4; A.6.5.20; A.6.5.21; A.13.10.1; B.13.10.1; A.10.1.9; A.10.1.10; Sa.2.3.3; Sa.24.3.3; A.16.9.1; Ca.9.1.1; Cb.5.1.1; G.23.5.1; J.23.1.1; A.4.1.1; D.14.10.1; E.14.10.1; Fb.14.10.1; G.14.10.1; H.14.10.1; I.14.10.1; J.14.10.1; Ja.14.10.1

Gen. R. **14.10**

[→ *1.8.b.2*

R.18. *Buttock(s) with Animal Attributes*

R.18.1. *Buttock(s) with tail*

(1) Adam is created with a tail, but the tail is later removed by God because of the dignity owing to man.

see Cb.9.1.1; F.5.1.1; A.9.1.2; R.14.1.1; A.12.1.1; A.6.1.19; A.6.1.20; A.6.3.4; A.6.5.20; A.6.5.21; A.13.10.1; B.13.10.1; A.10.1.9; A.10.1.10; Sa.2.3.3; Sa.24.3.3; A.16.9.1; Ca.9.1.1; Cb.5.1.1; G.23.5.1; J.23.1.1; A.4.1.1; D.14.10.1; E.14.10.1; Fb.14.10.1; G.14.10.1; H.14.10.1; I.14.10.1; J.14.10.1; Ja.14.10.1

Gen. R. **14.10**

[→ *1.8.b.2*

Ra. The Anus

Ra.23. *Disease, Paralysis or Malfunction of Anus*

Ra.23.1. *Anus closed up*

(1) The anus of each of the Philistines, and their beasts, is closed up when King Abimelech takes Sarah as a wife.

see Ga.23.2.1; Ha.23.1.1; I.23.4.1; J.23.2.1; Sa.23.2.1; Sb.23.2.1
GL 1, 258; GL 5, 243 n.190; GL 5, 244 n.202   [→ *2.10.a.2*

Rb. The Excrement

Rb.6. Unusual Size or Quantity of Excrement

Rb.6.1. *Abnormally large quantity of excrement*

(1) Zedekiah has extreme diarrhoea after Nebuchadnezzar has given him food for this very purpose, intending to shame him and expose him to ridicule.

see Rb.13.2.1
GL 6, 384 n.8   [→ *2.24.16; 2.25.a.1; 1.14.d.5*

Rb.13. Peculiarity of Texture of Excrement

Rb.13. *Unusually soft excrement*

(1) Zedekiah has diarrhoea after Nebuchadnezzar has given him food for that very purpose, intending to shame him and expose him to ridicule.

see Rb.6.1.1
GL 6, 384 n.8   [→ *2.24.16; 2.25.a.1; 1.14.d.5*

S. THE GENITALS

Sa *The Male Genitals*

Sa.2 *Absence of Male Genitals*

Sa.2.1 *Absence of testicle(s)*

(1) Noah is castrated by his son, Ham (or by his grandson Canaan), as he lies drunk and exposed.
    see A.11.2.5; A.11.3.2; G.10.2.7; Sa.2.3.6; Sa.24.3.6; E.11.2.1; T.23.1.1;
    I.10.4.1; Sa.24.10.1; Va.24.1.1; If.26.1.1; B.11.2.1; B.11.3.2; Sa.24.2.1
    Gen. R. 36.3; *Gen. R.* 36.7; *Lev. R.* 17.5   [→ *2.14.b.2*

(2) Potiphar (or Poti-phera) is castrated by the angel Gabriel (or by God) because he has bought Joseph for sexual purposes.
    see Sa.24.2.2
    Gen. R. 86.3; *Jub.* 34.11; *Jub.* 39.2; *Cant. R.* 1.1 §1
                                                    [→ *1.26.b.15; 2.23.b.2*

(3) Eunuchs act as servants and messengers for Potiphar and his wife.
    see Sa.24.2.3
    Jub. 39.14; GL 2, 40-42; GL 5, 337 n.99   [→ *2.22.a.13*

(4) Eunuchs bring food mixed with enchantments to Joseph from Pentephris's wife, but Joseph looks up and sees a frightening angel with a sword and a bowl and realizes it is a trick to lead him astray.
    see Sa.24.2.4
    T. Jos. 6.2 (T12P)   [→ *4.1.c.1*

(5) A eunuch tells Pentephris's wife about Joseph, and she goes to see him.
    see Sa.24.2.5
    T. Jos. 12.1 (T12P)   [→ *4.1.c.2*

(6) A eunuch is sent by Pentephris's wife to buy Joseph.
    see Sa.24.2.6
    T. Jos. 16.1f. (T12P)   [→ *4.1.c.3*

(7) The Egyptians are emasculated by frogs. These frogs also leap around, croaking, in their entrails.

see Sa.24.2.7; B.24.3.1; B.23.1.1; P.23.1.2; B.24.3.2; B.24.4.2; B.23.2.4; Ie.27.1.1; W.4.2.2; A.23.3.1; A.23.6.1
Cant. R. **10.3, 6;** *Cant. R.* **15.27; GL 2, 342, 345, 349-351**
[→ *1.26.b.25; 2.5.3*

(8) Agag is castrated by Samuel because he has taken the circumcised members of slain Israelites and thrown them upwards, exclaiming 'This is what thou hast chosen'.

see Sa.24.2.8
Lam. R. **3.64 §9**   [→ *1.26.b.35*

(9) Seventy eunuchs guard Solomon's daughter in the high tower in which he has imprisoned her.

see Sa.24.2.9
GL 4, 175-176; GL 6, 303 n.100   [→ *2.22.a.14*

(10) Johanan brings back the eunuchs from Gibeon.

see Sa.24.2.10
Jer. 41.16   [→ *4.1.c.16*

(11) A eunuch who is in command of the fighting men is taken prisoner by Nebuzaradan, an officer of the king of Babylon, who enters Jerusalem to sack it.

see Sa.24.2.11
2 Kgs 25.19; Jer. 52.25   [→ *4.1.c.9*

(12) Eunuchs leave Jerusalem for Babylon together with King Jeconiah and the queen mother, the nobility of Judah and Jerusalem and the blacksmiths and metal workers.

see Sa.24.2.12
Jer. 29.2   [→ *4.1.c.18*

(13) King Ahab employs eunuchs.

see Sa.24.2.13
1 Kgs 22.9; 2 Chron. 18.8   [→ *4.1.c.7*

(14) The king of Israel employs eunuchs.

see Sa.24.2.14
2 Kgs 8.6   [→ *4.1.c.5*

(15) Two or three eunuchs throw Jezebel out of a window at Jehu's command.

see Sa.24.2.15
2 Kgs 9.32-33 [→ *4.1.c.6*

(16) King Jehoiachin's eunuchs are deported to Babylon after the siege of Jerusalem.
see Sa.24.2.16
2 Kgs 24.12, 15 [→ *4.1.c.8*

(17) The seven eunuchs who attend King Ahasuerus—Mehuman, Biztha, Harbona, Bigtha, Abagtha, Zethar and Carkas—are commanded to bring Queen Vashti before the king, who wishes to display her beauty.
see Sa.24.2.17
Est. 1.10-11 [→ *4.1.c.14*

(18) Harbona, a eunuch who attends King Ahasuerus, reminds the king that Haman has erected a gallows.
see Sa.24.2.18
Est. 7.9 [→ *4.1.c.13*

(19) The two eunuchs Hegai and Shaashgaz are the custodians of King Ahasuerus's harems.
see Sa.24.2.19
Est. 2.3,14,15 [→ *2.22.a.15*

(20) Bigthan and Teresh, two of King Ahasuerus's eunuchs, who guard the palace, prepare to assassinate the king until Mordecai uncovers the plot.
see Sa.24.2.20
Est. Introduction 1m-1r; Est. 2.21-23 [→ *4.1.c.11*

(21) Esther is served by a eunuch called Hegai, chief of the eunuchs of the harem.
see Sa.24.2.21
Est. R. **5.3; GL 4, 386; GL 6, 460 n.75** [→ *2.22.a.17*

(22) Hathach, a eunuch whom the king has appointed to wait on Esther, is sent by her to Mordecai to obtain information.
see Sa.24.2.22
Est. 4.5 [→ *4.1.c.12*

(23) Ebed-melech the Cushite, a eunuch attached to the palace, intervenes to save Jeremiah's life and helps to rescue him from the well.

see Sa.24.2.23
Jer. 38.7-13　　　　　　　　　　　　　　　　　　[→ *4.1.c.15*

(24) Hezekiah is castrated by God for revealing the secrets of David and Solomon.

see Sa.24.2.24; A.25.30.1; B.2.2.1; E.1.1.4; B.15.1.1
Liv. Proph. (Isaiah) **1.13**　　　　　　　　　　　[→ *1.26.b.47*

(25) Isaiah announces to Hezekiah that his sons will be eunuchs in the palace of the king of Babylon.

see Sa.24.2.25
2 Kgs 20.18; GL 3, 359; GL 6, 125 n.730　　　　[→ *1.6.b.2*

(26) Bagoas is a eunuch who is in charge of the 'personal affairs' of Holofernes.

see Sa.24.2.26
Jdt. 12.11　　　　　　　　　　　　　　　　　　[→ *2.22.a.16*

(27) Daniel and his friends, Hananiah, Mishael and Azariah, mutilate themselves when they are accused by King Nebuchadnezzar of leading an unchaste life.

see Sa.24.2.27; A.6.1.31
Liv. Proph. (Daniel) **4.2; GL 4, 326; GL 6, 415 n.78**　　[→ *2.3.9*

(28) Ashpenaz, the chief eunuch of King Nebuchadnezzar, is ordered to select from the Israelites a certain number of boys suitable for service in the palace of the king.

see Sa.24.2.28
Dan. 1.3-21　　　　　　　　　　　　　　　　　[→ *4.1.c.10*

(29) The eunuchs, priests and nobles of Judah and Jerusalem and all the people of the country who have 'passed between the parts of the calf' will be put into the power of their enemies.

see Sa.24.2.29
Jer. 34.19　　　　　　　　　　　　　　　　　　[→ *4.1.c.17*

Sa.2.3. *Absence of foreskin*

(1) Certain classes of angels are created circumcised.

see Sa.24.3.1
GL 5, 66 n.6　　　　　　　　　　　　　　[→ *3.3.a.17; 3.11.1*

(2) The giant Og, also known as Eliezer, Abraham's servant, is circumcised by Abraham.

see Sa.24.3.2; A.6.3.3; A.6.5.19; Va.6.5.1; Ic.6.5.2; Ic.7.2.1; Ic.7.3.1;

Ic.2.8.1; Ic.5.11.1; U.6.5.3; A.6.1.16
GL 6, 119 n.691 [→ *3.11.2; 2.13.a.2*

(3) Adam is created circumcised.
see Cb.9.1.1; F.5.1.1; A.9.1.2; R.14.1.1; R.18.1.1; A.6.1.19; A.6.1.20;
A.6.3.4; A.6.5.20; A.6.5.21; A.13.10.1; B.13.10.1; A.10.1.9; A.10.1.10;
A.12.1.1; Sa.24.3.3; A.16.9.1; Ca.9.1.1; Cb.5.1.1; G.23.5.1; J.23.1.1;
A.4.1.1; D.14.10.1; E.14.10.1; Fb.14.10.1; G.14.10.1; H.14.10.1; I.14.10.1;
J.14.10.1; Ja.14.10.1
GL 5, 99-100 n.78 [→ *3.3.a.19; 3.10.1; 3.11.3*

(4) Esau is circumcised (but he later removes the sign of the covenant
by means of an operation).
see A.13.6.3; B.18.3.1; E.4.1.3; O.13.6.1; P.13.6.1; B.11.3.1; B.13.6.1;
E.26.1.1; Ic.26.1.1; A.11.3.3; Sa.24.3.4; A.13.1.1; B.13.1.1
GL 5, 273 n.25 [→ *3.11.17; 2.13.a.3*

(5) Seth is born circumcised.
see Sa.24.3.5
GL 1, 121; GL 5, 149 n.51, 52 [→ *3.3.a.20; 3.10.2; 3.11.4*

(6) Noah is born circumcised.
see A.11.2.1; A.11.3.2; G.10.2.7; E.11.2.1; Sa.24.3.6; Sa.2.1.1; T.23.1.1;
I.10.4.1; Sa.24.10.1; Va.24.1.1; If.26.1.1; B.11.2.1; B.11.3.2; Sa.24.2.1
GL 1, 146-147; GL 5, 168-169 n.6 [→ *3.10.17*

(7) All the males in Abraham's household are circumcised.
see Sa.24.3.7
Gen. R. **47.7f.**; *Gen. R.* **48.3f.**; Gen. **17.23, 27**
[→ *3.11.14; 2.13.a.5*

(8) Ishmael is circumcised at the age of thirteen.
see Sa.24.3.8
Gen. R. **46.2**; *Gen. R.* **47.7f.**; *Gen. R.* **43**; *Gen. R.* **55.4**; Gen.
17.25-26 [→ *3.11.26; 2.13.a.23; 2.4.11*

(9) Abraham is circumcised at the age of ninety-nine or one hundred.
see Sa.24.3.9; A.10.1.12; Pc.10.5.1; Pc.10.6.1; A.6.5.23; T.25.1.1; F.10.1.8
Gen. **17.23-26**; *Gen. R.* **42.8**; *Gen. R.* **46.1f.**; *Gen. R.* **47.7f.**;
Gen. R. **48.2f.** [→ *3.11.13; 2.13.a.4; 2.14.a.4; 2.31.b.1*

(10) The children of the people whom Abraham recaptures when he
sets out to recapture Lot are circumcised.
see Sa.24.3.10
Gen. R. **43.4** [→ *3.11.15; 2.13.a.6*

(11) Isaac is circumcised on the eighth day after his birth.
    see Sa.24.3.11; A.25.3.2; A.8.1.3; G.23.4.6
    Gen. 21.4; *Gen. R.* 55.4   [→ *3.11.16; 2.13.a.7*

(12) Jacob is born circumcised.
    see A.6.1.23; G.23.4.7; Ta.23.1.1; Ta.24.1.1; K.13.10.1; Sa.24.3.12; O.6.1.1;
    Q.6.1.1; K.16.5.1; T.23.1.3; G.23.5.3
    ***Gen. R.* 63.7; *Num. R.* 14.5**   [→ *3.3.a.21; 3.10.3; 3.11.5*

(13) Gad, Jacob's son, is born circumcised.
    see Sa.24.3.13
    GL 1, 365; GL 5, 297 n.185   [→ *3.3.a.22; 3.10.4; 3.11.6*

(14) Joseph is born circumcised.
    see Sa.24.3.14; A.10.1.14; Va.3.1.2; Va.27.2.1; Va.3.1.3; Va.10.10.1
    ***Gen. R.* 84.6; *Num. R.* 14.5**   [→ *3.3.a.23; 3.10.5; 3.11.7*

(15) During the famine in Egypt, the Egyptians coming to beg for grain are persuaded by Joseph to circumcise themselves.
    see Sa.24.3.16
    ***Gen. R.* 90.6; *Gen. R.* 91.5**   [→ *2.32.4*

(16) Ephraim and Manasseh, Joseph's sons, are circumcised.
    see Sa.24.3.14
    GL 2, 136; GL 5, 365 n.366   [→ *3.11.11; 2.13.a.8*

(17) The sons of Machir (the grandson of Joseph) are circumcised.
    see Sa.24.3.117
    GL 2, 169; GL 5, 373 n.429   [→ *3.11.19; 2.13.a.9*

(18) Shechem, his father, his five brothers and all the men in his city (645 men and 276 lads) are circumcised.
    see Sa.24.3.18
    **Gen. 34.15, 22-24; *Gen. R.* 80.8; *T. Levi* 6.6 (T12P);
    Theod. Fragments 4, 5, 6**   [→ *2.5.1; 2.4.8; 2.16.5*

(19) Moses is born circumcised or, alternatively, he is circumcised on the eighth day after his birth.
    see F.10.1.11; A.25.9.1; Sa.24.3.19; A.6.5.25; A.6.4.2; P.23.1.1; P.25.4.1;
    I.10.1.5; G.10.2.9; F.11.3.2; Fb.10.1.7; F.10.1.11; G.25.4.1; If.6.1.3;
    Fb.14.2.3; I.23.3.3; P.11.2.2; G.17.20.1; Ib.13.2.1; Ib.24.4.1; Ia.24.4.1;
    E.6.1.1; Ga.10.2.1; E.12.10.1; P.13.2.1; P.24.4.1; K.13.10.2; B.16.12.2;
    Ib.16.12.3; Ia.13.2.1; A.26.1.3
    ***Cant. R.* 1.20, 22, 24; *Lev. R.* 21; *Qoh. R.* 4.9 §1; *Qoh. R.* 9.2 §1;
    Deut. R. 11.10**   [→ *3.11.21; 2.13.a.10; 3.10.6; 3.3.a.24; 3.11.8*

(20) Zipporah takes a flint, cuts off her son's foreskin, and touches Moses' genitals with it when Yahweh meets them on the road and tries to kill Moses.

see Sa.24.3.20

Exod. **4.24-26;** *Cant. R.* **5.8;** GL **2, 295, 328;** GL **5, 412 n.97, 99;**
GL **5, 423 n.146-148**   [→ *2.15.b.10; 3.11.20; 2.18.a.4; 2.13.a.12*

(21) The sons of the Jews (as well as previously uncircumcised Jews) are circumcised before they leave Egypt.

see Sa.24.3.21

Cant R. **19.5;** *Num. R.* **11.3;** *Cant R.* **3.7 §4;** *Cant R.* **1.12 §3**
                                                                          [→ *2.32.6; 2.4.16*

(22) At Gilgal, on the west bank of the River Jordan, Joshua performs the rite of circumcision on those born in the desert who have remained uncircumcised because of the rough weather or for other reasons.

see Sa.24.3.22

Josh. **5.2-10;** GL **4, 7;** GL **6, 172 n.16**
                              [→ *3.11.22; 2.13.a.13; 1.16.b.6; 2.31.b.3*

(23) Achior the Ammonite is circumcised after he recognizes the mighty works of the God of Israel.

see Sa.24.3.23

Jdt. **14.10**   [→ *2.13.a.18; 3.11.23*

(24) Obed, the pious son of Ruth, is born circumcised.

see Sa.24.3.24

GL **6, 194 n.68**   [→ *3.3.a.25; 3.10.8; 3.11.10*

(25) David is born circumcised.

see E.11.3.1; F.11.1.7; Sa.24.3.25; B.11.3.3; T.23.2.1; O.23.2.1; A.25.15.3; A.23.1.16; G.25.1.1; A.25.9.2

GL **6, 247-248 n.13**   [→ *3.10.7; 3.11.11*

(26) Circumcised and uncircumcised men are brought to Solomon as a test to see whether he can distinguish between them. (He opens the door of the ark and the uncircumcised fall prostrate before the Shekinah, while the faces of the circumcised are filled with radiance.)

see Sa.24.3.26; F.10.1.16

GL **4, 146;** GL **6, 290 n.43**   [→ *2.1.b.1*

(27) The king of Salem is born circumcised.

see Sa.24.3.27
Gen. R. **43.6**   [→ *5.1.6*

(28) Jonah is circumcised. The sight of the sign of the covenant
makes Leviathan flee in terror.
see Sa.24.3.28; E.1.1.5; A.25.3.9
GL 4, 249; GL 6, 350 n.31   [→ *2.24.17*

(29) All the uncircumcised boys in the territories of Israel are circumcised forcibly by Mattathias, a priest of the line of Joarib.
see Sa.24.3.29
1 Macc. 2.46   [→ *2.13.a.19; 3.11.24*

(30) Shem-Melchizedek is born circumcised.
see Sa.24.3.30
Gen. R. **26.3; GL 5, 226 n.102**   [→ *3.11.9; 3.10.10; 3.3.a.26*

(31) Jeremiah is born circumcised.
see Sa.24.3.31; If.26.1.3; Gf.27.5.1
GL 4, 294; GL 6, 384-385 n.12   [→ *3.10.9; 3.11.12*

(32) The babies of two women are circumcised although this is forbidden by Antiochus Epiphanes.
see Sa.24.3.32
2 Macc. 6.10   [→ *3.11.25; 2.13.a.20*

Sa.6. *Abnormal Size of Male Genitals*

Sa.6.1. *Abnormally large male genitals*

(1) The Egyptians have huge penes.
Lev. R. **25.7; Ezek. 16.26; Ezek. 23.20**   [→ *3.6.b.12*

Sa.10. *Unusual Emission or Emanation from Male Genitals*

Sa.10.1. *Emission of noxious substance from male genitals*

(1) The male Israelites are afflicted with an issue (gonorrhoea) and
with leprosy after the making of the golden calf.
see A.23.1.9
Lev. R. **17.3;** *Num. R.* **7.1-6;** *Num. R.* **8.3;** *Num. R.* **7.10;**
Num. R. **13.8; GL 3, 213; GL 6, 79 n.112, 113**   [→ *1.26.a.11*

(2) Joab and his descendants are cursed with gonorrhoea by David
after Joab has killed Abner, son of Ner.

see A.23.1.17

2 Sam. 3.28-29; *Lev. R.* 16.1; *Lev. R.* 17.3; *Num. R.* 8.5

[→ *1.26.b.41*

Sa.13. *Peculiarity of Skin of Male Genitals*

Sa.13.1. *Tattooed genitals*

(1) Jehoiakim's penis is tattooed with the name of God (and his body with the names of idols).

see A.13.1.2

Lev. R. 19.6; GL 4, 284; GL 6, 379 n.125   [→ *2.13.b.1*

Sa.18. *Animal Genitals in Place of Human*

Sa.18.2. *Genitals of sheep*

(1) Baruch sees men with the loins of sheep in the first heaven.

see D.14.2.3; D.18.11.1; U.18.2.1; F.18.4.2

3 Bar. 2.3 (Slavonic and Greek)   [→ *1.26.b.7*

Sa.18.5. *Genitals of horses*

(1) The stars (who are fallen angels) have the sexual organs, hands and feet of horses.

see P.18.5.1; U.18.5.1

1 En. 88.1, 3   [→ *3.7.1*

Sa.23. *Disease, Paralysis or Malfunction of Male Genitals*

Sa.23.2. *Uretha closed up*

(1) The uretha of each of the Philistines and their beasts, and all the other apertures of their bodies, are closed up when King Abimelech takes Sarah as a wife.

see Ga.23.2.1; Ha.23.1.1; I.23.4.1; J.23.2.1; Ra.23.1.1; Sb.23.2.1

GL 1, 258; GL 5, 243 n.190; GL 5, 244 n.202   [→ *2.10.a.2*

Sa.24 *Wounded or Mutilated Male Genitals*

Sa.24.2 *Severed testicle(s)*

(1) Noah is castrated by his son, Ham (or by his grandson Canaan), as he lies drunk and exposed.

see A.11.2.5; A.11.3.2; G.10.2.7; Sa.2.3.6; Sa.24.3.6; E.11.2.1; T.23.1.1;
I.10.4.1; Sa.24.10.1; Va.24.1.1; If.26.1.1; B.11.2.1; B.11.3.2; Sa.2.1.1
Gen. R. **36.3**; *Gen. R.* **36.7**; *Lev. R.* **17.5**   [→ *2.14.b.2*

(2) Potiphar (or Poti-phera) is castrated by the angel Gabriel (or by God) because he has bought Joseph for sexual purposes.
see Sa.2.1.2
Gen. R. **86.3**; *Jub.* **34.11**; *Jub.* **39.2**; *Cant. R.* **1.1 §1**
[→ *1.26.b.15; 2.23.b.2*

(3) Eunuchs act as servants and messengers for Potiphar and his wife.
see Sa.2.1.3
Jub. **39.14**; GL 2, 40-42; GL 5, 337 n.99   [→ *2.22.a.13*

(4) Eunuchs bring food mixed with enchantments to Joseph from Pentephris's wife, but Joseph looks up and sees a frightening angel with a sword and a bowl and realizes it is a trick to lead him astray.
see Sa.2.1.4
T. Jos. **6.2** (T12P)   [→ *4.1.c.1*

(5) A eunuch tells Pentephris's wife about Joseph, and she goes to see him.
see Sa.2.1.5
T. Jos. **12.1** (T12P)   [→ *4.1.c.2*

(6) A eunuch is sent by Pentephris's wife to buy Joseph.
see Sa.2.1.6
T. Jos. **16.1f.** (T12P)   [→ *4.1.c.3*

(7) The Egyptians are emasculated by frogs. These frogs also leap around, croaking, in their entrails.
see Sa.2.1.7; B.24.3.1; B.23.1.1; P.23.1.2; B.24.3.2; B.24.4.2; B.23.2.4;
Ie.27.1.1; W.4.2.2; A.23.3.1; A.23.6.1
Cant. R. **10.3, 6**; *Cant. R.* **15.27**; GL 2, 342, 345, 349-351
[→ *1.26.b.25; 2.5.3*

(8) Agag is castrated by Samuel because he has taken the circumcised members of slain Israelites and thrown them upwards, exclaiming 'This is what thou hast chosen'.
see Sa.2.1.8
Lam. R. **3.64 §9**   [→ *1.26.b.35*

(9) Seventy eunuchs guard Solomon's daughter in the high tower in which he imprisons her.

see Sa.2.1.9
GL 4, 175-176; GL 6, 303 n.100   [→ *2.22.a.14*

(10) Johanan brings back the eunuchs from Gibeon.
see Sa.2.1.10
Jer. 41.16   [→ *4.1.c.16*

(11) A eunuch who is in command of the fighting men is taken prisoner by Nebuzaradan, an officer of the king of Babylon who enters Jerusalem to sack it.
see Sa.2.1.11
2 Kgs 25.19; Jer. 52.25   [→ *4.1.c.9*

(12) Eunuchs leave Jerusalem for Babylon together with King Jeconiah and the queen mother, the nobility of Judah and Jerusalem and the blacksmiths and metal workers.
see Sa.2.1.12
Jer. 29.2   [→ *4.1.c.18*

(13) King Ahab employs eunuchs.
see Sa.2.1.13
1 Kgs 22.9; 2 Chron. 18.8   [→ *4.1.c.7*

(14) The king of Israel employs eunuchs.
see Sa.2.1.14
2 Kgs 8.6   [→ *4.1.c.5*

(15) Two or three eunuchs throw Jezebel out of a window at Jehu's command.
see Sa.2.1.15
2 Kgs 9.32-33   [→ *4.1.c.6*

(16) King Jehoiachin's eunuchs are deported to Babylon after the siege of Jerusalem.
see Sa.2.1.16
2 Kgs 24.12,15   [→ *4.1.c.8*

(17) The seven eunuchs who attend King Ahasuerus—Mehuman, Biztha, Harbona, Bigtha, Abagtha, Zethar and Carkas—are commanded to bring Queen Vashti before the king, who wishes to display her beauty.
see Sa.2.1.17
Est. 1.10-11   [→ *4.1.c.14*

(18) Harbona, a eunuch who attends King Ahasuerus, reminds the

king that Haman has erected a gallows.
see Sa.2.1.18
Est. 7.9   [→ *4.1.c.13*

(19) The two eunuchs, Hegai and Shaashgaz, are the custodians of King Ahasuerus's harems.
see Sa.2.1.19
Est. 2.3, 14, 15   [→ *2.22.a.15*

(20) Bigthan and Teresh, two of King Ahasuerus's eunuchs, who guard the palace, prepare to assassinate the king until Mordecai uncovers the plot.
see Sa.2.1.20
Est. Introduction 1m-1r; Est. 2.21-23   [→ *4.1.c.11*

(21) Esther is served by a eunuch called Hegai, chief of the eunuchs of the harem.
see Sa.2.1.21
Est. R. 5.3; **GL 4, 386; GL 6, 460 n.75**   [→ *2.22.a.17*

(22) Hathach, a eunuch whom the king has appointed to wait on Esther, is sent by her to Mordecai to obtain information.
see Sa.2.1.22
Est. 4.5   [→ *4.1.c.12*

(23) Ebed-melech the Cushite, a eunuch attached to the palace, intervenes to save Jeremiah's life and helps to rescue him from the well.
see Sa.2.1.23
Jer. 38.7-13   [→ *4.1.c.15*

(24) Hezekiah is castrated by God for revealing the secrets of David and Solomon.
see Sa.2.1.24; A.25.30.1; B.2.2.1; E.1.1.4; B.15.1.1
Liv. Proph. (Isaiah) 1.13   [→ *1.26.b.47*

(25) Isaiah announces to Hezekiah that his sons will be eunuchs in the palace of the king of Babylon.
see Sa.2.1.25
2 Kgs 20.18; GL 3, 359; GL 6, 125 n.730   [→ *1.6.b.2*

(26) Bagoas is a eunuch who is in charge of the 'personal affairs' of Holofernes.
see Sa.2.1.26
Jdt. 12.11   [→ *2.22.a.16*

(27) Daniel and his friends, Hananiah, Mishael and Azariah, mutilate themselves when they are accused by King Nebuchadnezzar of leading an unchaste life.

see Sa.2.1.27; A.6.1.31

Liv. Proph. (Daniel) 4.2; GL 4, 326; GL 6, 415 n.78   [→ *2.3.9*

(28) Ashpenaz, the chief eunuch of King Nebuchadnezzar, is ordered to select from the Israelites a certain number of boys suitable for service in the palace of the king.

see Sa.2.1.28

Dan. 1.3-21   [→ *4.1.c.10*

(29) The eunuchs, priests and nobles of Judah and Jerusalem and all the people of the country who have 'passed between the parts of the calf' will be put into the power of their enemies.

see Sa.2.1.29

Jer. 34.19   [→ *4.1.c.17*

Sa.24.3. *Absence of foreskin*

(1) Certain classes of angels are created circumcised.

see Sa.2.3.1

GL 5, 66 n.6   [→ *3.3.a.17; 3.11.1*

(2) The giant Og, also known as Eliezer, Abraham's servant, is circumcised by Abraham.

see Sa.2.3.2; A.6.3.3; A.6.5.19; Va.6.5.1; Ic.6.5.2; Ic.7.2.1; Ic.7.3.1; Ic.2.8.1; Ic.5.11.1; U.6.5.3; A.6.1.16

GL 6, 119 n.691   [→ *3.11.2; 2.13.a.2*

(3) Adam is created circumcised.

see Cb.9.1.1; F.5.1.1; A.9.1.2; R.14.1.1; R.18.1.1; A.6.1.19; A.6.1.20; A.6.3.4; A.6.5.20; A.6.5.21; A.13.10.1; B.13.10.1; A.10.1.9; A.10.1.10; A.12.1.1; Sa.2.3.3; A.16.9.1; Ca.9.1.1; Cb.5.1.1; G.23.5.1; J.23.1.1; A.4.1.1; D.14.10.1; E.14.10.1; Fb.14.10.1; G.14.10.1; H.14.10.1; I.14.10.1; J.14.10.1; Ja.14.10.1

GL 5, 99-100 n.78   [→ *3.3.a.19; 3.10.1; 3.11.3*

(4) Esau is circumcised (but he later removes the sign of the covenant by means of an operation).

see A.13.6.3; B.18.3.1; E.4.1.3; O.13.6.1; P.13.6.1; B.11.3.1; B.13.6.1; E.26.1.1; Ic.26.1.1; A.11.3.3; Sa.2.3.4; A.13.1.1; B.13.1.1

GL 5, 273 n.25   [→ *3.11.17; 2.13.a.3*

(5) Seth is born circumcised.
  see Sa.2.3.5
  GL 1, 121; GL 5, 149 n.51, 52   [→ *3.3.a.20; 3.10.2; 3.11.4*

(6) Noah is born circumcised.
  see A.11.2.5; A.11.3.2; G.10.2.7; E.11.2.1; Sa.2.3.6; Sa.2.1.1; T.23.1.1;
  I.10.4.1; Sa.24.10.1; Va.24.1.1; If.26.1.1; B.11.2.1; B.11.3.2; Sa.24.2.1
  GL 1, 146-147; GL 5, 168-169 n.6   [→ *3.10.17*

(7) All the males in Abraham's household are circumcised.
  see Sa.2.3.7
  Gen. R. 47.7f.; Gen. R. 48.3f.; Gen. 17.23, 27
                                          [→ *3.11.14; 2.13.a.5*

(8) Ishmael is circumcised at the age of thirteen.
  see Sa.2.3.8
  Gen. R. 46.2; Gen. R. 47.7f.; Gen. R. 43; Gen. R. 55.4; Gen.
  17.25-26   [→ *3.11.26; 2.13.a.23; 2.4.11*

(9) Abraham is circumcised at the age of ninety-nine or one hundred.
  see Sa.2.3.9; A.10.1.12; Pc.10.5.1; Pc.10.6.1; A.6.5.23; T.25.1.1; F.10.1.8
  Gen. 17.23-26; Gen. R. 42.8; Gen. R. 46.1f.; Gen. R. 47.7f.;
  Gen. R. 48.2f.   [→ *3.11.13; 2.13.a.4; 2.14.a.4; 2.31.b.1*

(10) The children of the people whom Abraham recaptures when he
sets out to recapture Lot are circumcised.
  see Sa.2.3.10
  Gen. R. 43.4   [→ *3.11.15; 2.13.a.6*

(11) Isaac is circumcised on the eighth day after his birth.
  see Sa.2.3.11; A.25.3.2; A.8.1.3; G.23.4.6
  Gen. 21.4; Gen. R. 55.4   [→ *3.11.16; 2.13.a.7*

(12) Jacob is born circumcised.
  see A.6.1.23; G.23.4.7; Ta.23.1.1; Ta.24.1.1; K.13.10.1; Sa.2.3.12; O.6.1.1;
  Q.6.1.1; K.16.5.1; T.23.1.3; G.23.5.3
  Gen. R. 63.7; Num. R. 14.5   [→ *3.3.a.21; 3.10.3; 3.11.5*

(13) Gad, Jacob's son, is born circumcised.
  see Sa.2.3.13
  GL 1, 365; GL 5, 297 n.185   [→ *3.3.a.22; 3.10.4; 3.11.6*

(14) Joseph is born circumcised.
  see Sa.2.3.14; A.10.1.14; Va.3.1.2; Va.27.2.1; Va.3.1.3; Va.10.10.1
  Gen. R. 84.6; Num. R. 14.5   [→ *3.3.a.23; 3.10.5; 3.11.7*

(15) During the famine in Egypt, the Egyptians coming to beg for grain are persuaded by Joseph to circumcise themselves.
see Sa.2.3.15
Gen. R. 90.6; Gen. R. 91.5 [→ *2.32.4*

(16) Ephraim and Manasseh, Joseph's sons, are circumcised.
see Sa.2.3.16
GL 2, 136; GL 5, 365 n.366 [→ *3.11.11; 2.13.a.8*

(17) The sons of Machir (who is the grandson of Joseph) are circumcised.
see Sa.2.3.17
GL 2, 169; GL 5, 373 n.429 [→ *3.11.19; 2.13.a.9*

(18) Shechem, his father, his five brothers and all the men in his city (645 men and 276 lads) are circumcised.
see Sa.2.3.18
Gen. 34.15, 22-24; *Gen. R.* 80.8; *T. Levi* 6.6 (T12P); Theod. Fragments 4, 5, 6 [→ *2.5.1; 2.4.8; 2.16.5*

(19) Moses is born circumcised or, alternatively, circumcised on the eighth day after his birth.
see F.10.1.11; A.25.9.1; Sa.2.3.19; A.6.5.25; A.6.4.2; P.23.1.1; P.25.4.1; I.10.1.5; G.10.2.9; F.11.3.2; Fb.10.1.1; F.10.1.11; G.25.4.1; If.6.1.3; Fb.14.2.3; I.23.3.3; P.11.2.2; G.17.20.1; Ib.13.2.1; Ib.24.4.1; Ia.24.4.1; E.6.1.1; Ga.10.2.1; E.12.10.1; P.13.2.1; P.24.4.1; K.13.10.2; B.16.12.2; Ib.16.12.3; Ia.13.2.1; A.26.1.3
***Cant. R.* 1.20, 22, 24; *Lev. R.*21; *Qoh. R.* 4.9 §1; *Qoh. R.* 9.2 §1; *Deut. R.* 11.10** [→ *3.11.21; 2.13.a.10; 3.10.6; 3.3.a.24; 3.11.8*

(20) Zipporah takes a flint, cuts off her son's foreskin, and touches Moses' genitals with it when Yahweh meets them on the road and tries to kill Moses.
see Sa.2.3.20
Exod. 4.24-26; *Cant. R.* 5.8; GL 2, 295, 328; GL 5, 412 n.97, 99; GL 5, 423 n.146-148 [→ *2.15.b.10; 3.11.20; 2.18.a.4; 2.13.a.12*

(21) The sons of the Jews (as well as previously uncircumcised Jews) are circumcised before they leave Egypt.
see Sa.2.3.21
***Cant. R.* 19.5; *Num. R.* 11.3; *Cant. R.* 3.7 §4; *Cant. R.* 1.12 §3**
[→ *2.32.6; 2.4.16*

(22) At Gilgal, on the west bank of the River Jordan, Joshua performs the rite of circumcision on those born in the desert who have remained uncircumcised because of the rough weather or for other reasons.
　　see Sa.2.3.22
　　Josh. 5.2-10; GL 4, 7; GL 6, 172 n.16
　　　　　　　　　　　　　[→ *3.11.22; 2.13.a.13; 1.16.b.6; 2.31.b.3*

(23) Achior the Ammonite is circumcised after he recognizes the mighty works of the God of Israel.
　　see Sa.2.3.23
　　Jdt. 14.10　　　　　　　　　　[→ *2.13.a.18; 3.11.23*

(24) Obed, the pious son of Ruth, is born circumcised.
　　see Sa.2.3.24
　　GL 6, 194 n.68　　　　　[→ *3.3.a.25; 3.10.8; 3.11.10*

(25) David is born circumcised.
　　see E.11.3.1; F.11.1.7; Sa.2.3.25; B.11.3.3; T.23.2.1; O.23.2.1; A.25.15.3; A.23.1.16; G.25.1.1; A.25.9.2
　　GL 6, 247-248 n.13　　　　　　　[→ *3.10.7; 3.11.11*

(26) Circumcised and uncircumcised men are brought to Solomon as a test to see whether he can distinguish between them. (He opens the door of the ark and the uncircumcised fall prostrate before the Shekinah, while the faces of the circumcised are filled with radiance.)
　　see Sa.2.3.25; F.10.1.16
　　GL 4, 146; GL 6, 290 n.43　　　　　　　[→ *2.1.b.1*

(27) The king of Salem is born circumcised.
　　see Sa.2.3.27
　　Gen. R. 43.6　　　　　　　　　　　　[→ *5.1.6*

(28) Jonah is circumcised. The sign of the covenant makes Leviathan flee in terror.
　　see Sa.2.3.28; E.1.1.5; A.25.3.9
　　GL 4, 249; GL 6, 350 n.31　　　　　　[→ *2.24.17*

(29) All the uncircumcised boys in the territories of Israel are circumcised forcibly by Mattathias, a priest of the line of Joarib.
　　see Sa.2.3.29
　　1 Macc. 2.46　　　　　　　　[→ *2.13.a.19; 3.11.24*

(30) Shem-Melchizedek is born circumcised.

see Sa.2.3.30
Gen. R. 26.3; GL 5, 226, 102   [→ *3.11.9; 3.10.10; 3.3.a.26*

(**31**) Jeremiah is born circumcised.
see Sa.2.3.31; If.26.1.3; Gf.27.5.1
GL 4, 294; GL 6, 384-385 n.12   [→ *3.10.9; 3.11.12*

(**32**) The babies of two women are circumcised although this is forbidden by Antiochus Epiphanes.
see Sa.2.3.32
2 Macc. 6.10   [→ *3.11.25; 2.13.a.20*

Sa.24.10. *Unspecified wound to, or mutilation of, male genitals*

(**1**) Noah's sexual organs are mutilated when the lion mauls him as he is leaving the ark (with the result that when he has sexual relations his seed scatters).
see A.11.2.5; A.11.3.2; G.10.2.7; Sa.2.3.6; Sa.24.3.6; Sa.2.1.1; T.23.1.1; I.10.4.1; E.11.2.1; Va.24.1.1; If.26.1.1; B.11.2.1; B.11.3.2; Sa.24.2.1
Gen. R. 36.4   [→ *1.20.3; 1.13.2*

(**2**) Reuben is struck with a severe wound in the loins as a punishment for sleeping with his father's wife, Bilhah.
T. Reub. 1.7 (T12P)   [→ *1.26.b.18*

Sb. *The Vulva*

Sb.10. *Unusual Emission or Emanation from Vulva*

Sb.10.3. *Emission of unusually large quantity of blood from vagina*

(**1**) Large quantities of blood pour from the vaginas of the daughters of Zion so that the gentiles are unable to mix with them.
see W.5.1.1; D.23.1.1; E.23.1.1
Lam. R. 4.15 §18   [→ *2.23.b.4; 2.21.5*

Sb.23. *Disease, Paralysis or Malfunction of Vulva*

Sb.23.2. *Vagina closed up*

(**1**) The vaginas of the Philistines and their beasts and all the other apertures of their bodies are closed up when King Abimelech takes Sarah as a wife.
see Ga.23.2.1; Ha.23.1.1; I.23.4.1; J.23.2.1; Ra.23.1.1; Sa.23.2.1
GL 1, 258; GL 5, 243 n.190; GL 5, 244 n.202   [→ *2.10.a.2*

Sc. *Urine*
[No references in sources]

Sd. *Semen*

Sd.4. *Semen in Unusual Place on Body*

Sd.4.1 *Semen from fingernails*

(1) Joseph's semen is diffused and emerges from his fingernails when Potiphar's wife tries to seduce him.

   see Pd.10.16.1

Gen. R. **87.7;** *Gen. R.* **98.20**   [→ *2.14.b.3*

T. THE LEGS

T.5. *Unusual Number of Leg(s)*

T.5.3. *Four legs*

(1) Tebel, the second earth, is inhabited by humans with four legs.
see D.5.1.5; O.5.3.2; P.5.3.1; U.5.3.1; D.18.4.2; D.18.5.1; D.18.6.1;
D.21.4.1; D.21.5.1; D.21.6.1
GL 1, 10   [→ *1.16.b.8; 3.2.7*

T.6. *Abnormal Size of Leg(s)*

T.6.4. *Abnormally thin leg(s)*

(1) The Antichrist is a skinny-legged young man with a tuft of grey
hair on the front of his bald head. His eyebrows reach to his ears and
there is a leprous bare spot on the palms of his hands. He can appear
as a young child or an old man, but is unable to change the signs on
his head. He has fiery wings.
see E.2.1.1; E.11.4.1; Gb.6.5.1; M.14.2.19; M.20.1.19; Pa.23.1.1
Apoc. Elij. **3.15-17**; *Apoc. Elij.* **5.20**   [→ *3.1.26*

T.13. *Peculiarity of Skin of Leg(s)*

T.13.6. *Hairy legs*

(1) The queen of Sheba has hairy legs and feet.
see U.13.6.1; E.9.3.1
GL 6, 289 n.41   [→ *1.1.a.8*

T.16. *Leg(s) of Unusual Substance*

T.16.2. *Leg(s) of bronze, copper or brass*

(1) Daniel sees a man with legs and arms as if of burnished bronze, a
body like beryl, chrysolite or topaz, a face like lightning and eyes like

fiery torches (and a voice like the voice of a crowd).
> see A.16.18.1; F.16.12.3; G.16.12.3; O.16.2.1
> **Dan. 10.6** [→ *3.1.14*]

T.16.18. *Leg(s) of jewel or precious stone*

(1) The legs and body of Iaoel, the angel who takes the right hand of Abraham, are like a sapphire, his face is like chrysolite and his hair is white like snow.
> see A.16.18.2; E.11.2.1; F.16.18.1
> *Apoc. Abr.* **11.2** [→ *3.3.a.11*]

T.18. *Animal Leg(s) in Place of Human*

T.18.1. *Leg(s) of mule, donkey or ass*

(1) Onoskelis has the body of a beautiful woman but the legs of a mule; she is a spirit generated from an unexpected voice which is called 'a voice of the echo of a black heaven'.
> *T. Sol.* **4.2-4, 8** [→ *3.1.20*]

T.23. *Disease, Paralysis or Malfunction of Leg(s)*

T.23.1. *Lameness*

(1) Noah is struck and lamed by a lion in the Ark because he forgets to feed it, or is late in feeding it.
> see A.11.2.5; A.11.3.2; G.10.2.7; Sa.2.3.6; Sa.24.3.6; Sa.2.1.1; E.11.2.1;
> I.10.4.1; Sa.24.10.1; Va.24.1.1; If.26.1.1; B.11.2.1; B.11.3.2; Sa.24.2.1
> *Qoh. R.* **9.2 §1**; *Lev. R.* **20.1** [→ *1.20.3; 1.13.2*]

(2) Many Israelites are maimed and lamed during the building work in Egypt. (But all the lame, blind and deaf are healed in the time between the Exodus and the Revelation on Mount Sinai so that they are fit to receive the Torah.)
> see P.1.1.1; G.23.4.10; I.23.3.4; J.23.1.3
> *Num. R.* **7.1**; GL 3, 78; GL 6, 30 n.176; GL 3, 13 [→ *1.23.1*]

(3) Jacob limps after being struck in the hollow of his thigh during his fight with the angel (or God, or the guardian spirit of Esau); his thigh is put out of joint, or his sciatic nerve is injured; or the sinew and the hip are dislocated, flattened, cut open like a fish, or separated.
> see A.6.1.23; G.23.4.4; Ta.23.1.1; Ta.24.1.1; Sa.2.3.12; Sa.24.3.12; O.6.1.1;

Q.6.1.1; K.16.5.1; K.13.10.1; G.23.5.3
Gen. **32.24-26, 32-33;** *Gen. R.* **77.3;** *Gen. R.* **68.5;** *Gen. R.* **79.5;**
Dem. **Fragment 2.7; GL 1, 385, 389; GL 5, 305 n.248; GL 5, 308**
n.258   [→ *1.20.4; 1.26.b.13; 2.16.4*

(4) All the lame are made whole at the birth of Isaac.
see G.23.4.5; I.23.3.1
GL 1, 262; GL 5, 245 n.203   [→ *2.4.5*

(5) The Pharaoh Necho (which means 'hobbler') is injured and lamed
by one of the lions on the throne of Solomon.
Qoh. R. **9.2 §1;** *Lev. R.* **20.1**   [→ *1.23.3; 1.29.1*

(6) A parable: a lame man rides on the back of a blind man while
they guard the king's orchard and they are thus able to steal the king's
early figs. The king realizes what has happened and takes both men to
task.
see G.23.4.30
Lev. R. **4.5;** *Apoc. Ezek.* **1.1f.**   [→ *4.1.a.2*

T.23.2. *Trembling or agitated leg(s)*

(1) David's limbs never cease from trembling after the day he sees an
angel slay his four sons, the prophet Gad, and the elders who accompany him, and then wipe his dripping sword on the king's garments.
see E.11.3.1; Sa.2.3.25; Sa.24.3.25; B.11.3.3; F.11.1.7; O.23.2.1; A.25.15.3;
A.23.1.16; G.25.1.1; A.25.9.2
GL 4, 113; GL 6, 271 n.124   [→ *1.12.a.27; 1.14.a.8*

T.24. **Wounded Mutilated, or Maimed Leg(s)**

T.24.3. *Broken leg(s)*

(1) Nebuchadnezzar breaks a leg while attempting to ascend the
throne of Solomon.
see U.23.1.4; A.27.2.3; Cc.27.1.1; Cc.27.4.1; A.6.2.5; A.2.4.1; Pd.12.1.1;
Pd.6.5.1; E.6.5.6; Ib.1.1.2
GL 6, 415 n.80   [→ *1.29.2*

T.25. *Unusual Abilities of Leg(s)*

T.25.1. *Leg(s) that can cover vast distances at a single stride*

(1) Abraham can march with giant strides, each of his steps measuring four miles.
see A.6.5.23; A.10.1.12; Sa.2.3.9; Sa.24.3.9; Pc.10.5.1; Pc.10.6.1; F.10.1.8
GL 1, 232; GL 5, 225 n.97   [→ *3.3.a.27*

(2) When the spirit is upon him, Samson is able, in one stride, to cover a distance equal to that between Zorah and Eshtaol.
see E.8.1.2; E.25.5.1; A.6.1.29; Ie.17.3.1; I.10.20.1; G.24.1.2; G.1.3; U.23.1.2; M.6.3.1; E.6.5.4; G.23.4.16
Lev. R. 8.2   [→ *1.19.b.10*

Ta. *The Thigh(s)*

Ta.6. *Abnormal Size of Thigh(s)*

Ta.6.1. *Abnormally large thigh(s)*

(1) The thighs of the Gibborim measure eighteen ells.
GL 1, 151; GL 5, 172 n.13   [→ *1.1.b.2*

Ta.13. *Peculiarity of Skin of Thigh(s)*

Ta.13.2. *Birthmark on thigh(s)*

(1) The Messiah has small birthmarks on his thigh, and red hair.
see E.11.3.1
'Horoscope of the Messiah', Vermes, 270   [→ *3.1.29*

Ta.23. *Disease, Paralysis or Malfunction of Thigh(s)*

Ta.23.1. *Lameness*

(1) Jacob limps after being struck in the hollow of his thigh during his fight with the angel (or God, or the guardian spirit of Esau); his thigh is put out of joint, or his sciatic nerve is injured; or the sinew and the hip are dislocated, flattened, cut open like a fish, or separated.

see A.6.1.23; G.23.4.7; T.23.1.3; Ta.24.1.1; Sa.2.3.12; Sa.24.3.12; O.6.1.1;
Q.6.1.1; K.16.5.1; K.13.10.1; G.23.5.3
Gen. 32.24-26, 32-33; *Gen. R.* **77.3;** *Gen. R.* **68.5;** *Gen. R.* **79.5;**
**Dem. Fragment 2.7; GL 1, 385, 389; GL 5, 305 n.248; GL 5, 308
n.258** [→ *1.20.4; 1.26.b.13; 2.16.4; 1.14.c.7*

Ta.24. *Wounded, Mutilated or Maimed Thigh(s)*

(1) Jacob limps after being struck in the hollow of his thigh during
his fight with the angel (or God, or the guardian spirit of Esau); his
thigh is put out of joint, or his sciatic nerve is injured; or the sinew
and the hip are dislocated, flattened, cut open like a fish, or separated.
see A.6.1.23; G.23.4.7; T.23.1.3; T.24.1.3; Sa.2.3.12; Sa.24.3.12; O.6.1.1;
Q.6.1.1; K.16.5.1; K.13.10.1; G.23.5.3
Gen. 32.24-26, 32-33; *Gen. R.* **77.3;** *Gen. R.* **78.5;** *Gen. R.* **79.5;**
**Dem. Fragment 2.7; GL 1, 385, 389; GL 5, 305 n.248; GL 5, 308
n.258** [→ *1.20.4; 1.26.b.13; 2.16.4; 1.14.c.7*

Ta.24.3. *Broken thigh(s)*

(1) The thighs of the Israelites in Egypt are broken when they go out
to look for straw for making bricks.
Cant. R. **5.19** [→ *1.20.8*

Tb. *The Knee(s)*

Tb.13 *Peculiarity of Skin of Knee(s)*

Tb.13.1. *Tattoo or writing on knee(s)*

(1) A bill of sale whereby Haman sells himself to Mordecai in return
for provisions for Haman's army, is written upon Mordecai's knee-
cap.
GL 4, 398; GL 6, 464 n.105 [→ *2.33.1*

Tc. *The Shin(s)*
[No references in sources]

Td. *The Ankles*
[No references in sources]

U. THE FEET

U.1 *Absence of Foot/Feet*

(1) The feet, hands and tongue of Eleazer, his six brothers and his mother are cut off, their heads are scalped and the pupils of their eyes are pierced by King Antiochus Epiphanes as he tries to persuade them to taste pig's flesh. When they refuse they are fried alive.

see P.1.1.2; D.2.2.1; Ib.1.1.3; Ga.24.1.1

2 *Macc.* 7; *4 Macc.* 6.6, 25; *4 Macc.* 7.13-14; *4 Macc.* 9.28; *4 Macc.* 10.5-8, 17-21; *4 Macc.* 11.18-19; *4 Macc.* 18.21

[→ *2.5.12; 2.25.a.2; 1.24.4*

U.2 *Absence of Part of Foot/Feet*

U.2.4 *Absence of sole of foot/feet*

(1) The fifty men whom Adonijah, the pretender to the throne, prepares to run before him, cut out the flesh of the soles of their feet and their spleens to fit themselves for the function of heralds.

see Vi.1.1.1; U.13.5.1; U.24.4.1; V.2.9.1

GL 4, 118; GL 6, 275 n.139 [→ *2.22.a.12*

U.3 *Vital Foot/Feet*

(1) A physician who has recommended a milk cure for the Persian king has a dream in which his feet, hands, mouth, eyes and tongue quarrel with one another, each claiming the greatest credit in procuring the remedy for the king.

see G.3.1.1; I.3.1.1; Ib.3.1.1; P.3.1.1

GL 4, 174; GL 6, 302 n.97 [→ *2.5.13*

U.5 *Unusual Number of Foot/Feet*

U.5.3 *Four feet*

(1) The inhabitants of Tebel, the second earth, have four feet.
see D.5.1.5; O.5.3.2; P.5.3.1; T.5.3.1; D.18.4.2; D.18.5.1; D.18.6.1; D.21.4.1;
D.21.5.1; D.21.6.1
GL 1, 10   [→ *1.16.b.8; 3.2.7*

U.6 *Unusual Size of Foot/Feet*

U.6.5 *Abnormally long foot/feet*

(1) The soles of the feet of the Antichrist measure two span, his teeth
one span, his mouth one cubit. His fingers are like scythes, his right
eye like the rising morning star, his left eye unmoving, and on his
forehead is written the inscription 'Antichrist'.
see Fb.13.2.2; G.10.2.5; G.23.3.1; I.6.1.1; Ic.6.5.1; Pc.12.1.1; Pc.12.2.1
Gk Apoc. Ezra 4.29f.   [→ *3.1.24*

(2) The feet of the Antichrist measure three cubits, he himself is ten
cubits tall. His hair reaches to his feet and he is three-crested. His eyes
are like the rising morning star, his right eye like a lion's. His lower
teeth are made of iron, his lower jaw of diamond. His right arm is
made of iron, his left of copper. His right hand is three cubits long.
He is long-faced, long-nosed and disorderly, with three letters written
on his forehead: A, K and T, signifying denial, rejection and the
befouled dragon. His mother conceives him by touching the head of a
fish.
see A.6.5.13; E.6.5.1; Fb.13.2.3; Fc.16.5.1; G.10.2.6; G.18.1.1; Ic.16.1.1;
O.16.1.1; O.16.2.3
Apoc. Dan. 9.11,16-26   [→ *3.1.25; 1.3.c.1*

(3) The feet of the giant Og are eighteen cubits long.
see A.6.3.3; Va.6.5.1; Ic.6.5.2; Ic.7.2.1; Sa.2.3.2; Sa.24.3.2; Ic.2.8.1;
Ic.5.11.1; A.6.5.19; A.6.1.16
Deut. R. 1.24   [→ *1.1.a.15*

U.10 *Unusual Emission or Emanation from Foot/Feet*

U.10.3 *Foot/feet that emits flames*

(1) Sparks shoot from the feet and hands of the angel (probably

Michael) seen by Aseneth, and they are like molten iron. The hairs of his head are like a flaming torch, his face is like lightning and his eyes resemble sunshine.

see E.10.2.1; F.10.1.3; G.10.2.4; P.10.3.2; P.16.1.1; U.16.1.1
Jos. Asen. **14.9** (8, 9); *Jos. Asen.* **16.12, 13** (7)   [→ *3.1.8*

U.13 *Peculiarity of Skin of Foot/Feet*

U.13.1 *Tattoo or writing on foot/feet*

(1) Six verses of a psalm are inscribed on Joab's foot, the first verse running 'The Lord answers thee in the day of trouble, the name of the God of Jacob is thy defence'.

see P.23.6.2; W.25.2.1
GL 4, 101; GL 6, 258-259 n.77   [→ *2.11.e.4*

U.13.5 *Wounded or lacerated skin or flesh of foot/feet*

(1) The fifty men whom Adonijah, the pretender to the throne, prepares to run before him, cut out the flesh of the soles of their feet and their spleens to fit themselves for the function of heralds.

see U.2.4.1; U.24.4.1; V.2.9.1; Vi.1.1.1
GL 4, 118; GL 6, 275 n.139   [→ *2.22.a.12*

U.13.6 *Hairy foot/feet*

(1) The queen of Sheba has hairy feet and legs.

see T.13.6.1; E.9.3.1
GL 4, 145; GL 6, 289 n.41   [→ *1.1.a.8*

U.16 *Foot/Feet of Unusual Substance*

U.16.1 *Foot/feet of iron*

(1) The feet and hands of an angel (probably Michael) seen by Aseneth are like glowing iron emitting sparks, while his face is like lightning, the hairs of his head like a flaming torch and his eyes resemble sunshine.

see E.10.2.1; F.10.1.3; G.10.2.4; P.10.3.2; P.16.1.1; U.10.3.1
Jos. Asen. **14.9** (8, 9); *Jos. Asen.* **16.12, 13** (7)   [→ *3.1.8*

U.16.2 *Foot/feet of copper or bronze*

(1) The angel Eremiel, a great angel, has feet like molten bronze and a face which shines like the sun's rays.

   see F.10.1.5

   Apoc. Zeph. **6.11-12**   [→ *3.3.a.10*

(2) The myriads of angels who reside in the seventh heaven, called Arabot, have feet and arms like burnished bronze, eyes like torches of fire and faces like lightning.

   see F.16.13.1; G.16.12.4; O.16.2.2

   3 En. **35.1-2**; *3 En.* **22B.6** (Appendix)   [→ *3.3.a.9*

U.18 *Animal Foot/Feet or Foot/Feet with Animal Attributes*

U.18.2 *Foot/feet of goat*

(1) Men with the feet of goats, the loins of sheep, the faces of cattle and horns of deer are seen by Baruch in the first heaven.

   see Sa.18.2.1; F.18.4.2; D.14.2.3; D.18.11.1

   3 Bar. **2.3** (Slavonic and Greek)   [→ *1.26.b.7*

(2) Men with the feet of goats and deer, horns of deer and faces of dogs are seen by Baruch in the second heaven.

   see D.14.2.7; D.18.11.2; F.18.2.2; U.18.4.1

   3 Bar. **3.3** (Slavonic and Greek)   [→ *1.26.b.6*

U.18.3 *Foot/feet of calf, ox or cow*

(1) The cherubim seen by Ezekiel have hoofs like oxen, glittering like polished brass, in place of feet.

   see F.18.5.2; F.20.1.1; F.18.4.1; M.20.1.8; M.14.2.8; F.5.3.1; P.21.1.1; A.14.10.1; G.4.1.4; G.5.15.5

   Ezek. 1.7   [→ *3.1.16*

(2) The seraphim have calves' feet and six wings.

   see M.14.2.12; M.20.1.12; G.4.1.4; D.14.2.1; G.5.15.5; F.6.1.2; F.10.1.1; G.10.2.2

   Lev. R. **27.3**; *Hell. Syn. Pr.* **82**; GL 6, 359 n.36

                             [→ *3.1.2; 2.2.b.1; 2.8.1*

U.18.4 *Foot/feet of deer*

(1) Men with the feet of deer and goats, horns of deer and faces of dogs are seen by Baruch in the second heaven.

see D.14.2.4; D.18.11.2; F.18.2.2; U.18.2.2
3 Bar. **3.3 (Slavonic and Greek)** [→ *1.26.b.6*]

U.18.5 *Horse's hoof(s)*

(1) The stars (who are fallen angels) have feet, hands and sexual organs like those of horses.
see P.18.5.1; Sa.18.5.1
1 En. **88.1;** *1 En.* **88.3** [→ *3.7.1*]

U.20 Bird's Claw/Claws or Foot/Feet with Bird Attributes

U.20.1 *Hen's or cock's foot/feet*

(1) The demon Asmodeus has feet resembling those of a cock.
see A.22.1.3
GL 4, 172; GL 6, 301 n.92 [→ *1.1.a.7; 3.1.23*]

U.21 Human Foot/Feet on Unusual Creature

U.21.6 *Human foot/feet on body of serpent or dragon.*

(1) The angel Azazel has human feet and hands and the body of a dragon or serpent with wings.
see P.21.6.1; M.20.1.20; M.14.2.20
Apoc. Abr. **23.7; GL 5, 123-124 n.131** [→ *3.1.28*]

(2) Solomon summons up a winged demon in the form of a dragon but with the feet and face of a man.
see F.21.6.1
T. Sol. **14.1-2** [→ *3.1.19*]

(3) Before the Fall, the serpent has human feet, hands, ears and tongue, and stands erect like a reed. It also has wings.
see P.21.6.2; Ib.21.6.1; J.21.6.1
Gen. R. **19.1;** *Gen. R.* **20.5;** *LAE (Apoc. Mos.)* **26.2-3;** *Qoh. R.* **10.11 §1** [→ *3.3.a.44; 3.5.a.4; 1.16.a.6*]

U.23 Disease, Paralysis or Malfunction of Foot/Feet

U.23.1 *Lameness*

(1) Balaam is lame of one foot (and later becomes blind of one eye).
see G.23.4.12; If.6.1.5; A.25.15.1; I.23.3.6; Va.27.1.1; G.1.2; G.5.1.2
GL 3, 359; GL 6, 126 n.731 [→ *4.1.c.4*]

(2) Samson is lame of both feet and can only crawl.
see E.8.1.2; E.25.5.1; A.6.1.29; Ie.17.3.1; I.10.20.1; G.24.1.2; G.1.3; E.6.5.4;
M.6.3.1; T.25.1.2; G.23.4.16
Num. R. **14.9**   [→ *4.2.d.2; 3.3.b.2*

(3) Meribbaal has crippled feet and is lame after falling from his
nurse's arms when a child.
2 Sam. 4.4; 2 Sam. 9.3, 13; 2 Sam. 19.27   [→ *1.23.2*

(4) Nebuchadnezzar, ignorant of the mechanism of Solomon's throne,
is struck on the left foot by the right paw of a golden lion so that he
becomes lame.
see T.24.3.1; A.27.2.3; Cc.27.1.1; A.6.2.5; A.2.4.1; Pd.6.5.1; Pd.12.1.1;
E.6.5.6; Ib.1.1.2
GL 6, 453 n.13   [→ *1.29.2; 1.23.4*

U.24 *Wounded, Mutilated or Maimed Foot/Feet*

U.24.4 *Flesh of soles cut off*

(1) The fifty men whom Adonijah, the pretender to the throne, prepares to run before him, cut out the flesh of the soles of their feet and
their spleens to fit themselves for the function of heralds.
see U.2.4.1; U.13.5.1; V.2.9.1; Vi.1.1.1
GL 4, 118; GL 6, 275 n.139   [→ *2.22.a.12*

Ua. *The Heel(s)*

Ua.15 *Abnormal Puncture or Opening in Heel(s)*

(1) A hole is bored through Shebnah's heels (by which he is tied to
the tail of a horse).
GL 4, 270; GL 6, 365 n.65   [→ *2.22.b.6; 2.15.a.13*

Ub. *The Toe(s)*

Ub.1 *Absence of Toe(s)*

(1) Adoni-zedek's big toes and thumbs are cut off by the tribe of
Judah.
see Pc.1.2.1
Judg. 1.6-7   [→ *1.26.b.36*

Ub.5 *Unusual Number of Toe(s)*

Ub.5.5 *Six toes on foot/feet*

(1) One of the Philistines who fights at Gath has six toes on each foot
and six fingers on each hand.

see Pc.5.5.1; A.6.1.28

2 Sam. 21.20; 1 Chron. 20.6   [→ *1.1.b.8*

Ub.23 *Disease, Paralysis or Malfunction of Toe(s)*

Ub.23.3 *Gout*

(1) Asa, Solomon's son, has gout and leans on a staff after Solomon
has transferred David's curse against Joab's descendants to his own
issue.

GL 4, 127; GL 6 278 n.10; GL 4, 184; GL 6, 309 n.22

[→ *1.7.6; 1.26.b.49*

Uc. *The Toenail(s)*
[No reference in sources.]

V THE INTERNAL PARTS

V.1 *Absence of Internal Part(s)*

(1) The bodies of the soldiers of Sennacherib are burned within but their arms and clothes are preserved.

2 Bar. 63.8 [→ *2.4.2*

V.2 *Partial Absence of Internal Part(s)*

V.2.9 *Absence of spleen*

(1) The fifty men whom Adonijah, the pretender to the throne, prepares to run before him, cut out their spleens and the flesh of the soles of their feet to fit themselves for the function of heralds.

see Vi.1.1.1; U.2.4.1; U.13.5.1; U.24.4.1

GL 4 118; GL 6, 275 n.139 [→ *2.22.a.12*

V.16 *Internal Organs of Unusual Substance*

V.16.12 *Viscera of fire*

(1) Enoch's internal organs become burning sparks at his transformation into Metatron.

see A.6.3.2; A.6.5.12; G.5.13.2; G.10.2.3; M.14.2.13; M.20.1.13; A.16.12.6; B.16.12.1; E.16.4.1; G.16.12.5; Va.16.12.1; A.10.1.7 V.16.12.1)

3 En. **15.1;** *3 En.* **48c.6 (Appendix)** [→ *1.35.2*

Va. *The Bone(s)*

Va.2 *Absence of Part of Bone(s)*

Va.2.1 *Absence of joints*

(1) Angels have no joints, except the angels of destruction. In a different version, only the angels of destruction have no joints in their feet.

Gen. R. 65.21; *Lev. R.* 6.3   [→ *2.22.a.1*

Va.3 *Vital Bone(s)*

(1) Judah's bones join together again when Moses prays to God to forgive Judah (for not redeeming his promise to bring Benjamin back to his father).

see E.13.1.2; G.10.4.1; Gf.16.3.1; Ic.18.5.1; F.18.5.3; J.23.1.2; I.23.3.2; E.8.1.1; F.11.6.2; If.6.1.2; A.10.1.15

GL 3, 456; GL 6, 155 n.922   [→ *1.14.b.4; 1.19.b.8*

(2) The scattered bones of Joseph unite themselves into an entire body.

see Va.10.10.1; A.10.1.14; Sa.2.3.14; Sa.24.3.14; Va.3.1.3; Va.27.2.1

Deut. R. 11.7   [→ *1.15.1; 1.19.b.7*

(3) Joseph's bones, wrapped by Moses in a sheep's skin on which the name of God is written, come alive again and, assuming the form of a sheep, follow the Israelites during their wanderings through the wilderness.

see Va.27.2.1; Sa.2.3.14; Sa.24.3.14; A.10.1.14; Va.3.1.2; Va.10.10.1

GL 5, 376 n.442   [→ *1.11.a.2; 2.19.a.4*

(4) The bones (or skull) of a slain Jew made into a drinking vessel, come to life and strike a blow in Nebuchadnezzar's face, while a voice announces 'A friend of this man is at this moment reviving the dead'.

see D.3.1.1

GL 4, 330; GL 6, 418 n.90   [→ *1.15.3; 2.2.c.11*

(5) Dry bones join together when Ezekiel prophesies over them, and sinews, flesh and skin grow on them.

Ezek. 37.7   [→ *2.4.12; 1.19.b.22*

(6) A thigh-bone rolls of its own accord between the feet of a government courier bringing bad tidings for the Jews of Caesarea, so that he stumbles and dies.

Qoh. R. 5.8 §5; *Num. R.* 18.22   [→ *2.2.b.3*

Va.6 *Unusual Size of Bone(s)*

Va.6.5 *Abnormally long bone(s)*

(1) The giant Og is of immense stature: his thigh-bone alone measures more than three parasangs.
see A.6.3.3; A.6.5.19; Ic.6.5.2; Ic.7.2.1; Ic.7.3.1; Sa.2.3.2; Sa.24.3.2; Ic.2.8.1; Ic.5.11.1; U.6.5.3; A.6.1.16.
GL 3, 344; GL 6, 119 n.686 [→ *1.1.a.15*

Va.10 *Unusual Emission or Emanation from Bone(s)*

Va.10.10 *Unusual scent or fragrance from bone(s)*

(1) Joseph's bones exude fragrance.
see Va.3.1.2; A.10.1.14; Sa.2.3.14; Sa.24.3.14; Va.3.1.3; Va.27.2.1
GL 3, 5; GL 6, 1 n.2 [→ *2.6.b.4*

Va.11 *Unusual Colour of Bone(s)*

Va.11.1 *Black bone(s)*

(1) Someone who drinks water has black bones, someone who drinks wine has red bones, and someone who drinks hot water has white bones.
see Va.11.2.1; Va.11.3.1
Gen. R. 89.2 [→ *1.14.d.7*

Va.11.2 *White bones*

(1) Someone who drinks hot water has white bones, someone who drinks wine has red bones, and someone who drinks cold water has black bones.
see Va.11.1.1; Va.11.3.1
Gen. R. 89.2 [→ *1.14.d.7*

Va.11.3 *Red bones*

(1) Someone who drinks wine has red bones, someone who drinks cold water has black bones and someone who drinks hot water has white bones.
see Va.11.1.1; Va.11.2.1
Gen. R. 89.2 [→ *1.14.d.7*

Va.16 *Bone(s) of Unusual Substance*

Va.16.12 *Bone(s) of fire*

(1) Enoch's bones and veins become glimmering coals at his transformation into Metatron.

see A.6.3.2; A.6.5.12; G.5.13.2; G.10.2.3; M.14.2.13; M.20.1.13; A.16.12.6; B.16.12.1; E.16.4.1; G.16.12.5; V.16.12.1; A.10.1.7

3 En. **15.1;** *3 En.* **48c.6 (Appendix)** [→ *1.35.2*

Va.24.1 *Racked or broken bones*

(1) Noah's bone is broken when a lion bites him as he is about to leave the ark.

see A.11.2.5; A.11.3.2; G.10.2.7; Sa.2.3.6; Sa.24.3.6; Sa.2.1.1; T.23.1.1; I.10.4.1; Sa.24.10.1; E.11.2.1; If.26.1.1; B.11.2.1; B.11.3.2; Sa.24.2.1

Gen. R. **30.6** [→ *1.20.3*

(2) Antiochus Epiphanes' bones are racked when he is hurled from his chariot.

see A.10.10.2; B.23.6.1; G.23.20.1

2 Macc. 9.7 [→ *1.26.b.50; 2.4.15*

Va.27 *Transformation of Bone(s)*

Va.27.1 *Transformation of bone(s) into serpent*

(1) From Balaam's bones arise several species of harmful snakes.

see If.6.1.5; A.25.15.1; U.23.1.1; G.23.4.12; I.23.3.6; G.5.1.2; G.1.2

GL 3, 411; GL 6, 145 n.856 [→ *3.6.b.10*

(2) The human backbone is transformed into a serpent.

GL 5, 58 n.190 [→ *1.26.b.62*

Va.27.2 *Transformation of bone(s) to assume the shape of a sheep*

(1) Joseph's bones, wrapped by Moses in a sheep's skin upon which the name of God is written, come alive and assume the form of a sheep.

see Va.3.1.2; A.10.1.14; Sa.2.3.14; Sa.24.3.14; Va.3.1.3; Va.10.10.1

GL 5, 376 n.442 [→ *1.11.a.2; 2.19.a.4*

Vb. *The Brain*
[No references in sources]

Vc. *The Heart*
[No references in sources]

Vd. *The Liver*

Vd.23 *Disease, Paralysis or Malfunction of Liver*

Vd.23.10 *Unspecified disease of liver*

(1) Gad is afflicted with a disease of the liver as a punishment for his hatred towards Joseph.
T. Gad 5.9(T12P)   [→ *1.26.b.16*

Ve. *The Lung(s)*
[No references in sources]

Vf. *The Intestine(s)*

Vf.1 *Absence of Intestine(s)*

(1) The Philistines' entrails are eaten by mice when they go to ease nature.
see F.13.2.1; F.24.3.1
GL 4, 62-63; GL 6, 223 n.34   [→ *1.26.b.32*

(2) Jehoram's bowels drop out with disease.
2 Chron. 21.18-19   [→ *1.10.1; 1.26.a.13; 1.26.b.45*

Vg. *The Womb*

Vg.1 *Absence of Womb*

(1) Sarah has no womb.
see Vg.23.1.3; A.10.1.13; F.10.1.9; Nd.5.1.1
GL 5, 231 n.117   [→ *1.4.1*

(2) Rebecca has no ovary and is therefore barren (until Isaac prays to the Lord and He makes an ovary for her).
Gen. R. 47.2; *Gen. R.* 53.5; *Gen. R.* 63.5; *Gen. R.* 68.5   [→ *1.4.2*

(3) Ruth lacks the main portion of the womb until God shapes a womb for her.
Ruth R. 7.14   [→ *1.4.3*

Vg.23 *Disease, Paralysis or Malfunction of Womb*

Vg.23.1 *'Closed' or barren womb*

(1) One of the two wives of the men of the generation of the Deluge is sterilized.

GL 1, 117   [→ *2.14.b.1; 2.23.a.2*

(2) All the women of Abimelech's household become barren while Sarah remains with Abraham.

Gen. 20.17-18   [→ *1.26.b.10*

(3) Sarah is barren (but gives birth when she is past the age of ninety).

see Vg.1.1.1; A.10.1.13; F.10.1.9; Nd.5.1.1

Gen. 11.30   [→ *4.1.b.9*

(4) Rachel, Jacob's wife, is barren for a long time (until she gives birth to Joseph.

Gen. 29.31-32   [→ *2.24.11*

(5) Hannah, wife of Elkanah, is barren until the age of 130, when she gives birth to Samuel.

1 Sam. 1.5f.; GL 4, 58-59; GL 4, 215-218 n.6-15   [→ *4.2.c.1*

(6) Samson's mother is barren for most of her life (until an angel tells her that she will bear a son).

Judg. 13.2; *Num. R.* 10.5   [→ *4.2.c.2*

(7) Sopanim, the wife of Nir, is sterile but when she is past the menopause she conceives without contact with her husband.

2 *En.* 71.1-2   [→ *4.2.c.5*

(8) An allegory: a barren woman gives birth after thirty years, but her son dies on her wedding day. Then her face suddenly shines and flashes like lightning; she utters a loud cry and is no longer visible, but in her place there is an established city.

see F.10.1.20

4 Ezra 9.43f.; *4 Ezra* 10.25-27, 44, 50   [→ *4.1.a.4*

Vg.24 *Wounded or Mutilated Womb*

Vg.24.1 *Torn or lacerated womb*

(1) Rebecca has a torn womb after Esau fights with Jacob over who is to be born first (and threatens to kill her if he does not get his way).
   GL 5, 271 n.16; GL 1, 313-314   [→ *1.20.2*

Vi. *The Spleen*

Vi.1 *Absence of Spleen*

(1) The fifty men whom Adonijah, the pretender to the throne, prepares to run before him, cut out their spleens and the flesh of the soles of their feet to fit themselves for the function of heralds.
   see U.2.4.1; V.2.9.1; U.13.5.1; U.24.4.1
   GL 4, 118; GL 6, 275 n.139   [→ *2.22.a.12*

W. THE BLOOD

W.1 *Absence of Blood*

(1) No blood flows from the pierced bodies of Zimri and Cozbi.
see A.23.6.7; I.23.2.4
Num. R. 20.25 [→ *2.31.c.1*

W.3 *Vital Blood*

(1) The blood of the murdered prophet Zechariah seethes and reeks and does not congeal for 250 years until his death is avenged.
Lam. R. 4.13 §16; Lam. R. §23 (Proems); *Lam. R. 2.2 §4; Qoh. R. 3.16 §1; Qoh. R. 10.4 §1* [→ *2.4.14*

W.4 *Blood in Unusual Place in Body*

W.4.1 *Blood in eyes*

(1) The ugly angels, who carry off the souls of ungodly men, have eyes mixed with blood; their faces are like those of a leopard, with tusks like those of a boar outside their mouths, and hair loose like the hair of a woman.
see F.18.9.1; Ic.18.1.1; E.9.5.1
Apoc. Zeph. 4.2-4 [→ *2.24.9*

W.4.2 *Blood in mouth*

(1) Eve has a vision in which Abel's blood is in the mouth of Cain who is gulping it down.
LAE (Apoc. Mos.) 2.1-3; LAE (Vita) 23.2 [→ *3.10.19*

(2) The water drunk by the Egyptians becomes blood in their mouths.
see Ie.27.1.1; B.24.3.2; B.23.2.4; B.24.3.1; B.23.1.1; P.23.1.2; Sa.24.2.7; Sa.2.1.7; A.23.3.1; A.23.6.1
Cant. R. 9.10-11 [→ *1.26.b.24; 2.5.8; 2.24.13*

W.5 *Unusual Quantity of Blood*

W.5.1 *Unusual quantity of menstrual blood*

(1) Vast quantities of blood pour from the vaginas of the daughters of Zion so that the gentiles are unable to mix with them.
   see D.23.1.1; E.23.1.1; Sb.10.3.1
   Lam. R. **4.15 §18**   [→ *2.23.b.4; 2.21.5*

W.21 *Human Blood in Unusual Creature*

W.21.1 *Idol with human blood*

(1) Blood drips from the idols of the Egyptians.
   GL 2, 349; GL 5, 428 n.177   [→ *1.26.b.24; 2.5.8; 2.24.13*

W.25 *Unusual Abilities of Blood*

W.25.1 *Speaking blood*

(1) Abel's blood cries out to God from the ground.
   see A.10.1.2
   Gen. 4.10; *Gen. R.* 22.9   [→ *2.2.c.2*

W.25.2 *Blood that unfastens*

(1) The blood of an unborn child unfastens the sword from Joab's hand.
   see P.23.6.2; U.13.1.1
   GL 4, 100; GL 6, 258-259 n.77   [→ *2.27.a.3*

(2) The warm blood of a slain Amorite frees Kenaz's hand from his sword.
   see G.23.4.13; G.23.4.14; A.6.5.15
   Ps-Philo 27.11   [→ *2.27.a.2*

W.25.5 *Blood that permeates bone*

(1) The blood of a true heir permeates the bone of his father's corpse (while the blood of an impostor shows no affinity with the bone).
   GL 4, 131; GL 6, 284 n.27   [→ *2.2.c.10; 2.3.4; 2.6.b.9*

PART TWO

1. ABNORMALITY, DEFORMITY OR DISABILITY AS A RESULT

1.1. *Abnormality, Deformity or Disability as a Result of Having Unusual Ancestors*

1.1.a. *Abnormality, deformity or disability as a result of belonging to an unusual race*

(1) Angels have no backs.
Gen. R. **49.7**   [← *M.1.1.1*

(2) Spirits have no hair.
Ruth R. **6.1**   [←*E.1.1.1*

(3) Angels have six wings (including those who accompany the sun and moon).
Gen. R. **65.21;** *2 En.* **11.4-5** (J); *2 En.* **16.7** (J, A); GL 5, 52 n.155; GL 5, 110 n.101; GL 1, 63, 132-134
                                          [← *M.14.2.10; M.20.1.10*

(4) The 200 myriads of Grigori who lust after the daughters of men and descend to earth are larger than giants.
2 En. **18.1-5** (J, A)   [← *A.6.1.3*

(5) Demons and angels have wings (and can assume any form they desire).
Gen. R. **65.21;** *1 En.* **93.12;** GL 5, 108 n.98
                    [← *M.14.2.1; M.14.2.16; M.20.1.1; M.20.1.16*

(6) Demons, both male and female, have bodies and faces covered with hair but bald heads.
GL 6, 192 n.58
          [← *A.13.6.2; B.13.6.2; E.1.1.2; E.4.1.1; E.4.2.1; F.13.12.1*

(7) Demons have cocks' feet—hence Asmodeus keeps his feet well-hidden when he assumes the role of king.
see 3.1.23
GL 4, 172; GL 6, 301 n.92   [← *U.20.1.1*

(8) The queen of Sheba has hairy legs because she is a demon.
   GL 6, 289 n.41   [← *T.13.6.1; U.13.6.1; E.9.3.1*

(9) The seventh generation are Titans.
   Sib. Or. 1. 9   [← *A.6.1.7*

(10) Four hundred and nine thousand giants or, in another version, one hundred and four thousand giants, are destroyed in the Flood.
   3 Bar. **4.10 (Slavonic and Greek)**   [← *A.6.1.11*

(11) The Nephilim, the generation of Noah, are giants due to the union between the descendants of Seth and the descendants of Cain, and they possess the physical strength and stature of Cainites.
   GL 1, 148, 151, 152, 158-160; GL 5, 172, 173 n.13-15; GL 5, 178 n.26; GL 5, 181 n.35   [← *A.6.1.6*

(12) The children of the generation of Nephilim, or ante-diluvians, can run around while still connected to the mother by the navel cord.
   GL 1, 151, 152; GL 5, 173 n.16   [← *A.25.10.1*

(13) The Raphaim are giants ten, nine, eight or seven cubits tall. They dwell in the region between the land of the Ammonites and Mount Hermon until destroyed by God because of their evil deeds.
   Jub. **29.9-11**   [← *A.6.5.14*

(14) The Amorites (including Sihon and Og, their kings) are eighteen cubits tall.
   GL 3, 346; GL 6, 120 n.699   [← *A.6.5.15*

(15) The giant Og, last survivor of the race of giants, the Rephaim, is of immense stature, his breadth is one half of his height, his thigh-bone alone measures more than three parasangs, his teeth are sixty cubits long and his feet eighteen. He is so tall that the waters of the Flood do not reach him.
   Deut. 3.1-18; *Deut. R.* **1.24;** *Deut. R.* **11.10; GL 3, 343-348; GL 6, 119 n.685-687, 691; GL 6, 120 n. 694-695; GL 6, 121 n.704**
            [← *A.6.3.3; A.6.1.16; A.6.5.19; Va.6.5.1; Ic.6.5.2; U.6.5.3*

(16) The ancestors of Abraham are giants. They built the Tower of Babel (or, alternatively, one of them, Belos, built it) and the city of Babylon, and taught astrology. They were scattered when the Tower was destroyed, or perished for lack of wisdom.
   Ps.-Eupol. Preparatio Evangelica 9.17.2-3; 9.18.2   [← *A.6.1.5*

17) Cainites are dwarfs or giants and have two heads.
  see 1.16.b.2; 3.2.2
  GL 1, 114; GL 5, 143 n.34; GL 4, 132
                              [← *A.6.1.4; A.6.2.1; A.6.1.8; D.5.1.2*

(18) The nail of a giant is sufficient to stop up a spring of water, according to a report given by Israelites who have been on a reconnaissance mission into Canaan.
  GL 3, 275-276; GL 6, 96 n.532   [← *Pd.6.1.1*

(19) The Neshiah, the fifth earth, is inhabited by dwarfs without noses.
  see 1.16.b.3; 3.2.4
  GL 1, 114; GL 5, 143 n.36   [← *A.6.2.3; H.1.1.1*

(20) The 'sons of the sea', or dolphins, are half-man and half-fish.
  see 1.9.1
  GL 1, 35; GL 5, 53-54 n.168   [← *Cc.19.1.1*

1.1.b. *Abnormality, deformity or disability as a result of having unusual parents or ancestors*

(1) The union of fallen angels with mortal women results in a race of giants 3,000 ells tall.
  1 En. **6-7;** *1 En.* **9.7-9;** *1 En.* **15.3;** *1 En.* **15.8;** *2 En.* **18.5 (J); BR 26.7;** *Jub.* **5.1-2;** *Jub.* **7.21-22**   [← *A.6.1.10*

(2) As a result of their alliances with angels, the Cainite women give birth to the Gibborim, whose thighs measure eighteen ells.
  GL 1, 151; GL 5, 172 n.13   [← *Ta.6.1.1*

(3) Ahiah, whose father Shemhazai is one of the fallen angels, seduces Ham's wife so that she gives birth to the giants Og and Sihon. Sihon is the king of the Amorites and is so tall that the waters of the Flood do not reach him.
  Deut. R. **11.10; GL 3, 340; GL 6, 117 n.667-668**   [← *A.6.5.16*

(4) The giant Anak springs from the union of the fallen angels with mortal women; hence he is half-mortal, half-immortal. After a long life half his body withers away (or becomes paralysed), while the other half stays alive.
  GL 3, 269; GL 6, 94 n.515   [← *Cd.23.1.1; A.6.5.17*

(5) Three giants, sons of Anak, as well as several of his daughters, are seen by the Israelites on their reconnaissance mission into Canaan.

The three sons of Anak are called Talmai, Sheshai and Ahiman.
Num. 13.33; *Num. R.* **16.11; GL 3, 268-270; GL 6, 94 n.512-516**
[← *A.6.1.15; A.6.5.18*]

(6) Abner, the son of the witch of Endor, is a giant of extraordinary size.
GL 4, 73; GL 6, 239 n.84-85   [← *A.6.1.17*]

(7) The son of the angel Sammael, Cain, is born with a luminous face and inherits part of Sammael's light.
see 5.1.3
LAE (Apoc. Mos.) **1.1-3;** *LAE (Vita)* **21.3; GL 1, 105-106; GL 5, 133 n.3; GL 5, 135 n.6; GL 5, 137 n.13**   [← *F.10.1.7*]

(8) A Philistine, a descendant of Rapha (founder of a race of giants), has six toes on each foot and six fingers on each hand.
2 Sam. 21.20; 1 Chron. 20.6   [← *Pc.5.5.1; Ub.5.5.1; A.6.1.28*]

1.1.c. *Abnormality, deformity or disability as a result of having unusual foster parents*
[No reference in sources]

1.2 *Abnormality, Deformity or Disability as a Result of Supernatural or Cosmic Forces*

1.2.a *Abnormality, deformity or disability as a result of fate*
[No reference in sources]

1.2.b *Abnormality, deformity or disability as a result of supernatural intervention or agent*

(1) As a punishment for Ham's sexual relations with a dog whilst in the ark, God causes Ham's descendants to have a black skin.
see 1.6.a.2
Gen. R. **36.7; GL 5, 55 n.178; GL 5, 188 n.54**
[← *A.11.1.3; B.11.1.2*]

1.2.c. *Abnormality, deformity or disability at birth as a result of cosmic forces*
[No reference in sources]

1.3. Abnormality, Deformity or Disability at Birth as a Result of Unusual Manner of Creation or Birth

1.3.a. *Abnormality, deformity or disability as a result of birth from or conception by unusual object*

[No reference in sources]

1.3.b. *Abnormality, deformity or disability as a result of unusual time or place of conception or birth*

[No reference in sources]

1.3.c. *Abnormality, deformity or disability as a result of unusual manner of conception or birth*

(1) The Antichrist is conceived by his mother touching the head of a fish.

see 3.1.25; 3.6.b.3

Apoc. Dan. 9.11, 16-26   *[← A.6.5.13; E.6.5.1; Fb.13.2.3;*
Fc.16.5.1; G.10.2.6; G.18.1.1; Ic.16.1.1; O.16.2.3; O.16.1.1;
U.6.5.2

1.3.d. *Artificial being*

(1) Moulded wax figures are animated by being plunged into magic water and allowed to swim.

see 1.14.c.2; 2.11.b.1

GL 2, 159; GL 5, 372 n.425   *[← A.16.14.1*

(2) A life-like statue calls out in a loud voice, 'Hither, ye Satans, Solomon has come to undo you' when Solomon approaches it.

see 2.10.1.1; 1.32.2

GL 4, 165; GL 6, 298 n.79   *[← A.16.20.1*

(3) Nebuchadnezzar places the golden diadem of the high priest, on which is inscribed the holy name, into the mouth of an idol, and the idol speaks, saying 'I am thy God'.

see 1.11.a.1; 2.9.5

GL 4, 338; GL 6, 427 n.111   *[← A.16.20.2*

(4) An image of dust and clay made by Enosh is animated by Satan entering it.

see 1.32.1

GL 1, 122-123; GL 5, 150-151 n.54   *[← A.16.6.1; A.16.13.1*

(5) Idols of wood, brass and stone speak for three days, to give wise men news of future events, at the time of the coming of the Messiah.
see 2.2.c.1
Lad. Jac. **7.17**   [← *A.16.2.2; A.16.5.1; A.16.7.1*

1.4. *Abnormality, Deformity or Disability as a Result of an Accident of Birth*

(1) Sarah is born without a womb.
GL 5, 231 n.117   [← *Vg.1.1.1*

(2) Rebecca is born without a womb, and remains barren until Isaac prays for his wife to conceive. Alternatively, Yahweh makes an ovary for her.
Gen. R. **68.5;** *Gen. R.* **63.5;** *Gen. R.* **47.2;** *Gen. R.* **53.5**
                                                              [← *Vg.1.1.2*

(3) Ruth is born without the main portion of her womb, but God shapes a womb for her.
Ruth R. **7.14**   [← *Vg.1.1.3*

1.5. *Abnormality, Deformity or Disability as a Result of an Experience of Mother during Conception or Pregnancy*

(1) The women who, whilst copulating with their husbands, lust after the Watchers—who appear before them in the form of men as tall as the heavens—give birth to giants.
see 1.14.a.14
T. Reub. **5.6** (*Test. XII Patr.*); *Gen. R.* **26.7;** **GL 5, 155 n.57**
                                                              [← *A.6.1.13*

(2) A black woman who fixes her eyes upon some white-painted figures during intercourse with her black Arab husband, gives birth to a white child.
see 1.14.a.12
Num. R. **9.34**   [← *A.11.2.6; B.11.2.5*

1.6. *Abnormality, Deformity or Disability of Child or Descendant as Punishment for Transgression by Parents or Ancestors or Reward for Positive Act of Same*

1.6.a. *Abnormality, deformity or disability as punishment for violation of prohibition or taboo, pledge or oath, by parents or ancestors*

(1) As a punishment for Enosh's adultery, the countenances of the men of succeeding generations resemble apes and centaurs.
   Gen. R. 23.6; *Gen. R.* 24.6; GL 1, 123; GL 5, 152 n.55
                                        [← *F.18.3.1; Cc.18.1.1*

(2) Because Ham did not observe the law of sexual abstinence whilst in the ark, his descendants are black.
   see 1.2.b.1
   Gen. R. 36.7; GL 1, 166; GL 5, 55 n.178; GL 5, 188 n.54
                                        [← *A.11.1.3; B.11.1.2*

1.6.b. *Abnormality, deformity or disability as punishment for certain act by parents or ancestors*

(1) Because the Pathrusim and the men of Casluhim organized bazaars and snatched one another's wives, their descendants, the Philistines, are giants and the Caphtorim (also descendants) are dwarfs.
   Gen. R. 37.5   [← *A.6.1.9; A.6.2.2*

(2) As a punishment for Hezekiah's lie to Isaiah, his sons become eunuchs in the palace of the king of Babylon.
   GL 3, 358-359; GL 6, 125 n.730   [← *Sa.2.1.25; Sa.24.2.25*

(3) Because Gehazi has accepted money from the leprous Naaman, his descendants are cursed with leprosy by Elisha.
   see 1.7.a.8
   GL 4, 244-245; GL 6, 346 n.15   [← *A.23.1.11*

1.6.c. *Abnormality, deformity or disability as a reward for positive act by parents or ancestors*

(1) As a reward for travelling four miles (or forty steps) with Naomi, her mother-in-law, when she departs for Palestine, Orpah gives birth to the giant Ishbi.
   see 1.6.c.2
   Ruth R. 2.20; GL 4, 31, 86   [← *A.6.1.18*

(2) As a reward for shedding four tears when Naomi, her mother-in-law, departs for Palestine, Orpah gives birth to the giant Ishbi and his three brothers.
   see 1.6.c.1
   Ruth R. 2.20; GL 4, 86   [← *A.6.1.18*

(3) As a reward for walking four miles with Naomi, when she

departs for Palestine, Orpah gives birth to Goliath.
Ruth R. **2.20; GL 4, 31; GL 6, 190 n.44**   [← *A.6.1.26*

1.7. *Abnormality, Deformity or Disability of Child or Descendant as a Result of Curse, Malice or Blessing*

1.7.a. *Abnormality, deformity or disability of child or descendant as a result of curse or malice*

(1) As a result of Noah's curse after Ham has looked at his father's nakedness, Ham's descendants have red eyes.
GL 1, 169; GL 5, 191-192 n.60, 61   [← *G.11.3.1*

(2) As a result of Noah's curse after Ham has spoken to his brothers of his father's drunkenness and lechery, Ham's descendants have mis-shapen lips.
GL 1, 169; GL 5, 191-192 n.60, 61   [← *Ia.12.1.1*

(3) As a result of Noah's curse after Ham has turned his head to see the nakedness of his father, Ham's descendants have twisted, curly hair.
GL 1, 169; GL 5, 191-192 n.60, 61   [← *E.12.3.2*

(4) As the result of a curse called down by Abimelech upon Sarah's children, Isaac is blinded.
    see 1.12.a.8; 1.14.a.4; 1.14.c.6; 1.19.b.6; 1.26.b.12; 2.7.3; 4.1.b.10; 1.14.a.2; 1.31.1; 2.20.1; 2.6.a.7
GL 5, 281-282 n.74   [← *G.23.4.6*

(5) Uzziah, the son of Solomon, is smitten with leprosy because Solomon transfers David's curse against Joab's descendants to his own issue.
    see 1.19.b.17; 1.26.a.12
Num. R. **23.13; GL 4, 127; GL 6, 278 n.10**   [← *A.13.4.1;*
                    A.23.1.14; B.13.4.1; B.23.1.2; Fb.23.1.1; Fb.13.4.1

(6) Asa, the son of Solomon, leans on a staff when he walks because Solomon has transferred David's curse against Joab's descendants to his own issue.
    see 1.26.b.49
Num. R. **23.13; GL 4, 127; GL 6, 278 n.10**   [← *Ub.23.3.1*

(7) Rehoboam, the son of Solomon, is afflicted with gonorrhoea after

Solomon has transferred David's curse against Joab's descendants to his own issue.
   Num. R. **23.13; GL 4, 127; GL 6, 278 n.10**   [← *A.10.15.1*

(8) Elisha curses the descendants of Gehazi with leprosy.
   see 1.6.b.3
   GL 4, 244-245; GL 6, 346 n.15   [← *A.23.1.11*

1.7.b. Abnormality, deformity or disability of child or descendant as a result of blessing
                    [No reference in sources]

1.8. *Abnormality, Deformity or Disability as a Result of Incomplete Development*

1.8.a. Abnormality, deformity or disability of race or species as a result of incomplete development

(1) Because the Sabbath has already begun, God has no time to create bodies for the demons and they consist of souls only, which he has made first.
   Gen. R. **7.5**   [← *A.1.1.4*

(2) Before Noah, the hands of human beings consist of one piece, without separated fingers.
   GL 5, 168   [← *P.12.1.1*

1.8.b. Abnormality, deformity or disability of individual as a result of incomplete development

(1) Adam is created as an unformed mass, spread from one end of the world to the other.
   Gen. R. **8.1;** *Gen. R.* **14.8;** *Gen. R.* **24.2**   [← *A.12.1.1*

(2) Adam is created with a tail which is later removed by God on account of the dignity owing to man.
   Gen. R. **14.10**   [← *R.14.1.1; R.18.1.1*

(3) God creates the first man as an androgyne with two faces, then saws him in two and makes a back for each half.
   Gen. R. **8.1;** *Apoc. Adam* **1.2-5;** *Lev. R.* **14.1; GL 5, 88-89 n.42**
                    [← *Ca.9.1.1; Cb.9.1.1; Cb.5.1.1; F.5.1.1; A.9.1.2*

1.9. *Abnormality, Deformity or Disability as a Result of Unusual Environment in which Character Lives*

(1) The 'sons of the sea', or dolphins, are half-man, half-fish.
see 1.1.a.20
GL 1, 35; GL 5, 53-54 n.168   [← *Cc.19.1.1*

(2) In the belly of the fish the heat is so intense that Jonah's hair falls out.
see 1.14.c.17
GL 4, 252; GL 6, 351 n.36   [← *E.1.5*

(3) While Nebuchadnezzar lives like an animal in the desert, feeding on grass like an ox and drenched by the dew of heaven, his hair grows long like an eagle's feathers and his nails resemble birds' claws.
Dan. 4.30   [← *E.6.5.6; Pd.6.5.1; Pd.12.1.1*

1.10. *Abnormality, Deformity or Disability as a Result of Disease*

(1) A disease causes the bowels of Jehoram, king of Judah, to drop out.
see 1.26.a.13; 1.26.b.45
2 Chron. 21.18,19   [← *Vf.1.1.2*

(2) King Hezekiah has an ulcer but recovers when Isaiah applies a fig poultice to the wound.
2 Kgs 20.7; Isa. 38.1-8   [← *B.15.1.1*

(3) A disease causes the skin of Hezekiah to peel off as a punishment for his having 'peeled off' the gold of the temple.
see 1.26.b.46
GL 4, 272; GL 6, 366 n.72   [← *B.2.2.1*

(4) A disease attacks Haman's daughter, making her repulsive.
see 2.21.4
GL 6, 77 n.173   [← *A.22.1.6*

(5) Job is smitten with leprosy which causes his nails and fingers to drop off and boils and wounds, swarming with worms and vermin, to appear on his body, which exudes a terrible stench.
see 2.1.a.2
Job 2.7; 7.5; 17.7; 18.13; 19.20; 30.17; 30.30; *T. Job* 31.2; 34.4;

GL 2, 235; GL 5, 386 n.24,25   [← *A.23.20.2; B.24.1.4;*
        Cc.23.3.1; Cc.23.3.2; Pc.2.1.1; Pd.1.1.1; A.10.10.1

(6) Diseases, sent by God, disfigure the coquettish maidens of Jerusalem and make them repulsive.
see 1.19.b.23; 1.26.b.61
GL 4, 312-313; GL 6, 404 n.45   [← *A.22.1.7*

1.11. Abnormality, Deformity or Disability as a Result of Magic Words

1.11.a. *Abnormality, deformity or disability as a result of spell or charm*

(1) The golden diadem of the high priest is inscribed with the holy name and when placed in the idol's mouth, the idol speaks, saying 'I am thy God'.
see 1.3.d.3; 2.9.5
Cant. R. 7.9 §1; GL 4, 338; GL 6, 427 n.111
     [← *A.16.20.2; If.21.1.1*

(2) The bones of Joseph, when wrapped by Moses in a sheep's skin upon which 'the name of God' is written, come alive again and, assuming the form of a sheep, follow the camp of the Israelites during their wanderings through the wilderness.
see 2.19.a.4
GL 5, 376 n.442   [← *Va.3.1.3; Va.27.2.1*

(3) After reciting the name, Balaam flies through the air.
see 2.18.a.5
GL 3, 409-410; GL 6, 144 n.853, 854   [← *A.25.15.1*

(4) By pronouncing the name of God, Abishai causes David to be suspended in the air and thus avoid being transfixed by Ishbi's lance.
see 2.15.b.11
GL 4, 108; GL 6, 268 n.110   [← *A.25.15.3*

(5) As a result of the witchcraft of her enemies, Esther becomes ugly (but regains her former beauty through a miracle).
GL 6, 460 n.78   [← *A.22.1.5*

(6) After Daniel pronounces the name of God, the face of Vashti is marred and her beauty vanishes.
see 2.25.b.2
GL 4, 378; GL 6, 457 n.45   [← *F.22.1.2*

(7) The name of God, written down and placed upon the body of the dead boy, Micah, who has been used as building material by the

Egyptians, brings him back to life.
GL 4, 49; GL 6, 209 n.126 [← *A.25.3.3*

(8) 'The name', written upon small tablets of copper or gold and placed under the tongues of the heads of slain men enables them to speak and have oracular powers.
see 2.2.c.9
GL 1, 371-372; GL 5, 301 n.218 [← *D.3.2.1*

1.11.b. *Abnormality, deformity or disability as a result of curse*

(1) After Gehazi has accepted money from Naaman, Elisha, his master, curses him with the words 'May the disease of Naaman afflict thee and thy descendants for evermore', and, like Naaman, he becomes leprous.
see 1.26.b.43
2 Kgs 5.25-27 [← *F.23.1.1; A.23.1.10*

1.11.c. *Abnormality, deformity or disability as a result of blessing*
[No references in sources]

1.11.d. *Abnormality, deformity or disability as a result of satire*
[No references in sources]

1.12. Abnormality, Deformity or Disability as a Result of Excess

1.12.a. *Abnormality, deformity or disability as a result of emotion*

(1) The tears of God, shed for the suffering of Israel after the destruction of the temple, turn into pearls.
GL 6, 398 n.39 [← *Gf.27.2.1*

(2) God's sorrow over the destruction of the temple makes his right hand weep and rivers of tears flow from the five fingers into the Great Sea.
3 En. 48A.4 [← *P.10.7.1; Pc.10.7.1; Gf.4.1.1*

(3) Out of the fear of God, the holy Hayyot perspire and breathe fire (and a river of fire is formed from their perspiration).
Gen. R. 78.1; *Lam. R.* 3.23 §8; GL 3, 112; GL 6, 46 n.247
[← *Ba.16.4.2; I.10.1.1*

(4) When he weeps with compassion over the forthcoming death of Abraham, the angel Michael's tears turn into precious stones.
see 3.1.6
T. Abr. 3.9-12; *T. Abr.* 6.7 (Recension A and B) [← *Gf.27.2.2*

(5) The ministering angels are so distressed at seeing Isaac bound on the altar that their tears fall on the knife which is to be used on Isaac and dissolve it.

Gen. R. 56.7 [← *G.25.1.1*

(6) Eliezer, also known as the giant Og, is so frightened when Abraham shouts at him that he loses a tooth.

GL 3, 344; GL 6, 119 n.688, 689 [← *Ic.2.8.1; Ic.5.11.1*

(7) The weeping of Leah over the marriage proposed between herself and Cain causes her eyelashes to drop from their lids.

GL 1, 359; GL 5, 294 n.163 [← *Gc.1.1.1*

(8) The eyes of Leah are weakened by weeping when she fears to fall into the domain of the wicked Esau.

Gen. R. 70.16 [← *G.23.5.2*

(9) Isaac's grief at the idolatrous practices of his daughters-in-law (Esau's wives) makes him blind and prematurely old.

see 1.7.a.4; 1.14.a.2; 1.14.a.3; 1.14.a.4; 1.14.c.6; 1.19.b.6; 1.26.a.5; 1.26.b.12; 1.31.a; 2.6.a.7; 2.7.3; 2.20.1; 4.1.b.10

GL 1, 328; GL 5, 281 n.73, 74 [← *G.23.4.6*

(10) Jacob's weeping over his son, Joseph, makes him blind or partially sighted (but when he goes down to Egypt he can see clearly again).

see 1.31.3

T. Jac. 1.12 [← *G.23.4.7*

(11) After she has fasted for seven days as a penance for her sins, the eyes of Aseneth are inflamed with tears and shame.

see 1.13.3; 1.14.c.9; 2.31.b.2)

Jos. Asen. 11.1.1; *Jos. Asen.* 13.9.8; *Jos. Asen.* 18.3 [← *G.11.3.2*

(12) Certain Israelites tear out their hair in desperation when they are told by Moses to turn back to Pi-hahiroth.

GL 3, 10; GL 6, 3 n.12 [← *E.2.2.1*

(13) David is so distressed when he sees Uzzah touch the ark and die, that his face assumes the hue of a cake baked on coals.

Num. R. 4.20 [← *F.11.1.7*

(14) Zedekiah is blinded by the tears he sheds over the killing of his children by Nebuchadnezzar.

see 1.26.b.48; 1.24.3

GL 4, 293-294; GL 6, 383 n.6,7,8 [← *G.23.4.24*

(15) Ezra is so distressed when he hears that Israelites have married foreigners that he pulls out the hair from his head and beard.

Ezra 9.3   [← *E.2.3.1; E.2.2.2*

(16) The sorrow of the young men, seized and bound when the enemy enters the temple, is so great that their tears eat their way into their cheeks like the scars of boils.

Lam. R. **1.2** §25   [← *Gf.25.1.1; Fa.13.3.1*

(17) Rabbi Gamaliel, hearing a woman weep in the night, is reminded of the destruction of the temple and weeps until his eyelashes fall out.

Lam. R. **1.2** §24   [← *Gc.1.1.2*

(18) Cain's anger, when his offering is not accepted, makes his face turn red as a torch.

Gen. R. **22.6**   [← *F.11.3.1*

(19) When her father, Pentephres, tells Aseneth that he will give her in marriage to Joseph she is so angry that red sweat pours from her face.

Jos. Asen. **4.9(11)**   [← *Ba.11.3.1*

(20) In his rage, Judah sheds tears of blood from his right eye, the hair above his heart grows stiff and hot and stands on end (and becomes lethal, killing all who touch it), and his voice can destroy cities. In a variant, blood flows from both his eyes.

Gen. R. **93.6,7; GL 2, 106-108; GL 5, 354 n.277, 278**
[← *G.10.4.1; Gf.16.3.1; E.8.1.1; E.13.1.2*

(21) When Judah attacks the army from Nineveh he is inflamed with wrath and his countenance, teeth and voice are like a lion's.

GL 1, 404-406; GL 5, 314 n.291   [← *F.18.5.3; Ic.18.5.1*

(22) Balaam's frustration at not being able to touch the camps of the Israelites as he gazes upon them is so intense that his eye drops out.

see 1.26.b.33

Num. R. **2.4;** *Num. R.* **20.6**   [← *G.1.2; G.5.1.2*

(23) Haman's deranged hatred of Israel makes his eyes turn red like those of a serpent.

Gen. R. **16.4**   [← *G.11.3.3*

(24) People cast an 'evil eye' upon Hananiah, Mishael and Azariah when they emerge from the furnace unharmed.

see 2.15.a.12

Gen. R. 56.11; GL 6, 419 n.92 [← *G.25.1.2*

(**25**) Nehemiah tears out the hair of several Israelites in his anger over their marriage to foreigners.

Neh. 13.25 [← *E.2.2.3*

(**26**) Aaron's stature shrinks when he becomes aware of his approaching death.

GL 6, 111 n.636 [← *A.6.2.4*

(**27**) The Egyptians are paralysed with fear and become 'clamped to the spot' during the darkness of the sixth plague of Egypt.

Wis. 17.14, 15, 18 [← *A.23.6.1*

(**28**) David's limbs tremble in terror when he sees an angel slaying his four sons, the prophet Gad and the elders who accompany him, and wiping his dripping sword on the king's garments.

see 1.14.a.8

GL 4, 113; GL 6, 271 n.124 [← *O.23.2.1; T.23.2.1*

(**29**) The high priest of Jerusalem is so overwhelmed by fear and anguish that his body is seized with convulsions when Heliodorus, chancellor to the king, insists upon confiscating the temple funds for the royal exchequer.

2 Macc. 3.17 [← *A.23.2.2*

(**30**) A man's face turns green with fear when he meets the angel of death and hears of his impending demise.

BHM 6.14 no.8 (Hebrew texts, 133) [← *F.11.6.3*

(**31**) The hair of a man's head drops out with terror when, passing through the wilderness of Cub, he sees a sleeping serpent as thick as the beam of an olive press.

Exod. R. 24.4 [← *E.1.1.7*

(**32**) David's ruddy complexion and red hair are caused by Jesse's great passion at the time of begetting his youngest son.

see 3.10.18

GL 6, 247 n.13 [← *B.11.3.3; E.11.3.1*

(**33**) Judah's face turns green with shame when he publicly confesses his crime with Tamar.

GL 3, 170; GL 6, 69 n.357 [← *F.11.6.2*

1.12.b. *Abnormality, deformity or disability as a result of excessive exertion*

(1) Joab causes such bloodshed among the Amalekites that his gory weapon cleaves to his hand and his right hand loses all power of independent motion.

see 1.14.c.15

GL 4, 100; GL 6, 258-259 n.77 [← *P.23.6.2*

1.12.c. *Abnormality, deformity or disability as a result of excessive appetite*

(1) After his sojourn in Joseph's house in Egypt, Simon is so fat that he resembles a leather bottle.

GL 2, 95; GL 5, 350 n.240 [← *A.6.3.6*

(2) Excessive lust causes Samson to lose an eye.

see 2.18.b.1

Ps-Philo 43.5-6; *Num. R.* **9.24; GL 4, 48; GL 6, 208 n.121**
[← *G.1.3; G.24.1.2; G.23.4.16*

1.12.d. *Abnormality, deformity or disability as a result of other excesses*

[No reference in sources]

1.13. Abnormality, Deformity or Disability as a Result of Lack

(1) Because he lacks a head the demon called Murder sees through his breast.

see 3.9.4

T. Sol. **9.1-7** [← *G.4.5.2*

(2) A lack of food, either because Noah forgets to feed it, or is late in feeding it, makes the lion in the ark strike and wound him.

see 1.20.3

Lev. R. **20.1;** *Qoh. R.* **9.2 §1; GL 5, 182 n.37; GL 5, 187 n.51; GL 1, 165-166** [← *T.23.1.1; Sa.24.10.1; Va.24.1.1*

(3) After seven days of fasting in penance for her sins, Aseneth becomes emaciated while her face sags and her lips crack.

see 1.12.a.10; 1.14.c.9; 2.31.b.2

Jos. Asen. **11.1.1;** *Jos. Asen.* **13.9.8;** *Jos. Asen.* **18.3**
[← *A.6.4.1; Ia.15.1.1*

(4) A lack of food makes the skin of the sons of Zion dry as a stick; it shrinks against their bones, and their desiccated faces become darker than blackness itself.

Lam. 4.8; *Lam. R.* **4.8 §11**   [← *B.13.11.1;   F.11.1.4;   A.13.11.1*

(5) Fasting causes the face of Ashur to turn black.

Exod. R. **1.17**   [← *F.11.1.6*

(6) During the famine in Samaria the people are so hungry that they gnaw the flesh from their own bones.

GL 4, 191; GL, 6, 314 n.55   [← *B.2.1.1;   B.15.3.1;   B.24.4.3*

(7) The eyes of the Messiah are clearer than pure wine for 'they never behold unchastity and bloodshed' and his teeth are whiter than milk as they 'never bite aught that is taken by violence'.

GL 2, 143; GL 5, 367 n.388   [← *G.11.11.1;   Ic.11.2.1*

1.14. *Abnormality, Deformity or Disability as a Result of Certain Sight, Sound, Touch, Taste or Smell*

1.14.a. *Abnormality, deformity or disability as a result of a certain sight*

(1) Moses removes a beam of glory from between his eyes and blinds Sammael with it when the latter is sent to collect his soul.

see 5.1.1; 3.4.b.1
Deut. R. **11.10; GL 3, 468-471; GL 6, 160 n.947**   [← *G.23.4.1*

(2) Isaac is blinded by looking too often at Esau as looking at wickedness causes blindness.

see 1.7.a.4; 1.12.a.8; 1.14.a.4; 1.14.a.3; 1.14.c.6; 1.19.b.6; 1.26.a.5 1.26.b.12; 2.6.a.7; 2.7.3; 2.20.1; 1.31.1; 4.1.b.10
GL 5, 281 n.74   [← *G.23.4.6*

(3) Isaac is blinded when he looks at the Shekinah at the time of the Akedah.

see 1.14.a.2; 1.14.a.4; 1.7.a.4; 1.12.a.8; 1.19.b.6; 1.26.a.5; 1.26.b.12; 1.31.1; 2.6.a.7; 2.7.3; 2.20.1; 4.1.b.10; 1.14.c.6
GL 5, 281 n.74   [← *G.23.4.6*

(4) The sight of the Shekinah makes Isaac's eyes grow dim.

see 1.14.a.2; 1.14.a.3; 1.7.a.4; 1.12.a.8; 1.14.c.6; 1.19.b.6; 1.26.a.5; 1.26.b.12; 1.31.1; 2.7.3; 2.20.1; 2.6.a.7; 4.1.b.10
Gen. R. **65.10; GL 3, 479; GL 6, 166 n.962**   [← *G.23.4.6*

(5) Lot's wife is transformed into a pillar of salt when she looks behind her and beholds the Shekinah.

see 1.26.a.4; 1.26.b.9

GL 1, 254-255; GL 5, 241 n.174, 180   [← *A.27.7.1*

(6) When God hands Moses the tables of the law, God holds them by the top third, Moses takes hold of the bottom third and one third remains open, shedding its radiance upon Moses' face. Alternatively, the sparks from the Shekinah cause the rays on the countenance of Moses.

see 1.14.a.7; 1.14.f.2; 1.35.7; 1.14.c.12; 2.24.12; 3.3.a.30; 3.3.a.38

Exod. R. **47.6;** *Deut. R.* **3.12; GL 3, 119; GL 6, 50, 260**

           [← *F.10.1.11*

(7) The face of Moses shines from the reflection of the divine light when God passes in review before the cave in which Moses conceals himself.

see 1.14.a.6; 1.14.c.12; 1.14.f.2; 1.35.7; 2.24.12; 3.3.a.30; 3.3.a.38

Exod. R.   **47.6; GL 3, 137; GL 6, 57 n.295**   [← *F.10.1.11*

(8) David's limbs never cease from trembling after he sees an angel slay his four sons, the prophet Gad, and the elders who accompany him, and then wipe his dripping sword on the king's garments.

see 1.12.a.27

GL 4, 113; GL 6, 271 n.124   [← *O.23.2.1; T.23.2.1*

(9) Goliath is afflicted with leprosy and remains rooted to the ground when David casts his evil eye upon him.

see 1.26.b.38

Lev. R. **17.3; GL 4, 87; GL 6, 251 n.39**   [← *A.23.1.15; A.23.6.4*

(10) When Solomon opens the doors of the ark, the faces of the circumcised men are filled with the radiance of the Shekinah.

see 2.1.b.1

GL 4, 146; GL 6, 290 n.43   [← *F.10.1.16*

(11) A scholar loses his eyesight after he looks at the fiery chariots in which the pious ascend to the heavenly academy and beholds the blinding lustre of the chariot of Rabbi Hiyyah.

GL 6, 332 n.84   [← *G.23.4.21*

(12) The sight, during intercourse, of some white-painted figures causes the black wife of a black Arab king to give birth to a white child.

see 1.5.2

Num. R. 9.34   [← *A.11.2.6; B.11.2.5*

(13) The faces of kings, lords and princes receive a radiance from the glowing brazier into which the angel Raziel puts the coals of Rigyon.
see 2.24.18

GL 3, 112; GL 6, 46 n.247   [← *F.10.1.19*

(14) The sight, during intercourse, of the Watchers—who appear in the form of men as tall as the heavens—causes women to give birth to giants.
see 1.5.1

T. Reub. 5.6 (*Test. XII Patr.*); *Gen. R.* 26.7; GL 5, 155 n.57[← *A.6.1.*

1.14.b. *Abnormality, deformity or disability as a result of a certain sound*

(1) When the heavenly voice admonishes Abraham not to slaughter his son, the body of Isaac, who had died of fear, comes to life again.

GL 1, 281-282; GL 5, 251 n.243   [← *A.25.3.2*

(2) Simon's loud cry makes his seventy assailants fall to the ground and lose their teeth.

GL 2, 86; GL 5, 348 n.218   [← *Ic.1.1.2*

(3) At the sound of Judah's outcry, Joseph's 300 heroes lose their teeth and their heads remain fixed facing backwards, as they have turned to discover the cause of the tumult.

Gen. R. 93.7; GL 2, 106, 112; GL 5, 354-355 n.275, 281
[← *D.7.1.1; D.23.6.1; Ic.1.1.1*

(4) When Moses prays to God, saying 'Hear, Lord, the voice of Judah', the bones of Judah, scattered because he never redeemed the promise to bring Benjamin back to his father, join together again.
see 1.19.b.8

GL 3, 456; GL 6, 155 n.922   [← *Va.3.1.1*

(5) When Moses hears God's voice, his face turns red.

Num. R. 12.1; GL 3, 185; GL 6, 74 n.381   [← *F.11.3.2*

(6) When Moses hears God's voice, he becomes slow of speech.
see 1.26.b.22; 2.4.7

GL 5, 422 n.140   [← *I.23.3.3*

(7) The dead in Sheol are revived by the sound of the divine voice.
see 2.7.7

GL 3, 97; GL 6, 39-40 n.215   [← *A.25.3.16*

1.14.c. *Abnormality, deformity or disability as a result of a certain touch*

(1) When Enoch is anointed with the oil which is greater than the greatest light and resembles the rays of the glittering sun, his body becomes radiant.
    see 1.35.2
    2 En. 22.8-10 (J and A)   [← *A.10.1.7*

(2) The moulded wax figures of men are animated by being plunged into magic water and allowed to swim.
    see 1.3.d.1; 2.11.b.1
    GL 2, 159; GL 5, 372, 425   [← *A.16.14.1*

(3) After doing penance by standing in water, Adam's body becomes like sponge.
    P.R.E. 20   [← *A.16.9.1*

(4) After doing penance by standing in water, Eve's body becomes like sponge.
    GL 5, 115 n.106   [← *A.16.9.2*

(5) After doing penance by standing in water, Eve's body becomes like grass or algae.
    LAE (Vita) 6.1-2; 7; 9.1-5; 10.1   [← *A.16.8.1*

(6) The tears of the angels, weeping for grief to see Isaac bound to the altar and about to be sacrificed, fall upon Isaac's eyes and mark them, so that his sight fails later in life.
    Gen. R. **65.10**   [← *G.23.4.6*

(7) An angel touches the hollow of Jacob's thigh as they wrestle together at the ford of Jabbok, and lames him (but the angel Raphael cures Jacob of the injury inflicted by Michael).
    see 1.20.4; 1.26.b.13; 2.16.4
    Gen. 32.24-26, 32-33; GL 1, 385, 389; GL 5, 305 n.248; GL 5, 308 n.258   [← *Ta.24.1.1; Ta.23.1.1*

(8) After being blessed by Isaac, Jacob is bathed in celestial dew which fills his bones with marrow and transforms him into a giant.
    see 1.17.5
    GL 1, 332, 336; GL 5, 283 n.88; GL 5, 285 n.98   [← *A.6.1.23*

(9) The hair of Aseneth becomes lank and straggly from the load of ashes she places upon it during her seven days of fasting and penance for her sins.

see 1.12.a.10; 1.13.3; 2.31.b.2

Jos. Asen. **11.1.1;** *Jos. Asen.* **13.9.8;** *Jos. Asen.* **18.3** [← *E.22.1.2*

(10) When a child, Moses burns his tongue, lips and hand when he reaches out for a burning coal and holds it to his lips.

see 2.3.3; 2.6.a.8; 2.9.6; 2.20.2

Exod. R. **1.26; GL 2, 274; GL 5, 402 n.65**
[← *I.23.3.3; Ia.13.2.1; Ia.24.4.1; Ib.13.2.1; Ib.24.4.1; P.13.2.1; P.24.4.1*

(11) Moses lays both his hands upon Joshua and thereby bestows upon him a countenance radiant like the moon (as well as insight and understanding).

see 3.3.a.39

GL 3, 400; GL 6, 141-142 n.835, 836   [← *F.10.1.15*

(12) The scroll on which the Torah is to be written is made of a parchment of white fire, written upon with black fire, and sealed and swathed with bands of fire, and as he writes upon it, Moses dries his hands on his hair and thus acquires a lustrous appearance.

see 1.14.a.6; 1.14.a.7; 1.14.f.2; 1.35.7; 2.24.12; 3.3.a.30; 3.3.a.38

Exod. R. **47.6;** *Deut. R.* **3.12**   [← *Fb.10.1.1*

(13) The blains and leprosy of the skin suffered by the Egyptians are caused by the handful of ashes which Moses sprinkles towards heaven and which scatter over the whole land of Egypt.

see 1.26.b.28; 2.5.7

GL 2, 354; GL 5, 431 n.191, 192
[← *B.23.1.1; B.23.2.4; B.24.3.2*

(14) The Egyptians suffer from boils after the soot thrown into the air by Moses and Aaron lands on them.

see 2.4.6; 2.5.6

Exod. 9.8-12   [← *A.23.3.1*

(15) Joab causes such bloodshed among the Amalekites that his gory weapon cleaves to his right hand which loses all power of motion.

see 1.12.b.1

GL 4, 100; GL 6, 258-259 n.77   [← *P.23.6.2*

(16) The anointing of a king causes an increase in stature so that the clothes of Saul fit David even though Saul stands a head and shoulders above any other man.

see 3.3.a.33

Lev. R. **26.9**   [← *A.6.5.32*

(17) The intense heat in the belly of the fish makes Jonah's hair fall out.

see 1.9.2

GL 4, 252; GL 6, 351 n.36   [← *E.1.1.5*

(18) An eagle touches a corpse and it comes to life (as a sign that Jeremiah's mission is true).

see 2.3.7

4 Bar. 7.18; GL 4, 320   [← *A.25.3.8*

(19) Hezekiah is fireproof after he is rubbed with the blood of a salamander.

GL 4, 266; GL 6, 361 n.47   [← *A.25.30.1*

(20) Elisha revives the son of a woman from Shunem by stretching himself on top of the child, putting his mouth on its mouth, his eyes to its eyes, and his hands on its hands, and repeating this seven times until the child sneezes and opens its eyes.

see 1.35.10

2 Kgs 4.33-35; *Cant. R.* 2.5 §3   [← *A.25.3.5*

(21) A dead man revives at the touch of Elisha's bier (or bones) and stands up on his feet.

2 Kgs 13.21; GL 4, 246; GL 6, 347 n.21   [← *A.25.3.6*

(22) The hot droppings from sparrows make white spots on Tobit's eyes. When doctors use ointments to try and remove the spots, the spots make him completely blind.

see 1.30.1

Tob. 2.10   [← *G.23.4.23; G.11.2.1*

(23) The bodies of the Israelites are restored to life by 'the dew that will hereafter revive the dead' which God lets fall upon them.

see 1.17.4; 1.19.b.22; 2.3.5; 2.4.12

GL 3, 95; GL 6, 38-39 n.210; also *2 Bar.* 29.7; *2 Bar.* 73.2
[← *A.25.3.14*

(24) A drop of ink which God lets fall upon a man while he is signing the decree of that man's death, causes a radiance to envelop him.

GL 6, 61 n.309   [← *A.10.1.20*

(25) A foolhardy wight scalds himself by jumping into a scalding hot tub.

see 4.1.a.5

GL 3, 62; GL 6, 25 n.147   [← *B.24.3.3*

1.14.d. *Abnormality, deformity or disability as a result of a certain taste*

(1) The size of Adam's body is reduced to one hundred ells after he eats the fruit of the forbidden tree.
see 1.26.a.1; 3.6.b.5
Num. R. 13.2; *Num. R.* 13.12; *Gen. R.* 19.8; *Gen. R.* 12.6;
Cant. R. 3.7 §5   [← *A.6.1.20; A.6.5.2]*

(2) After eating from the honeycomb which she finds in her store-room (and which is the food of paradise and eternal life), Aseneth's face becomes like the sun, her eyes like the rising morning star, her cheeks red like the blood of the son of man, her lips like the rose of life, her teeth like fighting men lined up for fight, her hair like the vine in paradise, her neck like a cypress, her appearance like light and her bones strong like cedars.
see 1.35.5
Jos. Asen. 16.16; *Jos. Asen.* 18.7; *Jos. Asen.* 20.6
                    [← *F.10.1.10; Fa.11.3.1; G.10.2.8; Ia.11.3.1*

(3) After he has eaten honey, the eyes of Jonathan brighten.
1 Sam. 14.27-29   [← *G.10.2.10*

(4) The idolaters are unable to open their mouths after they drink the water which Samuel gives them.
see 2.6.b.8
GL 4, 64; GL 6, 225-226 n.40   [← *Ia.23.3.2*

(5) Zedekiah has diarrhoea after eating the food which Nebuchadnezzar has given him precisely for this purpose.
see 2.24.16; 2.25.a.1
GL 6, 384 n.8   [← *Rb.6.1.1; Rb.13.2.1*

(6) Sinners in hell are forced to drink venom from scorpions and this causes them such anguish that their eyes melt in their sockets.
see 1.26.b.64
GL 2, 312; GL 5, 418-419 n.118   [← *G.13.10.1*

(7) Black bones result from drinking water, red bones from drinking wine and white bones from drinking hot water.
Gen. R. 89.2   [← *Va.11.1.1; Va.11.2.1; Va.11.3.1*

1.14.e. *Abnormality, deformity or disability as a result of a certain smell*

[No reference in sources]

1.14.f. *Abnormality, deformity or disability as a result of an unusual meeting*

(1) The angels who bring the good news to Sarah (that she shall conceive) make her face shine like an olive.
  Gen. R. 53.3   [← *F.10.1.9*

(2) Moses' skin is radiant after his meeting with Yahweh on Sinai where he has been bathed with invisible light.
  see 1.14.a.6; 1.14.a.7; 1.14.c.12; 1.35.7; 2.24.12; 3.3.a.30; 3.3.a.38
  Ps-Philo 12.1; Exod. 34.29, 30, 35   [← *F.10.1.11*

1.15. Abnormality, Deformity or Disability as a Result of Mimicry or Sympathetic Magic

(1) When Moses throws a silver leaf with an image of a man engraved upon it into the Nile, the scattered bones of Joseph unite themselves into an entire body so that Moses can take him with him when he leaves Egypt.
  see 1.19.b.7
  Deut. R. 11.7; **GL 3, 122; GL 6, 51 n.266**   [← *Va.3.1.2*

(2) Egyptians imitate Moses by placing their hands within their bosoms and then withdrawing them, but in their case the ensuing leprosy is permanent.
  GL 2, 355; GL 5, 431 n.193   [← *P.23.1.2*

(3) While Ezekiel is reviving the dead, the bones or skull of a slain Jew, which have been made into a drinking vessel, come to life and strike a blow in Nebuchadnezzar's face, while a voice announces, 'A friend of this man is at this moment reviving the dead'.
  see 2.2.c.11
  GL 4, 330; GL 6, 418 n.90   [← *Va.3.1.4; D.3.1.1*

1.16. Abnormality, Deformity or Disability as a Result of Time or Place

1.16.a. *Abnormality, deformity or disability as a result of time*

(1) On the first day of the summer season no creature has a shadow.
Gen. R. 6.6 [← *A.2.1.1*

(2) Adam's body, before the Fall, has gigantic dimensions, reaching from heaven to earth and the same distance from east to west.
see 3.5.a.2
Lev. R. 14.1; Lev. R 18.2; Gen. R. 8.1; Gen. R. 19.9; Gen. R. 21.3; Gen. R. 24.2; Job 20.6; Apoc. Abr. 23.5
[← *A.6.1.19; A.6.3.4; A.6.5.20*

(3) Eve's body, before the Fall, is of a very great height and terrible breadth, incomparable in aspect and size.
see 3.5.a.3
Apoc. Abr. 23.5 [← *A.6.1.21; A.6.3.5; A.6.5.22*

(4) Adam and Eve have a horny skin (and are enveloped with a cloud of glory) before the Fall.
see 3.5.a.1
GL 1, 74; GL 5, 97 n.69
[← *A.13.10.1; A.13.10.2; B.13.10.1; B.13.10.2*

(5) In the days of the sons of Noah, children can run, speak and obey orders while still attached by the umbilical cord to the mother.
Gen. R. 36.1; Lev. R. 5.1 [← *A.26.1.1; Qa.14.1.1*

(6) The serpent, before the Fall, has human hands, feet, tongue and ears (as well as an upright posture and wings). They are later cut off by an angel.
see 3.3.a.44; 3.5.a.4
Gen. R. 19.1; Gen. R. 20.5; LAE (Apoc. Mos.) 26.2-3; LAE (Vita) 38.1; Qoh. R. 10.11 §1; Deut. R. 5.10
[← *P.21.6.2; U.21.6.3; J.21.6.1; Ib.21.6.1*

1.16.b. *Abnormality, deformity or disability as a result of place*

(1) In the wilderness Anah, a descendant of Esau, meets beasts (which are really demons) that are half-man, half-ape or bear.
see 3.2.1
GL 1, 423; GL 5, 322 n.321, 322 [← *Cc.18.2.1; Cc.18.3.1*

(2) The Cainites, inhabitants of the Arka, the third earth, have two heads and are giants or dwarfs.
see 1.1.a.2; 3.2.17
GL 1, 114; GL 5, 143 n.34; GL 4, 132
[← *A.6.1.4; A.6.2.1; A.6.1.8; D.5.1.2*

(3) The Neshiah, the fifth earth, is inhabited by dwarfs without noses.
see 1.1.a.19; 3.2.4
GL 1, 114; GL 5, 143 n.36   [← *A.6.2.3; H.1.1.*

(4) The dwellers of Paradise walk on their heads.
see 1.34.5; 3.2.5
GL 5, 263 n.301   [← *A.8.1.2*

(5) Isaac continues to walk on his head even after he has left Paradise.
GL 5, 263 n.301   [← *A.8.1.3*

(6) The Israelites cannot be circumcised on their journey through the wilderness so they are circumcised when they have crossed the Jordan river, at Gilgal.
see 3.11.22; 2.31.b.3; 2.13.a.13
Josh. 5.2-10   [← *Sa.2.3.22; Sa.24.3.22*

(7) Adne Sadeh, the 'man of the mountain', has the form of a human being, but is fastened to the ground by means of his navel string upon which his life depends.
see 3.2.6
GL 1, 31-32; GL 5, 50 n.147-149   [← *Qa.14.1.1*

(8) Some inhabitants of Tebel, the second earth, have two heads, four arms and hands and four legs and feet, and some have the head of an ox, lion or snake on a human body, or a human head on the body of an ox, serpent or lion.
see 3.2.7
GL 1, 10   [← *D.5.1.5; D.18.4.2; D.18.5.1; D.18.6.1; D.21.4.1;*
         D.21.5.1; D.21.6.1; O.5.3.2; P.5.3.1; T.5.3.1; U.5.3.1

1.17. *Abnormality, Deformity or Disability as a Result of the Influence of the Elements*

(1) It is so cold during the rains of the Flood that Noah coughs up blood while in the ark.
Gen. R. 32.10   [← *1.10.4.1*

(2) The hail that is sent as the seventh plague of Egypt sears the flesh of the Egyptians.
see 1.26.a.7; 1.26.b.26; 2.5.4
GL 2, 342, 344, 346, 356, 357; GL 5, 426 n.171; GL 5, 427 n.172, 173; GL 5, 431 n.194   [← *B.24.3.1*

(3) The sun darkens the faces of the women who accompany Nehemiah from the Exile.

    Gen. R. **18.5**   [← *F.11.1.4*

(4) The dew of heaven, dropped by God upon the dry bones in the Valley of Dura, causes sinews, flesh and skin to grow upon them and restores the dead Israelites to life.

    see 1.19.b.22; 1.14.c.23; 2.3.5; 2.4.12

    GL 3, 95; GL 4, 332-333; GL 6, 38-39 n.210; GL 6, 421-422 n.94, 95; also *2 Bar.* **29.7**; *2 Bar.* **73.2**   [← *A.25.3.14*

(5) The celestial dew in which Jacob is bathed fills his bones with marrow and transforms him into a giant.

    see 1.14.c.8

    GL 1, 332, 336; GL 5, 283 n.88; GL 5, 285 n.98   [← *A.6.1.23*

1.18. *Abnormality, Deformity or Disability as a Result of Altered Consciousness*

(1) When the spirit of God is upon him, Samson's hair begins to move and emit a bell-like sound, which can be heard from far off.

    see 1.19.b.9

    Lev. R. **8.2**; GL 4, 48; GL 6, 207 n.116   [← *E.25.5.1; E.8.1.2*

1.19. *Abnormality, Deformity or Disability as a Result of Supernatural or Cosmic Forces*

1.19.a. *Abnormality, deformity or disability as a result of fate*
[No reference in sources]

1.19.b. *Abnormality, deformity or disability as a result of supernatural intervention or agent*

(1) The garments of light which God makes for Adam and Eve make them luminous.

    see 5.1.2

    Gen. R. **20.12**   [← *A.10.1.9; A.10.1.11*

(2) A letter of God's holy name is placed upon Cain's forehead to protect him from the onslaught of the beasts.

    see 2.11.e.2

    GL 1, 111-112; GL 5, 141 n.27, 28   [← *Fb.13.2.4*

(3) Cain is marked by God with a horn on his forehead as a

punishment for the killing of Abel.
see 1.26.b.4
Gen. R. 22.12; GL 5, 141 n.28   [← *Fb.14.2.2; Fb.18.11.2*

(4) God strikes with blindness those who built the Tower of Babel.
see 1.26.b.8; 2.22.c.1
3 Bar. 3.8 (Greek)   [← *G.23.4.3*

(5) Abraham's dead servants (killed by fear when Death reveals his ferocious aspect) are revived, at Abraham's request, by God.
T. Abr. 18.11; *T. Abr.* 14.5-6 (Recension B)   [← *A.25.3.1*

(6) Isaac's blindness is the first disease which comes upon men after Isaac has prayed to God to send bodily ailments upon men that they might atone for their sins.
see 1.7.a.4; 1.12.a.8; 1.14.a.2; 1.14.a.3; 1.14.a.4; 1.14.c.6; 1.26.a.5; 1.26.b.12; 1.31.1; 2.6.a.7; 2.7.3; 2.20.1; 4.1.b.10
Gen. R. 65.9; GL 5, 281-282 n.74   [← *G.23.4.6*

(7) When Moses throws a silver leaf with the image of a man engraved upon it into the Nile, God causes the scattered bones of Joseph to unite into an entire body so that Moses can take it with him when he leaves Egypt.
see 1.15.1
Deut. R. 11.7; GL 3, 122; GL 6, 51 n.266   [← *Va.3.1.2*

(8) At the intercession of Moses, God joins Judah's bones together.
see 1.14.b.4
GL 3, 456; GL 6, 155 n.922   [← *Va.3.1.1*

(9) When the spirit of God is upon him, Samson's hair begins to move and emit a bell-like sound.
see 1.18.1
Lev. R. 8.2; GL 4, 48; GL 6, 207 n.116   [← *E.25.5.1; E.8.1.2*

(10) When the spirit is upon him, Samson is able, with one stride, to cover a distance equal to that between Zorah and Eshtaol.
Lev. R. 8.2; GL 4, 48   [← *T.25.1.2*

(11) An angel prevents Zimri and Cozbi, caught in the act of copulation, from moving apart or crying out.
see 2.18.b.2; 2.3.8
Num. R. 20.25; GL 3, 387; GL 6, 137 n.798 [← *A.23.6.1; I.23.2.4*

(12) An angel blinds the Amorites so that they fall upon and kill one another.

see 2.16.9
Ps-Philo 25.12; GL 4, 26; GL 6, 184 n.18   [← *G.23.4.13*

(13) The angel Nathaniel blinds Jair and his servants so that the seven pious men can escape from the furnace.
see 2.18.a.8
Ps-Philo 38.3; GL 4, 42; GL 6, 202 n.105   [← *G.23.4.19*

(14) The gold plate of the mitre on the high priest's forehead makes the Midianite women of marriageable age grow pale as they are led past it.
see 2.2.a.1
GL 3, 413; GL 6, 145 n.861   [← *F.11.2.1*

(15) When the Holy Spirit rests upon him, the face of Phinehas flames like a torch, making him look like an angel.
Lev. R. 1.1; Lev. R. 21.12   [← *F.10.2.1*

(16) The demon, Ornias, sucks the thumb of the right hand of a boy who is helping Solomon to build the temple and as a result the boy becomes thin and emaciated.
T. Sol. 1.2-4   [← *A.6.4.3*

(17) A heavenly voice commands that King Uzziah be stricken with leprosy when he tries to offer sacrifices upon the altar in the place of the high priest.
see 1.26.a.12; 1.7.a.5
GL 3, 214, 303; GL 4, 127, 262; GL 5, 141 n.28; GL 6 357-358 n.29, 30; 2 Chron. 26.19-23   [← *A.13.4.1; A.23.1.14; B.13.4.1; B.23.1.2; Fb.13.4.1; Fb.23.1.1*

(18) God raises the dead Jonah (through Elijah) to show that it is not possible to run away from God.
see 2.4.10
Liv. Proph. (Jonah) 10.6   [← *A.25.3.9*

(19) God hears the prayer of Elijah begging him to revive a widow's dead son, and his soul is returned to him.
see 1.35.11
1 Kgs 17.17-24; Cant. R. 2.5 §3   [← *A.25.3.10*

(20) Yahweh blinds the Aramaeans after Elisha has prayed to him to do so.
see 2.9.8; 2.18.a.9; 2.18.c.1
2 Kgs 6.18   [← *G.23.4.22*

(21) Yahweh strikes Ezekiel dumb (literally, Ezekiel's tongue sticks to the roof of his mouth) so that he will stop warning the Israelites and only be Yahweh's mouthpiece.
see 2.10.b.1
Ezek. 3.26-27; Ezek. 24.27; Ezek. 33.22   [← *I.23.3.8; Ib.23.2.1*

(22) God revives the dead when Ezekiel prophesies over them.
see 1.17.4; 2.3.5; 2.4.12; 1.14.c.23
Ezek. 37.7   [← *A.25.3.11; A.25.3.12; A.25.3.13; A.25.3.14; A.25.3.15; Va.3.1.5*

(23) God sends diseases to disfigure the coquettish maidens of Jerusalem and make them repulsive.
see 1.10.6; 1.26.b.61
GL 4, 312-313; GL 6, 404 n.45   [← *A.22.1.7*

(24) A demon in the form of a three-headed dragon with awful skin attacks children while they are still in the womb, turning their ears around backward and making them deaf, blind and dumb.
T. Sol. 12.1-2   [← *G.23.4.27; I.23.3.12; J.7.1.1; J.23.1.9*

(25) The angels of destruction make the teeth of the sinners in hell grow to a length of one parasang so that they can break them again the following day.
see 2.22.b.7; 1.26.a.14; 1.26.b.65
GL 2, 312; GL 5, 418-419 n.118   [← *Ic.25.1.1; Ic.6.5.3*

(26) God tosses Theodotus Ptolemy IV Philopator, king of Egypt, to the ground with a stroke to prevent him destroying the temple of Jerusalem and the Jews.
see 1.26.b.51; 2.15.b.13
3 Macc. 2.22   [← *A.23.6.6; I.23.2.6*

1.19.c *Abnormality, deformity or disability as a result of cosmic forces*
[No reference in sources]

1.20. Abnormality, Deformity or Disability as a Result of Battle, Fight or Other Physical Attack

(1) A stone thrown at Eliezer, a bondsman of Adam, by a Sodomite causes a serious wound to his forehead.
GL 1, 247-248   [← *Fb.24.1.1*

(2) Esau tears his mother's womb and threatens her life while arguing with Jacob about who is to be born first.

GL 1, 313-314; GL 5, 271 n.16   [← *Vg.24.1.1*

(3) Noah is struck by a lion in the ark with the result either that he is lamed, or his bone is broken, or his sexual organs are mutilated.
see 1.13.2

Gen. R. 36.4; Gen. R. 30.6; Lev. R. 20.1; Qoh. R. 9.2 §1
                    [← *T.23.1.1; Sa.24.10.1; Va.24.1.1*

(4) Jacob is struck in the hollow of his thigh by God, or an angel, or the guardian spirit of Esau, during the struggle at the ford of Jabbok.
see 1.26.b.13; 2.16.4; 1.14.c.7

**Gen. 32.24-26, 32-33; Gen. R. 77.3; Gen. R. 78.5; Gen. R. 79.5;
Dem. Fragment 2.7**   [← *T.23.1.3; Ta.23.1.1; Ta.24.1.1*

(5) Benjamin throws a pebble at the son of Pharaoh and seriously wounds him on the forehead.

GL 2, 177; GL 5, 374-375 n.432   [← *Fb.24.1.2*

(6) The blows received by the Israelites in Egypt make their breath putrid.

Exod. R. 5.21   [← *I.10.10.1*

(8) The Egyptians break the thigh-bones of the Israelites when they go out to look for straw for making bricks.

Exod. R. 5.19   [← *Ta.24.3.1*

(9) Jehoram, son of Ahab, king of Israel, is wounded in the battle against Hazael, king of Aram.

2 Chron. 22.5   [← *A.24.10.4*

(10) Judas, son of Simon, high priest and ethnarch of Jews, is wounded in a battle against Cendebaeus.

1 Macc. 16.9   [← *A.24.10.2*

(11) The shoulder of Dositheus (one of the Tubians) is slashed by one of the Thracian cavalry when he grasps Gorgias.

2 Macc. 12.35   [← *M.24.1.1*

1.21. *Abnormality, Deformity or Disability as a Result of Acquiring an Unusual Organ as a Replacement for One Lost*
[No reference in sources]

1.22. *Abnormality, Deformity or Disability as a Result of Borrowing, Buying or Stealing Organs of Another*
[No reference in sources]

1.23. *Abnormality, Deformity or Disability as a Result of an Accident*

(1) The vast majority of the Israelites become maimed during the building work in Egypt. Falling stones, beams and clay sever their hands, blind them, or otherwise injure them. (However, all the blind, lame, deaf and dumb are healed by an angel before they receive the Torah at Sinai.)
Num. R. **7.1;** GL 3, 13, 78; GL 6, 30 n.176
[← *G.23.4.10; I.23.3.4; J.23.1.3; P.1.1; T.23.1.2*

(2) Meribbaal has crippled feet after his nurse drops him when she flees after hearing of the death of Saul and Jonathan (Meribbaal's father).
2 **Sam. 4.4;** 2 **Sam. 9.3, 13;** 2 **Sam. 19.27**   [← *U.23.1.3*

(3) Ignorant of the wondrous mechanism of the throne of Solomon, the Pharaoh Necho is crippled by one of the lions on the throne the first time he attempts to mount it.
see 1.29.1
Lev. R. **20.1;** *Qoh. R.* **9.2** §1   [← *T.23.1.5*

(4) Nebuchadnezzar is struck on the left foot by the right paw of the golden lion and becomes lame when he tries to ascend the throne of Solomon without understanding its mechanism.
see 1.29.2
GL 6, 415 n.80   [← *U.23.1.4*

1.24. *Abnormality, Deformity or Disability as a Result of Cruelty or Malice*

(1) The serpent (Satan) maliciously bites and wounds Seth, since after the primal sin animals no longer fear man.
LAE (Vita) **37.1; 39.3;** *LAE (Apoc. Mos.)* **12.2; 10.1** [← *B.24.4.1*

(2) Nebuchadnezzar daily cuts off a piece of flesh from Hiram's body and forces him to eat it, until he finally perishes.
see 2.15.a.11
GL 4, 336; GL 6, 424-425 n.105   [← *B.2.3.1*

(3) The cruelty of the king of Babylon is such that he has the sons of Zedekiah slaughtered before his eyes, and then puts out Zedekiah's eyes.

see 1.26.b.48; 1.12.a.13

2 Kgs 25.7; Jer. 39.7; Jer. 52.11   [← *G.1.4; G.24.1.3; G.23.4.24*

(4) The cruelty of King Antiochus Epiphanes is such that he tortures Eliezer and his mother and six brothers, cutting off their extremities, cutting out their tongues, piercing their eyes and scalping their heads before he fries them alive.

see 2.5.12; 2.25.a.2

2 Macc. 7; *4 Macc.* 6.6, 25; *4 Macc.* 7.13-14; *4 Macc.* 9.28; *4 Macc.* 10.5-8, 17-21; *4 Macc.* 11.18-19; *4 Macc.* 18.21   [← *D.2.2.1; Ib.1.1.3; Ga.24.1.1; P.1.1.2; U.1.1.1*

1.25. *Abnormality, Deformity or Disability as a Result of Capture or Imprisonment*
[No references in sources]

1.26. *Abnormality, Deformity or Disability as a Punishment for Transgression*

1.26.a. *Abnormality, deformity or disability as a punishment for violation of prohibition or taboo*

(1) The size of Adam's body is reduced to one hundred ells or cubits after he has violated God's injunction concerning the forbidden fruit.

see 1.14.d.1; 3.6.b.5

***Cant. R.* 3.7 §5; *Gen. R.* 19.8; *Gen. R.* 12.6; *Num. R.* 13.12; *Num. R.* 13.2**   [← *A.6.1.20; A.6.5.21*

(2) Because he has had sexual relations in the ark with a dog, thus violating the rule of abstinence, Ham emerges 'dusky'.

***Gen. R.* 36.7**   [← *A.11.1.2; B.11.1.1*

(3) Those who had wanted to ascend the Tower of Babel and set up idols are transformed into apes.

GL 1, 180; GL 5, 203-204   [← *A.27.2.1*

(4) Lot's wife is transformed into a pillar of salt when she disobeys the angels and looks behind her.

see 1.14.a.5; 1.26.b.9

Gen. 19.17-26   [← *A.27.7.1*

(5) Isaac is blinded when he looks at the Shekinah at the time of the Akedah.

see 1.7.a.4; 1.12.a.8; 1.14.a.2; 1.14.a.3; 1.14.a.4; 1.14.c.6; 1.19.b.6; 1.26.b.12; 1.31.1; 2.6.a.7; 2.7.3; 2.20.1; 4.1.b.10

Gen. R. 65.10; GL 5, 281 n.74   [← *G.23.4.6*

(6) Pharaoh and his court are afflicted with leprosy because Pharaoh lusts after Sarah, who is another man's wife.

see 2.23.b.1

Gen. R. 41.2; *Gen. R.* 52.13; *Lev. R.* 16.1; GL 1, 224; GL 5, 221 n.75-77

[← *A.23.1.5*

(7) The flesh of the Egyptians is seared by hail after they ignore a prohibition on allowing animals to remain out of doors.

see 1.17.2; 1.26.b.26; 2.5.4

GL 2, 356; GL 5, 431 n.194   [← *B.24.3.1*

(8) Those who break the Sabbath are transformed into apes by Moses

GL 6, 85 n.452   [← *A.27.2.2*

(9) The lips of those who have worshipped the golden calf become tightly closed 'like gold'.

GL 6, 54-55 n.281   [← *Ia.23.3.1*

(10) The tongues of those who have willed in their minds that the golden calf should be made are cut off by drinking the water into which they are thrown (the sea having left its bed and threatening to flood the world because of the disregard for the Torah).

see 2.6.b.5

Ps.Philo 12.7; GL 6, 55 n.281   [← *Ib.1.1.1; Ib.24.1.1*

(11) Because of the idolatry of the golden calf, leprosy breaks out in the camp of the Israelites and the men are afflicted with gonorrhoea.

Lev. R. 17.3; *Num. R.* 7.1-6; *Num. R.* 8.3; *Num. R.* 13.8; GL 3, 213; GL 6, 79 n.112, 113   [← *A.23.1.9; Sa.10.1.1*

(12) When king Uzziah tries to usurp the rights of the priesthood, to burn incense and offer sacrifices upon the altar, he is stricken with leprosy.

see 1.7.a.5; 1.19.b.17

2 Chron. 26.19-23; *Lev. R.* 17.3 [← *A.13.4.1; A.23.1.14; B.13.4.1 B.23.1.2; Fb.13.4.1; Fb.23.1.1*

(13) Because Jehoram, king of Judah, has 'set up high places in the highlands of Judah and caused the inhabitants of Jerusalem to prostitute themselves and Judah to go astray' as well as murdering his own brothers, Yahweh makes his bowels drop out with disease.

see 1.10.1; 1.26.b.45

2 Chron. 21.13-19   [← *Vf.1.1.2*

(**14**) Sinners in hell are punished for eating taboo foods, eating on the Day of Atonement, and drinking blood, by having their teeth broken by the angels of destruction with fiery stones from morning until evening. The teeth regrow at night and thus the punishment is perpetuated.

see 1.19.b.25; 1.26.b.65; 2.22.b.7

GL 2, 312; GL 5, 418-419 n.118

[← *Ic.24.1.1; Ic.25.1.1; Ic.6.5.3*

1.26.b. *Abnormality, deformity or disability as a punishment for certain act or omission of required act*

(**1**) As a punishment for failing to recite the 'Holy', a devouring fire issues from the little finger of God and splits the ranks of the angels into 496,000 myriads of parts, and devours them.

see 2.15.a.3

3 En. **35.6;** *3 En.* **40.3;** *3 En.* **47.1-3**   [← *Pc.10.3.1*

(**2**) The body of Adam is subjected to afflictions of the eyes and hearing and sixty-eight other plagues as a punishment for his sin.

LAE (Apoc. Mos.) **8.2; 5.2-4;** *LAE (Vita)* **30; 34.1-2**

[← *G.23.5.1; J.23.1.1*

(**3**) Cain is afflicted with leprosy and boils as a punishment for the murder of Abel.

see 2.2.c.4; 3.6.b.6

Num. R. **7.5**   [← *A.23.1.1*

(**4**) Cain is marked by God with a horn on his head as a punishment for the killing of Abel.

see 1.19.b.3

Gen. R. **22.12**   [← *Fb.18.11.2; Fb.14.2.2*

(**5**) After his unsatisfactory offering, Cain's face becomes as black as smoke.

GL 1, 107-108; GL 5, 136-137 n.12,13   [← *F.11.1.2*

(**6**) As a punishment for having planned to build the Tower of Babel, those responsible have the feet of deer and goats, the faces of dogs, and the horns of deer.

3 Bar. **3.3 (Slavonic and Greek)**
[← *D.14.2.4; D.18.11.2; F.18.2.2; U.18.2.2; U.18.4.1*

(7) As a punishment for having built the Tower of Babel, those responsible have the faces of cattle, the horns of deer, the feet of goats and the loins of sheep.

3 Bar. **2.3 (Slavonic and Greek)**
[← *D.14.2.3; D.18.11.1; F.18.4.2; U.18.2.1; Sa.18.2.1*

(8) The builders of the Tower of Babel are struck with blindness by God.

see 1.19.b.4; 2.22.c.1
3 Bar. **3.8 (Greek)**   [← *G.23.4.3*

(9) Lot's wife is transformed into a pillar of salt because she 'sins in connection with salt': while borrowing salt from a neighbour she reveals the presence of forbidden guests in her home. Alternatively, it happens because she fights with Abraham when he asks her to bring the guests salt.

see 1.14.a.5; 1.26.a.4
Gen. R. **50.4;** *Gen. R.* **51.5; GL 1, 254-255; GL 5, 241 n.174, 180**
[← *A.27.7.1*

(10) All the women of Abimelech's household become barren because Abimelech has had Sarah, Abraham's wife, brought to him.

Gen. 20.17-18   [← *Vg.23.1.2*

(11) Abimelech, king of Gerar, is stricken with leprosy and covered in scabs for having instigated Isaac's removal from Gerar.

Gen. R. **64.9; GL 1, 324; GL 5, 280 n.65**   [← *A.23.1.2*

(12) Isaac's blindness is a punishment for preferring the wicked Esau to the God fearing Jacob.

see 1.7.a.4; 1.12.a.8; 1.14.a.2; 1.14.a.3; 1.14.a.4; 1.14.c.6; 1.19.b.6; 1.26.a.5; 1.31.1; 2.6.a.7; 2.7.3; 2.20.1; 4.1.b.10
Gen. R. **65.5-7**   [← *G.23.4.6*

(13) Jacob is injured by the angel as a punishment for his lack of trust in God, as he had intended to flee from Esau.

see 1.14.c.7; 1.20.4; 2.16.4
GL 5, 311 n.273   [← *T.23.1.3; Ta.23.1.1; Ta.24.1.1*

(14) Judah sits deaf and dumb in the heavenly academy as a punishment for not redeeming his promise to bring Benjamin back to his father.

GL 3, 456; GL 6, 155 n.922   [← *I.23.3.2; J.23.1.2*

(15) Potiphar, or Poti-phera, is made a eunuch as a punishment for his evil intentions towards Joseph. (In another version he is castrated because he has only bought Joseph for sexual purposes.)

see 2.23.b.2

Gen. R. 86.3; *Jub.* 34.11; *Jub.* 39.2; *Cant. R.* 1.1 §1   [← *Sa.2.1.2*

(16) As a punishment for his hatred towards Joseph, Gad is afflicted with a disease of the liver.

T. Gad 5.9 (*Test. XII Patr.*)   [← *Vd.23.10.1*

(17) The right hand of Simon withers for seven days as a punishment for his envy and consequent evil treatment of Joseph (and also to prevent him from harming Judah with whom he is angry for allowing Joseph to escape alive).

see 2.15.b.5

T. Sim 2.12 (*Test. XII Patr.*); GL 2, 192; GL 5, 397 n.8[← *P.23.7.1*

(18) As a punishment for sleeping with his father's wife, Bilhah, Reuben is struck in the loins with a severe wound for seven months.

T. Reub. 1.7 (*Test. XII Patr.*)   [← *Sa.24.10.2*

(19) As a punishment for not having sympathy for a heifer going to slaughter, Judah the Patriarch has toothache for thirteen years (until he is cured by Elijah).

Gen. R. 33.3   [← *Ic.23.1.1*

(20) Miriam becomes a leper, white as snow, as a punishment for complaining about Moses in connection with the Cushite woman he has taken. (Aaron and Moses intercede with God on her behalf and after seven days she is healed.)

Num. 12.10; *Lev. R.* 17.3; *Num. R.* 7.5   [← *A.23.1.3; B.11.2.3*

(21) Aaron is afflicted with leprosy as a punishment for his slander against Moses.

GL 3, 259; GL 6, 91 n.494, 495   [← *A.23.1.8*

(22) God causes Moses to remain slow of speech (when he might have cured him) as a punishment for complaining about his impediment.

see 1.14.b.6; 2.4.7

GL 2, 326; GL 5, 422 n.140   [← *I.23.3.3*

(23) The hand of Moses turns leprous and white as snow when he places it in his bosom and withdraws it as a punishment for having suspected God's children of lack of faith.

> see 2.7.4; 2.5.2; 2.3.2
> *Num. R. 7.5*; GL 2, 321; GL 5, 421 n.132   [← *P.11.2.2; P.23.1.1*

(24) The first plague of Egypt—the water changing into blood—is a punishment upon the Egyptians for forcing the Israelites to draw water for them and hindering them from taking ritual baths. It is also a punishment for the pride of Pharaoh who has said 'My Nile river is mine own, and I have made it for myself'.

> see 2.5.8; 2.24.13
> *Exod. R. 9.10-11*; GL 2, 343-345, 348, 349; GL 5, 426-427 n.172, 173; GL 5, 428 n.176-178   [← *Ie.27.1.1; W.4.2.2; W.21.1.1*

(25) The Egyptians are mutilated and emasculated by frogs (who leap around croaking in their entrails) as a punishment for having said to the Israelites 'Go and catch fish for us'.

> see 2.5.3
> *Exod. R. 10.3, 6; Exod. R. 15.27*; GL 2, 342, 345, 350, 351; GL 5, 426 n.171; GL 5, 427-429 n.172, 179-182.
> [← *Sa.2.1.7; Sa.24.2.7*

(26) The flesh of the Egyptians is seared by hailstones as a punishment for having desired to destroy a nation 'whose sins shall be white'.

> see 1.17.2; 1.26.a.7; 2.5.4
> *Exod. R. 12.4*; GL 2, 342, 344, 346, 356, 357; GL 5, 426-427 n.171-173; GL 5, 431 n.194   [← *B.24.3.1*

(27) The Egyptians are infested with lice as a punishment for saying to the Israelites 'Go and clean our houses, our courtyards and our streets'. God says 'Let the lice made of the dust of the earth take vengeance upon the Egyptians for having desired to destroy the nation whose seed is like unto the dust of the earth'.

> see 2.5.5
> GL 2, 342-343, 346, 351, 352; GL 5, 426-429 n.171-173, 183-185   [← *B.24.4.2*

(28) Burning blains and leprosy break forth among the Egyptians because they have said to the Israelites 'Go and prepare a bath for us unto the delight of our flesh and our bones'. The burning blains (caused by the ashes from the furnace) are also a punishment for the Egyptians having desired to destroy a nation 'whose ancestor,

Abraham, walked into the fiery furnace for the glorification of the name of God'.

see 1.14.c.13; 2.5.7

Exod. R. **11.5-6; GL 2, 342, 344, 346, 354, 355; GL 5, 426-427 n.171-173; GL 5, 431 n.191-193** [← *B.23.1.1; B.23.2.4; B.24.3.2*

(29) Pharaoh is afflicted with leprosy and boils as a punishment for his cruelty towards the children of Israel. As a further punishment he is later thrown from his horse and his flesh is ripped from his body.

Exod. R. 1.34; GL 2, 296-297; GL 5, 412-413 n.101, 104
[← *A.23.1.6; B.23.2.3; B.24.1.1*

(30) The names of the plagues with which the Egyptians are punished become engraved upon their bodies.

Deut. R. **7.9** [← *B.13.2.2; A.13.2.3*

(31) The tongues of the spies who have tried to dissuade the Israelites from going to Canaan are stretched out to so great a length that they touch their navels (and worms crawl out of their tongues and pierce their navels).

GL 3, 283; GL 6, 98 n.552 [← *Ib.6.5.2; Ib.23.20.1; Qa.15.1.1*

(32) As a punishment for their victory over the Israelites (and their pride and contempt of God) the entrails of the Philistines are pulled out of them by mice when they go to ease nature.

GL 4, 62-63; GL 6, 223 n.34 [← *Vf.1.1.1*

(33) Balaam becomes blind of one eye as a punishment for wishing to curse the Israelites.

see 1.12.a.21

Num. R. **2.4** [← *G.23.4.12*

(34) Eli ages prematurely and his eyes grow dim as a punishment for not being strict enough with his sons, whose misdeeds recoil upon him.

see 1.31.4

GL 4, 61; GL 6, 221 n.27 [← *G.23.4.15; G.23.3.2*

(35) As a punishment for taking the circumcised members of slain Israelites and throwing them towards heaven exclaiming 'This is what thou hast chosen', Agag is castrated by Samuel.

Lam. R. **3.64 §9** [← *Sa.2.1.8; Sa.24.2.8*

(36) As a punishment for using seventy kings with their thumbs and big toes cut off to pick up the crumbs from under his table, the

thumbs and big toes of Adoni-zedek are cut off.
Judg. 1.6-7   [← *Pc.1.2.1; Ub.1.1.1*

(37) As a punishment for retaining the ark, the Philistines of Ashdod, Gath and Ekron are afflicted with tumours.
see 2.24.15
1 Sam. 5.6-12; 1 Sam. 6.4-11   [← *A.14.1.1*

(38) Goliath is stricken with leprosy because he reviles God, or, alternatively, because he lusts after David.
see 1.14.a.9
Lev. R. **17.3;** *Lev. R.* **21.2;** *Num. R.* **7.5; GL 3, 214; GL 6, 78**
n.413   [← *A.23.1.15*

(39) Doeg dies a leper or is eaten alive by worms as a punishment for the impious use he has made of the law. Alternatively he is punished for telling Saul that Ahimelech has made plans with David.
Ps-Philo 63.4; GL 4, 76; GL 6, 242 n.106
                              [← *A.23.1.22; A.23.20.3*

(40) David is punished with leprosy after his transgression with Bathsheba.
GL 4, 104; GL 6, 266 n.96   [← *A.23.1.16*

(41) Joab and his descendants are punished with leprosy and gonorrhoea by David after Joab has killed Abner, son of Ner.
2 Sam. 3.28-29; *Lev. R.* **16.1;** *Lev. R.* **17.3;** *Num. R.* **8.5**
                              [← *A.23.1.17; Sa.10.1.2*

(42) Leprosy falls upon Naaman as a punishment for his arrogance over his heroic deeds, before his conversion.
see 4.1.b.19
2 Kgs 5; GL 3, 214; GL 6, 78 n.413; GL 6, 346 n.15 [← *A.23.1.12*

(43) As a punishment for accepting money from Naaman, Gehazi is cursed with 'the disease of Naaman', that is, leprosy, and becomes white as snow.
see 1.11.b.1
2 Kgs 5.25-27; *Lev. R.* **16.1;** *Lev. R.* **17.3;** *Num. R.* **7.5**
                     [← *F.23.1.1; A.23.1.10; B.11.2.4*

(44) As a punishment for sacrificing to idols and trying to seize the man of God who condemns the altar, the hand of King Jeroboam withers and he cannot withdraw it.
see 2.3.10
1 Kgs 13.14   [← *P.23.6.3; P.23.7.2*

(45) Yahweh causes the bowels of Jehoram, king of Judah, to drop out with disease because Jehoram has murdered his brothers and 'better men than himself', and worshipped idols.
see 1.10.1; 1.26.a.13
2 Chron. **21.13-19** [← *Vf.1.1.2*

(46) As a punishment for Hezekiah having 'peeled off' the gold from the temple, his skin becomes diseased and peels off.
see 1.10.3
GL 4, 272; GL 6, 366 n.72 [← *B.2.2.1*

(47) Hezekiah is made sterile as a punishment for having shown the gentiles the secrets of David and Solomon and having defiled the bones of the place of his fathers.
Liv. Proph. **1.13** *(Isaiah)* [← *Sa.2.1.24; Sa.24.2.24*

(48) The eyes of Zedekiah are pierced with iron lances as a punishment for perjury.
see 1.12.a.13; 1.24.3
Gen. R. **22.12** [← *G.1.1.4; G.23.4.24; G.24.1.3*

(49) As a punishment for trusting in his own skill rather than in God, King Asa is afflicted with gout. (He who is distinguished by the strength residing in his feet is punished through his feet.)
see 1.7.a.6
GL 4, 184; GL 6, 309 n.22 [← *Ub.23.3.1*

(50) As a punishment for his excessive pride and his evil acts towards the Jews, Antiochus Epiphanes is seized with an incurable pain in his bowels, he is hurtled from his chariot and every bone in his body is racked by the fall, his eyes teem with worms and his flesh rots away, and the stench of his decay sickens the whole army.
see 2.4.15
2 Macc. **9.5-10** [← *A.10.10.2; B.23.6.1; G.23.20.1; Va.24.1.2*

(51) As a punishment for trying to enter the temple in Jerusalem, Theodotus Ptolemy IV Philopator, king of Egypt, is tossed to the ground with a stroke, has paralysed limbs and is unable to speak.
see 1.19.b.26; 2.15.b.13
3 Macc. **2.22** [← *A.23.6.6; I.23.2.6*

(52) As a punishment for deeming himself more than a man, Nebuchadnezzar is forced to live for forty days (or, alternatively, seven years) as a beast. His upper body is transformed into that of an

ox and his lower half into a lion's. His tongue is removed from him so that he loses the power of speech.
see 2.7.6; 2.22.b.3
Liv. Proph. (Daniel) **4.5; GL 4, 334; GL 6, 423-424 n.102,103**
[← *A.27.2.3; Cc.27.1.1; Cc.27.4.1; Ib.1.1.2*

(53) Nebuchadnezzar is half consumed by the fire of the furnace into which he orders Hananiah, Mishael and Azariah to be cast.
Cant. R. **7.9 §1; GL 6, 418 n.90**   [← *A.2.4.1*

(54) King Darius is blinded by an angel because he keeps Daniel in prison. His sight is restored when he releases Daniel and, on the advice of Daniel, washes his eyes.
GL 4, 347; GL 6, 434 n.9   [← *G.23.4.26*

(55) As a punishment for her evil ways, encouraging her son to worship idols, worms crawl from the body of Delilah, Micah's mother, while she is still alive.
Ps-Philo 44.9; Ps-Philo 47.12; GL 4, 53; GL 6, 213 n.136
[← *A.23.20.1*

(56) Shebnah, a high priest, is punished with leprosy for his evil deeds, having made illicit use of the sacrifices, the properties of the sanctuary, and having dealt in a slighting manner with the sacrifices.
Lev. R. **5.5;** *Lev. R.* **17.3; GL 6, 364-365 n.64**   [← *A.23.1.21*

(57) Chenephres is attacked by elephantiasis as a punishment for ordering the Jews to wear linen garments and forbidding them to wear woollen clothing so that they may be conspicuous and be punished by him.
Art Moses Fragment 3; GL 5, 412, 413 n.101   [← *A.23.30.1*

(58) As a punishment for his evil deeds Haman becomes a leper on the day that Mordecai is honoured.
GL 6, 477 n.174   .   [← *A.23.1.18*

(59) A ravager of Ezekiel's grave becomes blind and sick.
GL 4, 326; GL 6, 413 n.75   [← *G.23.4.25*

(60) Leprous scabs appear on the crowns of the heads of the daughters of Zion and their hair becomes infested with lice as a punishment for their pride and unchastity.
Lev. R. **16.1;** *Lev. R.* **17.3;** *Num. R.* **7.5**   [← *D.23.1.1; E.23.1.1*

(61) God punishes the coquettish maidens of Jerusalem by sending

diseases that disfigure them and make them repulsive.
see 1.10.6; 1.19.b.23
GL 4, 312-313; GL 6, 404 n.45 [← *A.22.1.7*

(**62**) The backbones of those who did not formerly bow down at the time of prayer are transformed into serpents when God transforms nature (which he does once every seven years).
GL 5, 58 n.190 [← *Va.26.1.2*

(**63**) As a punishment for his unlawful deeds, a man is transformed into a demon in the form of a gigantic dog.
T. Sol. **10.1-2** [← *A.27.2.5*

(**64**) The sinners in hell who have caused the Israelites to lose their money, exalted themselves above the community, put their neighbours to shame in public, delivered their fellow Israelites into the hands of the Gentiles, denied the Torah, and maintained that God is not the creator of the world, are punished by having to drink the venom from scorpions which makes their eyes melt in their sockets.
see 1.14.d.6
GL 2, 312; GL 5, 418-419 n.118 [← *G.13.10.1*

(**65**) The sinners in hell are punished for eating carrion and forbidden flesh, lending money at usury, writing the name of God on amulets for Gentiles, using false weights, stealing money from their fellow Israelites, eating on the Day of Atonement, and drinking blood, by having their teeth broken by the angels of destruction with fiery stones from morning until evening. The teeth regrow during the night and thus the punishment is perpetuated.
see 1.26.a.14; 1.19.b.25; 2.22.b.7
GL 2, 312; GL 5, 418-419 n.118 [← *Ic.24.1.1; Ic.25.1.1; Ic.6.5.3*

(**66**) The sinners in hell are punished by worms breeding in their flesh for the sins of murder, idolatry, incest, cursing parents and teachers and calling themselves god.
GL 2, 313; GL 5, 418-419 n.118 [← *B.23.20.2*

(**67**) The eyes of sinners are pricked out by the angels of hell.
Vis. Ezra **40** [← *G.1.5*

1.26.c. *Abnormality, deformity or disability as a result of self-punishment*
[No reference in sources]

1.27. *Abnormality, Deformity or Disability as a Result of Trickery or Deception*
[No reference in sources]

1.28. *Abnormality, Deformity or Disability as a Result of False Logic or Stupid Act*
[No reference in sources]

1.29. *Abnormality, Deformity or Disability as a Result of Ignorance or Forgetfulness*

(1) Ignorant of the wondrous mechanism of Solomon's throne, the Pharaoh Necho is injured by one of the lions on the throne when he attempts to mount it, and limps forever after.
see 1.23.3
Qoh. R. **9.2** §1; *Lev. R.* **20.1;** **GL 4, 160; GL 6, 297 n.71**
[← *T.23.1.5*

(2) Ignorant of the mechanism of Solomon's throne, Nebuchadnezzar is struck on the left foot by the right paw of the golden lion, breaks a leg and becomes lame.
see 1.23.4
GL 6, 415 n.80; GL 6, 453 n.13   [← *T.24.3.1; U.23.1.4*

1.30. *Abnormality, Deformity or Disability as a Result of Strange Adventure or Misadventure*

(1) Tobit is blinded when the hot droppings of sparrows fall into his eyes and cause white spots.
see 1.14.c.22
Tob. 2.10   [← *G.23.4.23; G.11.2.1*

1.31. *Abnormality, Deformity or Disability as a Result of Extreme Old Age*

(1) When Isaac grows old his eyes become so weak that he can no longer see.
see 1.7.a.4; 1.12.a.8; 1.14.a.2; 1.14.a.3; 1.14.a.4; 1.14.c.6; 1.19.b.6; 1.26.a.5; 1.26.b.12; 2.6.a.7; 2.7.3; 2.20.1; 4.1.b.10
Gen. 27.1; *T. Isaac* 4.8-9   [← *G.23.4.6*

(2) Israel's (Jacob's) eyes grow heavy with age so that he no longer sees clearly.
Gen. 48.10; *T. Jac.* **2.3;** *T. Jac.* **4.10**   [← *G.23.5.3*

(3) Jacob's extreme old age (combined with his constant weeping for his son, Joseph) causes his blindness.
see 1.12.a.9
T. Jac. **1.12; GL 2, 92; GL 5, 350 n.234**   [← *G.23.4.7*

(4) At the age of ninety-eight, the gaze of Eli becomes fixed and he goes blind.
see 1.26.b.34
1 Sam. 3.2, 15; 1 Sam. 2.27-36   [← *G.23.4.15; G.23.3.2*

(5) The eyes of Ahijah, the prophet, have dimmed with age.
1 Kgs 14.4   [← *G.23.4.18*

1.32. *Abnormality, Deformity or Disability as a Result of Presence in Body of Parasite or Alien Object*

(1) Satan enters and animates an image of clay and dust made by Enosh.
see 1.3.d.4
GL 1, 122-123; GL 5, 150-151 n.54   [← *A.16.6.1; A.16.13.1*

(2) When Solomon approaches a life-like statue it calls out in a loud voice warning all the satans inhabiting the other statues. The statues are overthrown, and the sons of Satan run into the sea and are drowned.
see 1.3.d.2; 2.10.a.1
GL 4, 165; GL 6, 298 n.97   [← *A.16.20.1*

(3) The husbands of the she-devils take possession of Caleb and Phinehas and transform their appearance so frightfully that the residents of Jericho are struck with fear.
see 2.24.14
GL 4, 5; GL 6, 171 n.11   [← *A.22.1.4*

(4) Balaam is unable to speak when he wants to curse Israel because an angel settles in his throat.
see 2.21.3
GL 3, 372; GL 6, 130 n.762   [← *I.23.3.6*

1.33. *Abnormality, Deformity or Disability after Reincarnation*
[No reference in sources]

1.34. *Abnormality, Deformity or Disability as a Result of State of Being*

(1) Souls on their way to Sheol have human faces but bodies like eagles.
see 3.6.b.4
3 En. 44.5-6   [← *F.21.7.2*

(2) The dead and ghosts walk with their heads downward and their feet in the air; spirits appear likewise in necromancy, except when they are summoned by a king.
Lev. R. 26.7; **GL 4, 70; GL 6, 236 n.75**   [← *A.8.1.1*

(3) The soul when it leaves the body has the appearance of a glorious light but the form of the body, and it flies.
Hist. Rech. 15.10   [← *A.16.16.1*

(4) After his death a man killed in the age of the giants assumes the shadowy form of a man with gleaming eyes, and lives as a spirit, only returning to earth at midnight in order to kill and possess men.
T. Sol. 17.1-4   [← *A.17.1.1*

(5) The dwellers of paradise walk on their heads.
see 1.16.b.4; 3.2.4
GL 5, 263 n.301   [← *A.8.1.2*

1.35. *Abnormality, Deformity or Disability as a Result of Transfiguration or as a Reward*

(1) Abel in heaven appears like a wondrous man, bright as the sun, sitting on a throne between the two gates that lead to destruction, from where he judges and sentences souls.
T. Abr. 12.5   [← *A.10.1.1*

(2) When Enoch is transformed into the angel Metatron his height and breadth become equal to the height and breadth of the world, thirty-six wings are attached to him on each side, he receives 365,000

eyes, each 'brilliant as the sun', and his body is transformed into celestial fire.

see 1.14.c.1

3 En. **9.2-5;** *3 En.* **15.1;** *3 En.* **42.2;** *3 En.* **48C.6;** *T. Abr.* **10.8** (Recension B); **GL 1, 138-140; GL 5, 162-165 n.61**
[← A.6.3.2; A.6.5.12; A.10.1.7; A.16.12.6; B.16.12.1; E.16.4.1; G.5.13.2; G.10.2.3; G.16.12.5; M.14.2.13; M.20.1.13;V.16.12.1; Va.16.12.1

(3) Isaiah sees Adam, Abel, Enoch, and all the righteous from the time of Adam, without robes of flesh and in 'robes of above', like angels in glory.

Asc. Isa. (Vis. Isa.) **9.7-9** [← *A.10.1.19*

(4) Abraham, after his death, appears with a face 'luminous as lightning' and magnificent garments studded with gems radiant as the sun, before the beadle of Hebron.

see 2.6.b.3

GL 1, 307; GL 5, 269 n.319 [← *F.10.1.8*

(5) After eating from a honeycomb the face of Aseneth (emaciated by fasting and penance) becomes like the sun, with eyes like the rising morning star, lips like the rose of life, teeth like fighting men lined up to fight, hair like a vine in paradise, a neck like a cypress, bones like cedars and an appearance of light.

see 1.14.d.2

Jos. Asen. **16.16;** *Jos. Asen.* **18.7;** *Jos. Asen.* **20.6** [← *F.10.1.10;* *G.10.2.8; Fa.11.3.2; Ia.11.3.1; G.11.3.1*

(6) Those who did not will the golden calf to be made are rewarded with shining faces.

see 2.6.b.5

Ps-Philo 12.7; GL 6, 55 n.281 [← *F.10.1.13*

(7) The faces of Moses and the Israelites are made radiant as a reward for their willingness to accept the Torah before they know its contents. Moses is given a lustrous countenance as a reward for writing down the law.

see 1.14.a.6; 1.14.a.7; 1.14.f.2; 1.14.c.12; 3.3.a.30; 3.3.a.38; 2.24.12

Deut. R. **3.12; GL 3, 93; GL 6, 37 n.204** [← *F.10.1.14; F.10.1.11*

(8) When she re-marries Amram, Jochebed, though old, regains her youth.

GL 2, 263; GL 5, 396 n.38 [← *A.26.3.1*

(9) The Rechabites, sons of Jonadab, are transported to the Isles of

the Blessed, where they assume a shining appearance.
Hist. Rech. 11.5b; *Hist. Rech.* 12.(2)3   [← *A.10.1.16*

(**10**) The son of the woman of Shunem is brought back to life by Elisha as a reward for her feeding of him.
see 1.14.c.20
2 Kgs 4.33-35; *Cant. R.* 2.5 §3   [← *A.25.3.5*

(**11**) The son of the widow of Zarephath is revived from the dead by Elijah as a reward for the widow's maintainance of Elijah.
see 1.19.b.19
1 Kgs 17.17-24; *Cant. R.* 2.5 §3   [← *A.25.3.10*

(**12**) After fighting the Antichrist, Elijah and Enoch shine.
Apoc. Elij. 4.19   [← *A.10.1.17; A.10.1.18*

(**13**) Istehar is transformed into a star in the constellation of the Pleiades as a reward for her chastity.
BHM 5.21 (Midrash Fragments) no.4 (Hebrew texts, 156); GL 1, 149; GL 5, 169-170 n.10   [← *A.27.6.1*

(**14**) The bodies of the righteous in Paradise emit a shining light.
see 3.6.a.12
GL 1, 20   [← *A.10.1.22*

(**15**) The learned and virtuous will shine as brightly as the vault of heaven and the stars at the time of the resurrection.
1 En. 104.2; *2 En.* 65.10 (J); *2 En.* 65.11 (A); *2 En.* 66.7 (J); Dan. 12.3, 10; Dan. 11.35; *2 Bar.* 51.5, 9f.; *4 Ezra* 7.(97); *Num. R.* 30.2   [← *A.10.1.21*

(**16**) The hair and flesh torn from a martyr change into trees.
GL 6, 405 n.47   [← *B.27.15.1; E.27.15.1*

2. ABNORMALITY, DEFORMITY OR DISABILITY AS A MEANS

2.1. *Abnormality, Deformity or Disability as a Test*

2.1.a. *Abnormality, deformity or disability as a test of character*

(1) Purouel, the archangel, is m. ᵕ ᴏ. fire in order to test sinners with the all-consuming fire which issues from his trumpet when he blows it. (The sinners are destroyed by it, while the righteous are untouched.)

    T. Abr. **12.9-10, 12-13**   [← *A.16.12.3*

(2) To test Job's piety when under stress and adversity, Satan smites him with leprosy; his nails and fingers drop off, boils appear on his body and worms and vermin cover him, while his skin turns black and rots, cracks and oozes pus.

    see 1.10.5

    Job 2.7; 7.5; 17.7; 18.13; 19.20; 30.17; 30.30; *T. Job* 20.6-9; 24.3; 26.1; 34.4; 31.2; GL 2, 233-236; GL 5, 285-287 n.17-29

        [← *A.23.1.20; A.23.20.2; B.24.1.4; B.23.20.1; B.11.1.3; B.15.1.2; Pc.2.1.1; Pd.1.1.1; Cc.23.3.1; Pc.2.1.1; Pd.1.1.1*

(3) To test his army's fortitude, Bar Koziba orders each recruit to cut off a finger (and he then has with him at Bethar 200,000 men with an amputated finger).

    see 2.4.13

    Lam. R. **2.2 §4**   [← *P.2.1.2; Pc.1.1.2*

2.1.b. *Abnormality, deformity or disability as a test of ability*

(1) To test King Solomon, the queen of Sheba brings circumcised and uncircumcised men before him and asks him whether he can distinguish between them. He opens the doors of the ark and the uncircumcised fall prostrate while the circumcised are filled with the radiance of the Shekinah.

see 1.14.a.10
GL 4, 146; GL 6, 290 n.43   [← *Sa.2.3.26; Sa.24.3.26*

2.1.c. *Abnormality, deformity or disability as a test of other things*
[No reference in sources]

2.2 Abnormality, Deformity or Disability for Informational Reasons

2.2.a. *Abnormality, deformity or disability to extract information*

(**1**) In order to distinguish between the women of marriageable age and those that are too young to marry, Moses has the Midianite women led past the gold plate of the mitre on the high priest's forehead. The faces of those of marriageable age grow very pale.
see 1.19.b.14
GL 3, 413; GL 6, 145 n.861   [← *F.11.2.1*

(**2**) The bodies of pregnant women become transparent as glass so that God can communicate with the children in their wombs and ask them whether they will be surety for the observance of the Torah.
GL 3, 90; GL 6, 35 n.196   [← *A.13.20.1*

2.2.b. *Abnormality, deformity or disability to prevent spread of information*

(**1**) The six-winged seraphim use two of their wings to hide their calves' feet to keep secret Israel's transgression of the golden calf.
see 2.8.1
Lev. R. 27.3; **GL 2, 309; GL 5, 416-418 n.117**
                    [← *M.14.2.12; M.20.1.12; U.18.3.2*

(**2**) The troops of Pharaoh are stricken deaf, dumb or blind when they are ordered to pursue Moses so that they cannot pass on any information about the latter's abiding-place.
see 2.19.b.3; 2.22.c.3
Exod. R. 1.31; *Deut. R.* 2.26-27; **GL 2, 282; GL 5, 406 n.76**
                    [← *I.23.3.5; J.23.1.4; G.23.4.9*

(**3**) To prevent documents with bad tidings for the Jews of Caesarea from reaching the authorities, a thigh-bone rolls between the feet of the government courier making him stumble and die.
Qoh. R. 5.8 5; *Num. R.* §18.22   [← *Va.3.1.6*

2.2.c. *Abnormality, deformity or disability to give information*

(1) In order to give wise men news of future events at the time of the coming of the Messiah, idols of wood, brass and stone begin to speak (and then fall flat on their faces).

see 1.3.d.5
Lad. Jac. **7.17**   [← *A.16.2.2; A.16.5.1; A.16.7.1*

(2) The blood of Abel cries out to God from the ground.
Gen. 4.10; *Gen. R.* **22.9**   [← *W.25.1.1*

(3) Yahweh puts a mark on Cain to prevent those who meet him from killing him.

see 2.6.b.2; 2.11.e.1; 2.15.b.4
Gen. 4.13-16   [← *A.13.2.1; B.13.2.1*

(4) After Cain murders his brother, God afflicts him with leprosy to mark him as a sinner.

see 3.6.b.6; 1.26.b.3
Gen. R. **22.12; GL 1, 112; GL 5, 141 n.28**   [← *A.23.1.1*

(5) The hand of Moses proclaims what has happened to it after it has turned leprous in the bosom of Moses.
GL 5, 421 n.132   [← *P.25.4.1*

(6) To deliver a message from Yahweh to King Ahab, a prophet has himself wounded and pretends that he has been wounded in battle. Brought before the king he prophesies to him under the guise of relating his own experiences.

see 2.9.9
1 Kgs 20.37   [← *A.24.10.3*

(7) To inform the six angels sent as scourges of the city of Jerusalem which citizens are to be saved, an angel places a cross on the foreheads of the pious or, in a variant, the letter 'taw' is written in ink on the foreheads of the pious and the same letter is written in blood on those of the damned.

see 2.6.b.10; 2.15.b.14; 2.15.a.10
Ezek. 9.4-6; *Apoc. Elij.* **1.9;** *Lam. R.* **2.1 §3;** *Pss. Sol.* **15.6; GL 1, 6; GL 6, 392 n.26**   [← *Fb.13.2.5*

(8) A deaf-mute conveys information to Mordecai, who understands the language of deaf-mutes, and is directed to a locality where grain is found.

see 4.1.b.26
GL 4, 383; GL 6, 459 n.63
                              [← *I.23.3.10; I.23.3.11; J.23.1.7; J.23.1.8*

(9) The heads of slain men are animated by the placing of small gold
or copper tablets under their tongues so that they can impart information.
see 1.11.a.8
GL 1, 371-372; GL 5, 301 n.218   [← *D.3.2.1*

(10) The blood of the true heir permeates the bone of his father's
corpse while the blood of the impostor shows no affinity with the
bone.
see 2.3.4; 2.6.b.9
GL 4, 131; GL 6, 284 n.27   [← *W.25.5.1*

(11) The bones (or the skull) of a slain Jew, made into a drinking
vessel, come to life and strike a blow in Nebuchadnezzar's face while
a voice announces 'A friend of this man is at this moment reviving the
dead'.
see 1.15.3
GL 4, 330; GL 6, 418 n.90   [← *Va.3.1.4; D.3.1.1*

(12) A voice from a thorn bush admonishes Ezra to guard in his
heart the secrets revealed to him.
GL 4, 357; GL 6, 445 n.50   [← *If.21.10.1*

2.3. *Abnormality, Deformity or Disability to Prove a Certain Thing*

(1) To prove her fecundity, Sarah suckles all the babies present at
Isaac's circumcision.
see 2.32.3
Gen. R. 53.5; Gen. R. 53.9   [← *Nd.5.1.1*

(2) The hand of Moses turns leprous and white as snow when he
places it in his bosom and withdraws it, to prove to the Israelites and
the king of Egypt that God has appeared to him.
see 1.26.b.23; 2.5.2; 2.7.4
Exod. 4.6; *Ezek. Trag. Exagoge* **129-131**   [← *P.11.2.2; P.23.1.1*

(3) To prove to the Egyptians that the child Moses had acted without
comprehension when he had taken the Pharaoh's crown and placed it
upon his own head, the angel Gabriel guides Moses' hand towards a

burning coal—on which he burns his mouth and hand—instead of towards an onyx stone.

see 1.14.c.10; 2.6.a.8; 2.9.6; 2.20.2

Exod. R. **1.26; GL 2, 274; GL 5, 402 n.65**   [← *I.23.3.3;*
Ia.13.2.1; Ib.13.2.1; Ib.24.4.1; P.13.2.1; P.24.4.1; Ia.24.4.1

(4) To prove the identity of the true heir, Solomon dips a bone of the father's corpse in the blood of the two disputants. Only the blood of the true heir permeates the bone.

see 2.2.c.10; 2.6.b.9

GL 4, 131; GL 6, 284 n.27   [← *W.25.5.1*

(5) To prove the resurrection of the dead, Ezekiel revives those who had not believed in it.

see 1.19.b.22; 1.17.4; 2.4.12; 1.14.c.23

GL 4, 332; GL 6, 421-422 n.94-95   [← *A.25.3.15*

(6) To prove the resurrection of the dead, Jeremiah rises again three days after his death.

4 Bar. **9.7-14**   [← *A.25.3.7*

(7) To prove that the mission of Jeremiah is true, an eagle touches a corpse and it comes to life.

see 1.14.c.18

4 Bar. **7.18; GL 4, 320**   [← *A.25.3.8*

(8) An angel prevents the separation of the lovers, Zimri and Cozbi, so that, held up together on Phinehas's lance, all may see their guilt.

see 1.19.b.11; 2.18.b.2

Num. R. **20.25; GL 3, 387; GL 6, 137 n.798**   [← *A.23.6.1*

(9) To prove their piety, Daniel and his friends, Hananiah, Mishael and Azariah, castrate themselves when they are accused by Nebuchadnezzar of leading an unchaste life.

Liv. Proph. (Daniel) **4.2**   [← *Sa.2.1.27; Sa.24.2.27*

(10) As a proof that a man condemning the altar in Bethel is from God, the hand of King Jeroboam, stretched out to seize the man, withers and cannot be withdrawn.

see 1.26.b.44

1 Kgs 13.14   [← *P.23.6.3; P.23.7.2*

2.4. Abnormality, Deformity or Disability to Show or Demonstrate a Certain Thing

(1) To show his power to Jacob when he meets him at the ford, the angel sticks his finger into the ground and the ground emits fire.
    see 3.8.1
    Gen. R. **77.2**   [← *Pc.10.3.2*

(2) To reveal the marvellous works of the Mighty One, the angel Ramael causes the bodies of the soldiers of Sennacherib to be burned within while their arms and clothes remain untouched on the outside.
    2 Bar. **63.8**   [← *V.1.1.1*

(3) To show Adam, while he is still a lifeless mass, all the righteous people who will descend from him, God hangs them on his head: some hang on his hair, others on his forehead, eyes, ears, earlobes and mouth.
    Exod. R. **40.3**   [← *A.4.1.1; D.14.10.1; E.14.10.1; Fb.14.10.1;*
                    G.14.10.1; H.14.10.1; I.14.10.1; J.14.10.1; Ja.14.10.1

(4) The letter 'teth' (the ninth letter of the Hebrew alphabet) is placed on Cain's arm as a sign that he will not die until he has nine descendants.
    GL 5, 141 n.27   [← *O.13.2.1*

(5) To show God's joy at the birth of Isaac, all the blind are made to see, all the lame are made whole and the dumb are made to speak.
    GL 1, 262; GL 5, 245 n.203   [← *G.23.4.5; T.23.1.4; I.23.3.1*

(6) To show his power, Yahweh afflicts the Egyptians with boils.
    see 2.5.6; 1.14.c.14
    Exod. 9.16; Exod. 10.1   [← *A.23.3.1*

(7) God makes Moses slow of speech to show a miracle through him; namely, to make him speak without hesitation whenever God wills it.
    see 1.14.b.6; 1.26.b.22
    Exod. R. **3.15; GL 2, 324-325; GL 5, 421-422 n.136, 140**
                                        [← *I.23.3.3*

(8) Shechem, his father, his five brothers and all the men in his city (645 men and 276 lads), are circumcised to show their willingness to please the sons of Jacob (and persuade them to allow the marriage between Jacob's daughter, Dinah, and Shechem).

see 2.5.1; 2.16.5
Gen. 34.15, 22-24; *T. Levi* **6.6** (*Test. XII Patr.*); **BR 80.8; Theod.
Fragments 4-6**   [← *Sa.2.3.18; Sa.24.3.18*

(9) To show God's power, a miracle happens: a small quantity of water poured over Elijah's hands makes water flow from his ten fingers until the whole trench (dug out for the erection of the altar) is filled.

see 2.5.10; 2.7.5
GL 4, 199; GL 6, 320 n.18   [← *Pc.10.7.2*

(10) To show that it is not possible to run away from God, he raises the dead Jonah to life through Elijah.

see 1.19.b.18
Liv. Proph. (Jonah) **10.6**   [← *A.25.3.9*

(11) Ishmael circumcises himself when he is thirteen years old to show his obedience to God and his father.

see 2.13.a.23; 3.11.26
Gen. R. **46.2;** *Gen. R.* **47.7f.;** *Gen. R.* **43.3f.;** *Gen. R.* **55.4; GL 1,
273, 311**   [← *Sa.2.3.8; Sa.24.3.8*

(12) To show Ezekiel how the House of Israel will be revived, Yahweh makes dry bones (representing the House of Israel) join together, grow sinews and flesh, and come to life, while Ezekiel prophesies.

see 1.19.b.22; 1.14.c.23; 1.17.4; 2.3.5
Ezek. 37.7; GL 4, 332; GL 6, 421-422 n.94-95
                              [← *Va.3.1.5; A.25.3.11; A.25.3.12*

(13) To show their fortitude, 200,000 men amputate a finger when Bar Koziba orders them to.

see 2.1.a.3
Lam. R. **2.2 §4**   [← *P.2.1.2; Pc.1.1.2*

(14) To show that the Jews are guilty of the prophet Zechariah's murder, God makes his blood seethe and bubble for 250 years.

Lam. R. **4.13 §6;** *Lam. R.* **23** (**Proems**); *Lam. R.* **2.2 §4;** *Qoh. R.*
3.16 §1; *Qoh. R.* **10.4 §1**   [← *W.3.1.1*

(15) As a demonstration of the power of God, the evil king Antiochus Epiphanes is seized with an incurable pain in his bowels and he is hurled from his chariot so that every bone in his body is racked, while his eyes teem with worms, his flesh rots away and the stench of

his decay sickens the whole army.
    see 1.26.b.50
    2 Macc. 9.5-10   [← *A.10.10.2; B.23.6.1; G.23.20.1; Va.24.1.2*

(16) The sons of Jews and previously uncircumcised Jews undergo circumcision to demonstrate their piety, for the sake of which they will deserve release from their bondage.
    see 2.32.6
    GL 2, 362; GL 5, 432 n.201   [← *Sa.2.3.20; Sa.24.3.20*

2.5. *Abnormality, Deformity or Disability to Persuade or Dissuade*

(1) The men of Shechem are circumcised to persuade Jacob's sons to allow a marriage between Shechem and their sister, Dinah.
    see 2.16.5; 2.4.8
    Gen. 34.15, 22-24; *T.Levi* **6.6** *(Test. XII Patr.)*; **Gen. R. 80.8;**
    Theod. Fragments 4-6   [← *Sa.2.3.18; Sa.24.3.18*

(2) The hand of Moses turns leprous and white as snow when he places it in his bosom and withdraws it, to prove to the Israelites and the king of Egypt that God has appeared before him, and to persuade the latter to release the Israelites from captivity.
    see 1.26.b.23; 2.3.2; 2.7.4
    Ezek. Trag. Exagoge **129-131**   [← *P.11.2.2; P.23.1.1*

(3) To persuade the Egyptians to release the Israelites from bondage, frogs are sent to emasculate them.
    see 1.26.b.25
    Exod. R. **10.3, 6;** *Exod. R.* **15.27**   [← *Sa.2.1.7; Sa.24.2.7*

(4) To persuade the Egyptians to release the Israelites from bondage, their flesh is seared by hailstones.
    see 1.17.2; 1.26.a.7; 1.26.b.26
    Exod. R. **12.4**   [← *B.24.3.1*

(5) To persuade the Egyptians to release the Israelites, their bodies become infested with lice.
    see 1.26.b.27
    GL 2, 342, 343, 346, 351, 352; GL 5, 426, 427, 429 n.171-173,
    183-185   [← *B.24.4.2*

(6) To persuade the Egyptians to release the Israelites, their bodies are covered in boils.

see 1.14.c.14; 2.4.6
Exod. **9.8-12;** *Ezek. Trag. Exagoge* **137;** *Exod. R.* **11.5-6**
[← *A.23.3.1*

(7) To persuade the Egyptians to release the Israelites, they are afflicted with leprosy of the skin and burning blains.

see 1.26.b.28; 1.14.c.13
Exod. R. **11.5-6;** GL **2,** 342, 344, 346, 354, 355; GL **5,** 426, 427, 431 n.171-173, 191-193   [← *B.23.1.1; B.23.2.4; B.24.3.2*

(8) The water of the Nile and all the waters in Egypt, including drinking water, turns to blood to persuade the Egyptians to release the Israelites from their bondage.

see 2.24.13; 1.26.b.24
Exod. R. **9.10-11**   [← *Ie.27.1.1; W.4.2.2; W.21.1.1*

(9) To dissuade the Israelites from marching against the inhabitants of Canaan, those who have gone on a reconnaissance mission into Canaan with Caleb tell of the men of enormous size they have seen there.
Num. 13.32   [← *A.6.1.25*

(10) To persuade the people to give up their worship of idols, a miracle happens: a small quantity of water poured over Elijah's hands makes water flow from his ten fingers until the whole trench (dug out for the erection of the altar) is filled.

see 2.4.9; 2.7.5
GL **4,** 199; GL **6,** 320 n.18   [← *Pc.10.7.2*

(11) To persuade him to give a false prophesy, Zedekiah smites Micah's cheek with a rod, tearing out the hair.
Lev. R. **10.2;** Mic. **4.6**   [← *Fa.24.10.1; Fa.2.1.1*

(12) To persuade seven brothers and their mother to taste pig's flesh, King Antiochus Epiphanes has them tortured each in turn, cutting off their extremities, cutting out their tongues, piercing their eyes and scalping their heads, before they are fried alive.

see 1.24.4; 2.25.a.2
2 Macc. **7;** *4 Macc.* **6.6, 25;** *4 Macc.* **7.13-14;** *4 Macc.* **9.28;** *4 Macc.* **10.5-8, 17-21;** *4 Macc.* **11.18-19, 21**   [← *D.2.2.1;
Ga.24.1.1; Ib.1.1.3; P.1.1.2; U.1.1.1*

(13) The feet, hands, eyes, mouth and tongue of a physician quarrel when each tries to persuade the others that it has been the most

instrumental in effecting the cure for a Persian king.
GL 4, 174; GL 6, 302 n.97   [← *G.3.1.1; I.3.1.1; Ib.3.1.1;*
                                              P.3.1.1; U.3.1.1

2.6. *Abnormality, Deformity or Disability to Conceal or Reveal Identity*

2.6.a. *Abnormality, deformity or disability to conceal identity*

(1) The angel of death appears at a wedding banquet in the form of a ragged and dirty beggar with hair like nails.
GL 4, 227-229; GL 6, 335-336 n.96, 97   [← *A.22.1.2; E.13.1.1*

(2) Sammael (or Satanael) wears the skin of a serpent to conceal his identity when he deceives man.
see 2.9.1
3 Bar. **9.7 (Slavonic and Greek)**   [← *B.18.2.1*

(3) Satan assumes the brightness of angels and pretends to be one, telling Eve that her repentance—standing for thirty-nine days in the River Tigris—has been accepted after nineteen days, and luring her out of the water.
see 2.9.2
LAE (Vita) **6.1-2; 7; 9.1-5; 10.1;** *LAE (Apoc. Mos.)* **16** [← *A.10.1.8*

(4) To hide his true identity from Abraham and Isaac, Michael (disguised as commander-in-chief) becomes invisible when he goes to consult with God concerning the death of Abraham.
T. Abr. **8.1**   [← *A.1.1.2*

(5) The angel who appears to Sarah with a message from God is invisible to Pharaoh.
see 2.22.b.4
GL 1, 223; GL 5, 221 n.73   [← *A.1.1.3*

(6) To conceal the identity of Rabbi Meir, who is being pursued by Roman bailiffs, Elijah appears in the guise of a harlot and accompanies him. The Roman emissaries are unable to believe the rabbi would choose such a companion and desist from their pursuit.
see 2.9.3; 2.18.a.2
GL 4, 204; GL 6, 326 n.51   [← *A.9.2.1*

(7) Isaac's eyes are dimmed so that he will not go to the market-place and be identified as the father of wicked children.

see 1.7.a.4; 1.12.a.8; 1.14.a.2; 1.14.a.3; 1.14.a.4; 1.14.c.6; 1.19.b.6; 1.26.a.5; 1.26.b.12; 1.31.1; 2.7.3; 2.20.1; 4.1.b.10

Gen. R. 65.10 [← *G.23.4.6*

(8) To show the Egyptians that Moses is not the child prodigy who is about to snatch the government from Pharaoh's hands, the angel Gabriel makes Moses choose a burning coal in preference to an onyx stone.

see 1.14.c.10; 2.3.3; 2.9.6; 2.20.2

Exod. R. 1.26; **GL 2, 274; GL 5, 402 n.65** [← *I.23.3.3; Ia.13.2.1; Ia.24.4.1; Ib.24.4.1; P.13.2.1; P.24.4.1; Ib.13.2.1*

(9) Caleb and Phinehas pretend to be deaf and dumb so as not to arouse suspicions concerning their identities when they are spying in Jericho.

see 2.9.7

GL 6, 171 n.11 [← *I.23.3.7; J.23.1.6*

2.6.b. *Abnormality, deformity or disability to reveal identity*

(1) A heavenly being has the name 'Israel' engraved on his forehead.

GL 5, 307 n.253 [← *Fb.13.2.1*

(2) Yahweh puts a mark on Cain to prevent those who meet him from killing him.

see 2.2.c.3; 2.11.e.1; 2.15.b.4

Gen. 4.13-16 [← *A.13.2.1; B.13.2.1*

(3) Abraham appears after his death to some Jews of Hebron, dressed in shabby clothes. He is welcomed as the tenth man necessary for the divine service. Later he appears with a face 'luminous as lightning' and magnificent garments studded with gems and reveals that he is Abraham, their ancestor.

see 1.35.4

GL 1, 307; GL 5, 269 n.319 [← *F.10.1.8*

(4) The bones of Joseph exude fragrance, allowing Moses' mother to identify them.

GL 3, 5; GL 6, 1 n.2 [← *Va.10.10.1*

(5) In order to identify the sinners who had willed the golden calf to be made, Moses places the broken calf in water and makes the Israelites drink it. The tongues of the sinners drop out while the faces of those who had not willed the calf to be made (but who had been forced to consent) shine.

see 1.26.a.10; 1.35.6

Ps-Philo 12.7 [← *Ib.1.1.1; Ib.24.1.1; F.10.1.13*

(6) To identify the sinners, Joshua makes the people pass before the ark and the sinners remain rooted to the spot, unable to move.
GL 6, 176 n.28   [← A.23.6.2

(7) Milk flows from the breasts of his mother when, unwittingly, Joshua is about to marry her, having killed his father.
see 2.10.a.3
GL 4, 3; GL 6, 169 n.2   [← Nd.26.4.1

(8) To identify the idolaters, Samuel gives the Israelites water to drink, after which the idolaters are unable to open their lips.
see 1.14.d.4
GL 4, 64; GL 6, 225-226 n.40   [← Ia.23.3.2

(9) To reveal the identity of the true heir, Solomon dips a bone from the father's corpse in the blood of the two disputants. Only the blood of the true heir permeates the bone.
see 2.2.c.10; 2.3.4
GL 4, 131; GL 6, 284 n.27   [← W.25.5.1

(10) A cross is placed on the foreheads of the pious in Jerusalem so that they can be identified by the six angels sent as scourges of the city and not be killed. In a variant, those to be killed are marked with the letter 'taw' written in blood and those to be saved with a 'taw' written in ink.
see 2.2.c.7; 2.15.b.14; 2.15.a.10
Ezek. 9.4-6; *Apoc. Elij.* 1.9; *Lam. R.* 2.1 §3; *Pss. Sol.* 15.6; GL 1, 6; GL 6, 392 n.26   [← Fb.13.2.5

(11) To identify those enrolled in a census, Ptolemy declares that they should be branded with an ivy leaf, the emblem of Dionysus.
see 2.13.a.22
3 *Macc.* 2.29   [← B.13.2.4; A.13.2.4

2.7. *Abnormality, Deformity or Disability for Didactic Reasons*

(1) Yahweh appears as a voice from a fire to teach the Israelites that just as he appears without shape, so they should refrain from carving images of idols.
Deut. 4.12, 15, 33, 36   [← If.21.2.1

(2) To teach Tanna Eliezer a lesson in humility, Elijah takes the form of a hideously ugly man and, when told by Eliezer how ugly he is,

Elijah refers him to the master artificer who has fashioned him.

GL 4, 216; GL 6, 331 n.72, 73   [← *A.22.1.1*

(3) Isaac's blindness is the first disease to afflict mankind after Isaac himself has prayed to God to afflict mankind with bodily ailments as an atonement for its sins.

see 1.7.a.4; 1.12.a.8; 1.14.a.2; 1.14.a.3; 1.14.a.4; 1.14.c.6; 1.19.b.6; 1.26.a.5; 1.26.b.12; 1.31.1; 2.6.a.7; 2.20.1; 4.1.b.10

Gen. R. 65.9; GL 5, 281-282 n.74   [← *G.23.4.6*

(4) The hand of Moses turns leprous and white as snow when he places it in his bosom and withdraws it to teach him that just as a leper defiles, so the Egyptians defiled Israel, and just as Moses was healed of his uncleanness, so God would cleanse the children of Israel of the pollution the Egyptians had brought upon them.

see 1.26.b.23; 2.3.2; 2.5.2

GL 2, 321; GL 5, 421 n.132   [← *P.11.2.2; P.23.1.1*

(5) To teach the Israelites wisdom, miracles are displayed before their eyes, including the sprouting of ten springs of water from Elijah's fingers after a little water is poured over them by Elisha.

see 2.4.9; 2.5.10

GL 4, 197-199; GL 6, 320 n.18   [← *Pc.10.7.2*

(6) To teach Nebuchadnezzar that God rules over mankind and that no man equals God, Nebuchadnezzar is forced to live as a beast. His body is transformed, the upper part of his body into that of an ox, the lower part into the body of a lion.

see 1.26.b.52

Liv. Proph. (Daniel) 4.5; GL 4, 334; GL 6, 423-424 n.102, 103
                    [← *A.27.2.3; Cc.27.1.1; Cc.27.4.1*

(7) So that the Torah can be given to the living not the dead, God restores to life those Israelites whose souls had fled from them at the sound of his voice.

see 1.14.b.7

GL 3, 95, 97; GL 6, 39-40 n.215   [← *A.25.3.16*

2.8. *Abnormality, Deformity or Disability as an Aid to Memory or Oblivion*

(1) The seraphim use two of their wings to cover their calves' feet so that the Shekinah is not reminded of the sin of worshipping the golden calf.

see 2.2.1
Lev. R. **27.3;** *Hell. Syn. Pr.* **82;** GL **6,** 359,n.36
[← *M.14.2.12; M.20.1.12; U.18.3.2*

(2) To remind God of David's good deeds (and to plead for help in getting the ark into the sanctuary), Solomon brings David's coffin to the sanctuary, and David revives from the dead.
Exod. R. **8.1**   [← *A.25.3.4*

2.9. *Abnormality, Deformity or Disability to Deceive*

(1) To deceive man, Sammael (or Satanael) wears the skin of a serpent.
see 2.6.a.2
3 Bar. **9.7**   [← *B.18.2.1*

(2) Satan pretends to be an angel by assuming an angel's brightness and tells Eve that her penance—standing for thirty-nine days in the River Tigris—has been accepted after eighteen days, and lures her out of the water.
see 2.6.a.3
LAE (Vita) 6.1-2; 7; 9.1-5; 10.1; *LAE (Apoc. Mos.)* 16   [← *A.10.1.8*

(3) To deceive the Roman bailiffs who are chasing Rabbi Meir, Elijah appears in the guise of a harlot and walks beside him. The Roman emissaries cannot believe Rabbi Meir would choose such a companion and desist from their pursuit.
see 2.6.a.6; 2.18.a.2
GL **4,** 204; GL **6,** 326 n.51   [← *A.9.2.1*

(4) To deceive those stoning Jeremiah, a stone assumes his form and is stoned in his place. When, however, Jeremiah is ready to die, the stone cries out, saying 'Oh stupid children of Israel, why do you stone me thinking that I am Jeremiah? Behold, Jeremiah stands in your midst.'
see 2.18.a.1
4 Bar. **9.27-30**   [← *A.17.2.1*

(5) To deceive people into thinking that the idol has power, Nebuchadnezzar places the golden diadem of the high priest in its mouth, and the power of the holy name, which is inscribed upon the diadem, makes the idol say 'I am thy God'.
see 1.3.d.3; 1.11.a.1
GL **4,** 338; GL **6,** 427 n.111   [← *A.16.20.2*

(6) The Egyptians are deceived into thinking that Moses acted without comprehension when he removed the Pharaoh's crown and placed it upon his own head, by the angel Gabriel, who makes the child Moses reach for a burning coal—on which he burns his lips and mouth—in preference to an onyx stone.

see 1.14.c.10; 2.3.3; 2.6.a.8; 2.20.2

Exod. R. **1.26; GL 2, 274; GL 5, 402 n.65** [← *I.23.3.3; Ia.13.2.1; Ia.24.4.1; Ib.13.2.1; Ib.24.4.1; P.13.2.1; P.24.4.1*

(7) To mislead the inhabitants about their intentions, Caleb and Phinehas pretend to be deaf and dumb while they are spying in Jericho.

see 2.6.a.9

GL 6, 171 n.11   [← *I.23.3.7; J.23.1.6*

(8) To deceive the Aramaean warriors who have been sent to capture him in Dotham, Elisha prays to Yahweh to blind them, and then tells the Aramaeans that they are on the wrong road, leading them to their enemies.

see 1.19.b.20; 2.18.a.9; 2.18.c.1

2 Kgs 6.18-20   [← *G.23.4.22*

(9) A prophet is struck and wounded by a man at his own request and pretends to King Ahab that he has been wounded in battle.

see 2.2.c.6

1 Kgs 20.37   [← *A.24.10.3*

2.10. *Abnormality, Deformity or Disability to Warn or Prevent Warning*

2.10.a. *Abnormality, deformity or disability to warn*

(1) When Solomon approaches a life-like statue it calls out in a loud voice 'Hither ye satans, Solomon has come to undo you'.

see 1.3.d.2; 1.32.2

GL 4, 165; GL 6, 298 n.79   [← *A.16.20.1*

(2) The apertures of the bodies of the Philistines close up when King Abimelech takes Sarah as a wife, and he has a dream to warn him to return her to Abraham.

GL 1, 258; GL 5, 243 n.190; GL 5, 244 n.202   [← *Ga.23.2.1; Ha.23.1.1; I.23.4.1; J.23.2.1; Ra.23.1.1; Sa.23.2.1; Sb.23.2.1*

(3) Milk flows from the breasts of Joshua's mother as a warning to Joshua, who is unwittingly about to marry her.

  see 2.6.b.7

  GL 4, 3; GL 6, 169 n.2   [← *Nd.26.4.1*

(4) As a warning to the assembled nations of the consequences of their ungodliness, Ezra sees in a vision the Messiah with flames and fire streaming from his mouth: the flames symbolize their torture and destruction for the disobedience of the law.

  see 2.15.a.14

  4 Ezra **13.4, 10-11, 37-39**   [← *I.10.1.6; Ia.10.1.2; Ib.10.1.1*

2.10.b. *Abnormality, deformity or disability to prevent warning*

(1) Yahweh strikes Ezekiel dumb (literally, Ezekiel's tongue sticks to the roof of his mouth) so that he will only speak as the mouthpiece of Yahweh.

  see 1.19.b.21

  Ezek. 3.26-27; Ezek. 24.27; Ezek. 33.22   [← *I.23.3.8; Ib.23.2.1*

2.11. *Abnormality, Deformity or Disability for Magical Reasons*

2.11.a. *Abnormality, deformity or disability for acquisition of magical powers*

                    [No reference in sources]

2.11.b. *Abnormality, deformity or disability for acquisition of secret knowledge*

(1) To try and foretell the outcome of a future war between the African army and the Egyptians, Balaam moulds wax figures of men, representing the armies, and animates them by plunging them in magic water and allowing them to swim, to see which are the stronger.

  see 1.3.d.1; 1.14.c.2

  GL 2, 159; GL 5, 372 n.425   [← *A.16.14.1*

2.11.c. *Abnormality, deformity or disability as a demonstration of magical powers*

(1) The kings of Midian practise witchcraft together with Balaam and fly, but fall down on top of the slain Midianites when they see the

plate engraved with the holy name.
   Num. R. **20.20;** *Num. R.* **22.5**   [← *A.25.15.4*

2.11.d. Abnormality, deformity or disability for sympathetic or contagious magic
                    [No reference in sources]

2.11.e. Abnormality, deformity or disability for magical protection or as a prophylactic device

(1) Yahweh puts a mark on Cain to prevent those who meet him from killing him.
   see 2.2.c.3; 2.6.b.2; 2.15.b.4
   Gen. 4.13-16   [← *A.13.2.1; B.13.2.1*

(2) A letter of God's holy name is placed upon Cain's forehead to protect him from the attack of wild beasts.
   see 1.19.b.2
   GL 1, 111-112; GL 5, 141 n.27, 28   [← *Fb.13.2.4*

(3) The ineffable name engraved upon the Israelites when they leave Egypt means that no evil thing can touch them, neither the angel of death nor anything else.
   Num. R. **14.24**   [← *B.13.2.3; A.13.2.2*

(4) Six verses of a psalm are inscribed on Jacob's foot, the first verse running 'The Lord answers thee in the day of trouble, the name of the God of Jacob is thy defence'.
   GL 4, 101; GL 6, 258-259 n.77   [← *U.13.1.1*

2.12. *Abnormality, Deformity or Disability to Effect Disenchantment*
[No reference in sources]

2.13. *Abnormality, Deformity or Disability as Consecration to, or Denigration of, God*

2.13.a. Abnormality, deformity or disability as consecration to, or praise of, God

(1) The seraphim use two of their wings to praise God. In another version, they use their six wings for praising God on the six weekdays (while on the Sabbath Israel praises God).
   Lev. R. **27.3;** *Ques. Ezra* (Recension A) **29;** *BHM* **5.21** (Midrash Fragments) No.21 (Hebrew text, 162); **GL 6, 359 n.36**
                    [← *M.14.2.12; M.20.1.12*

(2) The giant Og, also known as Eliezer, Abraham's servant, is circumcised by Abraham.

see 3.11.2

GL 6, 119 n.691   [← *Sa.2.3.2; Sa.24.3.2*

(3) Esau is circumcised but removes this sign of the covenant by means of an operation.

see 3.11.17

GL 5, 273 n.25   [← *Sa.2.3.4; Sa.24.3.4*

(4) Abraham circumcises himself at God's command.

see 3.11(13; 2.14.a.4; 2.31.b.1

Gen. R. 42.7; *Gen. R.* 46.1f; *Gen. R.* 47.7f.; *Gen. R.* 48.2f.;
GL 1, 239,340; GL 5, 233 n.123-126   [← *Sa.2.3.9; Sa.24.3.9*

(5) All the males of Abraham's household are circumcised as a sign of the covenant between God and Abraham.

see 3.11.14

Gen. 17.23-27; *Gen. R.* 42.8f.; *Gen. R.* 43.3f.
                                          [← *Sa.2.3.7; Sa.24.3.7*

(6) The children of the people whom Abraham recaptures (when he goes to recapture Lot) are circumcised.

see 3.11.15

Gen. R. 43.4   [← *Sa.2.3.10; Sa.24.3.10*

(7) Isaac is circumcised when he is eight days old.

see 3.11.16

Gen. 21.4; *Gen. R.* 46.5f.; *Gen. R.* 55.4 [← *Sa.2.3.11; Sa.24.3.11*

(8) Ephraim and Manasseh, the sons of Joseph, are circumcised.

see 3.11.18

GL 2, 136; GL 5, 365 n.366   [← *Sa.2.3.16; Sa.24.3.16*

(9) The sons of Machir, grandson of Joseph, are circumcised.

see 3.11.19

GL 2, 169; GL 5, 373 n.429   [← *Sa.2.3.17; Sa.24.3.17*

(10) Moses is circumcised.

see 3.11.21

Exod. R. 1.24; GL 2, 267; GL 5, 399 n.51
                                          [← *Sa.2.3.19; Sa.24.3.19*

(11) Moses shaves off the hair of the head and body of Korah (and others).

GL 3, 288; GL 6, 100 n.564   [← *E.1.8*

(12) Zipporah takes a flint and cuts off her son's foreskin when Yahweh comes to kill Moses. Then she touches Moses's genitals with

it, saying that he is now truly a bridegroom of blood to her.
see 2.15.b.10; 2.18.a.4; 3.11.20
Exod. 4.24-26   [← *Sa.2.3.20; Sa.24.3.20*

(13) At Gilgal, on the west side of the River Jordan, Joshua performs the rite of circumcision on those born in the desert who have remained uncircumcised on account of the rough climate and for other reasons.
see 1.16.b.6; 2.31.b.3; 3.11.22
Josh. 5.2-10; GL 4, 7; GL 6, 172 n.16   [← *Sa.2.3.22; Sa.24.3.22*

(14) Samson is God's Nazirite and hence no razor is to touch his head.
Judg. 13.5-7   [← *E.6.5.4*

(15) Absalom allows his hair to grow long because (like Samson) he is a Nazirite, dedicated to God, and so no razor must touch his head.
see 3.4.a.9
Num. R. 9.24; Num. R. 10.5; Num. R. 10.17 [← *E.6.5.5; E.5.1.1*

(16) The name of Dagon, Goliath's God, is engraved upon his heart or breast.
Cant. R. 4.4 §5   [← *Na.13.2.1*

(17) During their hobbling dance to Baal, the Israelites gash their bodies with swords and spears until the blood flows.
1 Kgs 18.28   [← *B.24.1.3*

(18) Achior, the Ammonite, is circumcised after he recognizes the mighty works of the God of Israel (after the killing of Holofernes).
see 3.11.23
Jdt. 14.10   [← *Sa.2.3.23; Sa.24.3.23*

(19) Mattathias, a priest of the line of Joarib, forcibly circumcises all the uncircumcised boys in the territories of Israel.
see 3.11.24
1 Macc. 2.46   [← *Sa.2.3.29; Sa.24.3.29*

(20) The babies of two women are circumcised even though this is prohibited by Antiochus Epiphanes and results in the death of the women and their children.
see 3.11.25
2 Macc. 6.10   [← *Sa.2.3.32; Sa.24.3.32*

(21) The body of Jehoiakim is tattooed or etched with the names of idols.

Lev. R. **19.6; GL 4, 284; GL 6, 379 n.125**   [← *A.13.1.2; B.13.1.2*

(22) Ptolemy declares that the Jews should be enrolled in a census and that those enrolled should be branded with an ivy leaf, the emblem of Dionysus.

see 2.6.b.11
3 Macc. **2.29**   [← *B.13.2.4; A.13.2.4*

(23) Ishmael is circumcised at the age of thirteen.

see 2.4.11; 3.11.26
Gen. **17.25-26;** *Gen. R.* **43.f.;** *Gen. R.* **46.2;** *Gen. R.* **47.7f.;** *Gen. R.* **55.4**   [← *Sa.2.3.8; Sa.24.3.8*

2.13.b. *Abnormality, deformity or disability as denigration of God*

(1) The penis of Jehoiakim is tattooed with the name of God.
Lev. R. **19.6**   [← *Sa.13.1.1*

2.14. *Abnormality, Deformity or Disability to Create, Procreate or Prevent Such*

2.14.a. *Abnormality, deformity or disability to create or procreate*

(1) In order to create, God takes lightning from the flash in his eye.

see 2.15.a.1
2 En. **29.1 (J)**   [← *G.10.5.1*

(2) Nine hundred and fifty-five heavens are created from the rays issuing from the hand of the omnipresent one.

see 2.15.a.2
3 En. **5.3;** *3 En.* **48A.1; Hab. 3.3-4**   [← *P.10.1.1*

(3) A muse gives birth after becoming androgynous (and thereby satisfying her desire for herself).

see 2.23.a.1
Apoc. Adam   [← *A.9.1.1*

(4) Abraham must be circumcised before he can beget the son who is appointed to be the father of Israel.

see 2.13.a.4; 2.31.b.1; 3.11.13
Gen. R. **46.2**   [← *Sa.2.3.9; Sa.24.3.9*

2.14.b. *Abnormality, deformity or disability to prevent creation or procreation*

(1) One of the two wives of the men of the generation of the deluge is sterilized.

see 2.23.a.2
GL 1, 117   [← *Vg.23.1.1*

(2) Noah is castrated by his son Ham (or by his grandson Canaan) so that he will not beget a fourth son.

Gen. R. 36.3, 7; *Lev. R.* 17.5; GL 1, 168; GL 5, 191-192 n.60, 61
[← *Sa.2.1.1*; *Sa.24.2.1*

(3) To prevent the impregnation of Potiphar's wife, the semen of Joseph is diffused and emerges from his fingernails when she tries to seduce him.

Gen. R. 87.7; *Gen. R.* 98.20   [← *Pd.10.16.1*; *Sd.4.1.1*

2.15. *Abnormality, Deformity or Disability to Kill, Destroy or Prevent Such*

2.15.a. *Abnormality, deformity or disability to kill or destroy*

(1) The fiery eye of God will flash like lightning and men will be slowly destroyed by fire and their flesh perish forever.

see 2.14.a.1
Sib. Or. 6.28; 7.124-128   [← *G.10.5.1*

(2) The destruction of the temple is caused by rays which shine from the right hand of God (which, in consequence, is banished behind him).

see 2.14.a.2
3 En. 5.3; 48A.1; *Hab.* 3.3-4   [← *P.10.1.1*

(3) The ranks of the angels are split into 496,000 parts and consumed by a devouring fire that issues from the little finger of God when the angels fail to recite the 'Holy'.

see 1.26.b.1
3 En. 40.3; *3 En.* 47.1-3; *3 En.* 35.6   [← *Pc.10.3.1*

(4) All those who look at 'Opanni'el, prince of the Ophanim, are consumed by the lightning and blazing torches that flash from his eyes.

see 3.3.a.4; 3.12.2
3 En. 25.2-4   [← *G.10.1.1*; *G.10.5.2*

(5) The Assyrians are killed by the terrific noise made by the Angel Gabriel when he claps his wings together.
GL 4, 269; GL 6, 363 n.58   [← *M.14.2.7; M.20.1.7*

(6) Hadarniel, an angel of destruction who guards the gates of heaven, breathes fiery lightning flashes.
see 2.22.a.7; 3.3.a.3
GL 3, 110; GL 6, 46 n.247   [← *I.10.5.3*

(7) To destroy the world, the angel of the Face emits scorching fires and thick clouds from his eyes.
see 2.22.b.1
GL 1, 14; GL 5, 17-18 n.50   [← *G.10.3.1; G.10.1.3*

(8) Some of the angels of destruction are fashioned out of hail, others out of flames.
see 2.22.a.11
GL 2, 366; GL 5, 433-434 n.213   [← *A.16.11.2; A.16.12.9*

(9) The demon Keteb or Keteb Meriri ('Pestilence' or 'Bitter Destruction') has a single eye set on his heart that kills all who look upon it. His entire body is covered with eyes and scales and hairs, and he has the head of a calf with a single horn on his forehead.
see 3.1.22
Num. R. 12.3; *Lam. R.* 1.3 §29; GL 3, 186; GL 6, 74 n.381
                                             [← *G.4.5.1*

(10) So that the six angels sent as scourges of the city of Jerusalem may recognize and destroy the wicked, a letter 'taw', written in blood, is placed on their foreheads.
see 2.2.c.7; 2.6.b.10; 2.15.b.14
Lam. R. 2.1 §3; GL 1, 6; GL 6, 392 n.26   [← *Fb.13.2.5*

(11) Nebuchadnezzar daily cuts off a piece of flesh from the body of Hiram and forces him to eat it, until he dies.
see 1.24.2
GL 4, 336; GL 6, 324-425 n.105   [← *B.2.3.1*

(12) Hananiah, Mishael and Azariah are killed by the evil eye of the people after they emerge unharmed from the furnace.
see 1.12.a.23
Gen. R. 61.11; GL 6, 419 n.92   [← *G.25.1.2*

(13) To kill Shebnah, a hole is bored through his heels and he is tied with a rope through the hole to the tail of a horse.
see 2.22.b.6
GL 4, 270; GL 6, 365 n.65 [← *Ua.15.1.1*

(14) A multitude is burned by the flames streaming from the mouth, lips and tongue of the Messiah, so that only ashes and smoke remain. All who hear his voice melt like wax.
see 2.10.a.4
4 Ezra 13.4, 10-11, 37-39 [← *I.10.1.6; Ia.10.1.1; Ib.10.1.1*

2.15.b. *Abnormality, deformity or disability to prevent killing or destruction*

(1) Since no man can see God face to face and live, God speaks to Moses from a burning bush, but remains himself invisible. (The burning is a manifestation of the angel who heralds him.)
GL 1, 305; GL 5, 416 n.115, 117 [← *A.1.1.1*

(2) The pinions of the winged angel, Ben Nez, keep back the south wind, which brings fire, smoke, blasts and hurricanes, and thus prevent the consumation of the world.
see 2.22.a.2
GL 1, 12; GL 5, 14 n.36 [← *M.14.2.2; M.20.1.2*

(3) To prevent the Jews from being trampled to death by elephants, two angels clothed in glory and of awe-inspiring appearance terrify the enemy.
see 2.24.4
3 Macc. **6.18** [← *A.10.1.4*

(4) Yahweh puts a mark on Cain to prevent those who meet him from killing him.
see 2.2.c.3; 2.6.b.2; 2.11.e.1
Gen. 4.13-16 [← *A.13.2.1; B.13.2.1*

(5) Simon's right hand withers for seven days and this prevents him from harming Judah, with whom he is angry for allowing Joseph to escape alive.
see 1.26.b.17
T. Sim. **2.12** (*Test. XII Patr.*) [← *P.23.7.1*

(6) The hands of the Ishmaelites grow rigid when they raise them to inflict a blow upon Joseph.
GL 2, 20; GL 5, 330 n.59 [← *P.23.6.1*

(7) The flesh of Jacob's neck becomes as hard as ivory, or turns to stone, when Esau tries to sink his long teeth into it to bite him to death. (Esau hurts his mouth and his teeth are set on edge and melt like wax.)

Gen. R. 78.9; Cant. R. 7.5 §1; GL 1, 391; GL 5, 309 n.263, 264
[← K.13.10.1; K.16.5.1

(8) Moses' neck becomes as hard as ivory, or turns to marble, when the executioner strikes it ten times with a sharp sword.

Deut. R. 2.26-27; Exod. R. 1.31; Cant. R. 7.5 §1
[← K.13.10.2; K.16.5.2

(9) The flesh of Moses is changed by Metatron into torches of fire, his tongue is changed into a flame, his eyes into Merkabah wheels, and his strength becomes an angel's, so that he can look upon the countenance of an angel without being destroyed.

GL 2, 306; GL 5, 416-418 n.117
[← B.16.12.2; Ib.16.12.3; G.17.20.1

(10) Yahweh meets Moses and tries to kill him, but when Zipporah cuts off her son's foreskin and touches Moses' genitals with it, Yahweh lets Moses live.

see 2.13.a.12; 2.18.a.4; 3.11.20
Exod. 4.24-26; Exod. R. 5.8   **[← Sa.2.3.20; Sa.24.3.20**

(11) Abishai prevents David from being transfixed by Ishbi's lance by pronouncing the name of God, which causes David to remain suspended in the air.

see 1.11.a.4
GL 4, 108; GL 6, 268 n.110   **[← A.25.15.3**

(12) To prevent Alcimus from ordering the destruction of the walls of the inner court of the sanctuary, he is paralysed by a stroke and incapable of giving instructions.

see 2.22.c.4
1 Macc. 9.54-56   **[← A.23.6.5; I.23.2.5**

(13) To prevent the destruction of the temple and the Jews, Theodotus Ptolemy IV Philopator, king of Egypt, is tossed to the ground with a stroke, and becomes paralysed and unable to speak.

see 1.19.b.26; 1.26.b.51
3 Macc. 2.22   **[← A.23.6.6; I.23.2.6**

(14) To prevent the destruction of the pious of Jerusalem, a cross is placed upon their foreheads so that the six angels sent as scourges of the city will recognize them and do them no harm. In a variant, the pious are marked with a letter 'taw' written in ink, while the damned are marked with a 'taw' written in blood.

> see 2.2.c.7; 2.6.b.10; 2.15.a.10
> **Ezek. 9.4-6;** *Apoc. Elij.* **1.9;** *Lam. R.* **2.1** §3; *Pss. Sol.* **15.6; GL 1, 6; GL 6, 392 n.26** [← *Fb.13.2.5*

2.16. *Abnormality, Deformity or Disability for Superiority or Inferiority in Battle*

(1) Og is unable to throw a mountain at the Israelites as his teeth are suddenly pushed out and extend to left and right not allowing the mountain past his own head.

> **GL 3, 346; GL 6, 120 n.695, 696** [← *Ic.7.2.1; Ic.7.3.1*

(2) Sihon and his warriors are visited with convulsions so terrible that they roll up and writhe in pain, and the Israelites can cut them down while they lie half-dead on the ground.

> **GL 3, 342; GL 6, 118 n.679** [← *A.23.2.1*

(3) Jacob blinds the enemy army by grinding huge rocks into lime powder and throwing it at his opponents.

> **GL 1, 406; GL 5, 314 n.291** [← *G.23.4.8*

(4) When Jacob's opponent sees that he cannot prevail against him, he strikes him in the hollow of his thigh, injuring his sciatic nerve, which makes him limp.

> see 1.14.c.7; 1.20.4; 1.26.b.13
> **Gen. 32.24-26, 32, 33;** *Gen. R.* **77.3;** *Gen. R.* **78.5;** *Gen. R.* **79.5** [← *T.23.1.3; Ta.23.1.1; Ta.24.1.1*

(5) To weaken and thus defeat the men of Shechem more easily, Jacob's sons tell them to circumcise themselves on the pretext that only in this way will they be granted Dinah as a wife for Shechem.

> see 2.4.8; 2.5.1
> **Gen. 34.15, 22-24;** *Gen. R.* **80.8;** *T. Levi* **6.6** (*Test. XII Patr.*)
> **Theod. Fragments 4, 5, 6** [← *Sa.2.3.18; Sa.24.3.18*

(6) The enemies of Israel become petrified during the war between Joshua and the united kings of Canaan.

> **GL 6, 179 n.44** [← *A.23.6.3*

(7) The faces of the Philistines are scorched in the battle against Samuel, so that they drop their weapons from their hands in pain.

GL 4, 64; GL 6, 228 n.42   [← *F.13.2.1; F.24.3.1*

(8) David has the evil eye, by means of which he afflicts Goliath with leprosy and paralysis. (In a variant, it is the earth who holds Goliath fast, or God, who places 248 iron locks on his 248 limbs.)

GL 4, 87; GL 6, 251 n.39; *Lev. R.* 17.3; *Lev. R.* 21.2 [← *G.25.1.1*

(9) The Amorites are struck blind by the angel Ingethel, or the Angel Gabriel, so that they attack and kill one another.

see 1.19.b.12

Ps-Philo 25.12; GL 4, 26; GL 6, 184 n.18   [← *G.23.4.13*

(10) Zedekiah, the son of Chenaanah, makes himself iron horns, telling King Ahab that Yahweh has said 'With these you will gore the Aramaeans till you make an end of them'.

1 Kgs 22.11; 2 Chron. 18.10   [← *D.14.2.5; D.18.11.3*

2.17. *Abnormality Deformity or Disability for Superiority or Inferiority in Contest*
[No reference in sources]

2.18. *Abnormality, Deformity or Disability to Escape, Prevent Escape or Enable Capture*

2.18.a. *Abnormality, deformity or disability to escape*

(1) To allow Jeremiah to escape—so that he can tell the mysteries he has seen to Baruch and Abimelech—a stone takes on his appearance and is stoned instead of him.

see 2.9.4

4 Bar. 9.27-30   [← *A.17.2.1*

(2) To help Rabbi Meir escape from the Roman bailiffs who are pursuing him, Elijah appears in the guise of a harlot and accompanies him. Since the Roman emissaries cannot believe Rabbi Meir would choose such a companion, they desist from their pursuit.

see 2.6.a.6; 2.9.3

GL 4, 204; GL 6, 326 n.51   [← *A.9.2.1*

(3) To escape drowning in the Red Sea, the two Egyptian magicians, Jannes and Jambres, make wings for themselves, with which to fly to heaven.

GL 3, 28, 29; GL 6, 10 n.53   [← *M.14.2.22; M.20.1.22*

(4) To help Moses escape from an angel who has swallowed him down to his genitals, or, in a variant, from Satan in the guise of a serpent who has done likewise, or, in another variant, from the angels Af and Hemah who have swallowed him down to his feet, his wife Zipporah cuts off her son's foreskin with a flint and touches Moses' genitals with it (or, in the second variant, his feet).

see 2.13.a.12; 2.15.b.10; 3.11.20

Exod. R. **4.24-26; GL 2, 295, 328; GL 5, 412 n.97, 99; GL 5, 423 n.146-148; Exod. 4.24-26**   [← *Sa.2.3.20; Sa.24.3.20*

(5) To escape Israel's power, Balaam flies through the air.

see 1.11.a.3

GL 3, 409-410; GL 6, 143-144 n.851, 853, 854   [← *A.25.15.1*

(6) To escape from the army of Moses, the magicians Jannes and Jambres fly through the air.

GL 2, 287; GL 5, 407-410 n.80   [← *A.25.15.2*

(7) To escape capture by the bailiffs sent by the king of Jericho, Phinehas makes himself invisible in the house of Rahab.

Num. R. **16.1; GL 4, 5; GL 6, 171-172 n.13**   [← *A.1.1.2*

(8) The angel Nathaniel blinds Jair and his servants so that the seven pious men can escape from the furnace into which Jair's servants try to throw them.

see 1.19.b.13

Ps-Philo 38.3; GL 4, 42; GL 6, 202 n.105   [← *G.23.4.19*

(9) To escape from the Aramaeans who have been sent by the king of Aram to capture him, Elisha prays that Yahweh blind them and when his prayer is granted, misdirects them.

see 1.19.b.20; 2.9.8; 2.18.c.1

2 Kgs 6.18   [← *G.23.4.22*

(10) To escape capture by the king's hangman, Jochebed and her daughter, Miriam, become invisible.

GL 2, 261; GL 5, 396 n.35   [← *A.1.1.5*

(11) The Amalekites are great sorcerers and transform themselves into animals to escape the attacks of their enemies in war.

GL 6, 233 n.61   [← *A.27.2.4*

(12) Istehar is given wings with which she escapes from the angels who want to seduce her, and flies to the throne of God (where she is

changed into the constellation Virgo).

BHM 5.21 (Midrash Fragment no.4, Hebrew text, 156); BHM 4.3 (Shemchasai and Asael, Hebrew text, 156) [← *M.14.2.21; M.20.1.21*

2.18.b. *Abnormality, deformity or disability to prevent escape*

(1) After Samson is captured by the Philistines, his eyes are put out.
see 1.12.c.2
Judg. 16.21   [← *G.1.3; G.23.4.16; G.24.1.2*

(2) An angel prevents Zimri and Cozbi, caught in the act of copulation, from moving or crying out for help, and thus escaping.
see 1.19.b.11; 2.3.8
Num. R. 20.25; GL 3, 387; GL 6, 137 n.798 [← *I.23.2.4; A.23.6.7*

2.18.c. *Abnormality, deformity or disability to enable capture*

(1) To allow the Aramaeans to be captured, Elisha prays to Yahweh to blind them, and then directs them to Samaria and the king of Israel.
see 1.19.b.20; 2.9.8; 2.18.a.9
2 Kgs 6.18   [← *G.23.4.22*

2.19. Abnormality, Deformity or Disability to Reach or Prevent Reaching

2.19.a. *Abnormality, Deformity or Disability to Reach*

(1) To reach and take the keys of the temple which Jeconiah holds out standing on the temple roof, a fiery hand appears from the sky.
see 3.1.1
Lev. R. 19.6   [← *P.3.1.1*

(2) The corpse of Sammael's son weeps, even when cut up into pieces, in order to be ingested by Adam and Eve and reach their hearts.
GL 1, 154, 155; GL 5, 177 n.22   [← *A.25.2.1*

(3) Elijah, after his removal from earth, acquires wings, with four beats of which he can traverse the whole world.
see 2.22.a.9
GL 4, 203; GL 6, 326 n.46   [← *M.14.2.5; M.20.1.5*

(4) The bones of Joseph, wrapped in a sheep's skin upon which the 'name of God' is written, come alive and, assuming the form of a sheep, follow the camp of Israel through the wilderness in order to reach the land of Canaan.

see 1.11.a.2

GL 5, 376 n.442　　　　　　　　　　[← *Va.3.1.3; Va.27.2.1*

(5) Judah's roar travels 400 parasangs until Hushim, son of Dan, hears it and goes to help Benjamin.

***Gen. R.* 93.7**　　　　　　　　　　[← *If.6.1.2*

(6) The arm of Pharaoh's daughter lengthens miraculously so that she can grasp the ark containing Moses.

***Exod. R.* 1.23**　　　　　　　　　　[← *O.6.5.1*

2.19.b. *Abnormality, deformity or disability to prevent reaching*

(1) The angels of terror attempt to scorch Moses with their fiery breath and prevent him from reaching the throne of God.

see 2.24.6

GL 3, 112; GL 6, 46 n.247　　　　　　　　　　[← *I.10.1.2*

(2) The men of Sodom are stricken blind so that they cannot find the doorway to Lot's house.

***Gen.* 19.5, 9-11; *Gen. R.* 50.8**　　　　　　　　　　[← *G.23.4.4*

(3) To prevent the troops of Pharaoh from reaching Moses—who has just escaped from their custody and whom they have been ordered to pursue—they are stricken dumb, deaf or blind.

see 2.22.3; 2.2.b.2

***Exod. R.* 1.31; *Deut. R.* 2.26-27; GL 2, 282; GL 5, 406 n.76**
　　　　　　　　　　[← *G.23.4.9; I.23.3.5; J.23.1.4*

(4) Sammael stops the mouths of Joshua, Eleazar and Caleb to prevent their prayers for Moses' life from reaching heaven.

GL 3, 433; GL 6, 150 n.896　　　[← *I.23.2.1; I.23.2.2; I.23.2.3*

(5) To prevent anyone from reaching Eden, it is guarded by angels of fire.

2 En. 42.4　　　　　　　　　　[← *A.16.12.5*

2.20. *Abnormality, Deformity or Disability to Avoid Worse Fate*

(1) To avoid Isaac's death (which would result from his gazing too long at the Shekinah at the time of the Akedah), God blinds him.

see 1.7.a.4; 1.12.a.8; 1.14.a.2; 1.14.a.3; 1.14.a.4; 1.14.c.6; 1.19.b.6; 1.26.a.5;

1.26.b.12; 1.31.1; 2.7.3; 2.6.a.7; 4.1.b.10
Gen. R. **65.10**; GL **5**, 281 n.74   [← *G.23.4.6*

(2) To prevent the infant Moses being killed by the Egyptians, the angel makes him choose a burning coal, which burns his hand and mouth, in preference to an onyx stone, to show that the child's actions are inconsequential.
see 1.14.c.10; 2.6.a.8; 2.9.6; 2.3.3
Exod. R. **1.**26; GL **2**, 274; GL **5**, 402 n.65   [← *I.23.3.3; Ia.13.2.1;*
                          Ia.24.4.1; Ib.13.2.1; Ib.24.4.1; P.13.2.1; P.24.4.1

2.21 Abnormality, Deformity or Disability to Prevent Natural Course of Events

(1) The angel Gallizur, also called Raziel, stands behind the throne with outspread wings to arrest the breath of the Hayyot, the heat of which would otherwise scorch all the angels.
see 2.22.a.8
GL **3**, 112; GL **6**, 46 n.247   [← *M.14.2.6; M.20.1.6*

(2) The seraphim use two of their wings to cover their faces so as not to look at the Shekinah.
Hell. Syn. Pr. 82; *Lad. Jac.* 2.15   [← *M.14.2.12; M.20.1.12*

(3) Balaam is prevented from cursing Israel because an angel settles in his throat and he is unable to speak.
see 1.32.4
GL **3**, 372; GL **6**, 130 n.762   [← *I.23.3.6*

(4) Haman's daughter would have been chosen as a successor to Vashti if a disease had not made her repulsive.
see 1.10.4
GL **6**, 477 n.173   [← *A.22.1.6*

(5) To prevent the Gentiles from mixing with the daughters of Zion, large quantities of blood pour from their vaginas.
see 2.23.b.4
Lam. R. **4.15** §18   [← *W.5.1.1; Sb.10.3.1*

(6) To prevent Abraham being frightened or alarmed, Death assumes the form of a beautiful archangel with an appearance of sunlight and cheeks flashing with fire.
T. Abr. **16.**6-8   [← *A.10.1.24; Fa.10.2.1*

2.22. Abnormality, Deformity or Disability to Aid or Hinder Characteristic Duty or Specific Text

2.22.a. *Abnormality, deformity or disability to aid characteristic duty*
(1) Angels have no joints (except the angels of destruction), which enables them to fulfil their duties speedily. (In a variant, the angels of destruction have no joints in their feet.)
Gen. R. 65.21; Lev. R. 6.3; GL 5, 5 n.9 [← *Va.2.1.1*

(2) The pinions of the winged angel, Ben Nez, keep back the south wind (which brings fire, smoke, blasts and hurricanes) and thus prevent the consumation of the world.
see 2.15.b.2
GL 1, 12; GL 5, 14 n.36 [← *M.14.2.2; M.20.1.2*

(3) The ophan Sandalfon's height—reaching from earth to the holy Hayyot—aids his function as a mediator between Israel and God.
see 3.3.a.2
GL 5, 48 [← *A.6.5.11*

(4) The angel Sandalfon has 70,000 heads, each head has 70,000 mouths and each mouth has 70,000 tongues and each tongue has as many sayings, so as to praise and extol the Lord.
GL 2, 307; GL 5, 416-418 n.117 [← *D.5.13.1; I.5.14.1; Ib.5.14.1*

(5) The seraphim with six wings, seen by Isaiah and Moses in the seventh heaven, use two of their wings to fly and do the service of the Lord.
Isa. 6.2; Lad. Jac. 2.15; LAE (Apoc. Mos.) 37.3; Hell. Syn. Pr. 82 [← *M.14.2.12; M.20.1.12*

(6) The 200 angels who govern the stars use their wings to fly and do the rounds of the planets.
2 En. 4.2 (J and A) [← *M.14.2.3; M.20.1.3*

(7) The angel Hadarniel, who guards the gates of heaven, breathes fiery lightning flashes (and is sixty myriads of parasangs taller than his fellows).
see 2.15.a.6; 3.3.a.3
GL 3, 110; GL 6, 46 n.247 [← *I.10.5.3*

(8) The angel Gallizur, also called Raziel, stands behind the throne with outspread wings and arrests the breath of the Hayyot, the heat of which would otherwise scorch all the angels.

see 2.21.1
GL 3, 112; GL 6, 46 n.247   [← *M.14.2.6; M.20.1.6*

(9) To help anyone in need, Elijah, after his removal from earth, has wings with four strokes of which he is able to traverse the world.
see 2.19.a.3
GL 4, 203; GL 6, 326 n.46   [← *M.14.2.5; M.20.1.5*

(10) The guardians of the gates of hell are as large as serpents, and have faces like very large snakes with eyes aflame, or eyes like extinguished lamps, and fangs exposed to their breasts.
see 2.24.7
2 En. **42.1** (J and A); *2 En.* **42.1** (Appendix); *Apoc. Zeph.* **6.8**
[← *A.6.1.2; F.18.6.1; G.16.12.6; Ic.18.2.1*

(11) Some of the angels of destruction are fashioned out of hail, others out of fire.
see 2.15.a.8
GL 2, 366; GL 5, 433-434 n.213   [← *A.16.11.2; A.16.12.9*

(12) To prepare themselves for their duty as heralds, the fifty men whom Adonijah, the pretender to the throne, has chosen to run before him, cut out their spleens and the flesh of the soles of their feet.
GL 4, 118; GL 6, 275 n.139
[← *U.2.4.1; U.13.5.1; U.24.4.1; V.2.9.1; Vi.1.1.1*

(13) Eunuchs act as servants and messengers for Potiphar and his wife.
Jub. **39.14**; GL 2, 40-42, 46; GL 5, 337 n.99
[← *Sa.2.1.3; Sa.24.2.3*

(14) Seventy eunuchs are appointed by Solomon to guard his daughter whom he has imprisoned in a high tower.
GL 4, 175-176; GL 6, 303 n.100   [← *Sa.2.1.9; Sa.24.2.9*

(15) Two eunuchs, Hegai and Shaashgaz, are the custodians of Ahasuerus's harems.
Est. **2.3,14,15**   [← *Sa.2.1.19; Sa.24.2.19*

(16) Bagoas, who looks after the 'personal affairs' of Holofernes and attends Judith while she stays in his camp, is a eunuch.
Jdt. **12.11**   [← *Sa.2.1.26; Sa.24.2.26*

(17) Hegai, chief of the eunuchs of the harem, serves Esther.
Est. R. **5.3**; GL 4, 386; GL 6, 460 n.75 [← *Sa.2.1.21; Sa.24.2.21*

(18) The sun, represented as a bridegroom, has two faces: one of fire to warm the earth and one of hail to cool the heat that streams from his other face and prevent the earth from catching fire. (In winter the sun turns its fiery face upward and thus cold is produced.)

GL 1, 24-25; GL 5, 37 n.103   [← *F.5.1.2; F.16.12.4; F.16.11.1*

2.22.b. *Abnormality, deformity or disability to aid specific task*

(1) The angel of the Face emits scorching fires, and thick clouds, from his eyes to destroy the world at God's summons when certain parts of the waters refuse to obey his command.

see 2.15.a.7

GL 1, 14; GL 5, 17-18 n.50   [← *G.10.1.3; G.10.3.1*

(2) The two angels, Samuil and Raguil, are very tall with wings 'brighter than gold' on which they transport Enoch to the various heavens.

see 3.3.a.14

2 En. 1.4-6 (J and A); *2 En.* 3.1-3 (J and A); *2 En.* 33.6 (J and A);
GL 1, 130-131; GL 5, 158-162 n.60   [← *M.14.2.4; M.20.1.4*

(3) An angel with an appearance like snow and hands like ice, is sent to Enoch to chill his face (after he has ascended to heaven) so that men can endure the sight of him, or, in a variant, the angel's icy hands cool his face because he cannot endure the burning countenance of God.

2 En. 37.1-2(J); *2 En.* 37.1(A); GL 1, 136-137

[← *A.16.10.3; P.16.11.1*

(4) The angel who appears to Sarah to give her a message from God is invisible to Pharaoh.

see 2.6.a.5

GL 1, 223; GL 5, 221 n.73   [← *A.1.1.3*

(5) The Israelites who go on a reconnaissance mission into Canaan are sixty cubits tall.

GL 3, 268; GL 6, 94 n.513   [← *A.6.5.28*

(6) A hole is bored through the heels of Shebnah so that he can be tied to the tail of a horse and killed.

see 2.15.a.13

GL 4, 270; GL 6, 365 n.65   [← *Ua.15.1.1*

(7) To punish the sinners in hell, the angels of destruction make their teeth grow to a length of one parasang during the night so that they can break them again the following day.

see 1.19.b.25; 1.26.a.14; 1.26.b.65

GL 2, 312; GL 5, 418-419 n.118   [← *Ic.6.5.3; Ic.25.1.1*

(8) Two women use their stork-like wings to carry a bushel containing a woman (personifying wickedness) to the land of Shinar where they are to build a temple for it.

Zech. 5.5f.   [← *M.14.2.23; M.20.1.23*

2.22.c. *Abnormality, deformity or disability to hinder characteristic duty or specific task*

(1) To prevent people from completing the Tower of Babel, God strikes them with blindness.

see 1.19.b.4; 1.26.b.8
3 Bar. **3.8** (Greek)   [← *G.23.4.3*

(2) The Egyptian magicians are stricken with boils so that they cannot face Moses in a magical contest or perform any magic.

Gen. 9.11; *Jub.* **48.11**   [← *B.23.2.1*

(3) The troops of Pharaoh are stricken dumb, deaf or blind, when they are ordered to pursue Moses, and so they are unable to find him or give information of his whereabouts.

see 2.2.b.2; 2.19.b.3
Exod. R. **1.31;** *Deut. R.* **2.26-27**   [← *G.23.4.9; I.23.3.5; J.23.1.4*

(4) Alcimus is prevented from completing the demolition of the wall of the inner court of the sanctuary because he has a stroke which paralyses him and makes him incapable of giving instructions.

see 2.15.b.12
1 Macc. 9.54-56   [← *A.23.6.5; I.23.2.5*

2.23. *Abnormality, Deformity or Disability to Satisfy Certain Impulses or Prevent Satisfaction of Such*

2.23.a. *Abnormality, deformity or disability to satisfy certain impulses*

(1) To satisfy her desire for herself, a Muse becomes androgynous (and gives birth).

see 2.14.a.3
Apoc. Adam   [← *A.9.1.1*

(2) One of the two wives of the men of the generation of the deluge is sterilized to allow unhampered pursuit of carnal indulgences.

see 2.14.b.1
GL 1, 117   [← *Vg.23.1.1*

(3) The eyes of Moses are strengthened so that he can see the entire length and breadth of Israel before he dies.

> GL 3, 442; GL 6, 151 n.901   [← *G.25.4.1*

2.23.b. *Abnormality, deformity or disability to prevent satisfaction of certain impulses*

(1) Pharaoh is afflicted with leprosy and thus unable to indulge his carnal desires with Sarah, Abraham's wife.

> see 1.26.a.6
>
> *Gen. R.* **41.2;** *Gen. R.* **52.13;** *Lev. R.* **16.1**   [← *A.23.1.5*

(2) Potiphar (or Poti-phera) is castrated by the Angel Gabriel so that he cannot rape Joseph.

> see 1.26.b.15
>
> *Gen. R.* **86.3;** *Jub.* **34.11;** *Jub.* **39.2;** *Cant. R.* **1.1 §1**
>   [← *Sa.2.1.2; Sa.24.2.2*

(3) To prevent Nebuchadnezzar speaking, his tongue is taken from him when he is reduced to living like a beast.

> see 1.26.b.52
>
> *Liv. Proph. (Daniel)* **4.10**   [← *Ib.1.1.2*

(4) To prevent the Gentiles mixing with the daughters of Zion, large quantities of blood pour from their vaginas.

> see 2.21.5
>
> *Lam. R.* **4.15 §18**   [← *W.5.1.1; Sb.10.3.1*

2.24. *Abnormality, Deformity or Disability to Affect Emotionally*

(1) The angel Sammael is so tall that it would take 500 years to cover a distance equal to his height; he is covered from the crown of his head to the soles of his feet with glaring eyes at the sight of which the beholder falls prostrate in awe. His function is to take the soul away from man.

> GL 2, 308; GL 5, 416-418 n.117   [← *A.6.5.9; G.4.1.5; G.5.15.4*

(2) The angels Af, 'Anger', and Hemah, 'Wrath', are 500 parasangs tall and forged out of chains of red fire and black fire.

> GL 2, 308; GL 5, 416-418 n.117   [← *A.6.5.10; A.16.12.7*

(3) Balshazzar sees the awesome fingers of an angel writing 'Mene,

Mene, Tekel, Upharsin' on a wall, while the rest of the angel remains invisible.

   Dan. 5.5   [← *Pc.3.1.1*

(4) Two angels, clothed in glory and of awe-inspiring appearance, strike terror into the enemies of the Jews when they send elephants to trample them.

   see 2.15.b.3
   3 Macc. 6.18   [← *A.10.1.4*

(5) The glances of the angels of destruction strike terror in the heart of the beholder.

   GL 2, 366; GL 5, 433-434 n.213   [← *G.25.2.1*

(6) The angels of terror have a fiery breath and are the strongest and mightiest among the angels.

   see 2.19.b.1
   GL 3, 112; GL 6, 46 n.247   [← *I.10.1.2*

(7) The guardians of the gates of hell are as large as serpents and have faces like large snakes with eyes aflame, or, in a variant, with eyes like extinguished lamps, and fangs exposed down to their breasts.

   see 2.22.a.10
   2 En. **42.1 (J and A);** *2 En.* **42.1 (Appendix);** *Apoc. Zeph.* **6.8**
                    [← *A.6.1.2; F.18.6.1; G.16.12.6; Ic.18.2.1*

(8) In the lowest heaven (which is hell) sinners are punished by terrifying creatures who have the faces of lions, dogs, tigers, hyenas or camels, while some have only one eye.

   T. Isaac **5.7-10**   [← *F.18.1.1; F.18.2.1; F.18.5.1; F.18.7.1;*
                                      F.18.8.1; G.1.1 G.5.1.1

(9) The ugly angels who carry off the souls of ungodly men have a terrifying appearance: their faces are like leopards' with tusks outside their mouths like wild boars. Their eyes are mixed with blood and their hair is loose like the hair of women.

   Apoc. Zeph. **4.2-4;** *Apoc. Zeph* **6.8**
                    [← *E.9.5.1; F.18.9.1; Ic.18.1.1; W.4.1.1*

(10) The demon Asmodeus appears before Solomon in all his forbidding ugliness and terrifies the king so much that he surrounds his couch at night with valiant heroes.

   GL 4, 172; GL 6, 301 n.93   [← *A.22.1.3*

(11) Rachel remains barren after her marriage while Leah conceives because God, seeing how Leah is hated by Jacob, wants to correct this and make Jacob love Leah.

Gen. 29.31-32   [← *Vg 23.1.4*

(12) When Sammael tries to take Moses' soul he is terrified by Moses because his eyes and face are radiant like the sun and his mouth emits darts of fire and lightning flashes.

see 1.14.a.6; 1.14.a.7; 1.14.c.12; 1.14.f.2; 1.35.7; 3.3.a.30; 3.3.a.38
Deut. R. **11.10;** *Deut. R.* **3.12; GL 3, 467; GL 6, 160 n.947**
                        [← *F.10.1.11; G.10.2.9; I.10.1.5*

(13) All the water in Egypt, including drinking water, turns to blood in order to terrify the Pharaoh and his people and make them release the Israelites from their bondage.

see 1.26.b.24; 2.5.8
Exod. R. **9.10-11; GL 2, 348-349; GL 5, 426-428 n.172, 173, 176-178**   [← *Ie.27.1.1; W.4.2.2; W.21.1.1*

(14) To terrify the inhabitants of Jericho, the husbands of the she-devils Lilith and Mahlah take possession of Caleb and Phinehas and give them a frightful appearance.

see 1.32.3
GL 4, 5; GL 6, 171 n.11   [← *A.22.1.4*

(15) To terrify the Philistines of Ashdod and make them release the captured ark, God afflicts them with tumours.

see 1.26.b.37
1 Sam. 5.6-12; 1 Sam. 6.4-11   [← *A.14.1.1*

(16) To shame Zedekiah, Nebuchadnezzar feeds him food which gives him diarrhoea.

see 2.25.a.1; 1.14.d.5
Est. R. **3.1; GL 6, 384 n.8**   [← *Rb.6.1.1; Rb.13.2.1*

(17) To terrify Leviathan and prevent being swallowed, Jonah shows him the sign of the covenant on his body.

GL 4, 249; GL 6, 350 n.31   [← *Sa.2.3.28; Sa.24.3.28*

(18) Kings, lords and princes have radiant faces which make men fear them.

see 1.14.a.13
GL 3, 112; GL 6, 46 n.247   [← *F.10.1.19*

(19) At Abraham's request, Death shows him his face of ferocity and decay which includes seven fiery heads of dragons as well as a face of

burning fire, a dark face, a viper's face, the face of a precipice, a face of an asp, a face of a lion, a face of a cobra-horned serpent, a sword face, a face of thunder and lightning, a face of a turbulent river, a three-headed dragon face, a mixed cup of poisons, great ferocity and bitterness and every fatal disease.

see 3.9.8

T. Abr. 17.12-17; T. Abr. 19.5f. [← *D.5.6.1; D.17.1.1; D.18.6.2; D.5.2.1; F.17.2.1; F.17.3.1; F.17.4.1; F.17.5.1; F.17.6.1; F.17.10.1; F.18.5.4; F.17.1.1*

(20) To terrify Abraham, Death reveals his corruption, showing two heads, one with the face of a serpent and one like a sword.

see 3.9.7

T. Abr. 13.13-16; T. Abr. 14.1 (Recension B); GL 1, 306 [← *A.23.8.1; D.5.1.6; D.17.1.1; F.18.6.2*

2.25. Abnormality, Deformity or Disability for Entertainment or Play

2.25.a. *Abnormality, deformity or disability for entertainment or play*

(1) Nebuchadnezzar ridicules Zedekiah by giving him food to eat which gives him diarrhoea.

see 1.14.d.5; 2.24.16

Est. R. **3.1; GL 6, 384 n.8** [← *Rb.6.1.1; Rb.13.2.1*

(2) For the brutal amusement of himself and his followers, King Antiochus Epiphanes tortures Eleazar, his mother and his six brothers, cutting off their extremities, cutting out their tongues, piercing their eyes and scalping their heads, before frying them alive.

see 1.24.4; 2.5.12

2 Macc. 7; *4 Macc.* 6.6, 25; *4 Macc.* 7.13-14; *4 Macc.* 9.28; *4 Macc.* 10.5-8, 17-21; *4 Macc.* 11.18-19; *4 Macc.* 18.21 [← *D.2.2.1; Ib.1.1.3; Ga.24.1.1; P.1.1.2; U.1.1.1*

2.25.b *Abnormality, deformity or disability to prevent entertainment or play*

(1) The Levites bite off their own fingers when they are asked to play their harps for the Babylonians.

GL 4, 316-317; GL 6, 407 n.55 [← *Pc.1.1.1; P.2.1.1*

(2) Signs of leprosy appear on the forehead of Ahasuerus's wife, Vashti, as well as marks of other diseases on the rest of her body, so

she cannot appear naked before the guests of her husband.
see 1.11.a.6
GL 4, 375; GL 6, 455 n.35 [← *A.23.10.1; Fb.23.1.2*

2.26. Abnormality, Deformity or Disability for Aesthetic Reasons

2.26.*a. Abnormality, deformity or disability to beautify*

(1) Rebecca's nose is pierced by a nose-ring given to her by Abraham's servant.
Gn 24.22, 47 [← *H.15.1.1*

2.26.b. *Abnormality, deformity or disability to uglify*

(1) The Israelites blacken the faces of the Midianite women to hide their beauty and thus avoid temptation.
Cant. R. 1.6 §3; *Cant. R.* 4.4 §3; *Cant. R.* 6.6 §1 [← *F.11.1.3*

2.27. Abnormality, Deformity or Disability for Comfort or Relaxation, or to Prevent Such

2.27.a. *Abnormality, deformity or disability for comfort or relaxation*

(1) The hair of the babies born to Hebrew women in the fields (and subsequently abandoned to prevent their murder by the Egyptians) grows to their knees to serve as a protective garment.
GL 2, 258; GL 5, 394 n.25 [← *E.6.5.3*

(2) To free his hand from his own sword (to which it has become attached), Kenaz slays an Amorite whose warm blood releases it.
Ps-Philo 27.11; GL 4, 26; GL 6, 184 n.18 [← *W.25.2.2*

(3) The blood of an unborn child loosens the sword from Joab's hand.
GL 4, 100; GL 6, 258-259 n.77 [← *W.25.2.1*

2.27.b. *Abnormality, Deformity or Disability to Cause Discomfort or Prevent Relaxation*
[No reference in sources]

2.28. Abnormality, Deformity or Disability to Fit
[No reference in sources]

2.29. *Abnormality, Deformity or Disability for Altruistic Reasons*
[No reference in sources]

2.30. *Abnormality, Deformity or Disability for Medical Reasons*
[No reference in sources]

2.31. *Abnormality, Deformity or Disability to Cleanse or Prevent Pollution*

2.31.a. *Abnormality, deformity or disability to cleanse physically*
[No reference in sources]

2.31.b. *Abnormality, deformity or disability to cleanse spiritually*

(**1**) Abraham is commanded to remove his foreskin so that he can walk blamelessly before God.
see 2.13.a.4; 2.14.a.4; 3.11.13
Gen. R. 46.1-4   [← *Sa.2.3.9; Sa.24.3.9*

(**2**) To atone for her sins, Aseneth fasts for seven days until her body becomes emaciated, her face falls and her lips crack, while her eyes become inflamed and her hair becomes straggly from the ashes she has piled upon it.
see 1.12.a.10; 1.13.3; 1.14.c.9
Jos. Asen. **11.1.1;** *Jos. Asen* **13.9.8;** *Jos. Asen* **18.3**
[← *A.6.4.1; E.22.1.2; G.11.3.2; Ia.15.1.1*

(**3**) The shame of their sojourn in Egypt is removed from the Israelites when they are circumcised at Gilgal.
see 1.16.b.6; 2.13.a.13; 3.11.22
Josh. 5.2-10   [← *Sa.2.3.22; Sa.24.3.22*

(**4**) A seraph takes a live coal from the altar and touches Isaiah's lips with it to cleanse him from sin and iniquity.
Isa. 6.6-7   [← *Ia.13.2.2*

2.31.c. *Abnormality, deformity or disability to prevent pollution*

(**1**) To prevent Phinehas from being polluted by the blood of Zimri and Cozbi no blood flows from their bodies when Phinehas runs them through with his lance.
Num. R. **20.25; GL 3, 378; GL 6, 137 n.798**   [← *W.1.1.1*

2.32. *Abnormality, Deformity or Disability for Alimentary or Culinary Reasons*

(1) The lustre of God's presence nourishes Moses for forty days and nights while he is on Mount Sinai.
Exod. R. 47.5   [← *A.10.1.1*

(2) Milk and honey flow from the little finger of Abraham's right hand when he is left alone in a cave as a baby.
GL 1, 189; GL 5, 210 n.14   [← *Pc.10.5.1; Pc.10.6.1*

(3) Sarah has enough milk in her breasts to suckle all the babies present at Isaac's circumcision.
see 2.3.1
Gen. R. 53.5, 9; GL 1, 263; GL 5, 246 n.208   [← *Nd.5.1.1*

(4) To obtain food during the famine in Egypt, the Egyptians circumcise themselves, as Joseph will only give them food if they do so.
Gen. R. 90.6; Gen. R. 91.5   [← *Sa.2.3.15; Sa.24.3.15*

(5) Water flows from Samson's mouth as from a spring when he is about to perish from thirst after his first victory over the Philistines.
Gen. R. 98.13; Num. R. 9.24   [← *I.10.20.1; Ie.17.3.1*

(6) The sons of Jews are circumcised before they leave Egypt so that they can eat the Paschal lamb, whose paradisial scent attracts them.
see 2.4.16
Exod. R. 19.5; Num. R. 11.3; Cant. R. 3.7 §4; Cant. R. 1.12 §3
[← *Sa.2.3.21; Sa.24.3.21*

(7) Milk flows from Mordecai's breast to nourish Esther.
Gen. R. 30.8   [← *Nc.10.1.1; Nd.9.1.1*

(8) In exchange for three loaves of bread, Siti (Job's wife) allows her hair to be shaved off by Satan disguised as a bread seller.
T. Job 23.7-11   [← *E.1.6*

(9) The Israelites gash themselves for the sake of corn and wine.
Hos. 7.14   [← *B.24.1.2*

2.33. *Abnormality, Deformity or Disability for Commercial or Contractual Reasons*

(1) The bill of sale whereby Haman is to sell himself to Mordecai in return for provisions for Haman's army, is written upon Mordecai's knee-cap.

GL 4, 398; GL 6, 464 n.105   [← *Tb.13.1.1*

3. ABNORMALITY, DEFORMITY OR DISABILITY AS A SYMBOL

3.1. *Abnormality, Deformity or Disability as a Symbol of Self or Identity*

(1) A hand of fire takes the keys of the temple from Jeconiah, as he stands on the roof, and offers them back, declaring that his people are no fit custodians of the temple.

see 2.19.a.1

Lev. R. 19.6   [← *P.16.12.1*

(2) The seraphim have calves' feet and six wings. Each of their faces is as large as the rising sun and radiates light. The seraphim seen by Enoch are covered in eyes from which a brilliant light shines.

2 En. 20.1 (J); *2 En.* 19.6 (A); *2 En.* 21.1 (J); *2 En.* 1a.4 (J and A); *3 En.* 1.7-8; *3 En.* 2.1; *3 En.* 26.9-11; *3 En.* 25.6; *3 En.* 24.18 (Appendix); *Lev. R.* 27.3; *Hell. Syn. Pr.* 82

[← *F.6.1.2; F.10.1.1; G.4.1.4; G.5.15.5; G.10.2.2; U.18.3.2*

(3) The bodies, backs, hands, wings and wheels of the ophanim are covered in eyes and a brilliant light shines from their faces and eyes.

3 En. 1.7-8; *3 En.* 2.1; *3 En.* 25.6; *3 En.* 24.18 (Appendix); *1 En.* 71.1,7   [← *F.10.1.1; G.4.1.4; G.5.15.5; G.10.2.2*

(4) Enoch sees angels of flaming fire during his ascension.

1 En. 17.1   [← *A.16.12.4*

(5) The body of Michael is made of fire and Gabriel's of snow, or vice versa.

see 4.2.d.1

Num. R. 12.8; *Deut. R.* 5.12; *Cant. R.* 3.2 §1

[← *A.16.10.1; A.16.12.1; A.16.10.2; A.16.12.2*

(6) The angel Michael has tears which turn into pearls when he weeps over the forthcoming death of Abraham.

see 1.12.a.3

T. Abr. 3.9-12; *T. Abr.* 6.7 (Recension A and B)   [← *Gf.27.2.2*

(7) The angel Michael, though disguised as a commander-in-chief, is as bright as the sun.
T. Abr. 2.4; T. Abr. 7.3-5 (Recension A and B)   [← *A.10.1.3*

(8) An angel seen by Aseneth (probably Michael) has a face like lightning, eyes like sunshine, hair like a flaming torch and hands and feet like shining iron emitting sparks.
Jos. Asen. 14.9 (8, 9); Jos. Asen. 16.12-13 (7)   [← *E.10.2.1;*
F.10.1.3; G.10.2.4; P.10.3.2; P.16.1.1; U.10.3.1; U.16.1.1

(9) When Elijah is about to be born, angels of shining white appearance greet his father, Sobacha, wrapping him in fire and giving him flames of fire to eat.
Liv. Proph. (Elijah) 21.2   [← *A.10.1.5; A.11.2.2*

(10) The faces of the four 'Hayyot' consist of 240 faces each, and each of these has faces within faces (and wings within wings).
3 En. 21.1-3   [← *F.6.1.1*

(11) The Ishim are angels whose nether parts are snow and whose upper parts are fire.
GL 2, 308; GL 5, 416-418 n.117   [← *Cc.16.10.1; Cc.16.12.1*

(12) The angel Zagzagel has horns of glory.
GL 2, 309; GL 5, 416-418 n.117   [← *D.14.2.1*

(13) The angels called Erelim have white fire in place of a body. There are 70,000 of them in the retinue of Sandalfon.
GL 2, 307; GL 5, 416-418 n.117   [← *A.17.6.1*

(14) Daniel sees an angel with a body like beryl, topaz or chrysolite, a face like lightning, eyes like fiery torches and arms and legs like burnished bronze.
Dan. 10.6   [← *A.16.18.1; F.16.12.3; G.16.12.3;*
O.16.2.1; T.16.2.1

(15) Ezekiel sees an angel made of bronze, or partly of bronze, partly of fire.
Ezek. 1.27; Ezek. 8.2; Ezek. 40.3
[← *A.10.2.1; A.16.2.1; Cc.6.2.1; Cc.16.12.2*

(16) The four cherubim, seen by Ezekiel, Abraham and Enoch, have a human form with straight legs, four wings beneath which there are human hands, four faces of which one is human, one an eagle's, one a

bull's and one a lion's. They have hooves like oxen which glitter like polished brass. Beside each of them is a wheel with eyes round the rim. In a variant, the bodies, hands, wings and wheels are covered with eyes and in place of a bull's face there is a cherub's face. The cherubim have a brilliant light shining from their faces and eyes, and horns of glory. (In *2 Enoch* the cherubim have six not four wings.)

Ezek. 1.5-20; Ezek. 3.13; Ezek. 10.3-22; Ezek. 11.22-25; *Apoc. Abr.* 18.3-7; *Lad. Jac.* 2.7-8; *2 En.* 20.1 (J); *2 En.* 1a.4 (J and A); *2 En.* 19.6; *3 En.* 25.6; *3 En.* 24.18 (Appendix); *3 En.* 22.13-15; *Ques. Ezra* (A) 29

[← *A.14.10.1; D.14.2.2; F.5.3.1; F.10.1.1; F.18.5.2; F.20.1.1; F.18.4.1; M.20.1.8; M.14.2.8; G.4.1.4; G.5.15.5; G.10.2.2; P.21.1.1; U.18.3.1*

(**17**) Obyzouth is a female demon in the form of a woman with savage dishevelled hair. She strangles newborn infants, injures eyes, condemns mouths, destroys minds and causes pain.

T. Sol. 13.1; T. Sol. 13.5   [← *E.22.1.1*

(**18**) Enepsigos is a female demon with two separate heads and two pairs of arms on her shoulders. She hovers near the moon and can assume three different forms.

T. Sol. 15.1-5   [← *D.5.1.1; O.5.3.1*

(**19**) Solomon summons up a winged demon in the form of a dragon but with the face and feet of a man.

T. Sol. 14.1-2   [← *F.21.6.1; U.21.6.2*

(**20**) Onoskelis is a demon with the body of a beautiful woman but the legs of a mule. She is generated from an unexpected voice which is called 'a voice of the echo of a black heaven'.

T. Sol. 4.2-4, 8   [← *T.18.1.1*

(**21**) Abezethibou is a one-winged demon, an adversary of Moses in Egypt, who is trapped in the Red Sea when the parted waters return.

T. Sol. 6.3; T. Sol. 25.2-3   [← *M.14.2.18; M.20.1.18*

(**22**) The demon Keteb or Keteb Meriri ('pestilence' or 'bitter destruction') has the head of a calf with a single horn on his forehead. He is covered with scales and hair and full of eyes, with a single eye upon his heart that kills all who look at it.

see 2.15.a.9

Num. R. 12.3; *Lam. R.* 1.3 §29; GL 3, 186; GL 6, 74 n.381

[← *A.13.6.1; B.13.6.1; B.13.7.1; D.18.4.1; E.4.1.2; Fb.14.2.1; Fb.18.11.1; G.5.15.6; G.4.1.6; G.4.5.1*

(23) The demon Asmodeus has cock's feet.
see 1.1.a.7
GL 4, 172; GL 6, 301 n.92   [← *U.20.1.1*

(24) The Antichrist has feet measuring two span, a mouth that is one
cubit and teeth a span long. His right eye is like the rising morning
star, his left eye unmoving; his fingers are like scythes and he has the
inscription 'Antichrist' on his forehead.
Gk Apoc. Ezra 4.29f.   [← *Fb.13.2.2; G.10.2.5; G.23.3.1;*
I.6.1.1; Ic.6.5.1; Pc.12.1.1; Pc.12.2.1; U.6.5.1

(25) The Antichrist is ten cubits tall, the track of his feet is three
cubits and his right arm measures four and a half feet. The hair on his
head reaches to his feet and he is three-crested. His left eye is like the
morning star, his right eye like a lion's. His lower teeth are made of
iron, his lower jaw of diamond; his right arm is made of iron, his left
of copper. He is long-faced, long-nosed and has three letters written
on his forehead: A, K and T, signifying denial, rejection and the
befouled dragon. His mother conceives him by touching the head of a
fish.
see 1.3.c.1; 3.6.b.3
Apoc. Dan. 9.11, 16-26   [← *A.6.5.13; E.6.5.1; Fb.13.2.3;*
Fc.16.5.1; G.10.2.6; G.18.1.1; Ic.16.1.1; O.16.2.3; O.16.1.1;
U.6.5.2

(26) The Antichrist has fiery wings, skinny legs and a tuft of grey
hair at the front of a bald head, eyebrows reaching to his ears and a
leprous bare spot on the palms of his hands. He can appear as a child
or an old man, but cannot change the signs on his head.
Apoc. Elij. 3.15-17; *Apoc. Elij.* 5.20   [← *E.2.1.1; E.11.4.1;*
Gb.6.5.1; M.14.2.19; M.20.1.19; Pa.23.1.1; T.6.4.1

(27) Abraham sees a chariot with fiery wheels and each wheel is full
of eyes.
Apoc. Abr. 18.3-7,12   [← *G.21.1.1*

(28) The angel Azazel has human hands and feet and the body of a
serpent or dragon with twelve wings.
Apoc. Abr. 23.7; GL 5, 123-124 n.131
[← *M.14.2.20; M.20.1.20; P.21.6.1; U.21.6.1*

(29) The Messiah has red hair and small birthmarks on his thigh.
'Horoscope of the Messiah', Vermes, 270   [← *E.11.3.1; Ta.13.2.1*

3.2. *Abnormality, Deformity or Disability as a Symbol of 'The Other'*

(1) In the wilderness Anah, a descendant of Esau, meets beasts (really demons) which are half-man, half-ape or bear.

    see 1.16.b.1

    GL 1, 423; GL 5, 322 n.321, 322   [← *Cc.18.2.1; Cc.18.3.1*

(2) Arka, the third earth, is inhabited by Cainites who are dwarfs or giants with two heads.

    see 1.1.a.17; 1.16.b.2

    GL 1, 114; GL 4, 132; GL 5, 143 n.34

            [← *A.6.1.4; A.6.2.1; A.6.1.8; D.5.1.2*

(3) Solomon is told that there are heavenly bodies with a human form but heads like dogs.

    T. Sol. 18.1   [← *D.18.1.1*

(4) The Neshiah, the fifth earth, is inhabited by dwarfs without noses.

    see 1.16.b.3; 1.1.a.19

    GL 1, 114; GL 5, 143 n.36   [← *A.6.2.3; H.1.1*

(5) The dwellers of Paradise walk on their heads.

    see 1.16.b.4; 1.34.5

    GL 5, 263 n.301   [← *A.8.1.2*

(6) Adne Sadeh, 'the man of the mountain', has the form of a human being but is fastened to the ground by means of his navel cord upon which his life depends.

    see 1.16.b.7

    GL 1, 31-32; GL 5, 50 n.147-149   [← *Qa.14.1.2*

(7) Some inhabitants of Tebel, the second earth, have two heads, four arms and hands and four legs and feet, and some have the head of an ox, lion or snake on a human body, or a human head on the body of an ox, lion or snake.

    see 1.16.b.8

    GL 1, 10   [← *D.5.1.5; D.18.4.2; D.18.5.1; D.18.6.1;*

       D.21.4.1; D.21.5.1; O.5.3.2; P.5.3.1; T.5.3.1; U.5.3.1

3.3. *Abnormality, Deformity or Disability as a Symbol of Status*

3.3.a. *Abnormality, deformity or disability as a symbol of role or status*

(1) The voice of God reverberates throughout the world.
Exod. R. 5.9   [← *If.6.1.1*

(2) The angel Sandalfon, who guards the gates of heaven, towers above his fellows by so great a height that it would take 500 years to cross over it.
see 2.22.a.3
1 En. 71.1-7; *3 En.* 1.7-8; GL 2, 307; GL 3, 111; GL 5, 416-418 n.117; GL 6, 46 n.247   [← *A.6.5.11*

(3) The angel Hadarniel, who guards the gates of heaven, is sixty myriads of parasangs taller than his fellows (and breathes fiery lightning flashes).
see 2.22.a.7; 2.15.a.6
GL 3, 110; GL 6, 46 n.247   [← *A.6.5.6*

(4) Opanni'el, prince of the ophanim, has sixteen faces, the height of his body is a journey of 2,500 years, he has one hundred wings on each side and 8,766 eyes which flash lightning and fire.
see 2.15.a.4; 3.12.2
3 En. 25.2-4   [← *A.6.5.3; F.5.10.2; G.5.13.1; G.10.1.1; G.10.5.2; M.14.2.14; M.20.1.14*

(5) Serapi'el, prince of the seraphim, is as tall as the seven heavens, with a body full of eyes that resemble stars of lightning in their brightness. He has the face of an angel on the body of an eagle.
3 En. 27.3-7   [← *A.6.5.1; F.21.7.1; G.4.1.1; G.5.15.1; G.10.2.1*

(6) Soperi'el and Soperi-el, two princes of angels, have appearances like lightning; they are as tall as the seven heavens, with bodies full of eyes, as many wings as the days of the year and as big as the breadth of heaven, lips like the gates of the east and tongues as high as the sea's waves. Flames and lightning issue from their mouths, fire is kindled from their sweat and their tongues are blazing torches.
see 3.12.1
3 En. 18.25 [← *A.6.5.4; Ba.16.4.1; G.4.1.2; G.5.15.3; G.16.12.1; I.10.1.3; I.10.5.1; Ib.6.5.1; Ib.16.12.2; M.14.2.15; M.20.1.15*

(7) Kerubi'el, prince of the cherubim, is as tall and broad as the seven heavens, with a body full of burning coals, a mouth, face, tongue and eyes of fire, while flames blaze on his hands, his eyelashes are made of lightning, and his entire body is covered with wings and eyes.

 3 En. **22.3-9**   [← *A.6.3.1; A.6.5.2; A.14.5.1; A.14.10.2;*
 A.16.17.1; A.20.1.2; F.16.12.1; G.4.1.3; G.5.15.1; G.16.12.2;
       Gc.16.12.1;I.16.12.1; Ib.16.12.1; P.10.3.1

(8) Lightning and sparks stream from the bodies of the Hayyot who bear up the throne of God, and the length of each of their fingers is 8,766 parasangs.

 3 En. **29.2;** *3 En.* **33.3;** *3 En.* **34.1**   [← *A.10.5.1; Pc.6.5.1*

(9) The myriads of angels who live in Arabot, the highest of the heavens, have faces like lightning, eyes like torches of fire and arms and feet like burnished bronze.

 3 En. **35.1-2;** *3 En.* **22B.6** (Appendix)
      [← *F.16.13.1; G.16.12.4; O.16.2.2; U.16.2.2*

(10) The angel Eremiel, a great angel, has a face which shines like the sun's rays and feet like bronze.

 Apoc. Zeph. **6.11-12**   [← *F.10.1.5; U.16.2.1*

(11) The great angel Iaoel has a face like chrysolite, body and legs like sapphire and hair like snow.

 Apoc. Abr. **11.2** [← *A.16.18.2; E.11.2.1; F.16.18.1; T.16.18.1*

(12) The chief of the angels called Irin and Kadishim ('Watchers' and 'Holy Ones') is so tall that it would take 500 years to walk a distance equal to his height, and he is made of hail.

 GL 2 308; GL 5, 416-418 n.117   [← *A.6.5.8; A.16.11.1*

(13) The angel Nuriel is 300 parasangs tall and he and his retinue of fifty myriads of angels are fashioned out of fire and water.

 GL 2, 306-307; GL 5, 416-418 n.117
      [← *A.6.5.7; A.16.12.8; A.16.15.1*

(14) The two angels, Samuil and Raguil, who accompany Enoch to heaven, are very tall, with eyes like burning lamps, faces shining like the sun, fire issuing from their lips, hands whiter than snow and wings brighter than gold.

 see 2.22.b.2
 2 En. **1.4-6** (J and A); *2 En.* **3.1-3** (J and A); *2 En.* **33.6** (J and A)
   [← *A.6.5.5; F.10.1.4; G.10.1.2; Ia.10.1.1; M.14.2.4;*
        M.20.1.4; P.11.2.1

(15) The Lord of the spirits has four wings, on which a multitude of angels stand and beneath which the righteous will dwell.
 1 En. **39.7;** *1 En.* **40.1-2**   [← *M.14.2.9; M.20.1.9*

(16) The size of the angel with whom Jacob struggles is one third of the world.
 see 3.4.a.5
 Gen. R. **97.4;** *Gen. R.* **68.12**   [← *A.6.1.1*

(17) Certain superior classes of angels are created circumcised.
 see 3.11.1
 GL **5,** 66 n.6   [← *Sa.2.3.1; Sa.24.3.1*

(18) The angel Sammael, or Satan, has twelve wings before his fall instead of six (as most angels have) to indicate his important place in the heavenly hierarchy.
 GL **1, 63;** GL **5, 52 n.155;** GL **5, 84 n.34**
        [← *M.14.2.17; M.20.1.17*

(19) Adam is created circumcised.
 see 3.10.1; 3.11.3
 GL **5,** 99-100 n.78   [← *Sa.2.3.3; Sa.24.3.3*

(20) Seth is born circumcised.
 see 3.10.2; 3.11.4
 GL **1, 121;** GL **5,** 149 n. 51, 52   [← *Sa.2.3.5; Sa.24.3.5*

(21) Jacob is born circumcised.
 see 3.10.3; 3.11.5
 Gen. R. **63.7;** *Num. R.* **14.5**   [← *Sa.2.3.12; Sa.24.3.12*

(22) Gad, the son of Jacob, is born circumcised.
 see 3.10.4; 3.11.6
 GL **1, 365;** GL **5,** 297 n.185   [← *Sa.2.3.13; Sa.24.3.13*

(23) Joseph is born circumcised.
 see 3.10.5; 3.11.7
 Gen. R. **84.6;** *Num. R.* **14.5**   [← *Sa.2.3.14; Sa.24.3.14*

(24) Moses is born circumcised.
 see 3.10.6; 3.11.8
 Exod. R. **1.20, 22;** *Lev. R.* **20.1;** *Qoh. R.* **4.9** §1; *Qoh. R.* **9.2** §1;
 Deut. R. **11.10**   [← *Sa.2.3.19; Sa.24.3.19*

(25) Obed, the son of Ruth, is born circumcised.
 see 3.10.8; 3.11.10
 GL **6,** 194 n.68   [← *Sa.2.3.24; Sa.24.3.24*

(26) Shem-Melchizedek is born circumcised.
see 3.10.10; 3.11.9
Gen. R. 26.3; GL 5, 226 n.102   [← *Sa.2.3.30; Sa.24.3.30*

(27) Abraham is as tall as seventy men set on end and he can march with giant strides, each of his steps measuring four miles.
GL 1, 232; GL 5, 225 n.97; GL 5, 267 n.317
[← *A.6.5.23; T.25.1.1*

(28) The loins of Jacob are like a giant's and his arms are 'like the pillars supporting the bath-house of Tiberias'.
Gen. R. 65.17   [← *O.6.1.1; Q.6.1.1*

(29) Moses is ten cubits tall and as slender as a palm tree.
GL 6, 120 n.695   [← *A.6.5.25; A.6.4.2*

(30) When Moses and Aaron enter Pharaoh's presence they resemble angels: in stature they are like the cedars of Lebanon, their countenances radiate splendour like the sun, the pupils of their eyes are like the sphere of the morning star, their beards are like palm branches and their mouths emit flames when they open them to speak.
see 3.3.a.38; 1.14.a.6; 1.14.a.7; 1.14.f.2; 1.14.c.12; 2.24.12; 1.35.7
GL 2, 332; GL 5, 425 n.157   [← *A.6.5.25; A.6.5.26; E.6.1.1;*
E.6.1.2; E.12.10.1;E.12.10.2; F.10.1.11; F.10.1.12; Ga.10.2.1;
Ga.10.2.2; I.10.1.1; I.10.1.2

(31) Joshua is five ells tall.
GL 4, 14; GL 6, 179 n.45   [← *A.6.5.27*

(32) Saul stands head and shoulders taller than the rest of the people.
1 Sam. 9.2; 1 Sam. 10.23   [← *A.6.5.31*

(33) When a king is anointed he grows in stature: Saul's royal garments fit David even though Saul stands head and shoulders above the rest of the people.
see 1.14.c.16
Lev. R. 26.9   [← *A.6.5.32*

(34) Daniel is a giant in appearance.
Liv. Proph. (Daniel) 4.2   [← *A.6.1.31*

(35) Abraham is born with a luminous body.
Exod. R. 15.26   [← *A.10.1.12*

(36) Sarai's lustre makes the whole land of Egypt sparkle when the box in which Abram has hidden her is opened.
Gen. R. 40.5   [← *A.10.1.13*

(37) The rays which emanate from Joseph illuminate the house of Aseneth like 'the splendour of the sun'.
GL 2, 171; GL 5, 374 n.432   [← *A.10.1.14*

(38) Moses's face shines like the morning sun from one end of the world to the other. When he is born the whole house is flooded with light.
see 1.14.a.6; 1.14.a.7; 1.14.c.12; 1.35.7; 1.14.f.2; 2.24.12; 3.3.a.30
3 En. 15B.15 (Appendix); *Exod. R.* 1.20, 22; GL 2, 285
                                                                    [← *F.10.1.11*

(39) Joshua's face shines like the moon.
see 1.14.c.11
GL 3, 441; GL 6, 151 n.901   [← *F.10.1.15*

(40) The eye of the prophet Elisha is so awe-inspiring that no woman can look him in the face and live.
GL 4, 242; GL 6, 346 n.11   [← *G.25.2.2*

(41) Moses's voice is of a supernatural strength; it carries for twelve miles, from the house of study to the camp of the Israelites.
GL 6, 95 n.521   [← *If.6.1.3*

(42) The Messiah is one, two, three or nine hundred cubits tall.
Gen. R. 12.6   [← *A.6.5.33*

(43) The rays that emanate from the face of the Messiah spread a stronger lustre than the faces of Moses and Joshua.
GL 6, 141-142 n.836   [← *A.10.1.23*

(44) Before the Fall, the serpent has human hands, feet, ears and tongue (as well as an upright posture and wings), being created to be king over all the animals.
see 3.5.a.4; 1.16.a.6
Gen. R. 19.1; *Gen. R.* 20.5; *LAE (Apoc. Mos.)* 26.2-3; *LAE (Vita)* 38.1; *Deut. R.* 5.10; *Qoh. R.* 10.11 §1   [← *Ib.21.6.1; J.21.6.1; P.21.6.2; U.21.6.3*

3.3.b. *Abnormality, deformity or disability belies role or status*

(1) Moses, chosen by Yahweh to lead the Israelites out of Egypt, has a speech impediment.
Exod. 4.10; Exod. 6.12, 30; *Ezek. Trag. Exagoge* 113-115
                                                                    [← *I.23.3.3*

(2) Samson, the great hero, is lame in both feet and can only crawl.
see 4.2.d.2
Num. R. 14.9; GL 3, 204; GL 4, 47; GL 6, 76 n.398; GL 6, 207
n.115　　　　　　　　　　　　　　　　　　[← *U.23.1.2*

(3) The prophet Amos is chosen to proclaim the divine message even though he has a speech impediment.
see 4.2.d.4
Lev. R. 10.2; *Qoh. R.* 1.1 §2　　　　　　　　[← *I.23.3.9*

3.4. Abnormality, Deformity or Disability as a Symbol of Strength

3.4.a. *Abnormality, deformity or disability as a symbol of power*

(1) God is twelve-faced and lightning-eyed.
Lad. Jac. 2.17　　　　　　　　　　　　　　[← *F.5.10.1*

(2) God's lips are a furnace of fire, and his face is incandescent and emits sparks.
3 En. 39.3(A); *2 En.* 39.5(J)　　　　　[← *Ia.16.12.1; F.16.12.1*

(3) Thunder and lightning issue from God's mouth when he pronounces the first commandment.
Exod. R. 5.14　　　　　　　　　　　　　　[← *I.10.5.1*

(4) At God's command, an angel, whose size is one third of the world, can stretch his hand from heaven and touch the earth.
Exod. R. 3.6　　　　　　　　　　　　　　[← *P.6.5.1*

(5) The size of the angel with whom Jacob struggles is one third of the world.
see 3.3.a.16
Gen. R. 97.4; *Gen. R.* 68.12　　　　　　　[← *A.6.1.1*

(6) Balaam's voice is so powerful it carries as far as sixty miles.
GL 6, 133 n.781　　　　　　　　　　　　　[← *If.6.1.5*

(7) Caleb's voice is so powerful it can be heard twelve miles off and makes the three giants Ahiman, Sheshai and Talmai fall down in a swoon at the din.
GL 3, 273, 274; GL 6, 95-96 n.527　　　　　[← *If.6.1.4*

(8) Samson measures sixty ells between the shoulders.
GL 4, 47; GL 6, 206-207 n.114, 115　　　　[← *A.6.1.29; M.6.3.1*

(9) Absalom is of such gigantic proportions that a man, Abba Saul, himself of extraordinary size, standing in the eye-sockets of Absalom's skull, sinks in down to his nose. He also has an abundance of hair.

see 2.13.a.15
Num. R. **9.24**   [← *A.6.1.27; E.5.1.1; E.6.5.5*

3.4.b. *Abnormality, deformity or disability as symbol of weakness*

(1) Satan is blind at present, hence his power is weakened.

see 5.1.1; 1.14.a.1
GL 6, 449 n.57   [← *G.23.4.1*

3.5. *Abnormality, Deformity or Disability as a Symbol of Completeness*

3.5.a. *Abnormality, deformity or disability as symbol of wholeness*

(1) Adam and Eve have a horny skin (and are enveloped in a cloud of glory) before the Fall.

see 1.16.a.4
GL 1, 74; GL 5, 97 n.69   [← *A.13.10.1; A.13.10.2; B.13.10.1; B.13.10.2*

(2) Before the Fall, Adam's body is of gigantic dimensions, reaching from heaven to earth, and the same distance from east to west.

see 1.16.a.2
Lev. R. **14.1;** *Lev. R.* **18.2;** *Gen. R.* **19.9;** *Gen. R.* **21.3;** *Gen. R.* **8.1;** *Gen. R.* **24.2;** Job **20.6**   [← *A.6.1.19; A.6.3.4; A.6.5.20*

(3) In Paradise, Eve's body is of a very great height and terrible breadth, incomparable in aspect and size.

see 1.16.a.3
Apoc. Abr. **23.5**   [← *A.6.1.21; A.6.3.5; A.6.5.22*

(4) Before the Fall, the serpent has human hands, feet and ears (as well as an upright posture and wings), being created to be king over all the animals.

see 3.3.a.44; A.16.a.6
Gen. R. **19.1;** *Gen. R.* **20.5;** *LAE (Apoc. Mos.)* **26.2-3;** *Qoh. R.* **10.11 §1**   [← *P.21.6.2; U.21.6.3; J.21.6.1*

3.5.b. *Abnormality, deformity or disability as symbol of incompleteness*

[No reference in sources]

3.6. *Abnormality, Deformity or Disability as a Symbol of Moral Quality*

3.6.a. *Abnormality, deformity or disability as symbol of positive moral quality*

(1) Enoch sees God in the form of a snow-white person with hair as white as pure wool.
  1 En. **87.2**   [← *A.11.2.1; E.11.2.1*

(2) The first angels are known as the seven snow-white ones.
  1 En. **90.21-22**   [← *A.11.2.3*

(3) The archangels, who harmonize all existence, both heavenly and earthly, have faces more radiant than the radiance of the sun.
  2 En. **19.1 (J and A)**   [← *F.10.1.2*

(4) The 300 angels who look after Paradise are extraordinarily bright.
  2 En. **8.8 (J)**   [← *A.10.1.6*

(5) Methusalam's face is radiant like the sun at midday, or the morning star, when he approaches the altar to offer sacrifice.
  2 En. **69.10**   [← *F.10.1.6*

(6) Adam's beauty—which reflects the wisdom with which God had endowed him—makes his face shine; even the balls of his feet outshine the sun.
  Qoh. R. **8.1 §2;** *Lev. R.* **20.2**   [← *A.10.1.10*

(7) Although in the grave, Moses' dead body is as fresh as when he was alive.
  GL 3, 473; GL 6, 164 n.953   [← *A.25.9.1*

(8) Celestial light radiates from Jochebed's face, who risks her life to save Hebrew children.
  GL 2, 261; GL 5, 396 n.34   [← *F.10.1.18*

(9) The face of David's corpse amazes Hadrian with its high colour; and when he presses the flesh with his finger, the blood begins to circulate.
  GL 6, 412-413 n.73   [← *A.25.9.2*

(10) Elisha's body exudes fragrance—since the bodies of all the pious exude fragrance.
GL 4, 242; GL 6, 346 n.12   [← *A.10.10.3*

(11) Baruch's corpse shows no sign of decay.
GL 4, 324; GL 6, 412 n.73   [← *A.25.9.3*

(12) The bodies of the righteous in Paradise emit a shining light.
see 1.35.14
GL 1, 20   [← *A.10.1.22*

3.6.b. *Abnormality, deformity or disability as symbol of negative moral quality*

(1) The fallen angels have the appearance of darkness itself.
2 En. 7.2   [← *A.11.1.1*

(2) The angels called Grigori, who rejected the Holy Lord, have withered faces.
2 En. 18.1-5 (J and A)   [← *F.13.11.1*

(3) The Antichrist has three letters written on his forehead: A, K and T, signifying denial, rejection and the befouled dragon.
see 3.1.25; 1.3.c.1
Apoc. Dan. 9.11, 16-26   [← *Fb.13.2.3; A.6.5.13; E.6.5.1;*
Fc.16.5.1; G.10.2.6; G.18.1.1; Ic.16.1.1; O.16.1.1; O.16.2.3;
U.6.5.2

(4) The faces of the souls of intermediate sinners on their way to Sheol are greenish on account of their deeds, while the faces of the souls of the wicked are black as the bottom of a pot.
see 1.34.1
3 En. 44.5-6   [← *F.11.1.1; F.11.6.1*

(5) The size of Adam's body is reduced to one hundred ells after the Fall.
see 1.26.a.1; 1.14.d.1
Num. R. 13.2, 12; *Gen. R.* 12.6; *Gen. R.* 19.8; *Cant. R.* 3.7 §5
[← *A.6.1.20; A.6.5.21*

(6) After Cain's murder of Abel, God afflicts him with leprosy to mark him as a sinner.
see 2.2.c.4; 1.26.b.3
Num. R. 7.5; *Gen. R.* 22.12   [← *A.23.1.1*

(7) Esau is born with the figure of a serpent upon his body, 'symbol

of all that is wicked and hated of God'.
GL 1, 315; GL 5, 274 n.27   [← *A.13.1.1; B.13.1.1*

(8) Esau is hairy—and therefore demonic.
see 3.7.2; 3.10.16
Gen. R. 65.15   [← *A.11.3.3; A.13.6.3; B.18.3.1; B.13.6.3;
                                         E.4.1.3; O.13.6.1; P.13.6.1*

(9) Laban, having brought villainy to a white-hot pitch, is white; that
is, he is an albino.
see 5.1.5
Gen. R. 60.7; *Num. R.* 10.5   [← *B.11.2.2*

(10) From the bones of the evil magician, Balaam, arise several
species of harmful snakes.
GL 3, 411; GL 6, 145 n.856   [← *Va.27.1.1*

(11) Nebuchadnezzar has a dwarfish figure.
see 4.2.d.3
Gen. R. 16.4   [← *A.6.2.5*

(12) The Egyptians have huge penes.
Lev. R. 25.7   [← *Sa.6.1.1*

(13) Adikam, the Pharaoh who surpasses his father, Malol, and all
the former kings in wickedness, is ungainly in appearance, very small
and fleshy, and has a beard that flows down to his ankles.
GL 2, 298-299; GL 5, 413 n.104   [← *A.6.3.7; A.6.6.1; E.6.5.2*

3.6.c. *Abnormality, deformity or disability belies moral quality*
[No reference in sources]

3.7. *Abnormality, Deformity or Disability as Symbol of Psychological Quality*

(1) The stars, that is, the fallen angels, who lusted after the daughters
of men, have the sexual organs and hoofs of horses.
2 En. 88.1, 3   [← *P.18.5.1; Sa.18.5.1; U.18.5.1*

(2) Esau is reddish and hairy, a symbol of his sanguinary, bestial and
violent nature.
see 3.6.b.8; 3.10.16
Gen. 25.25; *Gen.* 27.11,23; *Gen. R.* 63.6,8,12; *Gen. R.* 73.8
    [← *A.13.6.3; A.11.3.3; B.18.3.1; B.13.6.3; B.11.3.1; E.4.1.3;
                                         O.13.6.1; P.13.6.1*

(3) Baladan's father, the real king of Babylon, has a dog's face.
GL 4, 275; GL 6, 367-368 n.81, 82   [← *F.18.2.3*

(4) The Persians are hairy like bears.
Kid 72a; *Est. R.* **1.17**   [← *A.13.6.4; B.18.1.1; E.18.1.1*

3.8. *Abnormality, Deformity or Disability as Symbol of Material Condition*

(1) Angels being made of fire, the finger of an angel starts a fire when he sticks it into the ground.
see 2.4.1
Gen. R. **77.2**   [← *Pc.10.3.2*

3.9. *Abnormality, Deformity or Disability as Personification of Abstract Concept*

(1) The head of God is golden—representing the Torah—and his locks are curled—representing the ruled lines in the scroll—and black as a raven—representing the letters of the Torah. He is also described as white and ruddy—white to symbolize mercy, red to symbolize justice.
Cant. R. **5.11 §1;** *Cant. R.* **5.9 §1**
          [← *A.11.2.2; A.11.3.1; D.16.3.1; E.11.1.1; E.12.3.1*

(2) The demon of the wind, Lix Tetrax, bears his face on high while the remaining part of his body crawls along like a snail.
T. Sol. **7.1**   [← *F.3.1.1*

(3) The demon called Envy has all the limbs of a man but has no head. He says to Solomon: 'I am called Envy and I delight to devour heads, being desirous to secure for myself a head; but I do not eat enough, and I am anxious to have such a head as thou hast'.
GL 4, 152; GL 6, 292 n.55   [← *D.1.1; A.2.5.1*

(4) The demon called Murder has all his limbs but no head.
see 1.13.1
T. Sol. **9.1-7**   [← *A.2.5.2; D.1.2*

(5) The man created by Ben Sira and his father after studying the Book of Yezirah for three years, has 'Emet', 'truth', written on his forehead. The man thus created tells them to erase the first letter, leaving 'Met', 'dead', and he immediately turns into dust.
GL 6, 402 n.42   [← *Fb.13.1.1*

(6) Isaiah personifies the sinful nation of Judah as a sick body covered in wounds, bruises and open sores.
        Isa. 1.5,6   [← *A.23.10.2*

(7) Death appears before Abraham and reveals his corruption, showing him two heads, one like a sword and one with the face of a serpent or dragon.
        see 2.24.20
        T. Abr. **13.13-16;** *T. Abr.* **14.1** (Recension B)
                        [← *A.23.8.1; D.5.1.6; D.17.1.1; F.18.6.2*

(8) At Abraham's request, Death shows him his face of decay and ferocity which includes seven fiery heads of dragons (representing the seven ages in which Death ravages the world) as well as faces of venomous wild beasts (asps, cobras, leopards, lions, bears, vipers), of fire, a turbulent river, a precipice and thunder and lightning (all common causes of death).
        see 2.24.19
        T. Abr. **19.5f.** [← *D.5.6.1; D.5.2.1; D.17.1.1; D.18.6.2; F.17.1.1;*
                F.17.2.1; F.17.3.1; F.17.4.1; F.17.5.1; F.17.6.1; F.17.10.1;
                                                        F.18.5.1

3.10. *Abnormality, Deformity or Disability as Portent or Omen*

(1) Adam is created circumcised.
        see 3.3.a.19; 3.11.3
        GL 5, 99-100 n.78   [← *Sa.2.3.3; Sa.24.3.3*

(2) Seth is born circumcised.
        see 3.3.a.20; 3.11.4
        GL 1, 121; GL 5, 149 n.51, 52   [← *Sa.2.3.5; Sa.24.3.5*

(3) Jacob is born circumcised.
        see 3.3.a.21; 3.11.5
        Gen. R. **63.7;** *Num. R.* **14.5**   [← *Sa.2.3.12; Sa.24.3.12*

(4) Gad, the son of Jacob, is born circumcised.
        see 3.3.a.22; 3.11.6
        GL 1, 365; GL 5, 297 n.185   [← *Sa.2.3.13; Sa.24.3.13*

(5) Joseph is born circumcised.
        see 3.3.a.23; 3.11.7
        Gen. R. **84.6;** *Num. R.* **14.5**   [← *Sa.2.3.14; Sa.24.3.14*

(6) Moses is born circumcised.
see 3.3.a.24; 3.11.8
Lev. R. **20.1;** *Exod. R.* **1.20,22;** *Qoh. R.* **4.9 §1;** *Qoh. R.* **9.2 §1**
[← *Sa.2.3.19; Sa.24.3.19*

(7) David is born circumcised as a sign that he is destined for great
things.
see 3.11.11
GL 6, 247-248 n.13   [← *Sa.2.3.25; Sa.24.3.25*

(8) Obed, the son of Ruth, is born circumcised.
see 3.3.a.25; 3.11.10
GL 6, 194 n.68   [← *Sa.2.3.24; Sa.24.3.24*

(9) Jeremiah is born circumcised as a sign that he is destined for
great things.
see 3.11.12
GL 4, 294; GL 6, 384-385 n.12   [← *Sa.2.3.31; Sa.24.3.31*

(10) Shem-Melchizedek is born circumcised.
see 3.3.a.26; 3.11.9
Gen. R. **26.3; GL 5, 226 n.102**   [← *Sa.2.3.30; Sa.24.3.30*

(11) Moses is able to speak, walk and converse with his parents from
the day of his birth. When he is three months old he prophesies.
Deut. R. **11.10**   [← *A.26.1.3*

(12) Moses' voice is like a child's although he is only a baby.
Exod. R. **1.24**   [← *If.26.1.2*

(13) Jeremiah speaks with the voice of a youth when he is barely out
of the womb.
GL 4, 294; GL 6, 385 n.13   [← *If.26.1.3*

(14) Ben Sira, the 'son of Jeremiah' speaks immediately after his
birth.
GL 6, 401 n.42   [← *If.26.1.4*

(15) Melkisedek, a child born from the dead Sopanim, is born fully
developed (like a three-year-old).
2 En. **71.17-19**   [← *A.26.1.2*

(16) Esau is born blood-red as an omen of his sanguinary nature; he
is also born hairy, and with beard and teeth.
see 3.6.b.8; 3.7.2
Gen. **25.25;** *Gen.* **27.11, 23;** *Gen. R.* **63.6, 8, 12;** *Gen. R.* **73.8**
[← *A.11.3.3; A.13.6.3; B.11.3.1; B.13.6.3; B.18.3.1;*
E.4.1.3; E.26.1.1; Ic.26.1.1

(17) Noah is born with a body white as snow, red as a rose, with long white locks, eyes like the rays of the sun, and circumcised, as a sign that he is appointed for an extraordinary destiny. While still in the hands of the midwife he praises the Lord.

1 En. **106.2-3, 5, 10-11**

[← *A.11.2.5; A.11.3.2; B.11.2.1; B.11.3.2; E.11.2.1;*
G.10.2.7; If.26.1.1; Sa.2.3.6; Sa.24.3.6

(18) David's red hair and ruddy complexion indicate that he is destined to shed blood.

see 1.12.a.31

GL 6, 247 n.13   [← *B.11.3.3; E.11.3.1*

(19) Eve has a vision in which the blood of Abel is in the hands of Cain who is gulping it down through his mouth.

LAE (Apoc. Mos.) **2.1-3;** *LAE (Vita)* **23.2**   [← *W.4.2.1*

(20) In Naphtali's prophetic vision, Judah becomes luminous like the moon, with twelve rays under his feet, while Levi captures the sun and Joseph rides to the heights of heaven on a bull with horns and eagles' wings.

T. Naph. **5.5** *(Test. XII Patr.)*   [← *A.10.1.15*

(21) Nimrod's eye is put out by a chicken hatching from an egg thrown at him by a man resembling Abraham: a dream of Nimrod which portends the annihilation of his army by Abraham and his descendants.

GL 1, 204; GL 5, 215-216 n.45   [← *G.24.1.1*

(22) Children are born with grey temples as a sign of the End.
Sib. Or. **2.221-226**   [← *E.26.1.2*

(23) Esau is born with the figure of a serpent upon his body, 'symbol of all that is wicked and hated of God'.

see 3.6.b.7

GL 1, 315; GL 5, 274 n.27   [← *A.13.1.1; B.13.1.1*

3.11 *Abnormality, Deformity or Disability as Symbol of the Covenant*

(1) Certain classes of angels are created circumcised.

see 3.3.a.17

GL 5, 66 n.6   [← *Sa.2.3.1; Sa.24.3.1*

(2) The giant Og, also known as Eliezer, Abraham's servant, is circumcised by Abraham.
    see 2.13.a.2
    GL 6, 119 n.691   [← *Sa.2.3.2; Sa.24.3.2*

(3) Adam is created circumcised.
    see 3.3.a.19; 3.10.1
    GL 5, 99-100 n.78   [← *Sa.2.3.3; Sa.24.3.3*

(4) Seth is born circumcised.
    see 3.3.a.20; 3.10.2
    GL 1, 121; GL 5, 149 n.51, 52   [← *Sa.2.3.5; Sa.24.3.5*

(5) Jacob is born circumcised.
    see 3.3.a.21; 3.10.3
    Gen. R. 63.7; Num. R. 14.5   [← *Sa.2.3.12; Sa.24.3.12*

(6) Gad, the son of Jacob, is born circumcised.
    see 3.3.a.22; 3.10.4
    GL 1, 365; GL 5, 297 n.185   [← *Sa.2.3.13; Sa.24.3.13*

(7) Joseph is born cicumcised.
    see 3.3.a.23; 3.10.5
    Gen. R. 84.6; Num. R. 14.5   [← *Sa.2.3.14; Sa.24.3.14*

(8) Moses is born circumcised.
    see 3.3.a.24; 3.10.6
    Exod. R. 1.20,22; Lev. R. 20.1; Qoh. R. 4.9 §1; Qoh. R. 9.2 §1;
    Deut. R. 11.10   [← *Sa.2.3.19; Sa.24.3.19*

(9) Shem-Melchizedek is born circumcised.
    see 3.3.a.26; 3.10.10
    Gen. R. 26.3   [← *Sa.2.3.30; Sa.24.3.30*

(10) Obed, the son of Ruth, is born circumcised.
    see 3.3.a.25; 3.10.8
    GL 6, 194 n.68   [← *Sa.2.3.24; Sa.24.3.24*

(11) David is born circumcised.
    see 3.10.7
    GL 6, 247-248 n.13   [← *Sa.2.3.25; Sa.24.3.25*

(12) Jeremiah is born circumcised.
    see 3.10.9
    GL 4, 294; GL 6, 384-385 n.12   [← *Sa.2.3.31; Sa.24.3.31*

(13) Abraham circumcises himself at God's command. Alternatively, his foreskin is removed by the bite of a scorpion.

see 2.14.a.4; 2.13.a.4; 2.31.b.1
Gen. R. **42.8;** *Gen. R.* **46.1;** *Gen. R.* **47.7;** *Gen. R.* **48.2**
[← *Sa.2.3.9; Sa.24.3.9*

(14) All the males of Abraham's household are circumcised.
see 2.13.a.5
Gen. **17.23-27;** *Gen. R.* **42.8;** *Gen. R.* **43.3** [← *Sa.2.3.7; Sa.24.3.7*

(15) The children of the people whom Abraham recaptures (when he goes to recapture Lot) are circumcised.
see 2.13.a.6
Gen. R. **43.4**   [← *Sa.2.3.10; Sa.24.3.10*

(16) Isaac is circumcised when he is eight days old.
see 2.13.a.7
Gen. **21.4;** *Gen. R.* **46.5;** *Gen. R.* **55.4**   [← *Sa.2.3.11; Sa.24.3.11*

(17) Esau is circumcised (but later removes this sign by means of an operation).
see 2.13.a.3
GL 5, 273 n.25   [← *Sa.2.3.4; Sa.24.3.4*

(18) Ephraim and Manasseh, the sons of Joseph, are circumcised.
see 2.13.a.8
GL 2, 136; GL 5, 365 n.366   [← *Sa.2.3.16; Sa.24.3.16*

(19) The sons of Machir (grandson of Joseph) are circumcised.
see 2.13.a.9
GL 2, 169; GL 5, 373 n.429   [← *Sa.2.3.17; Sa.24.3.17*

(20) When Yahweh comes to kill Moses, Zipporah takes a flint, cuts off her son's foreskin and touches Moses' genitals with it, saying that he is now truly a bridegroom of blood to her.
see 2.13.a.12; 2.15.b.10; 2.18.a.4
Exod. **4.24-26**   [← *Sa.2.3.20; Sa.24.3.20*

(21) Moses is circumcised.
see 2.13.a.10
Exod. R. **1.24**   [← *Sa.2.3.19; Sa.24.3.19*

(22) Joshua circumcises the Israelites on the Hill of Foreskins at Gilgal.
see 1.16.b.6; 2.13.a.13; 2.31.b.3
Josh. **5.2-10**   [← *Sa.2.3.22; Sa.24.3.22*

(23) Achior, the Ammonite, is circumcised after he recognizes the mighty works of God.

see 2.13.a.18
Jdt. 14.10   [← *Sa.2.3.23; Sa.24.3.23*

(**24**) All the uncircumcised boys in the territories of Israel are forcibly circumcised by Mattathias, a priest of the line of Joarib.
see 2.13.a.19
1 Macc. 2.4-6   [← *Sa.2.3.29; Sa.24.3.29*

(**25**) The babies of two women are circumcised even though this is prohibited by Antiochus Epiphanes and results in the death of the women and their children.
see 2.13.a.20
2 Macc. 6.10   [← *Sa.2.3.32; Sa.24.3.32*

(**26**) Ishmael is circumcised aged thirteen.
see 2.4.11; 2.13.a.23
Gen. 17.25-26; *Gen. R.* **46.2;** *Gen. R.* **47.7;** *Gen. R.* **48;** *Gen. R.* **55.4**   [← *Sa.2.3.8; Sa.24.3.8*

3.12 *Abnormality, Deformity or Disability as Cosmic Symbolism*

(**1**) Soperi'el and Soperi-el, two princes of angels, have wings as numerous as the days of the year.
see 3.3.a.6
3 En. **18.25**   [← *M.14.2.15; M.20.1.15*

(**2**) Opanni'el, prince of the ophanim, has 8,766 eyes, corresponding to the number of hours in a year.
see 2.15.a.4; 3.3.a.4
3 En. **25.2-4**   [← *G.5.13.1*

4. ABNORMALITY, DEFORMITY OR DISABILITY AS A NARRATIVE DEVICE

4.1 Abnormality, Deformity or Disability as Part of the Development of the Plot

4.1.a. *Abnormality, deformity or disability as part of a parable or allegory*

(1) A parable: those who are blind walk on an evil road, so thorns add wound to wound; those who can see walk on a good road and they and their clothes become scented.

    Exod. R. 30.20   [← *G.23.4.29*

(2) A blind and a lame man guard the king's orchard; the lame man rides on the blind man's back and thus they manage to steal the king's early figs. The king realizes what has happened and takes both men to task. (A parable to show that body and soul are one and that one does not sin without the other).

    Lev. R. 4.5; *Apocr. Ezek.* 1.1f.   [← *G.23.4.30; T.23.1.6*

(3) A blind man is helped home by a sighted man, then the sighted man asks the blind man to light a lamp for him (so that the blind man will be under no obligation). (A parable in which the blind man represents Israel, the sighted man God, and the kindling of lamps refers to the building of the Tabernacle.)

    Num. R. 15.5; *Exod. R.* 36.2   [← *G.23.4.28*

(4) A barren woman gives birth after thirty years but her son dies on her wedding day. Her face suddenly shines and flashes like lightning; she utters a cry and becomes invisible, but in her place there is an established city. (An allegory in which the woman is Zion, the thirty years refers to the 3,000 years of the world before the first offering, the son is Solomon who built the city, the wedding is the destruction

of Jerusalem, and the established city is Zion in all her brightness and beauty.)

4 Ezra 9.43f.; *4 Ezra* 10.25-27, 44, 50   [← *F.10.1.20; Vg.23.1.8*

(5) A foolish wight scalds himself in a boiling tub but notices that the tub becomes a little cooler by his plunge. (An allegory for Amalek's attack on the Israelites; although Amalek is defeated, the fear of the invincibility of the Israelites is gone).

see 1.14.c.25
GL 3, 62; GL 6, 25 n.147   [← *B.24.3.3*

(6) Daniel has a vision of a horn with eyes and mouth on a beast with iron teeth and bronze claws. The beast represents the future kingdom, its ten original horns, ten kings, and the horn with eyes, a succeeding king who will bring down three kings and speak against the Most High. The eyes allude to the wicked realm which looks enviously on someone's wealth.

Dan. 7.7-8,19f.; *Gen. R.* 76.6   [← *G.21.10.1; I.21.10.1*

4.1.b. *Abnormality, deformity or disability essential to the plot*

(1) A double-headed Cainite comes up when Asmodeus sticks his finger into the ground.
GL 4, 132; GL 6, 286 n.28, 29   [← *D.5.1.3*

(2) Solomon pours hot water onto one of the heads of the double-headed son of a Cainite who is claiming two shares of his father's property. As both mouths scream and proclaim that they are one, Solomon decides that the double-headed son is only a single being.
GL 4, 132; GL 6, 286 n.29   [← *D.5.1.4*

(3) Giants put their feet over the great deep at the time of the Flood and keep the water shut up.
Gen. R. 31.12   [← *A.6.1.12*

(4) Three giants, Ahiman, Sheshai and Talmai are consulted by Sarah who asks them to look into the distance to try and see Abraham and Isaac. They inform her that they see an old man with a knife in his hand and next to him a youth bound as a sacrifice.
GL 5, 256 n.259   [← *A.6.1.14*

(5) A strange creature, man above, he-goat below, is discovered and killed by Zepho, the son of Eliphaz.
GL 2, 160; GL 5, 373 n.425   [← *Cc.18.4.1*

(6) Lamech, the great grandson of Cain, is blind and kills his ancestor by accidentally shooting him with his bow and arrow.
GL 1, 116-117; GL 5, 145-147 n.42, 44   [← *G.23.4.2*

(7) Lamech is wounded and kills the man who wounded him.
Gen. 4.23-24   [← *A.24.10.1*

(8) Because Eliezer, Abraham's servant, is a giant, Laban is unable to slay him and prevent him from completing his mission: to fetch a wife for Isaac.
GL 1, 295; GL 5, 261 n.292   [← *A.6.1.22*

(9) Sarai (later called Sarah) is barren but gives birth when she is over ninety.
Gen. 11.30   [← *Vg.23.1.3*

(10) Isaac's eyes grow dim so that Jacob can come and receive the blessing in place of Esau.
see 1.7.a.4; 1.12.a.8; 1.14.a.2; 1.14.a.3; 1.14.a.4; 1.14.c.6; 1.19.b.6; 1.26.a.5; 1.26.b.12; 1.31.1; 2.6.a.7; 2.7.3; 2.20.1
Gen. R. 65.8; GL 1, 329, 412; GL 5, 282 n.75   [← *G.23.4.6*

(11) Achor, the king of Tappual, a giant of a man, is killed by Judah.
T. Jud. 3.3-4 (*Test. XII Patr.*)   [← *A.6.1.24*

(12) Belisath, a giant of a man in strength, twelve cubits tall, is killed by Jacob.
T. Jud. 3.7 (*Test. XII Patr.*)   [← *A.6.5.24*

(13) Hushim, the son of Dan, is deaf, so he does not understand the dispute about Jacob's burial. When he inquires and discovers that Esau is responsible for the interruption, he seizes a club and kills Esau.
GL 2, 154; GL 5, 371 n.422   [← *J.23.1.5*

(14) Benaiah demonstrates his prowess in battle by killing an Egyptian who is five cubits tall.
1 Chron. 11.22, 23   [← *A.6.5.29*

(15) Thermutis, the daughter of the Pharaoh, seeks relief from the burning pain caused by leprosy and boils by bathing in the Nile and thus discovers Moses. She is instantly cured when she touches the ark.
Exod. R. 1.23; GL 2, 266; GL 5, 398 n.48 [← *A.23.1.4; B.23.2.2*

(16) Two lepers, marching outside the cover of the pillar of clouds (because they are unclean), are able to witness and report the miracle

of the levelling of the mountains and the annihilation of the Amorites which the other Israelites cannot see for the clouds.
GL 6, 116 n.662   [← *A.23.1.7*

(17) Goliath, from Gath, is six cubits and one span tall.
1 Sam. 17.4   [← *A.6.5.30*

(18) The two sons of Hezekiah ridicule their father's bald head and suggest offering sacrifices to idols upon it, whereupon the enraged father drops them from his shoulders, killing one of them.
GL 4, 277; GL 6, 370 n.94   [← *E.1.4*

(19) The leprous Naaman is healed after he follows Elisha's instructions to bathe seven times in the Jordan river.
see 1.26.b.42
2 Kgs 5   [← *A.23.1.12*

(20) Elisha curses the small boys who mock his bald head and two she-bears come out of the woods and savage forty-two of the boys.
2 Kgs 2.23-24   [← *E.1.3*

(21) The medicine administered by Elijah changes the monstrous face of a woman into a beautiful one.
GL 6, 328 n.59   [← *F.22.1.1*

(22) Because there is a famine in Samaria, four lepers go over to the Aramaean camp and discover that it has been abandoned.
2 Kgs 7.3-8   [← *A.23.1.13*

(23) While Asmodeus is being led to Solomon, he sets upon the right path a blind man who is going astray.
GL 4, 167-168   [← *G.23.4.17*

(24) Although Ahasuerus is blind, his eyes become bright as soon as he directs them towards Esther.
GL 6, 474 n.149   [← *G.23.4.11*

(25) The general Sisera, who is sent to fight the Israelites, has a body of vast dimensions, and at the sound of his voice the strongest of walls fall in a heap.
GL 4, 35; GL 6, 195 n.72   [← *A.6.1.30*

(26) A deaf-mute communicates with Mordecai, who understands the language of deaf-mutes, and directs him to a locality where grain can be found.

see 2.2.c.8
GL 4, 383; GL 6, 459 n.63

[← *I.23.3.10; I.23.3.11; J.23.1.7; J.23.1.8*]

(27) When a blind Amorite kisses one of seven idols made of precious stones and at the same time touches his eyes, his sight is restored.

Ps-Philo 25.12; GL 4, 23; GL 6, 182 n.10   [← *G.23.4.14*]

(28) A leper or a man with boils who bathes in the Sea of Tiberias is instantly healed when he touches the water of Miriam's well.

Lev. R. **22.4;** *Qoh. R.* **5.8 §5**   [← *A.23.1.19; B.23.2.5*]

(29) A blind man at Shihin comes across Miriam's well (which supplied the Israelites with water while they were in the wilderness), bathes in it, and is healed.

Num. R. **18.22**   [← *G.23.4.20*]

4.1.c. *Abnormality, deformity or disability not essential to the plot*

(1) A eunuch brings food mixed with enchantments to Joseph from Pentephris's wife, but Joseph looks up and sees a frightening angel with a sword and bowl and realizes it is a trick to lead him astray.

T. Jos. **6.2** *(Test. XII Patr.)*   [← *Sa.2.1.4; Sa.24.2.4*]

(2) A eunuch tells Pentephris's wife about Joseph and she goes to see him.

T. Jos. **12.1** *(Test. XII Patr.)*   [← *Sa.2.1.5; Sa.24.2.5*]

(3) Pentephris's wife sends a eunuch to buy Joseph.

T. Jos. **16.1** *(Test. XII Patr.)*   [← *Sa.2.1.6; Sa.24.2.6*]

(4) Balaam is lame of one foot (and later becomes blind of one eye).

GL 3, 359; GL 6, 126 n.731   [← *U.23.1.1*]

(5) The king of Israel is served by eunuchs.

2 Kgs 8.6   [← *Sa.2.1.14; Sa.24.2.14*]

(6) At Jehu's command, two or three eunuchs throw Jezebel out of the window.

2 Kgs 9.32-33   [← *Sa.2.1.15; Sa.24.2.15*]

(7) A eunuch works for King Ahab and delivers messages for him.

1 Kgs 22.19   [← *Sa.2.1.13; Sa.24.2.13*]

(8) The eunuchs of King Jehoiachim are deported to Babylon after the siege of Jerusalem.

2 Kgs 24.12,15   [← *Sa.2.1.16; Sa.24.2.16*

(9) A eunuch who is in command of the fighting men is taken prisoner by Nebuzaradan, an officer of the king of Babylon who enters Jerusalem to sack it.

2 Kgs 25.19; Jer. 52.25   [← *Sa.2.1.11; Sa.24.2.11*

(10) Ashpenaz, the chief eunuch of Nebuchadnezzar, is ordered to select from the Israelites a certain number of boys suitable for service in the palace of the king.

Dan. 1.3-21   [← *Sa.2.1.28; Sa.24.2.28*

(11) Bigthan and Teresh, two of King Ahasuerus's eunuchs, who guard the palace, are preparing to assassinate the king until Mordecai uncovers their plot.

Est. Introduction 1m-1r   [← *Sa.2.1.20; Sa.24.2.20*

(12) Hathach, a eunuch whom the king has appointed to wait on Esther, is sent by her to Mordecai to obtain information.

Est. 4.5   [← *Sa.2.1.22; Sa.24.2.22*

(13) Harbona is a eunuch who attends King Ahasuerus and reminds the king that Haman has erected a gallows.

Est. 7.9   [← *Sa.2.1.18; Sa.24.2.18*

(14) The seven eunuchs (Mehuman, Biztha, Harbona, Bigtha, Abagtha, Zethar and Carkas) who attend King Ahasuerus, are commanded to bring Queen Vashti, who wishes to display her beauty, before the king.

Est. 1.10-11   [← *Sa.2.1.17; Sa.24.2.17*

(15) Ebed-melech, the Cushite, a eunuch attached to the palace, intervenes to save Jeremiah's life and helps rescue him from the well.

Jer. 38.7-13   [← *Sa.2.1.23; Sa.24.2.23*

(16) Johanan brings back eunuchs, as well as men, women and children, from Gibeon.

Jer. 41.16   [← *Sa.2.1.10; Sa.24.2.10*

(17) 'Eunuchs, priests and nobles of Judah and Jerusalem and all the people of the country who have "passed between the parts of the calf." will be put by Yahweh into the power of their enemies' says Yahweh to Jeremiah.

Jer. 34.19   [← *Sa.2.1.29; Sa.24.2.29*

(18) Eunuchs leave Jerusalem together with King Jeconiah and the queen mother, the nobility of Judah and Jerusalem and the blacksmiths and metal workers.

Jer. 29.2   [← *Sa.2.1.12; Sa.24.2.12*

4.2. *Abnormality, Deformity or Disability to Introduce a Certain Narrative Mode into the Tale*

4.2.a. *Abnormality, deformity or disability to introduce the ridiculous*

[No reference in sources]

4.2.b. *Abnormality, deformity or disability to introduce the humorous*

[No reference in sources]

4.2.c. *Abnormality, deformity or disability to introduce the marvellous*

(1) Hannah, Samuel's mother and wife of Elkanah, is barren until the age of 130 when she gives birth to a son.

   1 Sam. 1.5f.; GL 4, 58-59; GL 6, 215-218 n.6-15   [← *Vg.23.1.5*

(2) Zelalponit, Samson's mother, is sterile for most of her life but bears a son, Samson, when she has given up hope of having children.

   Judg. 13.2; *Num. R.* **10.5**   [← *Vg.23.1.6*

(3) Two tears falling from the eyes of Jeremiah become fountains.

   GL 6, 405 n.47   [← *Gf.27.5.1*

(4) When Ruth the Moabitess is forty years old she looks like a girl of fourteen.

   Ruth R. **4.4**   [← *A.26.3.2*

(5) Sopanim, the wife of Nir, is sterile but conceives when she is past the menopause, without contact with her husband.

   2 En. 71.1-2   [← *Vg.23.1.7*

4.2.d. *Abnormality, deformity or disability to introduce paradox*

(1) Although the body of Michael is made of fire and Gabriel's of snow, or vice versa, they can stand next to each other without injury.

   see 3.1.5

   Num. R. **12.8;** *Deut. R.* **5.12;** *Cant. R.* **3.11 §1**

                    [← *A.16.10.1; A.16.12.1; A.16.10.2; A.16.12.2*

(2) Samson, the great hero, is maimed in both feet.
   see 3.3.b.2
   Num. R. **14.9**   [← *U.23.1.2*

(3) Though ruler of the whole world, Nebuchadnezzar has a dwarfish figure.
   see 3.6.b.11
   GL 6, 422 n.96   [← *A.6.2.5*

(4) God chooses to proclaim his divine message through Amos who has a speech impediment.
   see 3.3.b.3
   Lev. R. **10.2;** *Qoh. R.* **1.1** §2   [← *I.23.3.9*

4.2.e. *Abnormality, deformity or disability to introduce the tragic*
                     [No reference in sources]

5. ABNORMALITY, DEFORMITY OR DISABILITY RELATED TO ETYMOLOGY

5.1 *Abnormality, Deformity or Disability Suggested by Etymology*

(1) The angel Sammael is known as 'the blind one' who does not see the pious, because of the similarity between his name and the word for blind man, 'suma'.

see 1.14.a.1; 3.4.b.1
GL 5, 121 n.116   [← *G.23.4.1*

(2) A confusion between the Hebrew words for skin and light—both pronounced 'or' but spelt with a different initial letter—has led to the legend that God made garments of light not skin, for Adam and Eve.

see 1.19.b.1
Gen. R. 20.12   [← *A.10.1.9; A.10.1.11*

(3) The similarities between the name Cain, 'Qayin', and the word 'Kiyun' or 'Kaiwan', signifying the planet Saturn, has given rise to the legend about Cain's shining face which is found in *PRE* 21 and y. Targ. on Gen. 4.1.

see 1.1.b.7
LAE (Apoc. Mos.) 1.1-3; *LAE (Vita)* 21.3; GL 1, 105-106; GL 5, 133 n.3; GL 5, 135 n.6; GL 5, 137 n.13   [← *F.10.1.7*

(4) The interpretation of 'karan or', he cast forth or radiated light, as 'keren or', horns of light, has led to the iconographical motif of Moses with horns. (Jerome mistranslated the word as 'cornuta', horned, and this became the standard phrasing in the Latin Bible, later called the Vulgate.)

Mellinkoff, 1; 79f.; Exod. 34.29, 35   [← *Fb.14.2.3*

(5) The name Laban means white, hence the legend that he is an albino.

see 3.6.b.9
Gen. R. 60.7; *Num. R.* 10.5   [← *B.11.2.2*

(6) The fact that the consonants of the name Salem can also mean whole or complete has given rise to the legend that the king of Salem was born complete, in other words, already circumcised.
Gen. R. 43.6   [← *Sa.2.3.27; Sa.24.3.27*

5.2 Abnormality, Deformity or Disability Suggests Name

(1) Barak, the modest husband of Deborah, who makes the lamps for the sanctuary, has a face which shines like lightning (hence his name, which means lightning).
GL 6, 195 n.73   [← *F.10.1.17*

In this appendix, three points from the introduction are elaborated upon: the sources and argument inherent in the index, its relation to structural analysis, and finally, the directions future studies in this subject might take.

The present thesis derives from two main sources, Stith Thompson's *Motif-Index of Folk Literature*, and a dissertation of my own, entitled *Lame Gods*. Stith Thompson analyses tales according to 'constituent motifs' and considers a tale to be the sum of these motifs. As his intention was to include all known motifs (and in fact, motif-indexes specializing in the material from specific areas have been added to his own more general compilation) the ambition is clearly stupendous. The idea of dividing a tale into its various parts derives from linguistics: just as a language can be divided up into constituent units (phonemes, morphemes, sememes), so a myth may be regarded as being built up from constituent mythemes. While structuralists have criticised Stith Thompson's methodology (indeed, Alan Dundes has compared it to that of a 'philological atomist. . . who thought that language was simply an inventory or mechanical sum of the units used in speaking')[1], maintaining that it is the relationship of parts to each other and to the whole that is important, I think that they have misunderstood his intention. Rather than attempting to elucidate the underlying meaning of a tale through an analysis of its structure, he was merely creating a reference work, a thesaurus of motifs that would serve as a preliminary for any study of structure or meaning. This has also been my own intention. I have concentrated, however, on a single group of motifs with an identity and a persistency of their own, but which under Stith Thompson are frequently either subsumed in an arbitrary manner or impossible to classify with adequate specificity. Thus my own motif-index can be seen as an elaboration and a coherent and logical presentation of one aspect of Stith Thompson's more general work. At the same time, the combination of each motif with the reason or reasons for its presence within the tale, adds another dimension: instead of a mere list of motifs, it represents an analysis of motifs.

In my dissertation *Lame Gods*, rather than taking a synoptic view of the entire world of deformities, I concentrated on a single type, lameness, whether as a permanent feature of a god or a hero, or as a temporary or imaginary aberration as manifested, for example, in the ritual of the limping dance. Even the study of a single motif soon revealed the inadequacy of a one-dimensional theory or approach. Not only did the motif of 'lameness' prove itself to be far from simple (since it could be subdivided into distinct elements such as deformity of the foot, the ankle, the knee or

---

1. *The Morphology of North American Indian Folktales* (Folklore Fellows Communications, 195; Helsinki: Suomalainen), p. 39

the thigh, or of one or both of these), but it could only be understood in the context of a whole network of both 'natural' and culture-specific associations, none of which could be linked exclusively to the 'symbol' or 'archetype' of lameness. As a result of this study it was evident that a general theory of the 'meaning' even of a single motif should be regarded with extreme suspicion. As will become clear later, such theories as have been made, whether on a structuralist, linguistic or psychological basis, adopt either an extreme reductionism or simply gloss over the details of their evidence. Before any theory about the deformities of characters in folk tales can be made, the material upon which it is to be based must be made visible both in its entirety and in detail. For the present work, therefore, I decided upon what may be termed a phenomenology of the abnormalities, deformities, and disabilities of the human form as the only way to begin to investigate such a new and wide area of study.

My initial approach was entirely pragmatic. Rather than confining myself to the cultural limitations imposed, for reasons of space and time, on the present work, I studied narratives of all genres and from different regions of the world, including American Indian myths, Greek legends, Chinese, Celtic and Scandinavian folklore, as well as more specifically Jewish, Christian and Islamic material. It soon became clear that relevant motifs cross all boundaries of genre, culture and geography—while at the same time there was no clear indication of a universality or consistency of meaning, or, for that matter, a significant predominance of certain deformities. Given this fluidity in the material under scrutiny, it became necessary to take as a starting point the only fixed element present: the human body. For a systematic approach I first divided the body into its constituent parts, and secondly, drawing on my knowledge of folk tales as well as on my own imagination, deduced all possible permutations of the anatomy: size, shape, colour, substance, number of parts, place on body, animal attributes, and so on. These are divided into 'discrete' parts: no hierarchy or structural interdependence seemed relevant or possible. At this point, several options were discarded. A brief look at medical history showed that a possible division between natural and imaginary abnormalities, deformities, and disabilities would be arbitrary and impractical. Similarly, the distinction between permanent and temporary, and between voluntary and involuntary, seemed irrelevant.

The second part of the index lists the reasons for the abnormalities, deformities and disabilities. The aim was to be comprehensive, to create a definitive index capable of incorporating every possible circumstance; and since the reasons for motifs do not form a discrete whole such as the human body, which limits the first part of the index, but are limited only by the imagination of the storyteller, the sections into which the second part is divided are, to a certain extent, 'open'. To anticipate any surprises, both very specific categories and more abstract ones were used, the latter serving as a kind of 'catchment area' for unpredictable idiosyncracies. There are three main sections, abnormality as a result, as a means and as a symbol, and two minor ones for those motifs without stated or implicit reasons. The 'cradle to grave' (or rather, 'pre-conception to afterlife') scenario provides a rough framework for the first section; the second is necessarily more heterogeneous, but follows the range of basic human needs and desires. It should be stressed once more that my aim has been encyclopaedic, not taxonomic. There is no other significance in my arrangement than that all relevant motifs can find a place in it with an adequate attention to detail and without unnecessary repetition and overlap.

From the preceding description, it should be clear that the relationship between my own classificatory system and others, including structural analysis, is an oblique one. I have already discussed the shortcomings of Stith Thompson's index as far as the reasons for the presence of motifs is concerned, even though they are sometimes included in the description. Vladimir Propp, on the other hand, is very much concerned[1] with reasons, or, as he would express it, functions, of the tale roles. These functions, such as 'absentation', 'interdiction' and so on, are what propel the plot forward, and the sequence of functions, he argues, is always identical: all fairy tales are therefore of one type with regard to their structure. His method is structural in that each function is considered in relation to preceding and subsequent functions as well as the tale as a whole. One of the purposes of Propp's analysis is to create a model by means of which different tales and their variants can be compared and contrasted, even when a similarity of structure is obscured by the varying contents of the plots.

The irreconcilable difference between Propp's analysis and my own approach is obvious. Unlike Propp's, my attention is focused on only one aspect of the narrative: the abnormal appearance of the dramatis personae, and the function this abnormality serves in the plot. For Propp, however, it is these very dramatis personae, or 'tale roles', that are variables, changing their names and attributes from tale to tale. Propp does construct a model of the spheres of action of the tale roles (for instance, the sphere of action of the villain constitutes villainy) but is of necessity less interested in their physical attributes, except when they fulfill a tale function such as function 17 (branding) or function 29 (transfiguration). Moreover, Propp looks at a very narrow genre: the European Märchen, or fairy tale. It is doubtful whether his method could be extended to include all genres. My intention, on the other hand, has been to classify abormalities, deformities and disabilities of characters in traditional literature, whatever the genre. Nevertheless, could Propp's list of functions have been adapted? Certainly a lack (function 9) may include the lack of an eye or an arm, forcing the protagonist to travel to a distant place to retrieve the eye or buy an artificial limb. Then again, emaciation (lack of food) may initiate the action of a tale. But this would mean that a large proportion of the abnormalities, deformities and disabilities included in my index would have to be subsumed under Propp's ninth function. In other words, one would have to expand Propp's ninth function by subdivision to include all these possible motifs: and this would surely be helpful neither of Propp's analysis of the tale functions, nor for understanding the function of the motifs in the narrative. Conversely, branding (function 17) can be the means whereby a hero or a villain is recognized, as Propp suggests, but a brief look at any body of folk tales reveals that it may just as well be the result of torture, or an accident or a battle, or a means of repentance, mockery or punishment. In other words, it would be necessary

---

1.   *Morphology of the Folktale* (trans. L. Scott; rev. and ed. L.A. Wagner; Austin, TX: University of Texas Press, 2nd edn, 1979 [1928]).

both to expand each function and to add many more: thus little of the initial structure would be left intact. To sum up, I am concerned with only one aspect of the tale; each of the motifs in my index is both an interchangable variable in that it could occur anywhere in a tale, or in any genre (whereas the functions and the sequence of functions in Propp are supposed to be fixed); and a decription of a unique narrative fragment (whereas Propp's method, like all structural analysis, consists in divesting the narrative of its uniqueness).

Other structural models of the tale, such as those of Rina Drory, Pierre and Elli Köngäs Maranda, A.J. Greimas and Alan Dundes[1] are of little use for my purposes for similar reasons. Structural analysis can only be applied to a structure, that is, a complete entity or form. It may be employed to analyse a single tale, or a single genre such as the riddle, the joke or the proverb.

There is one structuralist who has discussed the meaning of abnormalities, deformities and disabilities of the human form in myth and folktale and that is Claude Lévi-Strauss. In *An Introduction to a Science of Mythology*, he proposes that the structure of myths of origin (and, by extension, all myths) involves a series of oppositions which are resolved through mediating agents, in accordance with Hegel's paradigm of thesis, antithesis and synthesis. The function of myth, he argues, is to create a model by means of which a community can resolve the disjunction that exists between tradition and renewal, nature and culture. Thus, cultural innovations, such as the art of cooking and fire making, are thought to provoke tensions that can be eased only if myths are created which introduce a mediating agent which, while not exactly reconciling the opposing terms, demonstrates a similarity of structure which serves as a makeshift bridge between them. To discover the underlying structure of a myth it must be divided into mythemes (akin to motifs) which must then be tabulated and read both diachronically and synchronically. To justify this twofold method, Lévi-Strauss uses the analogy of music, where harmony and melody are related in a similar manner. The abnormalities, deformities and disabilities that he encounters are invariably interpreted as a manifestation or a means of mediation. I do not intend here to analyse the validity of Lévi-Strauss's brilliant hypothesis, but only to show its limitations with regard to the present subject. He is concerned with the function of myths within society rather than with the purely narrative functions of motifs. In other words, while this motif-index can be used as a comparative tool in Lévi-Strauss's sense (allowing an examination of the prevalence of certain motifs in distinct regions, or of the combination of motifs and stated reasons for these motifs in relation to historical or cultural factors), a firm foundation must be laid by a detailed analysis of narrative functions. The neglect of this leads to glaring

1.   Rina Drory, 'Ali Baba and the Forty Thieves: An Attempt at a Model for the Narrative Structure of the Reward and Punishment Fairy Tale', pp. 31ff. Q.H. Jason and D. Segal (eds.), *Patterns in Oral Literature* (The Hague: Mouton, 1977); Algirdas J. Greimas *Sémantique structurale* (Paris: Larousse, 1966); Dundes, *Morphology of North American Folktales*; E. and P. Maranda (eds.), *Structural Analysis of Oral Tradition* (Philadelphia: University of Pennsylvania Press, 1971).

errors in Lévi-Strauss's work. In his essay 'The Structural Study of Myths'[1] he opposes the lameness of Oedipus, his father and grandfather, due, he thinks, to their emergence from the earth and indicative of the underrating of blood relations, with the overrating of blood relations expressed by the marriage of Oedipus to his mother, and the burying of Polynices by his sister Antigone in spite of a prohibition. However, just because certain mythical figures who emerge from the earth are lame, this is no reason to assert that all lame characters have acquired their disability in this way, or that emergence from the earth invariably leads to lameness. Indeed, the Spartoi, who are an important part of his analysis, are not said to be lame, even though they do emerge from the earth. Often he ignores the stated reason for an abnormality in favour of a more abstract one that fits his schema. Ostensibly commenting on the nature of myth, Lévi-Strauss describes his own methodology: ' . . . a discrete system is produced by the destruction of certain elements or their removal from the original whole'[2] He continues, 'Mythological figures who are blind or lame, one-eyed or one-armed are familiar the world over; and we find them disturbing because we believe their condition to be one of deficiency. But just as a system that has been made discrete through the removal of certain elements becomes logically richer, although numerically poorer, so myths often confer a positive significance on the disabled and the sick, who embody modes of mediation.' This may be the case; but just as often the myth about the disabled, the deformed, and the sick simply reflects what no amount of interpretation can disguise, the misery of the real thing.

Although I will not discuss any of the 'monolithic' theories that exist about specific abnormalities of folktale characters or about the mechanism by which these are formed, it is interesting to note that many of the reasons for deformities included in this index anticipate certain theories, whether of anthropological or psychological origin. Of the psychological theories that deal with deformities, I need only mention Jung's study of the androgyne in religion and alchemy as a symbol of perfection or wholeness (Category 3.5.a), Bruno Bettelheim's view of the beast-man in dreams and fairy tales as a symbol of a negative moral quality (Category 3.6.b), and Freud's opinion of the myth of the toothed vagina as a manifestation of a subconscious fear of the female (Category 3.7: Symbol of psychological quality).[3] There are many anthropological studies that mention abnormalities, deformities or disabilities in passing. I single out Lévi-Strauss's view of the limping dance of the American Indians as a technique to alter the balance of the cosmos and thereby cause rain (Category 2.11.d); Deonne's theory of the multiplication of bodily organs, ears,

---

1. In *Structural Anthropology* (trans. C. Jacobson and B. Grundfest Schoef; New York: Basic Books, 1963).

2. *The Raw and the Cooked* (trans. J. and D. Weightman; New York: Harper & Row, 1975), p. 53.

3. C.G. Jung, *Mysterium Coniunctionis* (trans. R.F.C.Hull; New York: Princeton University Press, 1977 [1955-56]; *idem., Psychology and Alchemy*; Bruno Bettelheim *The Uses of Enchantment*; C.J. Campbell, *The Masks of God*. I. *Primitive Mythology,* pp. 73-77.

arms and legs as well as their reduction to unity by a single organ or limb replacing one normally double as a means of obtaining magical powers (Category 2.11.a); Mary Douglas's view of abnormality as a symbol of the Other, blessed with a special kind of power, whether numinous or demonic (category 3.2 and 3.4.a); Cook's interpretation of the Cyclops as a symbol of the sun (Category 3.12); and Dumézil's conception of the single eye of the seer and the single hand of the lawgiver in Indo-European thought as a symbol of status (Category 3.3.a).[1]

This index is a comprehensive record including, or allowing space to include, every conceivable type of deformity and every possible reason for the deformity in the tale. It identifies an almost virgin territory, namely, the place of the human body in the imagination. While this subject has been broached by a number of writers, for example, Max Lüthi[2] and Mary Douglas,[3] it lacked the broad perspective and wealth of information needed for a thorough analysis. As such, this work is of use to all those from the fields of folklore, anthropology, literature and comparative religion who would study either a particular deformity and the significance of its occurrence, a custom or ritual involving deformities or mutilations of the body, or a particular tale or symbol including them. Documenting a vast range of deformities and their reasons, it deflates any theories based on an inadmissible simplification of the information presented. The index also provides a tool for investigating the historical, social and cultural perspectives of a region or a people by revealing the tension between the imagination and reality. In the area studied here, the prevalence of the disease of leprosy and the ritual of circumcision would provide an interesting basis for such a study. Of particular interest would be a correlation of abnormalities, deformities and disabilities documented in historical or medical records with their counterparts in folk literature. Future developments of the present work would involve the introduction of material from different cultures. This would make possible a comparative study of the concept of the body and the forms of the imagination, perhaps by means of statistical analysis. This in turn may make it possible to draw some conclusions about both the uniqueness and similarity of cultures.

1. Lévi-Strauss, *From Honey to Ashes*. Introduction to a Science of Mythology, II (trans. J. & D. Weightman; New York: Harper & Row, 1973), pp. 460-67; Mary Douglas, *Purity and Danger* (London: Routledge & Kegan Paul, 1984 [1966].); W. Deonne, 'Un divertissement de table "à cloche-pied', *Latomus* 40 (1959), pp. 37-3;. G. Dumézil, *Gods of the Ancient Norsemen* (ed. Einar Haugen; Berkley: University of California Press, 1973 [1959]); A.B. Cook, *Zeus*, I (3 vols.; Cambridge: Cambridge University Press, 1914).

2. In *The Fairy Tale as an Art Form and Portrait of Man* (trans. J. Erickson; Bloomington, IN: Indiana University Press, 1987).

3. In *Natural Symbols* (Harmondsworth: Penguin, 1973).

BIBLIOGRAPHY

Aarne, A.A., and Stith Thompson, *The Types of the Folktale* (2nd rev. edn; Folklore
Fellows Communications, 184; Helsinki: Academia Scientiarum Fennica, 1961).
Alter, R., *The Art of Biblical Narrative* (London: George Allen & Unwin, 1968).
Aptowitzer, V., *Kain und Abel in der Aggada der Apokryphen, der hellenistischen,
christlichen und mohammedanischen Literatur* (Vienna and Leipzig: R. Loewit, 1922).
Aycock, D.A., 'The Fate of Lot's Wife', in *Structuralist Interpretations of Biblical Myth*
(ed. Edmund Leach and D. A. Aycock; Cambridge: Cambridge University Press,
1983).
—'The Mark of Cain', in *Structuralist Interpretations of Biblical Myth* (ed. Edmund Leach
and D.A. Aycock; Cambridge: Cambridge University Press, 1983).
Babcock, B. (ed.), *The Reversible World* (Ithaca, NY: Cornell University Press, 1978).
Baring-Gould, S., *Curious Myths of the Middle Ages* (London: Rivingtons, 1876).
Barton, G.A., 'Semitic Circumcision', in *The Encyclopaedia of Religion and Ethics* (ed.
J. Hastings; Edinburgh: T. & T. Clark, 1910), pp. 679-80.
Bateson, G., *Naven* (Stanford: Stanford University Press, 1958 [1936]).
Beidelman, T.O., 'Circumcision', in *The Encyclopedia of Religion*, III (ed. Mircea Eliade;
New York: Collier & Macmillan, 1987), pp. 511-14.
Ben-Amos, D., and K. Goldstein (eds.), *Folklore: Performance and Communication* (The
Hague: Mouton, 1975).
Ben-Amos, D. (ed.), *Folklore Genres* (Publications of the American Folklore Society, 26;
Austin, TX: University of Texas Press, 1976).
Benwell, G., and A. Waugh, *Sea Enchantress* (London: Hutchinson, 1961).
Besserman, L.L., *The Legend of Job in the Middle Ages* (Cambridge, MA: Harvard
University Press, 1979).
Bet HaMidrash, collected by A. Jellinek (6 vols.; Jerusalem: Wahrmann Books, 3rd edn,
1967 [Vienna, 1887]).
Bettelheim, B., *The Uses of Enchantment* (London: Thames & Hudson, 1976).
Bowers, R.H., *The Legend of Jonah* (The Hague: Martinus Nijhoff, 1971).
Brown, R.N., 'Midrashim as Oral Traditions', *HUCA* 47, 1976, pp. 181-189.
Buchler, I.R., and H.A. Selby, *A Formal Study of Myth* (Center for Intercultural Studies in
Folklore and Oral History Monograph Series, 1; Austin, TX: University of Texas
Press, 1968).
Campbell, J., *The Masks of God* (4 vols.; New York: Viking, 1959–68).
Céard, J., *La nature et les prodiges* (Travaux d'humanisme et renaissance, 158; Geneva:
Droz, 1977).
Charlesworth, J.H. (ed.), *The Old Testament Pseudepigrapha* (2 vols.; London: Darton,
Longman & Todd, 1983).

Childs, B.S., *Myth and Reality in the Old Testament* (Studies in Biblical Theology, 27; London: SCM Press, 1960).

'Circumcision', *Enc Jud* V (1971), pp. 567-76.

Cirlot, J.E., *A Dictionary of Symbols* (trans. J. Sage; New York: Thames & Hudson, 1962).

Cohen, P.S., 'Theories of Myth', *Man* 4 (London, 1969), pp. 337-53.

Cook, A.B., *Zeus*, I (3 vols.; Cambridge: Cambridge University Press, 1914).

Crossley-Holland, K.(trans.), *The Exeter Book of Riddles* (Harmondsworth: Penguin, 1979).

Davidson, G., *A Dictionary of Angels* (London: Collier & Macmillan, 1967).

Dégh, L., H. Glassie and F.J. Oinas (eds.), *A Festschrift for Richard M. Dorson. Folklore Today* (Research Centre for Language and Semiotic Studies; Bloomington, IN: Indiana University Press, 1976).

Delcourt, M., *Héphaistos, ou la légende du magicien* (Paris: Société d'L'édition 'Les Belles Lettres', 1957).

—*Hermaphrodite* (Paris: Presses Universitaires de France, 1956).

Deonne, W., *Le symbolisme de l'oeil* (Paris: Éditions E. de Boccard, École Français d'Athènes Fasc. XV, 1965).

—'Un divertissement de table "à cloche-pied" ', *Latomus* 40 (1959), pp. 1-39.

—'Essai sur la genèse des monstres dans l'art', *Revue des études grecques* 28 (1971 [1915]).

Diel, P., *Le symbolisme dans la mythologie grecque* (Paris: Payot, 1952).

Douglas, M., *Natural Symbols* (Harmondsworth: Penguin, 1973).

—*Purity and Danger* (London: Routledge and Kegan Paul, 1984 [1966]).

Dowson, J., *A Classical Dictionary of Hindu Mythology and Religion, Geography, History and Literature* (London: Kegan Paul, Trench, Truebner and Co., 3rd edn, 1891).

Drory, R., 'Ali Baba and the Forty Thieves: An Attempt at a Model for the Narrative Structure of the Reward and Punishment Fairy Tale', in H. Jason and D. Segal (eds.), *Patterns in Oral Literature* (The Hague: Mouton, 1977), pp. 31ff.

Dumézil, G., *Gods of the Ancient Norsemen* (ed. Einar Haugen, Berkeley, CA: University of California Press, 1973 [1959]).

Dundes, A., *Analytical Essays in Folklore* (The Hague: Mouton, 1975).

—*The Morphology of North American Indian Folktales* (Folklore Fellows Communications, 195; Helsinki: Suomalainen, 1964).

—(ed.) *Sacred Narrative* (Berkeley, CA: University of California Press, 1984).

—(ed.) *Varia Folklorica* (Papers from the 9th Congress of Anthropological and Ethnological Sciences, Chicago 1973; The Hague: Mouton, 1978).

Eliade, M., *A History of Religious Ideas*, I & II (trans. W.R. Trask; 3 vols.; Chicago: Chicago University Press, 1978–86).

—*Patterns in Comparative Religion* (London: Sheed & Ward, 1979 [1958]).

—*The Sacred and the Profane* (trans. W.R. Trask; New York: Harcourt Brace Jovanovich, 1959 [1957]).

—*Shamanism* (trans. W.R. Trask; New York: Princeton University Press, 1972 [1951]).

—'Spirit, Light and Seed', in *Occultism, Witchcraft and Cultural Fashions* (Chicago: University of Chicago Press, 1976).

Epstein, Rabbi Dr I. (ed. and trans.), *The Babylonian Talmud* (London: Soncino Press, 1956).

Evans-Pritchard, E.E., *Theories of Primitive Religion* (Oxford: Clarendon Press, 1977 [1965]).

Firth, R., *Symbols: Public and Private* (London: George Allen Unwin, 1973).

Fohrer, G., *Introduction to the Old Testament* (trans. D.E. Green; London: SPCK, 1968).

Fokkelman, J.P., *Narrative Art in Genesis* (Assen: Van Gorcum, 1975).

Forsyth, N., 'More Notes on the World Upside Down', *Journal of American Folklore* 92 (1979), p. 65.

Frazer, J.G., *Folklore in the Old Testament* (3 vols.; London: Macmillan, 1918).

—*The Golden Bough* (London, abr. edn, 1971 [1922]).

Friedlaender, M., 'L'Anti-Messie', *REJ* 38 (1899).

Friedman, Rabbi Dr. H., and M. Simon (trans. and ed.), *The Midrash*, (9 vols.; London: Soncino Press, 1939).

Friedman, J.B., *The Monstrous Races in Medieval Art and Thought* (Cambridge, MA: Harvard University Press, 1981).

Gaer, J., *The Lore of the Old Testament* (Boston: Little, Brown, 1952).

Gennep, A. van, *The Rites of Passage* (trans. M.B. Vizedom and G.L. Caffe; London: Routledge & Kegan Paul, 1977 [1908]).

Gaster, M., *The Exempla of the Rabbis* (London: The Asia Publishing Co., 1924).

—*Studies and Texts in Folklore, Magic, Medieval Romance, Hebrew Apocrypha and Samaritan Archaeology* (3 vols.; London: Maggs, 1925–28).

Gaster, T.H., *Myth, Legend and Custom in the Old Testament* (New York: Harper and Row, 1969).

—*Thespis* (New York: Schumann, 1950).

Ginzberg, L., *The Legends of the Jews* (trans. H. Szold; 7 vols.; Philadelphia: The Jewish Publication Society of America, 1909–38).

—*On Jewish Law and Lore* (Philadelphia: The Jewish Publication Society of America, 1955).

Girard, R., 'Violence and Representation in the Mythical Text', in *To Double Business Bound* (Baltimore: Johns Hopkins University Press, 1978), pp. 178-98.

—*Violence and the Sacred* (trans. P. Gregory; Baltimore: Johns Hopkins University Press, 1977).

Goebel, F.M., *Jüdische Motive im märchenhaften Erzählungsgut* (Gleiwitz: Greifswald doctoral dissertation, 1932).

Gonzalez-Crussi, F., *Notes of an Anatomist* (London: Picador, 1986).

Goodenough, E.R., *Jewish Symbols in the Greco-Roman Period* (13 vols.; New York: Pantheon Books, 1953–68).

Gordon, C.H., 'Homer and the Bible', *HUCA* 26 (1955).

Gottwald, N.K., *The Hebrew Bible: A Socio-Literary Introduction* (Philadelphia: Fortress Press, 1985).

Graves, R., *The White Goddess* (London: Faber & Faber, 1971 [1961]).

Graves, R., and R. Patai, *Hebrew Myths* (London: Cassell, 1964).

Greimas, A.J., *Sémantique structurale: recherche de méthode* (Paris: Larousse, 1966).

Gunkel, H., *Das Märchen im Alten Testament* (Tübingen: Mohr, 1917).

Hartman, G.H., and S. Budick, *Midrash and Literature* (New Haven: Yale University Press, 1986).

Hayman, P. (trans.), 'Sefer Yetsira', *Shadow* 3.1, (1986) pp. 20-38.

Hays, P., *The Limping Hero: Grotesques in Literature* (New York: New York University Press, 1971).

Heinemann, J., and S. Werses, *Studies in Hebrew Narrative Art through the Ages* (Scripta Hierosolymitana, 27; Jerusalem: Magnes Press, 1978).

Holden, L., *Lame Gods* (unpublished BA dissertation, Stirling, 1982).

James, E.O., 'Initiatory Rituals', in *Myth and Ritual* (ed. S.H. Hooke; Oxford: Oxford University Press, 1933), pp. 147-71.

James, M.R. (trans.), *The Apocryphal New Testament* (Oxford: Clarendon Press, 1969 [1924]).

Jason, H., *Ethnopoetics* (Jerusalem: Israel Ethnographic Society, 1975).

—*Ethnopoetry* (Bonn: Linguistica Biblica, 1977).

—'The Genre in Oral Literature: an Attempt at Interpretation', *Temenos* 3 (1973), pp. 156-60.

—'The Poor Man of Nippur: an Ethnopoetic Analysis', *JCS* 31 (1979), pp. 189-215.

—'Precursors of Propp: Formalist Theories of Narrative in Early Russian Ethnopoetics', *PTL: A Journal for Descriptive Poetics and Theory of Literature* 3 (1977), pp. 471-516.

—'Proverbs in Society: The Problem of Meaning and Function', *Proverbium* 17 (1971), pp. 617-23.

—'The Russian Criticism of the "Finnish School" in Folktale Scholarship', *NORVEG* 14 (1970), pp. 285-94.

Jason, H., and A. Kempinski, 'How Old Are Folktales', *Fabula* 22 (1981), pp. 1-27.

Jason, H., and D. Segal (eds.), *Patterns in Oral Literature* (The Hague: Mouton, 1977).

The Jerusalem Bible (pop. edn; London: Darton, Longman & Todd, 1974).

Jobling, D., *The Sense of Biblical Narrative*. II. *Structural Analyses in the Hebrew Bible* (JSOTSup, 39; Sheffield: JSOT Press, 1986).

Jung, C.G., *Mysterium Coniunctionis* (trans. R.F.C. Hull; New York: Princeton University Press, 1977 [1955–56]).

—*Psychology and Alchemy* (trans. R.F.C. Hull; New York: Princeton University Press, 1980 [1953]).

Kirk, G.S., *Myth. Its Meaning and Functions in Ancient and Other Cultures* (Cambridge: Cambridge University Press, 1978 [1970]).

Kirkpatrick, P.G., *The Old Testament and Folklore Study* (JSOTSup, 62; Sheffield: JSOT Press, 1988).

Lambrechts, P., and L. Vanden Berghe, 'La divinité-oreille dans les religions antiques', *Bulletin de l'institut historique* 29 (1955).

Lauterbach, J.Z. (trans.), *Mekilta de Rabbi Ishmael* (3 vols.; Philadelphia: Jewish Publication Society of America, 1933–35).

Leach, E.R. (ed.), *The Structural Study of Myth and Totemism* (London: Tavistock, 1967).

Leibowitz, N., *Studies in the Book of Genesis in the Context of Ancient and Modern Jewish Bible Commentary* (trans. A. Newman; Jerusalem: World Zionist Organization, 1972).

Lévi-Strauss, C., *Introduction to a Science of Mythology*. I. *The Raw and the Cooked* (trans. J. and D. Weightman; New York: Harper & Row, 1975).

—*Introduction to a Science of Mythology*. II. *From Honey to Ashes* (trans. J. and D. Weightman; New York: Harper & Row, 1973).

—*Introduction to a Science of Mythology*. III. *The Origin of Table Manners* (trans. J. and D. Weightman; New York: Harper & Row, 1979).

Forms of Deformity

—'The Structural Study of Myth', in *Structural Anthropology* (trans. C. Jacobson and B. Grundfest Schoepf; New York: Basic Books, 1963).

Long, C. H., 'Creation, Myths and Doctrines of', in *Encyclopaedia Britannica: Macropedia*, V, (London, 1974), pp. 239-43.

Lord, A., *The Singer of Tales* (New York: Atheneum, 1976 [1960]).

Lüthi, M., *The Fairytale as an Art Form and Portrait of Man* (trans. J. Erickson; Bloomington, IN: Indiana University Press, 1987).

—*Once Upon a Time: On the Nature of Fairy Tales* (trans. L. Chadeayne and P. Gottwald; Bloomington, IN: Indiana University Press, 1976).

Maccoby, H., *The Sacred Executioner* (London: Thames & Hudson, 1982).

Maranda, E., and P. Maranda (eds.), *Structural Analysis of Oral Tradition* (Philadelphia: University of Pennsylvania Press, 1971).

—*Structural Models in Folklore and Transformational Essays* (The Hague: Mouton, 1971).

Marmorstein, A.,'Anges et hommes dans l'Agada', *REJ* 84 (1927), pp. 37-50.

Matthews, J.H., *The Imagery of Surrealism* (New York: Syracuse University Press, 1977).

Meir, O., 'The Narrator in the Stories of the Talmud and the Midrash', *Fabula* 22 (1981).

Meletinski, E., 'Structural-Typological Study of Folktales', in *Soviet Structural Folklorists* (ed. P. Maranda; The Hague: Mouton, 1974).

Meletinski, E., S. Nekludov, E. Novik and D. Segal, 'Problems of the Structural Analysis of Fairytales', in *Soviet Structural Folklorists* (ed. P. Maranda; The Hague: Mouton, 1974).

Mellinkoff, R., *The Horned Moses in Medieval Art and Thought* (Berkeley: University of California Press, 1970).

—*The Mark of Cain* (Berkeley: University of California Press, 1981).

Mendenhall, G.E., *The Tenth Generation* (Baltimore: Johns Hopkins University Press, 1973).

Merz, R., *Die Numinose Mischgestalt* (Berlin: de Gruyter, 1978).

Mode, H., *Fabeltiere und Dämonen* (Leipzig: Edition Leipzig, 1977).

Needham, R., 'Unilateral Figures', in *Reconnaissances* (Toronto: University of Toronto Press, 1980).

—(ed.) *Right and Left* (Chicago: Chicago University Press, 1973).

—*Symbolic Classification* (Santa Monica: Goodyear, 1979).

Neuman (Noy), D., *A Motif-Index of Talmudic-Midrashic Literature* (unpublished thesis, University of Indiana, 1954).

—'Folklore', *EncJud* (1971), pp. 1375-1410.

Neusner, J. (ed.), *Genesis Rabba* (3 vols.; Atlanta: Scholars Press, 1985).

—(trans.), *The Talmud of the Land Of Israel* (Chicago: University of Chicago Press, 1985).

Nickelsburg, G.W.E., *Jewish Literature between the Bible and the Mishna* (London: SCM Press, 1981).

Nikiforov, A.I., 'On the Morphological Study of Folklore', *Linguistica Biblica* 27/28 (1973), pp. 25-35.

Noth, M., *The History of Israel* (trans. S. Godman; London, 1960 [1950]).

Otzen, B., H. Gottlieb and K. Jeppesen, *Myths in the Old Testament* (trans. F. Cryer; London: SCM Press, 2nd edn, 1980).

Ovid, *Metamorphoses* (trans. R. Humphries; Bloomington, IN: Indiana University Press, 1969 [1955]).

Patai, R., *The Hebrew Goddess* (New York: Avon Books, 1978).

Patai, R., F. Lee Utley, and D. Neuman, *Studies in Biblical and Jewish Folklore* (Bloomington, IN: Indiana University Press, 1960).

Pritchard, J.B. (ed.), *Ancient Near Eastern Texts relating to the Old Testament* (Princeton: Princeton University Press, 3rd edn, 1969).

—*Solomon and Sheba* (London: Phaidon Press, 1974).

Propp, V., *Morphology of the Folktale* (trans. L. Scott; rev. and ed. L.A. Wagner; Austin, TX: University of Texas Press, 2nd edn, 1979 [1928]).

—*Theory and History of Folklore* (trans. A.Y. and R.P. Martin; ed. and intro. A. Lieberman; Minnesota: University of Minnesota Press, 1984).

Radin, P., *The Trickster* (New York: Schocken Books, 1976 [1972]).

Rappoport, A.S., *The Folklore of the Jews* (London: Soncino Press, 1937).

—*The Psalms in Life, Literature and Legend* (London: Centenary Press, 1935).

Rees, A., and B. Rees, *Celtic Heritage* (London: Thames & Hudson, 1961).

Robinson, J.M. (trans. and ed.), *The Nag Hammadi Library* (Leiden: Brill, 1984).

Robinson, T.H., 'Hebrew Myths', in *Myth and Ritual* (ed. S.H. Hooke, Oxford: Oxford University Press, 1933), pp. 172-96.

Rogerson, J.W., *Anthropology in the Old Testament* (Oxford: Basil Blackwell, 1978).

Rosner, F., *Medicine in the Bible and the Talmud* (New York: Ktav, 1977).

Russell, J.B., *The Devil* (Ithaca: Cornell University Press, 1977).

Sacks, O., *The Man who Mistook his Wife for a Hat* (London: Picador, 1986).

Sapadin, A., 'On a Monstrous Birth Occurring in the Ghetto of Venice', *Studies in Bibliography and Booklore* 6 (1964), pp. 153-58.

Schmidt, W.H., *Introduction to the Old Testament* (trans. M.J. O'Connell; London: SCM Press, 1984 [1979]).

Schwarz, H., 'The Aggadic Traditions', in *Gates to the New City* (ed. H. Schwarz; New York: Avon Books, 1983).

Scott-Littleton, C., *The New Comparative Mythology* (Berkeley, CA: University of California Press, 1973 [1966]).

Sebeok, T.A. (ed.), *Myth: A Symposium* (Bloomington, IN: Indiana University Press, 1958 [1955]).

Simpson, J., 'The World Upside Down Shall Be', *Journal of American Folklore* 91 (1978), pp. 559–67.

Sperber, D., 'Pourquoi les animaux parfaits, les hybrids et les monstres: sont-ils bons à penser symboliquement?', *L'Homme* 15 (1975), pp. 5-34.

—*Rethinking Symbolism* (trans. A.L. Morton; Cambridge: Cambridge University Press, 1975).

Sperling, H., and M. Simon (trans.), *The Zohar* (5 vols.; Jerusalem: Soncino Press, 1973 [1934]).

Strack, H.L., *Introduction to the Talmud and Midrash* (trans. from the fifth German edition; Philadelphia: Jewish Publication Society of America, 1931 [1887]).

Sydow, C.W. von, *Selected Papers on Folklore* (ed. L. Bødker; Copenhagen: Rosenkilde & Baggar, 1948).

Thompson, C.J., *The Mystery and Lore of Monsters* (London: Williams & Norgate, 1930).

370   *Forms of Deformity*

Thompson, S., *The Folktale* (Berkeley, CA: University of California Press, 1977 [1946]).

—*A Motif-index of Folk Literature* (6 vols.; Copenhagen: Rosenkilde & Baggar, 2nd edn, 1955–58).

Turner, V., *The Ritual Process* (Chicago: Aldine Publishing Co., 1969).

Turville-Petre, E.O.G., *Myth and Religion of the North* (London: Weidenfeld & Nicolson, 1964).

Utley, F. Lee, 'The Bible of the Folk', *California Folklore Quarterly* 4 (1945), pp. 1-17.

Vermes, G., *The Dead Sea Scrolls in English* (Harmondsworth: Penguin, 1984 [1962]).

Ward, D., *The Divine Twins: An Indo-European Myth in Germanic Tradition* (Berkeley, CA: University of California Press, 1968).

Waxman, M., *A History of Jewish Literature*, I (New York: Bloch Publishing, 2nd edn, (1938).

Werner, E.T.C., *Myths and Legends of China* (London: Harrap, 1956 [1922]).

Westman, H., *The Structure of Biblical Myths* (Dallas, TX: Spring Publications, 1983).

Wittkower, R., 'Marvels of the East: A Study in the History of Monsters', in *Allegory and the Migration of Symbols* (London: Thames & Hudson, 1977), pp. 45-74.

Wolfson, E.R., 'Circumcision, Vision of God and Textual Interpretation', *History of Religions* 27.2 (1987), pp. 189-215.

JOURNAL FOR THE STUDY OF THE OLD TESTAMENT

Supplement Series